IBM® Microcomputer Architecture and Assembly Language

IBM® Microcomputer Architecture and Assembly Language

A Look Under the Hood

Norman S. Matloff

University of California, Davis

Prentice Hall
Englewood Cliffs, New Jersey 07632

Library of Congress Cataloging-in-Publication Data

Matloff, Norman S.
   IBM microcomputer architecture and assembly language : a look
under the hood / Norman S. Matloff.
     p.   cm.
   Includes index.
   ISBN 0–13–451998–1
   1. IBM microcomputers. 2. Computer architecture. 3. Assembler
language (Computer program language) I. Title.
QA76.8.I259193M38 1992
004.2'565–dc20
                                 91–27994
                                     CIP

Acquisitions editor: *Marcia Horton*
Editorial/production supervision
  and interior design: *Kathleen Schiaparelli*
Copy editor: *Brian Baker*
Cover design: *Lundgren Graphics*
Prepress buyer: *Linda Behrens*
Manufacturing buyer: *Dave Dickey*
Editorial assistant: *Diana Penha*

© 1992 by Prentice-Hall, Inc.
A Simon & Schuster Company
Englewood Cliffs, New Jersey 07632

The author and publisher of this book have used their best efforts in preparing this book. These
efforts include the development, research, and testing of the theories and programs to determine
their effectiveness. The author and publisher make no warranty of any kind, expressed or
implied, with regard to these programs or the documentation contained in this book. The author
and publisher shall not be liable in any event for incidental or consequential damages in
connection with, or arising out of, the furnishing, performance, or use of these programs.

Apple and Macintosh are registered trademarks of Apple Computer, Inc.
Borland, Turbo-PASCAL, Turbo-C, Turbo Assembler, and Turbo-Debugger are trademarks of Borland International.
Codeview is a registered trademark.
Cray is a registered trademark of Cray Research.
IBM, PC-DOS, OS/2, and PS/2 are registered trademarks of International Business Machines Corporation.
Microsoft, Microsoft-PASCAL, Microsoft-C, Microsoft Assembler, and MS-DOS are registered trademarks of Microsoft
   Corporation.
Motorola is a registered trademark.
NEC is a registered trademark of Nippon Electric Company.
Sun and SPARC are trademarks for Sun Computers.
UNIX is a registered trademark of AT&T (Bell Labs).
VMS and VAX are registered trademarks of Digital Equipment Corporation.

Printed in the United States of America

10 9 8 7 6 5 4 3 2

ISBN 0-13-451998-1

Prentice-Hall International (UK) Limited, *London*
Prentice-Hall of Australia Pty. Limited, *Sydney*
Prentice-Hall Canada Inc., *Toronto*
Prentice-Hall Hispanoamericano, S.A., *Mexico*
Prentice-Hall of India Private Limited, *New Delhi*
Prentice-Hall of Japan, Inc., *Tokyo*
Simon & Schuster Asia Pte. Ltd., *Singapore*
Editora Prentice-Hall do Brasil, Ltda., *Rio de Janeiro*

Contents

PREFACE ix

INTRODUCTION: WHY LOOK UNDER THE HOOD? 1

1 REPRESENTATION AND STORAGE OF INFORMATION 6

1.1 Bits and Bytes 6

1.2 Representing Information as Bit Strings 9

 1.2.1 *Representing Integer Data, 9*
 1.2.2 *Representing Real Number Data, 12*
 1.2.3 *Representing Character Data, 14*
 1.2.4 *Representing Machine Instructions, 15*
 1.2.5 *What Type of Information Is Stored Here? 15*

1.3 Organization of Main Memory 18

 1.3.1 *Words and Addresses, 18*
 1.3.2 *Storage of Variables in HLL Programs, 21*
   Analytical Exercises, 29
   Programming Projects, 33

2 MAJOR COMPONENTS OF COMPUTER "ENGINES" 34

2.1 Major Hardware Components of the "Engine" 35

 2.1.1 *System Components, 35*

v

2.1.2   *General CPU Components, 38*
2.1.3   *iAPX CPU Components, 41*
2.1.4   *Motorola 68000 Family CPU Components, 48*
2.1.5   *The CPU Fetch/Execute Cycle, 49*

2.2   Software Components of the Computer "Engine"   53

2.3   Speed of a Computer "Engine"   56

2.3.1   *CPU Architecture, 56*
2.3.2   *Parallel Operations, 56*
2.3.3   *Clock Rate, 58*
2.3.4   *Memory-Access Time, 59*
2.3.5   *OS Efficiency, 62*
         Analytical Exercises, 63
         Programming Projects, 65

**3   INTRODUCTION TO THE iAPX INSTRUCTION SET
    AND ADDRESSING MODES**   **68**

3.1   An Introductory Program   68

3.2   A Brief Look at Instruction Formats   78

3.3   Allowable Combinations of Operations and Operands   83
         Analytical Exercises, 85
         Programing Projects, 86

4   GENERATING, LOADING, AND EXECUTING PROGRAMS   **89**

4.1   Use of DEBUG for Loading and Executing Programs   90

4.2   Introduction to iAPX Assembly Language   96

4.2.1   *Hire a Clerk! 96*
4.2.2   *A First MASM Example, 98*
4.2.3   *Command Sequence and Syntax for MASM
         and LINK, 118*
4.2.4   *Debugging Assembly Language Programs, 121*
4.2.5   *Further MASM Examples, 130*
4.2.6   *Tools Developed So Far, 138*

4.3   More on Program Loading and Transfer of Control   139

4.4   Loading and Executing Programs Derived from HLL
      Sources   143
         Analytical Exercises, 144
         Programming Projects, 147

**5   MODULAR PROGRAMMING: SUBPROGRAMS, LINKERS,
    AND MACROS**   **151**

5.1   Stacks   152

5.2   Procedures   156

5.3   Machine-Level Aspects of Procedures in High-Level
       Languages   170

       *5.3.1   What the Compiler Produces from HLL Procedure
       Calls, 171*
       5.3.2   Mixed-Language Programming, 179

5.4   Macros   193

5.5   MAKE: A Maintenance Utility for Program Modules   197

       Analytical Exercises, 199
       Programming Projects, 201

6   A FURTHER LOOK AT THE iAPX ARCHITECTURE   204

6.1   A Further Look at the iAPX Flags Register   204

       6.1.1   The Carry Flag, 205
       6.1.2   The Overflow Flag, 207
       6.1.3   Other Flags, 211

6.2   A Further Look at iAPX Addressing Modes   212

       6.2.1   Register Mode, 212
       6.2.2   Immediate Mode, 214
       6.2.3   Direct Mode, 214
       6.2.4   Indirect Mode, 215
       6.2.5   Indexed Addressing, 215
       6.2.6   Based Mode, 221
       6.2.7   Combined Indexed and Based Modes, 223
       *6.2.8   Use of the Addressing Modes in JMP and CALL
       Instructions, 224*
       6.2.9   Segment Override, 224

6.3   A Further Look at the iAPX Instruction Set   226

       6.3.1   Other Arithmetic Instructions, 226
       6.3.2   Logical (Boolean) Operations, 233
       6.3.3   String Instructions, 245
       6.3.4   Loop Instructions, 251
       6.3.5   Miscellaneous Instructions, 253
       Analytical Exercises, 256
       Programming Projects, 257

7   INPUT/OUTPUT   260

7.1   Introduction to I/O Ports and Device Structure   261

       7.1.1   I/O Address Space Approach, 262

7.1.2   *Memory-Mapped I/O Approach, 263*
7.1.3   *I/O Ports and Device Structure in the IBM
          Microcomputer Family, 266*

7.2   Interrupt-Driven I/O   277

7.2.1   *Basics of the Interrupt Sequence, 279*
7.2.2   *Arranging Priorities among Devices, 293*

7.3   I/O through System Calls   296

7.4   I/O in HLLs   306

Analytical Exercises, 309
Programming Projects, 310

8   INTRODUCTION TO OPERATING SYSTEMS   **315**

8.1   Mechanisms to Call OS Services   316

8.2   "Cooking" Services   319

8.3   File Systems   320

8.4   Process Management   334

8.4.1   *TSR Programming, 335*
8.4.2   *The Infrastructure of Time-Sharing, 340*

8.5   Memory Management   345

8.5.1   *Memory Sharing, 345*
8.5.2   *Virtual Addressing, 347*
Analytical Exercises, 351
Programming Projects, 352

Appendices   **354**

I   ASCII AND SCAN CODES   **354**

II   THE iAPX INSTRUCTION SET   **359**

**III   COMMANDS FOR ASSEMBLING, COMPILING, LINKING
       AND DEBUGGING**   **382**

IV   SELECTED DOS AND BIOS SERVICE ROUTINES   **385**

V   PASCAL/C TUTORIAL   **388**

INDEX   **395**

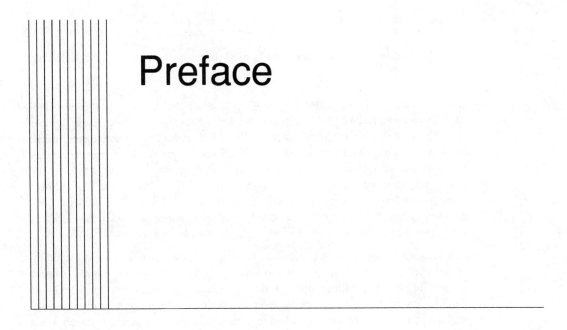

Preface

What is different about this book?

On the one hand, the book has the same central goal as do a number of other books: This book develops the skill of assembly-language programming on IBM PC-family microcomputers. Thus, as with other books, this text presents a thorough treatment of PC assembly language, covering essentially the entire 80×86 instruction set (except the instructions that involve protected mode). Though the approach taken here is different, the teaching of PC-family assembly language is still the central goal.

On the other hand, the point of view taken is that the traditional "assembly language course" should actually be more than just what that phrase implies, i.e., more than just a language course. In addition to developing the skill of assembly-language programming, this course should also integrate well with a modern computer science curriculum. For example, this course should prepare the student for, and point out to the student the connections to, subsequent courses in computer architecture/organization, operating systems, and compilers.

In other words, this course should comprise the student's first introduction to *computer systems*. This goal is summarized by the metaphor in the book's subtitle:

"A Look Under the Hood"

The student, having previously seen the computer only from a high-level viewpoint of languages such as Pascal or C, will now get a look at how the lower levels—machine architecture and system software—support the abstractions of those high-level languages.

This "look under the hood" metaphor is used throughout, such as in the following ways:

- There are many "looks under the hood" that consist of examining the machine-assembly code produced by the compilers from Pascal or C source code. In this way, the students develop an understanding of how high-level languages utilize machine resources, and how in some applications it is desirable or even necessary to bypass these languages and write code directly at the machine level. In the latter case, they see that we must not only "look under the hood," but also must in some cases program directly at the "under-the-hood" level. The students also develop insight into why an understanding of what happens "under the hood" is important even when we write entirely in high-level languages.

- The students "look under the hood" to develop at least a first-level understanding of how one machine differs from another, e.g., why one machine might be faster or have broader capabilities than another. The students learn that a knowledge of what is "under the hood" is needed even for such commonplace activities as reading newspaper advertisements when purchasing a PC, say reading descriptions such as "16 MHz 286 CPU; 1 megabyte main memory; 40 megabyte, 20 ms hard disk; includes VGA graphics ports..."

- The students learn that the world "under the hood" has both hardware and software components, and the students begin to delineate the different roles played by those two components. For example, they learn that the actions resulting from the user's hitting the backspace key—the most recently typed character disappears, and the cursor moves one space backward—are typically functions of *software* (the operating system), not the keyboard and monitor hardware. On the other hand, the students learn that some functions, such as memory protection afforded by protected mode, does require hardware support.

- The students also learn that some functions might be implemented either in hardware or software. For instance, this is the case for floating-point operations in PC-family microcomputers, in which the operations must be coded in software unless an 80×87 coprocessor is present (or the CPU is of the 80486 type). Putting these operations in hardware increases program speed substantially.

The author has found the "look under the hood" approach to be a powerful motivator for the students in this course, because it relates the material to the other courses the students have taken. For example, the text makes very frequent connections of the course material to what the students already know about high-level languages such as Pascal or C.* Chapter 1 is a good illustration of this. Although this chapter covers the standard material on bits, bytes, and addresses, it does so in an innovative way, which very much captures the attention of the students and provides important

*Knowledge of *either* Pascal or C is fully sufficient background for reading this book. Examples from both languages are presented but are quite readable by "speakers" of *either* language.

insight: The material is illustrated by relating it directly to Pascal or C, showing how the abstract data types of those languages—integer/int, char, arrays, and record/struct types, etc.—are represented and allocated memory by compilers, i.e., what these variables are like "*under the hood.*"

Additional motivation is developed in other ways, again typically relating to high-level languages. In the Introduction, which has as its purpose the development of student motivation, the student is immediately presented with a program "bug," one which is quite simple but which the author has found that the students consider to be very surprising: It is asserted that it is possible that the execution of the Pascal statement

```
Sum:=X+Y;
```

could result in Sum being negative, even if X and Y are positive. This anomaly is explained in Chapter 1, but the point is that the student is immediately presented with a reason why it *is* important to understand what happens at the machine level—"*under the hood*"—even when programming in a high-level language.

In spite of the different approach taken, make no mistake about it—this *is* a book on PC assembly language. As mentioned earlier, it does treat PC assembly language quite thoroughly, covering essentially the entire 80×86 instruction set, and its central goal is still to develop *programming skills* in PC assembly language. In fact, this text goes further than most others to develop such skills. For example, it gives extensive advice on program debugging at the assembly-language levels. Sections 4.2.4 and 5.3.2.2 are devoted to this—not just presenting the mechanics of how to use debugging tools, but actually giving specific tips that will help the student track down his/her bug. The text also emphasizes the use of such real-world programming tools as MAKE files (Section 5.5). And there are numerous Programming Projects: Some are straightforward and quick to implement while others are more challenging.

A major feature of the book is its numerous Analytical Exercises. These are "thought problems" that typically have a "What would happen if..." theme. The author has found these to be extremely valuable in ensuring that the student does not "miss the forest for the trees."

With any textbook, most instructors tend to skip some sections so as to be able to spend more time on others. The organization of this text has been designed to facilitate this. One certainly can cover Section 7.3, for example, without covering the earlier sections in Chapter 7.

Another point of central importance in this regard is that many sections can be read by students on their own, thus giving the instructor more lecture time with which he/she can cover the more difficult concepts in extra detail. The author, for example, teaches this course on a quarter system, with its attendant time constraints. He spends only two hours on Chapter 1, and about an hour and a half each on Chapters 2 and 3. He has the students read Sections 3.2, 3.3, and 4.1 on their own, for instance. His aim is to start Chapter 4 as early as possible, and he has designed the earlier chapters to facilitate this.

The students begin machine-level programming in Chapter 3, and then become immersed in such programming beginning in Chapter 4. The two main programming examples in Chapter 4 have been chosen to be simple enough to serve as a rapid introduction but rich enough to provide the student with a broad range of tools that he/she can use to write a wide variety of programs. This latter point is emphasized by the inclusion of a special subsection, Section 4.2.6, Tools Developed So Far. This subsection lists all the instructions, addressing modes, pseudo-ops, and DOS calls that have been introduced up to that point; the students find it helpful to keep this list in mind when writing their first few programs.

This text was class-tested for three years in manuscript form on more than 1,000 students. This has resulted in an abundance of valuable feedback, with many thanks being due, especially to Tom Schubert, Steve Snapp, Feiling Jia, and Mark Heckman, who translated many hours of student contact into suggestions that resulted in numerous improvements. Much credit must also be given to Jim Stabile and Eric Irby, who played a major role in implementing some of the examples early in the project. Scott Horne and Glenn Lai also gave highly detailed and valuable comments on the manuscript. Any errors, of course, are due to the author rather than to these individuals.

The author also wishes to thank Marcia Horton and Ray Henderson of Prentice Hall, as well as the following Prentice Hall reviewers: Keith Olson, Montana College of Mineral Sciences and Technology; Patricia Finch, CUNY Graduate School and University Center; Frank Gergelyi, New Jersey Institute of Technology; Peter Abel, British Columbia Institute of Technology; and Jim Peters, Kansas State University. Last but not least, the author is eternally grateful to his wife, Gamis, both for her PC expertise and for her patience and inspiration.

Norman Matloff
Davis, California

IBM® Microcomputer Architecture and Assembly Language

Introduction: Why Look under the Hood?

The title of this book, and of this introduction, suggests an analogy between computers and automobiles. A look under the hood of a car gives us a view of the engine, the source of power that we utilize when we drive the car. In the case of a computer, the analogue of driving is programming in a high-level language (HLL) such as Pascal or C, and there are two sources of power:

- The hardware, including the central processing unit which executes the computer's machine language, and
- The low-level software, consisting of various services that the operating system makes available to programs.

When you write a program in an HLL program on a certain computer, the compiler will translate your HLL statements into the machine language of that computer and into calls to subroutines within the computer's operating system. And of course, it is this translated version of your program that is actually executed, not your HLL program itself. Thus, the hardware and operating system do indeed form the "engine" of the computer.

It is the goal of this book to demystify this engine, by giving the reader an introductory "look under the hood." Note carefully that the engine consists of both hardware and software components, each of which is equally important.*

*The term **hardware** in this book will refer to the major physical components of a computer. Our discussion will concern the *functions* of these components, i.e., what is known as "computer architecture," but not the details of the electronic implementation, which are beyond the scope of the book. Thus, no background in electronics is needed or used.

The skeptical reader will point out here, quite correctly, that one does not need to know about automobile engines in order to be a good driver. This raises the question as to whether one needs to know about a computer's hardware and operating system in order to be a good programmer or software engineer. The answer to this question is that *such knowledge is actually vital to good programming.* Professional developers of software need much, much more than mere programming skills—they *do* need to know how the computer's "engine" works. And again, it is equally important to understand both the hardware and the software components of this "engine."

For example, consider the following Pascal code, which finds the sum of two variables X and Y of type **integer** and stores the total in an **integer** variable Sum:

```
Sum:=X+Y;
```

(Or in the language C, consider the statement Sum=X+Y; with X,Y and Sum of type int.*) Suppose that you know that both X and Y are nonnegative. Then you would expect that the value of Sum, after the statement is executed, will be nonnegative. But actually, *it is entirely possible that Sum will turn out to have a negative value.* For example, suppose that X is 28,502, Y is 12,344, and the program is run with a Microsoft Pascal compiler on an IBM PC. Then the resulting value of Sum will be –24,689!

How could Sum become negative? After you learn, in Chapter 1, how computer hardware stores positive and negative integers, a negative value for Sum will be no mystery to you at all. But imagine how helpless you would be without this knowledge. Suppose your program were more complex than this simplified example. Then you might spend hours or even days searching in vain for a bug, because the problem would be a *conceptual* error concerning the computer's engine, not a *programming* error.

As another example, I was once involved in a large software development project for a data-base application. After the development team finished the product and presented it to the client for testing, the client pronounced the product completely unacceptable. The programmers were shocked, since the client confirmed that the program was producing correct results. But the client, who had used similar products before, said that the program was too slow. The program was taking about 15 seconds to respond to his commands, while from experience with other programs of this type, he was expecting essentially instantaneous response. Upon looking closer at the program, the development team found a subtle problem which made the program's use of the operating system extremely inefficient, resulting in the 15-second delay that had been upsetting the client. After the team changed the manner in which the program was making calls to operating system services, the response time did become instantaneous, and the client was pleased. So, as in the last example, we again see that it is not enough to be just a good programmer—knowledge of the underlying "engine" can be crucial to the success of the program.

In the PC world, an important class of programs is that of the **terminate-and-stay-resident** (TSR) variety, an example of which is an "alarm clock" program, which would allow the user to arrange a beep sound to be emitted from the computer at a

---

*In this book it is assumed that the reader knows either Pascal or C, but not necessarily both.

specified time, to remind the user of a meeting or some other event. Once again, writing this type of program requires a very intricate understanding of the "under the hood" workings of the system. Yet another example in which this knowledge is important is the area of computer security, which is becoming of central interest in many organizations. Most attacks by "hackers" to invade computer systems are based on a thorough understanding of "under the hood" aspects of those systems, so a successful defense against those attacks requires an equally thorough understanding of those aspects.

The foregoing examples, which are just a few among the many that occur in real-world software development, show why an understanding of the computer's "engine" is important even when writing in an HLL. Furthermore, in some applications we must do our programming in the computer's machine language directly, rather than indirectly through an HLL. The reason for this is that some applications require that our program access some special feature of our particular hardware. This is impossible in an HLL, since HLLs are by definition machine-independent languages, so we must write such applications directly in our computer's machine language.

This kind of situation arises, for example, in **embedded applications**, in which a computer is used to control a machine, such as an automatic bank teller machine, a robot, or even a common household item such as a washing machine or an autofocus camera. Computers are in all these machines, and the programs that run on these computers need to access machine-specific items. Similarly, almost all programs involving computer graphics require direct manipulation of the specialized hardware of whatever computer is being used.

Another setting in which one needs to program directly in machine language is that in which the program's execution time is of special concern. It is likely that execution time has not been a problem in the classroom programs you have written so far, but in the real world there exist many applications that require very fast execution; thus, it is important to be able to write such programs so that they run as fast as possible. In many cases, use of an HLL does not produce the fastest possible program. The HLL compiler produces a machine-language program—and keep in mind, it is this latter program which actually is what is executed, not the HLL source—but the program might not make the most efficient use of the computer's engine. We can do much better if we write the machine-language program ourselves.

Thus, there are at least two good reasons for us to write our own machine-language programs or our own assembly-language programs (you will see in Chapter 4 that assembly language is actually equivalent to machine language):

(a) A need to have our program access special hardware in our computer, and

(b) A need to write an especially fast-executing program.

On the other hand, machine-language–assembly-language (MLAL) programming is inconvenient and hard for others to read. For this reason, the modern software engineering philosophy is as follows. Suppose a certain section of a program has special needs as described in (a) or (b) above. Then the idea is to write part of the program in MLAL, to accommodate (a) or (b), and the rest in an HLL, for convenience and clarity.

For example, suppose a given program will be doing a lot of sorting of arrays. Then we might write the sort algorithm in MLAL, to maximize its speed, but write the rest of the program, which does not have to be fast, in an HLL. This is one of the recurring themes in this book, with many of our sample programs being written partially in Pascal or C* and partially in the assembly language of the IBM PC microcomputer family.

Actually, programing in the language C itself requires knowledge of the computer's "engine." For example, pointer variables in C involve machine-level entities explicitly, while for Pascal pointers this involvement is only implicit. The same type of situation exists for parameters in calls to subprograms. In C the analog of a **var** parameter in Pascal uses explicit references to addresses in the computer's memory, whereas these addresses are essentially hidden to the Pascal programmer. Thus, programming in C requires the programmer to have a thorough understanding of the "engine under the hood." In fact, C is sometimes called a "middle-level language," since it combines the high-level features of Pascal with the ability to perform low-level operations; this versatility is one of the reasons for C's enormous popularity in today's computer and electronics industry. That popularity is yet another reason for the importance of understanding the "under the hood" material in this book.

Lastly, an understanding of the computer's "engine" is important in choosing the proper computer for a given development project. What are the differences between an IBM PC microcomputer, a VAX minicomputer, and a Cray supercomputer? Will the VAX necessarily be faster than the PC and the Cray faster than the VAX—on *all* applications? (The answer is "no.") And what do those advertisements for computers mean, such as the following, which is typical of what one sees in our daily newspapers? "16 MHz 286 CPU; 1 megabyte main memory; 40 megabyte, 20 ms hard disk; includes VGA graphics ports;..." These questions again involve an "under the hood" understanding of computer systems.

One must understand the differences among various computer "engines" when making decisions as to what computing equipment should be purchased for a given application—whether it involves recommending to an employer or client what workstations are most appropriate for his or her setting, or whether it means answering your uncle Bill's question as to what kind of personal computer he should buy for home use.

For all these reasons, the goal of this book is to get a thorough "look under the hood" of modern computer systems. It is of course vital that we make the concepts concrete, by using a real computer for our examples. The computer we will use is actually the whole family of IBM microcomputers, including the original IBM PC and XT models and ranging through the more advanced AT and PS/2 models. Though the advanced models have extra instructions, all models share the same basic instruction set.

This last point stems from the fact that the **central processing unit** (CPU)—the component of a computer in which the execution of programs occurs (more details will be presented in Chapter 2)—in any IBM microcomputer comes from the Intel Corporation's iAPX family, all of whose members have the same basic instruction set.

---

*Again, as long as the reader has knowledge of one of these two languages, he or she will be able to understand the examples in the other language.

The PC, XT, and PS/2 Models 25 and 30 machines use the iAPX 86 subfamily of CPUs, the AT and PS/2 Models 50 and 60 use the iAPX 286 subfamily, and the PS/2 Model 80 uses the iAPX 386 subfamily.

Through the material in this book, you will become proficient at using the iAPX instruction set, writing both stand-alone assembly language programs and also assembly-language procedures to be linked together with other modules that you write in Pascal or C or any other HLL. But, as emphasized above, our goal also extends beyond programming: an equally important goal is to learn what occurs "under the hood." Thus, you will also learn how the iAPX instruction set is utilized at the low levels of software and in input/output.

On the other hand, you will undoubtedly encounter many different kinds of computer systems. Thus, it is vital that we discuss commonalities and variations found in computer systems *in general*. For this reason, although we will concentrate on the IBM family of microcomputers, we will also make some comparisons among different kinds of hardware, e.g., between the IBM PC family's iAPX instruction set and the instruction sets of the VAX and Motorola 68000 family, and we will make occasional comparisons among different kinds of software, e.g., between the IBM PC family's familiar MS-DOS operating system* and the new OS/2, as well as Unix, operating systems.

We will begin our "look under the hood" with a discussion of how a computer stores data, in Chapter 1.

---

*The IBM product itself is called PC-DOS and is negligibly different from MS-DOS. Both are often known simply as DOS.

Representation and Storage of Information

A computer can store many types of information. A high-level language (HLL) will typ-ically have several data types, such as Pascal's **integer, real, char,** and **boolean,** or the C language's **int, float,** and **char.** Yet a computer cannot directly store any of these data types. Instead, a computer only stores 0's and 1's. Thus, the question arises as to how one can represent the abstract data types of Pascal, C, or other HLLs in terms of 0's and 1's. What, for example, does a **char** variable look like when viewed from "under the hood"? A related question is how we can use 0's and 1's to represent our program itself, meaning the machine language instructions that are generated when our Pascal, C, or other HLL program is compiled. In this chapter, we will discuss how to represent various types of information in terms of 0's and 1's. And, in addition to the question of *how* items are stored, we will also begin to address the question of *where* they are stored, i.e., where they are placed within the structure of a computer's main memory.

1.1 BITS AND BYTES

The 0's and 1's used to store information in a computer are called **bits.** The term comes from binary digit, i.e., a digit in the base-2 form of a number (though once again, keep in mind that not all kinds of items that a computer stores are numeric). The physical nature of bit storage, such as using a high voltage to represent a 1 and a low voltage to represent a 0, is beyond the scope of this book, but the point is that every piece of information must be expressed as a string of bits.

We will first need to define a shorthand notation to use for writing long bit strings. For example, imagine how cumbersome it would be for us humans to keep reading and writing a string such as 1001110010101110. So let us agree to use **hexadecimal** notation, which consists of grouping a bit string into four-bit substrings and then giving a single-character name to each substring.

For example, for the string 1001110010101110, the grouping would be

$$\underline{1001} \ \underline{1100} \ \underline{1010} \ \underline{1110}$$

To give a name to each four-bit substring, we treat each one as if it were a base-2 number. For example, the leftmost substring above, 1001, is the base-2 representation for the number 9, since

$$1(2^3) + 0(2^2) + 0(2^1) + 1(2^0) = 9$$

So, for convenience we call that substring "9." The second substring, 1100, is the base-2 form for the number 12, so we could call it "12." However, we want to use a single-character name, so if we let "A" represent 10, "B" 11, "C" 12, and so on until 15, which we denote by "F," then we will call the substring 1100 "C."

Accordingly, we will refer to the string 1001110010101110 as 9CAE. This is certainly much more convenient than writing the whole string out, since it involves writing only 4 characters instead of 16 0's and 1's. However, keep in mind that we are doing this only as a quick shorthand form, for use by us humans. The computer still stores the string in its original form, 1001110010101110, *not* 9CAE.

We say that 9CAE is the hexadecimal, or "hex," form of the the bit string 1001110010101110. Often we will append an "H" at the end of the hex form of a bit string, to make clear that it is the hex, and not the decimal form. For instance, 5207 has no "A," "B," "C," "D," "E," or "F" that would identify it as being in hex form, so we write 5207H so that no one will mistake it for a base-10 number. Even 9CAE would usually be written as 9CAEH, just to make sure that we remember that it is in hex form.

Recall that we use bit strings to represent many different types of information, some being numeric and others nonnumeric. If we happen to be using a bit string as a nonnegative number, then the hex form of that bit string has an additional meaning, namely, the base-16 representation of that number.

For example, the preceding string 1001110010101110, if representing a nonnegative base-2 number, is equal to

$$1(2^{15}) + 0(2^{14}) + 0(2^{13}) + 1(2^{12}) + 1(2^{11}) + 1(2^{10}) + 0(2^9) + 0(2^8) \qquad (1\text{--}1)$$
$$+ 1(2^7) + 0(2^6) + 1(2^5) + 0(2^4) + 1(2^3) + 1(2^2) + 1(2^1) + 0(2^0) = 40,110$$

If the hex form of this bit string, 9CAE, is treated as a base-16 number, its value is

$$9(16^3) + 12(16^2) + 10(16^1) + 14(16^0) = 40,110 \qquad (1\text{--}2)$$

confirming that the hex form is indeed the base-16 version of the number. That is in fact the origin of the term "hexadecimal," which means "pertaining to 16." (Note that there is no significance in the fact that this particular bit string is 16 bits long; we use hexadecimal notation for strings of any length.)

The fact that the hex version of a number is also the base-16 representation of that number comes in handy in converting a binary number to its base-10 form. We *could* do such conversion by expanding the powers of 2 as in Equation (1–1), but it is much faster to group the binary form into hex and then expand the powers of 16, as in Equation (1–2).

The opposite conversion—from base 10 to binary—can be expedited in the same way, by first converting from base 10 to base 16, and then disassociating the hex groups into binary form. The conversion from decimal to base 16 is done by repeatedly dividing by 16 until we get a quotient less than 16; the hex digits are then obtained as the remainders and the very last quotient. To make the procedure concrete, let us convert the decimal number 21602 to binary:

> Divide 21602 by 16, yielding 1350, remainder 2.
> Divide 1350 by 16, yielding 84, remainder 6.
> Divide 84 by 16, yielding 5, remainder 4.
> The hex form of 21602 is thus 5462.
> The binary form is thus 0101 0100 0110 0010, i.e., 0101010001100010.

The main ingredient here is the repeated division by 16; this builds up powers of 16. For example, in the line

> Divide 1350 by 16, yielding 84, remainder 6.

that is our second division by 16, so it is a *cumulative* division by 16^2. (Note again that this is why we are dividing by 16, not because the number has 16 bits.)

We need a little more notation and terminology before continuing. For most computers, it is customary to label individual bits within a bit string from right to left, starting with 0. For example, in the bit string 1101, we say bit $0 = 1$, bit $1 = 0$, bit $2 = 1$ and bit $3 = 1$.

If we happen to be using an *n*-bit string to represent a nonnegative integer, we say that bit $n - 1$, the leftmost bit, is the most significant bit (MSB). To see why this terminology makes sense, think of the base-10 case. Suppose the price of an item is $237. A mistake by a sales clerk in the digit 2 would be much more serious than a mistake in the digit 7; i.e., the 2 is the most significant of the three digits in this price. Similarly, in an *n*-bit string, bit 0, the rightmost bit, is called the least significant bit (LSB).

A bit is said to be **set** if it is 1 and **cleared** if it is 0. A string of eight bits is usually called a **byte**. Bit strings of eight bits are important for two reasons. First, in storing characters, we typically store each character as an eight-bit string. Second, computer storage cells are typically composed of an integral number of bytes—i.e., an even multiple of eight bits—with 16 bits and 32 bits being the most commonly encountered cell sizes.

The whimsical pioneers of the computer world extended the pun "byte" to the term **nibble**, meaning a four-bit string. So each hex digit is called a nibble.

1.2 REPRESENTING INFORMATION AS BIT STRINGS

We may now address the questions raised at the beginning of the chapter: how can the various abstract data types used in HLLs, and also the computer's machine instructions, be represented using 0's and 1's?

1.2.1 Representing Integer Data

Representing nonnegative integer values is straightforward: we just use the base-2 representation, such as 101 for the number +5. The C language data type **unsigned int** (also called simply **unsigned**) uses this representation.

But what about integers that can be either positive or negative, i.e., integers that are signed? That is, what about the data type **integer** in Pascal or **int** in C?

Suppose, for simplicity, that we will be using three-bit strings to store integer variables. (Note: We will assume this size for bit strings in the next few paragraphs.) Since each bit can take on either of two values, 0 or 1, there are $2^3 = 8$ possible three-bit strings. So we can represent eight different integer values. In other words, we could represent any integer from −4 to +3, or −2 to +5, or whatever. Most systems opt for a range in which about half the representable numbers are positive and about half are negative. The range −2 to +5, for example, has many more representable positive numbers than negative numbers. This might be useful in some applications, but since most computers are designed as *general-purpose* machines, they use integer representation schemes that are as symmetric around 0 as possible. The two major systems to be discussed shortly use ranges of −3 to +3 and −4 to +3.

But this still leaves open the question as to which bit strings represent which numbers. The two major systems, **signed-magnitude** and **two's-complement** answer this question in different ways. Both systems store the nonnegative numbers in the same way, by storing the base-2 form of the number: 000 represents 0, 001 represents +1, 010 represents +2, 011 represents +3, and so on. However, the two systems differ in the way they store the negative numbers.

The signed-magnitude system stores a three-bit negative number as a 1, followed by the base-2 representation of the magnitude—i.e., absolute value—of that number. For example, consider how the number −3 would be stored. The magnitude of this number is 3, whose base-2 representation is 11. So the three-bit signed-magnitude representation of −3 is 1 followed by 11, i.e., 111. Similarly, the number −2 would be stored as 1 followed by 10, i.e. 110, and so on. Under this system, the reader should verify that the resulting range of numbers representable in three bits would then be −3 to +3. The reader should also note that the number 0 has *two* representations, 000 and 100. The latter could be considered "−0," which of course has no meaning, so 000 and 100 should be considered identical. Note, too, that 100, which in an unsigned system would represent +4, does *not* do so here; indeed, +4 is not representable at all, since our range is −3 to +3.

The two's-complement system handles the negative numbers differently. To see how, think of strings of three decimal digits, instead of three bits—for concreteness, say, a three-digit odometer or trip meter in an automobile. Think about how we could store positive and negative numbers on this trip meter if we had the desire to do so. Since there are 10 choices for each digit (0, 1, . . . , 9), and there are three digits, there are $10^3 = 1,000$ possible patterns. So we would be able to store numbers approximately in the range –500 to +500.

Suppose we can wind the odometer forward or backward with some manual control. Let us initially set the odometer to 000—i.e., set all three digits to 0. If we were to wind *forward* from 000 once, we would get 001; if we were to wind forward from 000 twice, we would get 002; and so on. So we would use the odometer pattern 000 to represent 0, 001 to represent +1, 002 to represent +2, . . . , and 499 to represent +499. If we were to wind *backward* from 000 once, we would get 999; if we were to wind backward twice, we would get 998; and so on. So we would use the odometer pattern 999 to represent –1, 998 to represent –2, . . . , and 500 to represent –500 (since the odometer would read 500 if we were to wind backward 500 times). This would give us a range of representable numbers from –500 to +499.

Getting back to strings of three binary digits instead of three decimal digits, we apply the same principle. If we wind backward once from 000, we get 111, so we use 111 to represent –1. If we wind backward twice from 000, we get 110, so we use 110 to represent –2. Similarly, 101 will mean –3, and 100 will mean –4. If we wind backward one more time, we get 011, which we already reserved to represent +3, so –4 will be our most negative representable number. Hence, under the two's-complement system, three-bit strings can represent any integer in the range –4 to +3.

The two's-complement system may seem strange at first, but it has a very powerful feature: we can add two numbers without worrying about their signs; that is, whether the two addends are both positive, both negative, or of mixed signs, we will do addition in the same manner. For example, suppose we wish to add the base-10 numbers +23 and –6. These have the "trip meter" representations 023 and 994. Adding 023 and 994 yields 1,017, but since we are working with three-digit quantities, the leading 1 in 1,017 is lost, and we get 017. Now 017 is the "trip meter" representation of +17, so our answer is +17—exactly as it should be, since we wanted to add +23 and –6.

The importance of this uniformity of addition is that in building a computer, we can greatly simplify the hardware to do addition. The same hardware will work for all signs of addends. For this reason, most modern computers are designed to use the two's-complement system.

Although we have used the "winding backward" concept to informally define the two's-complement representation of negative integers, in actual computation—both by humans and by the computer hardware—it is inconvenient to find representations this way. For example, suppose we are working with eight-bit strings, which allow numbers in the range –128 to +127. If we wish to find the representation of –29, we *could* wind backward from 00000000 29 times, but this would be very tedious.

Fortunately, a "shortcut" method exists. To find the n-bit two's-complement representation of a negative number $-x$, do the following:

(a) Find the n-bit base-2 representation of $+x$, making sure to include any leading 0's.

(b) In the result of (a), replace all 0's by 1's and 1's by 0's.

(c) Add 1 to the result of (b), ignoring any carry coming out of the most significant bit.

For instance, suppose again that we want to find the representation of –29 in an eight-bit string. We first find the representation of +29, which is 00011101. (We include the three leading 0's, as specified in (a) above.) Applying step (b) to this result, we get 11100010. Adding 1, we get 11100011. So, the eight-bit two's-complement representation of –29 is 11100011. We would get this same string if we wound back from 000000 29 times, but the method here is much quicker.

This transformation is its own inverse; i.e., if you take the two's-complement representation of a negative number $-x$ and apply steps (b) and (c) above, you will get $+x$. The reader should verify this by applying steps (b) and (c) to the bit string 11100011 representing –29. The resulting bit string can be seen to represent +29. In this way, one can find the base-10 representation of a negative number that is in two's-complement form.

The n-bit representation of a negative integer $-x$ is equal to the base-2 representation of $2^n - x$. You can see this by looking at the base-10 example on page 10. The corresponding statement would be that $-x$ is represented as $10^n - x$, and since $n = 3$ in that example, the statement says that $-x$ is represented as $1,000 - x$. Thus, in that example, –2 was represented by 998, which is indeed $1,000 - 2$, and similarly, the number –3 was represented by 997, which is $1,000 - 3$, and so on.

Using this knowledge, you can now see why the foregoing "shortcut" works: Let Q denote the n-bit string consisting of all 1's, and let A, B, and C be the results of applying, respectively, steps (a), (b), and (c) to finding the n-bit two's-complement representation of a negative number $-x$. We then have the following results:

1. $A + B = Q$ [by definition of step (b) and Q].

2. $C = B + 1$ [by definition of step (c)].

3. $C = Q - A + 1$ [from steps 1 and 2].

4. $C = 2^n - A$ [since, from the definition of Q, $Q + 1 = 2^n$].

The right-hand side of step 4 is the n-bit two's-complement representation of $-x$, which is what we have been claiming for C.

The reader should also verify the following properties, true for general n, for the case of four-bit strings:

(i) The range of integers supported by the n-bit, two's-complement representation is -2^{n-1} to $2^{n-1}-1$.

(ii) The values -2^{n-1} and $2^{n-1}-1$ are represented by 10000...000 and 01111...111, respectively.

(iii) All nonnegative numbers have a 0 in bit $n-1$, and all negative numbers have a 1 in that bit position.

Incidentally, due to the slight asymmetry in the range in property (i), we cannot use the "shortcut" method if we need to find the two's-complement representation of the number -2^{n-1}; step (a) of that method would be impossible, since the number 2^{n-1} is not representable. Instead, we just use property (ii).

We can now solve the mystery of the Pascal statement

```
Sum:=X+Y;
```

discussed in the introduction. It was asserted there that the value of Sum might become negative, even if the values of both X and Y are positive. The reader should now be able to verify this: with 16-bit storage and with X = 28,502 and Y = 12,344, the resulting value of Sum will be –24,690. We will discuss this problem further, and solutions to it, in Chapter 6.

Again, most modern CPUs, including those in the iAPX family, use the two's-complement system for storing signed integers. We will assume this system from this point on, except where stated otherwise.

1.2.2 Representing Real Number Data

The main idea in representing real numbers is to use **scientific notation**, familiar from physics or chemistry, say,

$$3.2 \times 10^{-4}$$

for the number 0.00032. In this example, 3.2 is called the **mantissa** and –4 is called the **exponent**.

The representation of real numbers in a computer—i.e., numbers that are not necessarily integers (also called **floating-point** numbers)—is essentially of the form

$$m \times 2^n$$

with m and n stored as individual bit strings. If, for example, we were to store real numbers as 16-bit strings, we might devote 10 bits—say, bits 15–6—to the mantissa m, and 6 bits—say, bits 5–0—to the exponent n. Then the number 1.25 might be represented as

$$5 \times 2^{-2}$$

that is, with $m = 5$ and $n = -2$. As a 10-bit two's-complement number, 5 is represented by the bit string 0000000101, while as a 6-bit two's-complement number, –2 is represented by 111110. Thus, we would store the number 1.25 as the 16-bit string

$$0000000101111110 = 017\text{EH}.$$

The representation commonly used on IBM microcomputers features 32-bit storage, in order to provide a broad range of numbers and reasonably small roundoff error for individual computations. It consists of a sign bit, an 8-bit exponent field, and a 23-bit mantissa field. In explaining these fields, keep in mind the distinction between the terms *mantissa* and *mantissa field*, and between *exponent* and *exponent field*.

Recall that in base 10, digits to the right of the decimal point are associated with negative powers of 10. For example, 4.38 means

$$4(10^0)+3(10^{-1})+8(10^{-2})$$

The principle is the same in base 2, of course, with the base-2 number 1.101 meaning

$$1(2^0)+1(2^{-1})+0(2^{-2})+1(2^{-3})$$

that is, 1.625 in base 10.

Under the IBM microcomputer format, the mantissa must be in the form $\pm1.x$, where x is some bit string. In other words, the absolute value of the mantissa must be a number between 1 and 2. The number 1.625 is 1.101 in base 2, so it already has this form. Thus, we would take the exponent to be 0, that is, we would represent 1.625 as

$$1.101\times2^0$$

What about the number 0.375? In base 2, this number is 0.011, so we *could* write 0.375 as

$$0.011\times2^0$$

But again, the IBM format insists on a mantissa of the form $\pm1.x$. So we would write 0.375 instead as

$$1.1\times2^{-2}$$

which of course is equivalent to 0.011×2^0, but the point is that the former fits IBM's convention for the mantissa.

Now since that convention requires that the leading bit of the mantissa be 1, there is no point in storing it! Thus, the mantissa field only contains the bits to the right of the leading 1, so that the mantissa consists of $\pm1.x$, where x is the bit string stored in the mantissa field. The sign of the mantissa is given by the sign bit, 0 for positive and 1 for negative.

Suprisingly, the exponent field does *not* directly contain the exponent; instead, it stores the exponent plus a **bias** of 127. The exponent field itself is considered an eight-bit unsigned number and thus has values ranging from 0 to 255. However, the values 0 and 255 have a special meaning: 0 means that the floating-point number is 0, and 255 means that it is in a sense infinity, the result of dividing by 0, for example. Thus the exponent field actually has a range of 1 to 254, which, after accounting for the bias term, means that the exponent is a number in the range -126 to $+127$ ($1-127=-126$ and $254-127=+127$).

With all this in mind, let us find the representation of the number 1.625. We have found that the mantissa is 1.101 and the exponent is 0. Thus, the 23-bit mantissa field is

$$10100000000000000000000$$

(The mantissa is 1.101, but remember that we do not store the '1.' in the mantissa field.) The exponent field is $0 + 127 = 127$, or, in bit form,

$$01111111$$

The sign bit is 0, since 1.625 is a positive number.

Now, how are the three fields stored altogether in one 32-bit string? Well, 32 bits fill four bytes, say, at addresses n, $n+1$, $n+2$, and $n+3$. The format for storing the three fields is then as follows:

Byte n: least-significant eight bits of the mantissa field

Byte $n+1$: middle eight bits of the mantissa field

Byte $n+2$: least significant bit of the exponent field and most-significant seven bits of the mantissa field

Byte $n+3$: sign bit, and most-significant seven bits of the exponent field

Suppose for example, we have a variable, say, T, of type **real** in Pascal or **float** in C, which the compiler has decided to store beginning at byte 304A2H. Then if the current value of T is 1.625, the bit pattern will be

Byte 304A2: 00; byte 304A3: 00; byte 304A4: D0; byte 304A5: 3F

As another check, the reader should verify that if the contents of the four bytes are E1 7A 60 42, then the number represented is 56.12.

1.2.3 Representing Character Data

Representing character data is merely a matter of choosing which bit patterns will represent which characters. The two most famous systems are the American Standard Code for Information Interchange (ASCII) and the Extended Binary Coded Decimal Information Code (EBCDIC). ASCII stores each character as the base-2 form of a number between 0 and 127. For example, 'A' is stored as 65_{10} (01000001 = 41H) and '%' is stored as 37_{10} (00100101 = 25H).

A complete list of standard ASCII codes appears in Appendix I. Note that even keys such as the carriage return, line feed, and so on are considered characters and have ASCII codes.

Incidentally, those who have studied Pascal may recall the Pascal **ord** function. This function gives the numeric code of a character. For example, for a computer system that uses ASCII, ord('A') = 65.

Since ASCII codes are taken from base-2 numbers in the range 0 to $2^7-1 = 127$, each code consists of seven bits. By contrast, EBCDIC system consists of eight bits and thus can code 256 different characters, as opposed to ASCII's 128. In either system, a character can be stored in one byte.

From this point on, we will use the ASCII system unless otherwise specified, because most computers today, including those in the IBM microcomputer family, use that system. The IBM microcomputers themselves actually use an extension of the ASCII system that uses all eight bits; thus, codes for a number of non-ASCII characters are allowed. Interested readers should check their IBM manuals for details.

1.2.4 Representing Machine Instructions

Each type of computer has a set of binary codes used to specify various operations. For example, in the IBM microcomputer family, the code C7070100, i.e.,

$$1100011100000111000000000100000000$$

in binary, means that the value 1 is to be put into a certain cell of the computer's memory. The circuitry in the computer is designed to recognize such patterns and act accordingly. You will learn how to generate these patterns in later chapters, but for now, the thing to keep in mind is that a computer's machine instructions consist of patterns of 0's and 1's.

Note that we can get an instruction into the computer in one of two ways:

(a) We write a program in machine language (or assembly language, which we will see is essentially the same), directly producing instructions such as the foregoing.

(b) We write a program in a high-level language (HLL) such as Pascal or C, and the compiler translates that program into instructions such as the foregoing.

(The reader should keep in mind throughout what follows that compilers themselves are programs. Thus, they consist of machine-language instructions, although, of course, these instructions might themselves have been generated from an HLL source.)

1.2.5 What Type of Information Is Stored Here?

A natural question to ask at this point would be how the computer "knows" what kind of information is being stored in a given bit string. For example, suppose we have the 16-bit string 0111010000101011,—in hex form, 742B. Then

(a) If this string is being used to store a signed integer, its value will be 29,739.

(b) If this string is being used to store characters, its contents will be the characters 't' and '+'.

(c) If this string is being used to store a machine instruction, the instruction says to "jump" (like a **goto** in Pascal or C) forward 43 bytes.

(The reader should check the first two cases. Case (c) will become clear in Chapter 3, so we can only take it on faith for now; however, note again that this case, as opposed to (a) and (b), is highly machine specific, applying only to computers that use the iAPX family of CPUs.)

So, in this context, the question is,

How does the computer "know" which of the preceding three kinds (or other kinds) of information is being stored in the bit string 742BH? Is it 29,739? Is it 't' and '+'? Or is it a jump-ahead-43-bytes machine instruction?

The answer is, "The computer does *not* know!" As far as the computer is concerned, the information is just a string of 16 0's and 1's, with *no* special meaning. So the responsibility rests with the person who writes the program, who must remember what kind of information he or she stored in that bit string. If the programmer makes a mistake, the computer will not notice and will carry out the programmer's instruction, no matter how ridiculous it is. For example, suppose the programmer had stored *characters* in each of two bit strings, but forgets this and mistakenly thinks that *integers* were stored in the strings. If the programmer then tells the computer to multiply those two "numbers," the computer will dutifully obey and produce an erroneous result.

The discussion in the preceding paragraph refers to the case in which we program in machine language directly. What about the case in which we program in an HLL, say, Pascal or the C language? In that case, the *compiler* produces the machine language from our HLL source. Then, during the time the compiler is translating the HLL source to machine language, the compiler must "remember" the type of each variable and react accordingly. In other words, the responsibility for handling various data types properly is now in the hands of the compiler, rather than directly in the hands of the programmer—but still not in the hands of the hardware, which, as indicated before, remains ignorant of the type of data in question.

As an example, suppose that in a Pascal program X and Y are declared to be of types **char** and **integer**, respectively, and the program includes the statement

```
X:=X+Y;
```

The Pascal language is **strongly typed**, meaning that it reflects the philosophy that mixing types is a dangerous programming practice. Thus, the Pascal compiler would declare an error upon encountering the foregoing statement and would refuse to produce machine language from it.

But again, this refusal is in the software—the Pascal compiler—not in the hardware. To the hardware, X and Y are simply typeless bit strings, which of course can be summed, and thus the machine is indeed capable of adding them. In fact, the language C is *not* strongly typed, and a C compiler faced with the statement in question will uncomplainingly go ahead and produce machine instructions that perform the indicated addition.

As another example, consider the built-in Pascal procedure **writeln**, which is used to write the values of program variables to the terminal screen. Suppose again that we have a variable Y of type **integer**, and consider the Pascal statement

```
writeln(Y);
```

In translating this, the compiler will "recall" that Y is of type **integer** and thus produce appropriate machine code for this type. But what is "appropriate" here? Well, keep in mind that circuitry in the terminal screen is set up to receive eight-bit strings and to react to such a string by displaying on the screen whatever ASCII character the string denotes.

Thus, if the current value of Y is, say, 9,778 (base 10), so that the bit string stored in Y's memory location is 0010011000110010, then the machine instructions within the **writeln** procedure must send the *characters* '9', '7', '7', and '8' to the screen—that is, these machine instructions must first send the string 00111001, then the string 00110111, then 00110111, and finally 00111000. Note carefully that it would be disastrously wrong for these machine instructions within **writeln** to simply send the "raw" contents of Y's memory location—i.e., first send 00100110 and then send 00110010. The hapless screen circuitry would then obediently print the corresponding characters, '&' and '2', to the screen, instead of '9', '7', '7', and '8'! (The reader should pause at this point and take the time to understand fully why this would occur.)

Thus, the **writeln** procedure, innocent as it may seem at first glance, is actually a complicated program. It must go through a lot of work to extract the *characters* '9', '7', '7', and '8' from the *number* 9,778. We will see the details of how this is done in Chapter 7, but for now the point is that quite a few machine instructions are needed in **writeln** to do the work. If, on the other hand, Y had been of type **char**, a much, much simpler section in the **writeln** procedure would have been involved, since the bit string stored in Y's memory location would *already* be in the form needed for the screen circuitry. That string would be sent directly to the screen without any alteration.

Now, backing away a little from the details in the last paragraph, let us note once again that the major point here is that the computer *hardware* is not aware of what data type we intend for a bit string stored in any particular memory location; rather, the *software*, in this case the Pascal compiler, is enforcing types and acting upon them. In particular, in translating the Pascal statement

```
writeln(Y);
```

the compiler will use one section of the **writeln** procedure if Y is declared of type **integer**, and a different section of that procedure if Y is declared of type **char**.

By contrast, in the language C, some of this responsibility is left to the programmer, rather than the compiler. In writing out the value of a variable to the terminal screen, it is up to the *programmer* to decide how the bit string in that variable is to be interpreted. For example, consider the following C code:

```
Y = -32697;
printf("%d %u %c\n",Y,Y,Y);
```

Before determining what is printed, note that although Pascal has two types of subprograms, namely, **procedures** and **functions**, C uses the term **function** for both of these. The built-in C function **printf** is thus analogous to Pascal's built-in procedure **write**.

In the foregoing code, we are printing the bit string in Y to the screen three times, but are directing that this bit string be interpreted first as a decimal signed integer (%d), then as a decimal unsigned integer (%u), and then as an ASCII character (%c). We then instruct the computer to go to a new line (indicated by \n, making this like a Pascal **writeln** rather than a **write**). Assuming that the compiler stores integer variables in 16-bit words (see later), the output that would appear on the screen is

```
-32697  32839  G
```

The bit string in Y is 8047H. Interpreted as a 16-bit two's-complement number, the string represents the number –32,697. Interpreted as an unsigned number, the string represents 32,839. If the least significant eight bits of the string are interpreted as an ASCII character, they represent the character 'G'.

Remember, the key point in these examples is that the *hardware* is ignorant; it has no idea as to what type of data we intend to be stored in Y's memory location. The interpretation of data types is solely in the software. As far as the hardware is concerned, the contents of a memory location are just a bit string and nothing more.

In fact, the language C allows one to view the bit string in an uninterpreted manner, by using the %x format in the call to printf. This will result in the bit string itself being printed out (in hex notation).

A similar situation exists for disk storage. Disk hardware simply stores collections of bytes; it is ignorant as to whether those bytes represent numbers, characters, machine instructions, or whatever. It is also ignorant of the concept of files on the disk. The partitioning of the storage areas on the disk into files is done by the operating system (OS), again quite transparently to the disk hardware.

This idea of "who is responsible for what?"—e.g., asking whether a particular concept is in the domain of hardware versus software—is one of the themes running throughout this book.

1.3 ORGANIZATION OF MAIN MEMORY

1.3.1 Words and Addresses

During the time a program is executing, both the program's data and the program itself—i.e., the machine instructions—are stored in main memory. In this section, we introduce the structure of main memory. (We will usually refer to main memory simply as "memory.")

Memory can be viewed as a long string of consecutive bytes. Most modern machines, including those of the Intel, Motorola, and VAX families, give an identification number, called an **address**, to each individual byte. An address is just an "i.d. number," like a social security number, which identifies a person, a license number, which identifies a car, and an account number, which identifies a bank account. Byte addresses are consecutive integers, so that the memory of a computer consists of byte 0, byte 1, byte 2, and so on.

On typical machines, including those just mentioned, a certain number of consecutive bytes is called a **word**. The number of bytes or bits (there are eight times as many bits as bytes, since a byte consists of eight bits) in a word in a given machine is called the machine's **word size**. This is usually defined in terms of the size of operands on which the CPU addition circuitry is capable of operating. For example, the adder in iAPX 86 and iAPX 286 CPUs is capable of adding two 16-bit numbers together, so we say the word size for these machines is 16 bits. This is a common word size, also seen on the earlier Motorola 68000 family CPUs. Machines with 32-bit words such as the VAX, the iAPX 386 and 486, and the later 68000-series CPUs, are also common.

A characteristic of the iAPX 386 and 486 CPUs is that they can emulate CPUs of the iAPX 86 and 286 types, so that the same program can run on any iAPX machine. In particular, the 386 and 486 models can operate in a mode which treats words as being 16 bits wide instead of 32. For simplicity, we will assume this mode from now on.

Thus, each iAPX word consists of two bytes, and each word "inherits" an address from the first of those two bytes. Word 0 consists of byte 0 and byte 1, word 2 consists of byte 2 and byte 3, and so on. (Also, bytes 1 and 2 form word 1, etc., so that the odd-numbered words overlap their even-numbered neighbors.)

This raises a question: how can we tell the computer that we wish to refer to a byte rather than to a word, or vice versa? For example, how can we specify that we want to access byte 52 instead of word 52? The answer is that for machine instruction types which allow both byte and word access (some instructions do, while others do not), the instruction itself will indicate whether we want to access byte x or word x.

As an example, in Section 1.2.4, we mentioned that the instruction C7070100 puts the value 1 into a certain cell of memory. Since we now have the terms "word" and "byte" to work with, we can be more specific than simply using the word "cell" here: the instruction C7070100 puts the value 1 into a certain *word* of memory; by contrast, the instruction C60701 puts the value 1 into a certain *byte* of memory. Again, the details of these operations will be discussed in later chapters, but for now you can see that differentiating between byte access and word access *is* possible and is indicated in the bit pattern of the instruction itself.

Note that the word size determines the capacity of a computer, depending on what type of information we wish to store. For example:

(a) Suppose we are using an n-bit word to store a nonnegative integer. Then the range of numbers that we can store will be 0 to $2^n - 1$, which, for $n = 16$, will be 0 to 65,535 and, for $n = 32$, will be 0 to 4,294,967,295.

(b) If we are storing a signed integer in an n-bit word, then the range will be -2^{n-1} to $2^{n-1} - 1$, which will be $-32,768$ to $+32,767$ for 16-bit words and $-2,147,483,648$ to $+2,147,483,647$ for 32-bit words.

(c) Suppose we wish to store characters. Recall from Section 1.2.3 that a character will take up either seven or eight bits, depending on which coding system is used. But even if a seven-bit system is used, it is typical that the seven is "rounded off" to eight, with one bit left unused (or used for some other purpose, such as a feature called **parity**, which is used to help detect errors). So we will assume that a character takes up eight bits. In that case, machines with 16-bit words can store two characters per word, while 32-bit machines can store four characters per word.

(d) Suppose we are storing machine instructions. On most machines, instructions are of variable length. On iAPX 86 machines, for instance, instructions are of length one to six bytes. Since the word size on such machines is 16 bits (i.e., two bytes), in some cases a word might contain two instructions, while in other cases an instruction would be spread out over several words. The instruction C7070100 in Section 1.2.4, for example, takes up four bytes (count them!) and thus two words of memory.

In most cases, we will concentrate on IBM microcomputers which have a 16-bit word size.

It is helpful to make an analogy between memory cells (bytes or words) and bank accounts. Each individual bank account has an account number and a balance. Similarly, each memory cell has an address and contents.

As with anything else in a computer, an address is given in terms of 0's and 1's, i.e., as a base-2 representation of an unsigned integer. The number of bits in an address is called the **address size**. Among IBM microcomputers, the address size varies from 20 bits on the models based on the iAPX 86 CPU subfamily to 24 bits on the machines which use iAPX 286 CPUs and 32 bits for iAPX 386 and 486 CPUs. VAX and many other machines also have 32-bit addresses.

Once again, although the later iAPX models (286, 386, and 486) have address sizes greater than 20 bits, in their simpler running mode (called **real mode**), they still use only the 20-bit addresses. In order to exploit their 24-bit or 32-bit memory addressing capabilities, they must be switched to **protected mode**. This, will be discussed in Chapter 8, but until then, we will assume real-mode operation. Thus, all iAPX addresses will be assumed to be 20 bits long, through Chapter 7. And, as indicated earlier, we will assume all iAPX words to be 16 bits long, since even the 386/486 models, which have the capability of operating on 32-bit quantities, can be run in 16-bit mode.

A computer's address size is crucial, since it puts an upper bound on how many memory bytes the system can have. If the address size is n, then addresses will range from 0 to $2^n - 1$, so we can have at most 2^n bytes of memory in the system. The situation is similar to the case of automobile license plates. If for example, license plates in a certain state consist of three letters and three digits, then there will be only $26^3 10^3 = 17,560,000$ possible plates. That would mean that we could have only 17,560,000 cars and trucks in the state.

So, since many modern applications have very large memory requirements, and it is common to have many programs resident in memory together, the address size of a computer can be a very limiting factor. For example, the 20-bit addresses used on the IBM PC/XT limit the maximum memory size to 2^{20}, or approximately 1 million, bytes, i.e., about half a million words. When IBM PCs were first introduced in the early 1980's, this was considered to be a large memory size, but today that size is considered to be quite restrictive. We will discuss how later PC models can overcome such a size restriction in Chapter 8.

Keep in mind that an address is considered an unsigned integer. For example, suppose our address size is, to keep the example simple, four bits. Then the address 1111 is considered to be +15, not −1.

We will use the notation c( ) to mean "contents of"; e.g., c(2B410) means the contents of memory word 2B410.

1.3.2 Storage of Variables in HLL Programs

When you execute a program, both its instructions and its data are stored in memory. Keep in mind that the word "instructions" here means machine-language instructions. Again, these machine language instructions were either written by the programmer directly or produced by a compiler from a source file written by the programmer in Pascal, C, or some other HLL. Let us now look at storage of *data* in the Pascal/C/HLL case.

In an HLL program, we specify our data via names. For example, suppose the declaration section of a Pascal program is as given in Program 1.1. The compiler will assign each of the variables of the program a location in memory. Generally (but not always, depending on the compiler), these locations will be consecutive, in the same order as the order in which they are declared. In other words, Y will be stored right next to X, Z right next to Y, W[1] right next to Z, W[2] right next to W[1], and so on.

```
var X,Y,Z : integer;
    W : array[1..4] of integer;
    U,V : char;
    M,N : boolean;
    A,B,C : real;
```

Program 1.1

A variable might be stored in one byte, one word, or more than one word, depending on the data type and on the compiler. For example, the Microsoft Pascal compiler stores variables of type **integer** in one word, variables of type **char** in one byte, variables of type **boolean** in one byte, and variables of type **real** in two words. Suppose the data area of our program in memory starts at word 20050. Then a compiler might assign locations to variables as shown in Table 1.1. (It is possible on most systems for these addresses to be **relocated**, i.e., changed in some manner, by the time the program is loaded into memory. We will see what happens in one type of relocation in Chapters 2, 4 and 8, but for now, let us restrict our attention to a simple compiler-machine combination that does not allow relocation.)

The developers of a compiler will generally choose the storage size of a variable type in a way that is natural for the hardware. For example, the hardware that does integer addition and other arithmetic operations typically is set up to operate on one-word quantities. Thus, it is natural for the designer to assign one word of storage for Pascal **integer** and C **int** variables. For example, for the Pascal statement

```
Y:=25;
```

the compiler will produce machine code that puts 0019H (the 16-bit hex form of 25) into word 20052.

TABLE 1.1

Variable	Location
X	Word 20050
Y	Word 20052
Z	Word 20054
W[1]	Word 20056
W[2]	Word 20058
W[3]	Word 2005A
W[4]	Word 2005C
U	Byte 2005E
V	Byte 2005F
M	Byte 20060
N	Byte 20061
A	Words 20062, 20064
B	Words 20066, 20068
C	Words 2006A, 2006C

Note that the choice of a size for **integer** variables limits the range of such variables. Recall that for n-bit storage, this range will be -2^{n-1} to $2^{n-1} - 1$; the latter value is called **maxint** in Pascal. On machines of the iAPX 86 and iAPX 286 subfamilies (and even on 386/486 models, running in 16-bit mode), the compiler will produce **integer** variables that range from −32,768 to +32,767, with **maxint** having the latter value.

Since this range might be too restrictive, some compilers and languages offer alternative types for integer variables. The Microsoft Pascal compiler for iAPX 86 and iAPX 286 machines, for example, gives the programmer the option of declaring variables to be of a special type **integer4**, instead of **integer**. The "4" means four bytes, i.e., 32 bits, which would produce a range of −2,147,483,648 to +2,147,483,647. In the language C, there is a corresponding type called **long**, as opposed to the type **int**, which corresponds to Pascal's **integer**.

Of course, the increase in range gained by introducing special integer types is offset by a slowdown in execution speed, since the adders in these machines operate on only 16 bits at a time. As you will see in Chapter 6, the machine code produced by the compiler is correspondingly more complicated.

Another example is variables of type **char**. Recall from Section 1.2.3 that a character can easily be fit into the space of one byte. Thus, it would be wasteful to assign a whole word to each **char** variable, and as Table 1.1 shows, our compiler has indeed avoided such a waste: it does store **char** variables as individual bytes. For example, if Program 1.1 contains a statement

```
V:='A';
```

then the compiler will produce machine code that puts 41H, the ASCII code for 'A', in byte 2005F.

The C language allows one to store eight-bit integers that are near 0 in its **char** type. As remarked earlier, C is not a strongly typed language; thus, the compiler will not object to our using variables of type **char** to store integers. The eight-bit size will give us a range of −128 to +127. As long as our variables will not be outside this range, we save memory space by using **char** instead of **int**; if we have a large array of such variables, the space savings may be important. Also, for integers in the range 0 to +255—i.e., in the range of *unsigned* eight-bit quantities—C offers the type **unsigned char**.

What about variables of type **boolean**, which take on only two values, **true** and **false**? We can store such variables in one bit, setting the bit to 1 for **true** and 0 for **false**. However, in iAPX machines (and almost all others, for that matter), individual bits in memory do not have addresses; the smallest item that has an address is a byte, eight bits. Thus, it would be difficult to store **boolean** variables in individual bits. For example, if M and N in Program 1.1 were to be stored in consecutive bits, they both would be listed as being in byte 20060 in Table 1.1, which would be ambiguous.

Accordingly, in the table, the compiler has assigned M and N to one byte each, in spite of the waste that entails. Thus, if Program 1.1 contains a statement

```
N:=true;
```

then the compiler will produce machine code that puts 01H in Byte 20061; the corresponding value for 'false' is 00H.

If we are really worried about space, we might consider **packing** variables. Suppose, for instance, we have an array of 160,000 **boolean** variables and have a Pascal compiler that allows **packed arrays**. Then packing would result in using only 20,000 bytes of memory, instead of 160,000, since we could store each variable in one bit. You will see how this is done in Chapter 6. (Incidentally, you might think 160,000 is an outlandish size for an array, but it could arise quite easily. On a graphics screen, for example, each screen position—i.e., each **pixel**—is represented by a **boolean** variable, 1 meaning dark and 0 meaning light. Screens with 100,000 pixels or more are common, so an array of 160,000 elements is not at all something to be surprised at.)

What about variables of type **real**? The compiler assumed in Table 1.1 assigns two words, i.e., 32 bits, of storage for each **real** number. As explained in Section 1.2.2, this size is fairly commonly used in general-purpose computer systems, because it yields reasonably good accuracy, i.e., reasonably small computational roundoff errors for most ordinary applications.

Note that, unlike the preceding cases of **integer**, **char**, and **boolean** types, the choice of the 32-bit size was *not* made on the basis of the size of **real** data that the hardware works on. CPUs in the IBM microcomputer family, and in most other microcomputers, do *not* include instructions to do arithmetic on real numbers (although optional attachments to supplement such CPUs are available to do this, and the new 80486 CPU has this capability, as will be mentioned in Chapter 6). Instead, the compiler must synthesize these arithmetic operations from sequences of more primitive instructions. (Some earlier microcomputer CPUs did not even have integer-multiplication instructions, so compilers had to synthesize even that operation. For example, a Pascal statement like

```
Z:=26*Z;
```

could be translated into a machine-language loop, in which the original value of Z is added to Z 25 times.)

In the language C, the **sizeof** operator tells us how many bytes of storage the compiler will allocate for any variable type. For instance, the expression

```
sizeof(int)
```

will be equal to the number of bytes that the compiler allocates to a variable of type **int** (which is the same as the type **integer** in Pascal). An example in which knowledge of that number is useful is the **malloc** function, which is used in C to allocate extra memory **dynamically**, i.e., at the time the program is running rather than at compilation time, as in Table 1.1. Suppose we have a C program that needs to allocate memory space dynamically for 100 variables of type **int**. On an iAPX 86 or 286 machine, we would do this allocation with the C statement

```
P = malloc(200);
```

since each **int** variable needs two bytes of memory. (In executing this statement, the system will allocate the 200 bytes of memory and then set the variable P to contain the address of the memory space, so as to inform us where the space is.) On the other hand, on a VAX, with four-byte words, our statement would need to be

```
P = malloc(400);
```

It would be highly inconvenient to need to have a different version of our program for each different machine. The **sizeof** operator eliminates this need; we can use the single statement

```
P = malloc(100*sizeof(int));
```

on *any* machine. On an iAPX 86 machine, for example, the compiler "knows" that integers are two bytes in length, so it will set up machine code to allocate 200 bytes of memory space. On a VAX, the compiler "knows" that integers are four bytes long, so it will produce machine instructions to allocate 400 bytes. The point is that the same C-language program will be compilable and executable on either of these machines.

Note once again that the hardware is quite unaware of the data type of an HLL variable. As far as the hardware is concerned, each variable is simply a bit string. For example, suppose that in a C program we have the declaration

```
char c;
```

and the statement

```
c = 65;
```

If the reader is accustomed to Pascal, this second statement may look strange, since it assigns a value of type **int** to a variable of type **char**. But the language C allows this, and since the hardware does not know about data types anyway, the hardware will not "complain" either.

The Microsoft C compiler will translate this statement into the machine instruction

```
11000110000001101110000000000000101000001
```

Note the last eight bits here, 01000001; they are the binary representation of the number 65. If the instruction had instead been

```
c = 'A';
```

then the compiler would have produced *exactly the same machine instruction*, since the ASCII code for 'A' is again 01000001. The instruction itself says to copy this bit string, 01000001, to the memory byte allocated to the variable c. You will see later why this particular bit pattern denotes this copy operation, but the main point for now is that the 'A' is specified in bit form.*

In general, the language C is very liberal in allowing mixing of types. Sometimes it requires the programmer to confirm that he or she is deliberately doing so; confirmation is carried out with a **cast**, as will be seen in Chapter 2.

As implied in the foregoing examples, array variables are generally implemented by compilers as contiguous blocks of memory. For example, the array declared in Microsoft Pascal as

```
x : array[1..100] of integer;
```

*Again, it is important to remember that *everything* is in bit form when your program runs. In particular, all numeric quantities will be in their base-2 form. Suppose, for example, you have a Pascal program that includes the following lines:

```
var i:integer;

readln(i);
i:=i*18;
```

If, when you run the program you input the value 25 for i at the keyboard, the procedure **readln** will "see" the characters '2' and '5' and form the base-2 representation of 25, which is 11001. Earlier, when you compiled the program, the compiler had already translated the 18 to its base-2 form, which is 10001. The multiplication performed at execution-time will then be 11001 times 10001.

or in Microsoft C as

```
int x[100];
```

would be allocated to some set of 100 consecutive words in memory (words, because **integer** and **int** variables are implemented by these compilers as 16-bit quantities).

What about two-dimensional arrays? For example, consider the four-row, six-column Pascal array

```
g : array[1..4,1..6] of integer;
```

and its C equivalent

```
int g[4][6];
```

Again, these arrays will be implemented in blocks of consecutive words of memory—more specifically, 24 consecutive words—since these arrays consist of 4*6 = 24 elements. But in what order will those 24 elements be arranged? Most compilers use either **row-major** or **column-major** order. In row-major order, all elements of the first row are stored at the beginning of the block, then all the elements of the second row are stored, then the third row, and so on. In column-major order, it is just the opposite: all of the first column is stored first, then all of the second column, and so on.

In the preceding example, consider the Pascal element g[2,5], and its C counterpart g[1][4] (since all C array subscripts start at 0, the second row is called row 1 and the fifth column is called column 4). If the compilers use row-major order, this element would be stored as the 11th word in the block of words allocated to g. If column-major order is used, the element would be stored in the 18th word. (The reader should verify both of these statements.) C compilers use row-major order; no general convention exists for Pascal.

Advanced data types are handled similarly, again in contiguous memory locations. For example, **record** type in Pascal, say,

```
record
   X : integer;
   A,B : char
   end;
```

or its equivalent, **struct**, in C, as in

```
struct  {
   int X;
   char A,B;
}
```

would be stored on a 16-bit machine in four consecutive bytes, two for X and then one each for A and B.

As remarked in the introduction, the language C tends to get involved at the machine level more than do other HLLs. The **sizeof** operator mentioned on page 24 is an example of this, as are the operators **&** and *****, which act as inverses of each other. As an example of how these operators work, let us look at a C version of the declarations in Program 1.1. This is given in Program 1.2.

```
int X,Y,Z,W[4];

char U,V,M,N;

float A,B,C;
```

Program 1.2

Note that the language C has no explicit **boolean** type. In boolean expressions, it just treats 0 as **false** and any nonzero value as **true**. So C's **char** type, which is nominally for storage of characters but actually can be used to store eight-bit integers, is sufficiently large to informally store values corresponding to Pascal's **boolean** type. We have done this here. The memory storage could be the same as in Table 1.1. (We also assume that the declarations in Program 1.2 are global, not local to main (). In the latter case, storage of variables is in reverse order, e.g., with Y being stored at a lower address than X.)

Now, the C operators **&** and ***** stand for "address of" and "contents of," respectively. Thus, &Y would be 0x20052 (the prefix '0x' is C notation to indicate a bit string given in hexadecimal form), since Table 1.1 tells us that Y is that memory location. Conversely, *0x20052 would be whatever the current *value* of Y is. So ***** acts as the inverse of **&**, with *(&Y) being Y again.

To make this concrete, suppose our C program contains the code

```
Y = 12;
printf("%d %d %d %d\n",Y,&Y,*131154,*0x20052);
```

As mentioned before, the C function **printf** is analogous to Pascal's **write** procedure. A '%d' field means to print out to the screen as a signed, base-10 integer. Here, the values printed out on the screen would be 12, 131154, 12, and 12, where 131154 is the base-10 version of 20052H. (This is in general; in the case of iAPX machines, the situation is slightly more complex, as you will see in Chapter 2.)

The ***** operator in C is one of the reasons for C's popularity. Using it, a programmer can access specific words in memory from a high-level language program, instead of having to resort to assembly language. Our first concrete example of this will come in Chapter 2, in which we show how to write to the memory locations that control an IBM microcomputer's monitor screen.

We have not yet discussed how **pointer** variables in Pascal and C are stored. *A pointer is an address.* In C, for example, suppose we have the declaration

```
int *G,X;
```

The declaration instructs the compiler to allocate memory for two variables, one named G and the other named X. It also instructs the compiler as to what types these variables will have: X will be of integer type, while the '*' says that G will be of pointer-to-integer type—meaning that G will store the address of some integer. For instance, in our program, we might have the statement

```
G = &X;
```

which would place the address of X into G. If one then executed the statement

```
printf("%x\n",G);
```

the address of X would be printed to the monitor.

In Pascal, pointer variables consist of addresses too, but you can see them only at the machine-language level, i.e., when you inspect the compiled code. It is not possible in (standard) Pascal to print out the numerical value of a pointer, as it is in C.

In C, '&' is also needed for parameters in function calls. For example, to read the preceding variable X from the keyboard, we would have the following call to **scanf**, C's analogue of Pascal's **read** and **readln** procedures:

```
scanf("%d",&X);
```

The call to **scanf** passes the address of X, as opposed to a call to **printf** (C's analog of Pascal's **write** and **writeln** procedures), which passes the value of X:

```
printf("%d\n",X);
```

The reason for this will be discussed in detail in Chapter 5.

Just as C's **&** operator is useful in this way for pointers, the * operator indicates the "pointee," i.e., the object pointed to. So, in the foregoing example, we might have

```
*G = 3;
```

analogous to the Pascal statement

```
G^:=3;
```

In both cases, the meaning is "Put the value 3 into the object pointed to by G."

Another aspect of C pointers that explicitly exposes the way it stores program objects in memory is **pointer arithmetic**. For example, suppose p is of pointer type. Then $p+1$ would point to the next consecutive object of the type to which p points. To be specific, say the last line of Program 1.2 were to be changed to

```
float A,B,C,*Q;
```

and we executed the statement

```
Q = &B;
```

Then Q+1 would point to C, and if we were to execute the statement

```
printf("%d\n",(Q+1)-Q);
```

the value printed out would be 4, not 1.

Another very important thing to note is that the variable names in a Pascal, C, or other HLL program are just for the convenience of us humans. In the machine-language program produced from our HLL file by the compiler, all references to the variables are through their addresses in memory, with no references whatsoever to the original variable names. Those names are discarded when the compiler finishes its work.

For example, consider Program 1.1. As the compiler scans through that program, the first major section it will encounter is the declaration of variables. The compiler will then allocate memory for each of those variables and record the names, types, and memory locations in its **symbol table**. A symbol table is essentially what you see in Table 1.1 (but with a column for the data type of each variable added in). It is just an array in the compiler program. (Remember, the compiler *is* a program, and programs often have arrays.)

After the compiler finishes scanning the declaration section of the Pascal program and setting up the symbol table, it will scan the program's procedures and main section. Suppose it encounters the Pascal statement

```
X:=Y+4;
```

The compiler will then produce some machine-language instructions to implement this action. These instructions will *not* refer to X and Y—they will only refer to words 20050 and 20052, the *locations* the compiler chose for the Pascal variables X and Y.

For instance, the compiler might produce the following sequence of three machine language instructions from the foregoing line of Pascal:

```
copy word 20052 to a cell in the CPU
add 4 to the contents of that cell
copy that cell to word 20050
```

Note that there is no mention of X and Y at all! The names X and Y were just *temporary* entities, for communication between you and the compiler. The compiler chose memory locations for each variable and then translated all of your Pascal references to those variables to references to those memory locations. When the compiler is done compiling your program, it will discard the symbol table entirely.

ANALYTICAL EXERCISES

1. Give the hex notation for the string 01100100011000111001.
2. If we are working with six-bit strings, what is the range of representable signed integers under the signed-magnitude and two's-complement systems? Find the representation for +13

and -17 in each system. Determine which signed integer is represented by the string 101111 under each system.

3. Consider the Pascal program declaration in Section 1.3, whose "memory chart" is given in Table 1.1.

   (a) Suppose the program at some point sets the variables X, Y, Z, W[1], W[2], W[3], W[4], U, V, M, and N to the values 551, -66, 16, 0, 15, 92, 0, 'd', '*', **true**, and **false**, respectively. Give the hex contents of each byte from byte 20050 through byte 20061, inclusive. (Be careful: Keep in mind the nature of iAPX byte addressing, in which *word n* consists of *bytes n* and $n+1$. Also, in determining two's complement values, make sure to remember the length of the bit string you are supposed to work with.)

   (b) Suppose that between the declarations of V and M there had been a declaration

```
L : array[1..19] of integer;
```

   To what locations would M, N, A, B, and C then have been assigned?

4. Suppose we have a machine with 12-bit word size and a compiler that implements C **int** variables in one word. What would be the output of the C code

```
X = -202;
printf("%d %u %c %x\n",X,X,X,X);
```

   where X is of type **int**?

5. Consider the C statements

```
U = X;   V = Y;
if (X < Y) A = 1; else A = 2;
if (U < V) B = 1; else B = 2;
```

   Suppose X and Y (and A and B) were declared of type **int**, while U and V were declared of type **unsigned**. Will A and B necessarily be equal to each other after these three lines are executed? If yes, explain why; if no, give a counterexample. You should be able to do this problem without actually running it on a computer.

6. The MS-DOS files whose names have the .EXE ("executable") suffix are the actual machine-language programs we execute. Try using the TYPE command for one of these files. (There should be many such files in your \DOS directory.) Why does miscellaneous "random garbage" appear on the screen? Illustrate your answer using the following specific example. Suppose the program in the .EXE file contains the instruction 742B. What will TYPE do when it reads this instruction? (Hint: The TYPE command, just like the other commands which you submit at the DOS '>' prompt, is a *program*. That program could have been written in any language, say C or Pascal. Imagine how you would write such a program and the action it would take when it sees 742B.)

7. Show that in n-bit two's-complement storage of signed integers, the leading bit, bit $n-1$, can be considered the coefficient of -2^{n-1}, with the other bits being coefficients of $+2^k$, $k = n-2, n-3, \ldots, 1, 0$. This approach then gives an alternative way to get the base-10 form from the two's-complement form of a negative number, especially convenient if the latter has a lot of zeros. Use this approach to find the base-10 form of the signed number whose 16-bit, two's-complement representation is 1000000000000011.

8. Consider a computer with a word size of 12 bits and compilers that implement integer variables in one word.

(a) What would be the value of **maxint** in Pascal?

(b) What would be the number of bytes allocated by **malloc** in the C statement

```
p = malloc(100*sizeof(int));
```

9. Consider "four's-complement" storage of signed numbers, the analogue of two's-complement storage, but using base 4. Say we have three digits to work with. Then the decimal number +7 would be represented as 013, since $7 = 1(4^1) + 3(4^0)$. How would -3 be represented?

10. Suppose we already have found the m-bit, two's-complement representation for a negative number $-x$, and now wish to find the n-bit representation for that same number, where $n > m$. Suggest a quick way to find the n-bit form from the m-bit form. Using either the "winding backward" definition or the fact that $-x$ is represented in k-bit strings as $2^k - x$, give an informal proof that your suggested quick computational method works.

11. Suppose we have the Pascal array

```
q : array[1..16000] of 0..3;
```

where 0..3 means that the elements of q take on only the values 0, 1, 2, and 3. How much memory space could be saved if we could pack the array? Assume that without packing the compiler uses 16,000 bytes for this array. What if the range of the elements were 2..5?

12. Consider the C declaration

```
int x[3][4],i,j;
```

which sets up an array of three rows (numbered 0, 1, and 2) and four columns (numbered 0 through 3) and int variables i and j. What will be the output of the C statements

```
i = (int)&x[1,2];   j = (int)x[2,1];
printf("%d\n", i-j);
```

if it is run on a VAX? How would your answer change if the declaration had been for a 3×4 array of type **char**, instead of type **int**?

13. Suppose, in a C language program P, that the variable c is declared to be of type **char**. It was remarked in Section 1.3.1 that the statements

```
c = 65;
```

and

```
c = 'A';
```

would be translated into exactly the same machine instruction. Thus, P would have the same **execution time** in either case. However, the **compilation time**, i.e., the time needed to compile P, would be different for the two versions. Which one would result in a shorter compilation time? Explain your answer very carefully.

14. Suppose we have a machine with eight-bit words and a C compiler that stores integer variables in one word each.

(a) What would appear on the screen after the following code is executed?

```
int X,Y,Sum;

X = 12;   Y = 23;   Sum = X + Y;
printf("%d %u %x\n",Sum,Sum,Sum);
```

(b) Give an example of positive values of X and Y that would make Sum negative, i.e., values that would make the logical expressions $X > 0$, $Y > 0$, and *Sum* < 0 true, such as in the instruction

```
if (X > 0 ) ....
```

15. Suppose we were to use the simple 16-bit storage discussed in Section 1.2.2 as an introductory example of representations for real numbers.
    (a) What algebraic range of numbers could be represented?
    (b) What is the smallest positive number that could be represented?
    (c) Give an example of a number that is in the range of (a) but that cannot be represented exactly.
    (d) Give an example of numbers x and y such that x and y can be represented exactly and x, y, and $x + y$ are within the range of (a), but some roundoff error will occur in the computation of $x + y$. Find the roundoff error as a percentage of the true value of $x + y$.

16. Do the previous exercise for the 32-bit representation for floating-point numbers given in Section 1.2.2.

17. In the 32-bit representation for floating-point numbers given in Section 1.2.2, let S, E, and M denote the contents of the sign, exponent, and mantissa fields, respectively, for a real number x. Give a *mathematical formula* for the value of x in terms of S, E, and M.

18. Suppose we have a Pascal program in a file A.PAS, containing a variable Y of type **integer** and a statement

```
Y:=12
```

(or a C program in a file A.C, with Y of type **int** and a statement Y = 12). In the storage on disk of the file A.PAS (or A.C), state the exact bit string that corresponds to that number 12.

19. Suppose in a C program we have the global declaration

```
char x,y,*p;
```

Assume a non-Intel machine, but still with 16-bit words and individual byte addressability. Suppose that the compiler allocates storage similar to that of Table 1.1, starting at location 4000. What will appear on the screen after the following code is executed?

```
x = 'G'; y = 'Y'; p = &y;
print("%d %d %d\n",y,p,*(p-1));
```

20. Consider a base-8 number system consisting of digits 0–7, just as the base-10 system has digits 0–9 and the base-16 (hex) system has digits 0–F. Convert the base-16 number C148 to base-8. (Note: Almost no arithmetic is needed to do this problem.)

PROGRAMMING PROJECTS

1. Write a C or Pascal program to input an integer in base-10 form and display its binary—i.e., base-2—representation on the screen. The following parts (a), (b), and (c) will ask for several different versions of the program, each more complex than the last.

   (a) Write a program that handles the nonnegative case only, printing out a message "Sorry, negative number" if the number is negative. Assume that the size of an integer is 16 bits. (Hints: Use a binary version of the hex algorithm in Section 1.1. Keep dividing by two until you get a remainder that is less than two, storing each remainder you obtain and the final quotient in an array. These bits form the binary representation of the number, from right to left.)

   (b) Write an extended version of (a) that allows for both nonnegative and negative numbers. Assume two's-complement form. (Hints: First check whether the number is negative. If so, change it to positive and record the fact that you made this change. Then apply whatever code you developed for (a). Finally, if you recorded that the original number was negative, interchange 0's and 1's in the array and then "add 1." (You will have to write your own code to do this, including code for handling carries.)

   (c) Write an extended version of (b) in which the program does not assume a 16-bit size for integers. In other words, write the program so that it can be used on any machine, up to a size of 100-bit integers. (Hints: If you are using C, employ the **sizeof** operator. If you are using Pascal, check your compiler manual to see whether your compiler recognizes an equivalent operator. (Microsoft Pascal does.)

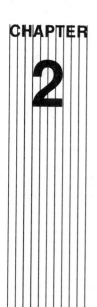

CHAPTER 2

Major Components of Computer "Engines"

From the introduction, the computer "engine" has two main components:

- The hardware, including the central processing unit, which executes the computer's machine language, and
- The low-level software, consisting of various services that the operating system makes available to programs.

This chapter presents a broad overview of both components of this "engine." The details will then unfold in succeeding chapters.

One of the major goals of this chapter, and a frequent theme in the chapters that follow, is to develop an understanding of the functions of the two computer components. In particular, questions to be addressed concern the various functions of computer systems:

- Which functions are typically implemented in hardware?
- Which functions are typically implemented in software?
- For which functions are both hardware and software implementations common? Why is hardware implementation generally faster, but software implementation more flexible?

Related to these questions are the following points concerning the **portability** of a program, i.e., the ability to move a program developed under one computing environment to another. What dependencies, if any, does the program have on that original environment? Potential dependencies are the following:

- *Hardware Dependencies:* A program written in machine language for the IBM PC's Intel 8088 CPU certainly will not run on an Apple Macintosh's Motorola 68000-family CPU. That same program, however, *will* run on the IBM AT's Intel 80286 CPU, since the capabilities of the 8088 form a subset of those of the 80286, but a program written for the 80286 might not run on an 8088.

- *Operating System (OS) Dependencies:* A program written to work on an IBM AT under the MS-DOS OS will probably not run on the same machine under the Minix OS, since the program will probably call OS procedures.

- *Compiler Dependencies:* Pascal, for example, has a recognized standard, but designers of commercial compilers usually extend the Pascal language by adding their own special capabilities. Thus, a Pascal-language file developed under, say, Borland's Turbo Pascal, might not be compilable under Microsoft Pascal, even on the same machine under the same OS.

And finally, we will discuss one of the most important questions of all: what aspects of the hardware and software components of the engine determine the overall speed at which a system will run a given program?

2.1 MAJOR HARDWARE COMPONENTS OF THE "ENGINE"

2.1.1 System Components

A block diagram of the setup of a typical computer system appears in Figure 2.1. The following subsections discuss these components.

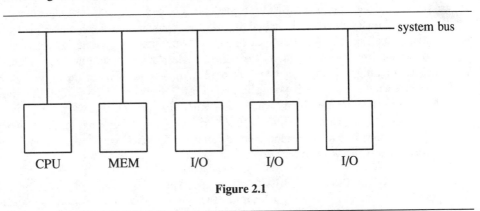

Figure 2.1

2.1.1.1 Central Processing Unit.   The **central processing unit** (CPU), often called simply the **processor**, is where the actual execution of a program takes place. (Since only machine language programs can be executed on a computer, the word

program in this book will usually mean a machine-language program. Recall that we might write such a program directly, or it might be produced indirectly, as the result of compiling a source program written in a high-level language (HLL) such as Pascal or C.)

Some special, high-performance computer systems are **multiprocessor** systems; that is, they have several CPUs that allow several programs—or several parts of the same program—to run simultaneously and thus achieve higher performance. However, most ordinary computer systems have only one CPU. The single-processor system is treated throughout this book; thus, there will be frequent references to "the" CPU.

As mentioned in the introduction, the CPUs in IBM microcomputers are made by the Intel Corporation and come from the iAPX 86, 286, and 386 subfamilies of CPUs produced by Intel. Each of these subfamilies is more powerful than the last: the 286 subfamily is faster and has more features than the 86 subfamily, and the 386 and 486 subfamilies are even more powerful. However, they all share the same core instruction set, which you will learn in this book. You will also learn the major advanced features of the 286/386/486 subfamilies.

Another popular CPU subfamily is the 68000 series, made by Motorola Corporation. This series is used in the Apple Macintosh and in the older Sun workstation computers. Again, the newer, more powerful members of this series, such as the 68020 and 68030, are **upward(ly) compatible** with the original 68000 CPU, meaning that programs written for the 68000 can be run on the more powerful models, too.

2.1.1.2 Memory.

A program's data and machine instructions are stored in **memory** (MEM) during the time the program is executing. Memory consists of cells called "words," each of which is identifiable by its "address."

If the CPU fetches the contents of some word of memory, we say that the CPU **reads** that word. On the other hand, if the CPU stores a value into some word of memory, we say that it **writes** to that word. Reading is analogous to listening to an audio cassette tape, while writing is analogous to recording onto the tape.

Ordinary memory is called **RAM**, for "random-access memory," a term which means that all words are accessible in the same amount of time. There is also **ROM** (read-only memory), which, as the name implies, can be read but not written. ROM is used for programs that need to be stored permanently in main memory, staying there even after the computer's power is turned off. For example, an autofocus camera typically has a computer in it, which runs only one program, a program to control the operation of the camera. Think of how inconvenient—to say the least—it would be if this program had to be loaded from a floppy disk drive every time you took a picture! It is much better to keep the program in ROM.

2.1.1.3 Input/Output Devices.

A typical computer system has several, possibly even hundreds, of **input/output** (I/O) devices. (Figure 2.1 shows a system with three of them.) Examples of I/O devices are keyboards, monitor screens, floppy and fixed disks, modems, printers, and "mice."

Specialized applications may have their own unique I/O devices. For example, consider a vending machine, say, for tickets for a regional railway system such as the

San Francisco Bay area's BART, which is capable of accepting dollar bills. The machine is likely to be controlled by a small computer. One of its input devices might be an optical sensor that senses the presence of a bill and collects data that will be used to analyze whether the bill is genuine. One of the system's output devices will control a motor that is used to pull in the bill; a similar device will control a motor to dispense the railway ticket. Yet another output device will be a screen to give messages to the person buying the ticket, such as "Please deposit 25 cents more."

The common feature of all of these examples is that they serve as interfaces between the computer and the "outside world." Note that in all cases they are communicating with a *program* that is running on the computer. Just as, in the past, you have written programs that input from a keyboard and output to a monitor screen, programs also need to be written in specialized applications to do input/output from special I/O devices, such as the railway ticket machine application. Input/output devices and I/O programming are discussed in Chapter 7.

2.1.1.4 System Bus.   A **bus** is a set of parallel wires (usually referred to as "lines") used as communication between components. The **system bus** in Figure 2.1 is the means by which the CPU communicates with memory and I/O devices. It is also possible for I/O devices to communicate directly with memory (i.e., without CPU involvement) an action which is called **direct memory access** (DMA), and again, this is done through the bus.

The bus may be broken down into the following three subbuses:

Data Bus.   As the name implies, the data bus is used for sending data. When the CPU reads a memory word, the memory sends the contents of that word along the data bus to the CPU; when the CPU writes a value to a memory word, the value flows along the data bus in the opposite direction.

Since the word is the basic unit of memory, a data bus usually has as many lines as there are bits in a memory word. For instance, IBM microcomputers whose CPUs are from the iAPX 86 or 286 families have 16-bit words; thus, most of these microcomputers have 16-line data buses.

The 8088 CPU, which was used in the original IBM PC and XT models, was an exception. It was set up for an eight-line data bus and thus needed to make two accesses to memory to read or write one word, resulting in slower performance than its "sister" CPU, the 8086, which was identical except for its data bus size of 16 bits. Similarly, the 386SX CPU is identical to the 386, except that the former is set up for a 16-line data bus, which is what the "SX" refers to, so it, too, must make two trips to fetch the 32-bit words that are characteristic of the 386 family. (On the other hand, for the many applications that run on 386-family machines in 16-bit mode, the effect is minor.)

Address Bus.   When the CPU wants to read or write a certain word of memory, it needs to have some mechanism by means of which to tell memory *which* word it wants to read or write. This is the role of the address bus. For example, if the CPU wants to read word 504 of memory, it will put the value 504 on the address bus, along which this value will flow to the memory, thus informing memory that word 504 is the word the CPU wants.

The address bus usually has the same number of lines as there are bits in the computer's addresses. For example, IBM microcomputers that use iAPX 286 subfamily CPUs have 24-bit addresses and thus 24-line address buses.

Control Bus. How will the memory know whether the CPU wants to read or write? This is one of the functions of the control bus. For example, the control bus in the IBM PC, XT, and AT models includes lines named MEMR and MEMW, for "memory read" and "memory write." If the CPU wants to read from memory, it will **assert** the MEMR line, by putting a low voltage on it, while for a write, it will assert MEMW. Again, this signal will be noticed by the memory, since it, too, is connected to the control bus, so it can act accordingly.

Control buses contain a number of other lines. We will look at some of these in Chapter 7.

As an example, consider an iAPX 86 machine. Let us denote the 20 lines in the address bus as A_{19} through A_0, corresponding to bits 19 through 0 of the 20-bit address, and denote the 16 lines in the data bus by D_{15} through D_0, corresponding to bits 15 through 0 of the word being accessed. Suppose the CPU executes an instruction to fetch the contents of word D0126 of memory. This will involve the CPU's putting the value D0126 onto the address bus. Remember, this is hex notation, which is just a shorthand abbreviation for the actual value, namely,

```
11010000000100100110
```

So the CPU will put a 1 on Line A_{19}, a 1 on Line A_{18}, a 0 on Line A_{17}, and so on; at the same time, it will assert the MEMR line in the control bus. The memory, which is attached to these bus lines, will sense these values and "understand" that we wish to read word D0126. Thus, the memory will send back the contents of that word on the data bus. If for instance c(D0126) = 0003, then the memory will put 0's on lines D_{15} through D_2, and 1's on lines D_1 and D_0, all of which will be sensed by the CPU.

2.1.2 General CPU Components

Figure 2.2 shows the components that make up a typical CPU. Included are an **arithmetic and logic unit** (ALU) and various **registers**.

The ALU, as the name implies, does **arithmetic** operations, such as addition, subtraction, multiplication, and division, and also several **logical** operations. The latter operations are similar to Pascal's **and**, **or**, and **not** operations (or the corresponding **&&**, **||**, and **!** operations in the language C) used in Boolean expressions such as those in the Pascal statement

```
if (a < b) and (c = 3) then x:=y;
```

How logical operations work is discussed in Chapter 6.

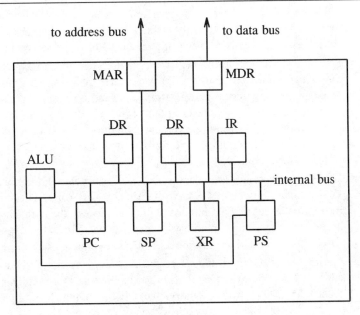

Figure 2.2

The ALU does not *store* anything. Values are input to the ALU, and results are then output from it, but it does not store anything, in contrast to memory words, which do store values. An analogy might be made to telephone equipment. A telephone inputs sound, in the form of mechanical vibrations in the air, and converts the sounds to electrical pulses to be sent to the listener's phone, but it does not store these sounds. A telephone tape-recording answering machine, on the other hand, does store the sounds that are input to it.

Registers are storage cells that are similar in function to memory words. The number of bits in a register is typically the same as that for memory words. We will even use the same c( ) notation for the contents of a register, as we have used for the contents of a memory word. For example, c(PC) will denote the contents of the register PC to be described momentarily, just as, for instance, c(322C4) means the contents of memory word 322C4. Keep in mind, though, that registers are not in memory; they are inside the CPU. The following are some details concerning the registers shown in Figure 2.2:

- PC: This is the **program counter**. Recall that a program's machine instructions must be stored in memory while the program is executing. The PC contains the address of the instruction that is currently executing.

- SP: The **stack pointer** contains the address of the "top" of a certain memory region called the **stack**. A stack is a type of data structure that the machine uses to keep track of subroutine calls and other information, as we will see in Chapters 5 and 7.

- XR: The **index register** helps programs access arrays. Its name comes from the fact that in a Pascal or C array element such as a[i], the subscript i is often called the **index**. The details of using this register will be presented in Chapter 6.

- PS: The **processor status register** contains miscellaneous pieces of information, including **condition codes**. The latter are indicators of information, such as whether the most recent computation produced a negative, positive, or zero result. Note that there are wires leading out of the ALU to the PS (shown as just one line in the figure). These lines keep the condition codes up to date. Each time the ALU is used, the condition codes are immediately updated according to the results of the ALU operation.

- DRs: **Data registers** are usually used as "fast memory," i.e., as temporary places to store data to which we need quick access. Because DRs are in the CPU, an instruction executing within the CPU can access them much faster than it can access memory, since memory is outside the CPU (see Figure 2.1). Different CPU types have different numbers of DRs; two are pictured in Figure 2.2.

- MAR: The **memory address register** is used as the CPU's connection to the address bus. For example, if the instruction that is currently executing needs to read word 20054 from memory, the CPU will put 20054 into the MAR, from which it will flow onto the address bus.

- MDR: The **memory data register** is used as the CPU's connection to the data bus. For example, if the instruction that is currently executing needs to read word 20054 from memory, the memory will put c(20054) onto the data bus, from which it will flow into the MDR in the CPU. On the other hand, if we are writing to word 20054—say, writing the value 19—the CPU will put 19 in the MDR, from which it will flow out onto the data bus and then to memory. At the same time, we will put 20054 into the MAR, so that the memory will know to which word the 19 is to be written.

- IR: This denotes the **instruction register**. When the CPU is ready to start execution of a new instruction, it fetches the instruction from memory. The instruction is returned along the data bus and deposited in the MDR. The CPU needs to use the MDR for further accesses to memory, so it copies the fetched instruction into the IR, so that the original copy in the MDR may be overwritten.

As regards the sizes of the various registers; the PC, SP, XR, and MAR all contain addresses, and thus typically have sizes equal to the address size of the machine. Similarly, DRs and the MDR typically have sizes equal to the word size of the machine. The PS stores miscellaneous information; thus, its size has no particular relation to the machine's address or word size. The IR must be large enough to store the longest possible instruction for the machine in question.

A CPU also has **internal buses**, similar in function to the system bus, which serve as pathways through which transfers of data from one register to another can be made. Figure 2.2 shows a CPU that has only one such bus, but some CPUs have two or more. Internal buses are beyond the scope of this book; thus, any reference to a bus from this point onward will be to the system bus.

The reader should pay particular attention to the MAR and MDR. They will be referred to at a number of points in the following chapters, both in the text and in the exercises—not because they are so vital in their own right, but rather because they serve as excellent vehicles for clarifying various concepts that we will cover in this book. In particular, phrasing some discussions in terms of the MAR and MDR will clarify the fact that some CPU instructions access memory while others do not.

2.1.3 iAPX CPU Components

Now let us look at a specific CPU structure, that of the iAPX family, depicted in Figure 2.3. Shown are the components of the basic iAPX 86 subfamily, which form a subset of the components found in the more sophisticated 286, 386, and 486 subfamilies. These latter subfamilies have additional components, but those components are not of concern to us at this point, because they are used only when a 286/386/486 CPU runs in **protected mode**. When such a CPU runs in **real mode**, it is essentially equivalent to a fast version of an iAPX 86 CPU. Protected mode is quite complex and will not be discussed until Chapter 8, and even then, only an introduction will be presented. Thus, Figure 2.3 is sufficiently detailed for our purposes now.

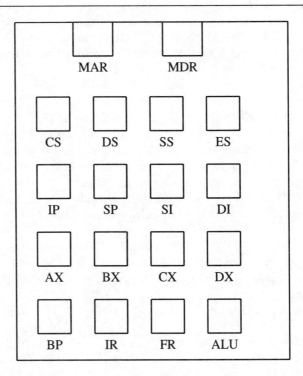

Figure 2.3

2.1.3.1 Nonsegment Registers. The MAR and MDR are part of a more complex entity called the **bus interface unit**, which will not be described here. For our purposes, the terms "MAR" and "MDR" as used in Section 2.1.2 are sufficiently detailed.

The registers BX, BP, SI, and DI all serve as index registers, similar to XR in Figure 2.2, but with much more variety than XR. They will be described in more detail in Chapter 6. AX and DX are used mainly as data registers, similar to the DRs in Figure 2.2, though the other registers can be used in this way, too. CX also has some special functions that will be presented in Chapter 6. AX, BX, CX, and DX are further broken down into their high bytes, bits 15 through 8, and their low bytes, bits 7 through 0: the high byte of AX is called AH, the low byte is called AL, and similarly on for BX, CX, and DX. The flags register FR is the iAPX version of the processor status register PS in Figure 2.2.

The **segment registers**, CS, DS, SS, and ES, and the IP register involve the way iAPX CPUs form addresses, which is the subject of the next subsection.

2.1.3.2 iAPX Segment Registers and Addressing. The iAPX IP ("Instruction Pointer") register is the analogue of the PC in Figure 2.2. However, there is a difference: the PC in Figure 2.2 gives the *absolute address* of the current instruction, while the iAPX IP gives the *relative address* of the current instruction, as a distance from the beginning of the code area of memory. The latter is indicated by the CS register. This is characteristic of iAPX CPUs and is a key aspect of their operation, so the reader should pay special attention to the material in the next few paragraphs, which will play a crucial role throughout the book.

Recall, from Chapter 1, that iAPX CPUs have address sizes varying from 20 bits on the earlier models to 32 bits on the most recent ones. But even on the more recent models, the default-mode (real-mode) address size is 20 bits. For example, on an iAPX 286 system, the address bus will have 24 lines, called $A_{23}, A_{22}, \ldots, A_0$, but in real mode, only lines $A_{19}-A_0$ are used. Since we will not discuss the other modes until Chapter 8, we will continue to assume a 20-bit address size until then.

With all this in mind, we can get to the main point: on iAPX CPUs, an address is *formed* differently than on other CPUs. For example, on an "ordinary" CPU, the address of the current instruction is obtained directly, from the PC register. But on an iAPX CPU, that address must be formed by combining values from two registers, the CS and IP registers. The CS register points to a certain place in memory, while the IP indicates how far the current instruction is from that place. So, to get the actual 20-bit address of the current instruction, the contents of the second register must be added to the contents of the first.

The CS register points to the beginning of the memory region in which our program's instructions are stored. This region is called the **code segment** (the word *code* means program instructions). Accordingly, CS is the *code segment* register.

For example, suppose our current instruction is in word 72B54 in memory. In a non-iAPX CPU, this would be indicated by having the value 72B54 in the PC. By contrast, in an iAPX CPU, the CS register would contain the memory address at which our program instructions start—say, 71A30—and the IP register would contain the distance that the current instruction is from this location—say, 1124. Since 71A30 + 1124 = 72B54, we see that CS and IP *jointly* indicate that the current instruction is at word 72B54. The final value that goes into MAR when we prepare to fetch the instruction from memory is 72B54, and the value that will go out onto the address bus is also 72B54, just as it would in an "ordinary" machine. In other words, the memory only sees the value 72B54, not the values 71A30 and 1124.   But the difference in iAPX machines is that this address is generated by combining the CS and IP values, as opposed to being given explicitly to begin with, as in "ordinary" machines.

Similarly, the DS register defines the beginning of the **data segment**, i.e., the memory region in which our program's data items are stored. Thus, Table 1.1, c(DS) might be 20050, and an instruction to access Y might refer to "the memory word that is two bytes from the place pointed to by DS," instead of referring directly to word 20052.

Again, note carefully that the address of Y in this example is still 20052. Thus, when the instruction to access Y is executed, the value 20052 will still go into the MAR and out onto the address bus. But what is different about iAPX machines is that the value 20052 would be *formed* by adding 2 to 20050, whereas on a non-iAPX machine the instruction would specify 20052 explicitly.

In addition to the CS and DS segment registers, there are two other segment registers: SS and ES. These will be described in Chapters 5 and 6, respectively. Note that segment/offset pairs are often written in the notation xxxx:yyyy, where xxxx is the value in the segment register and yyyy is the offset. Hence, we could write the address 72B54 as 71A3:1124.

In sum, in iAPX machines, the memory location of an instruction is specified by saying how far it is past the location pointed to by the CS register. On the other hand, the memory location of a data item is specified by saying how far it is past the location pointed to by the DS register. Any item's address is specified in terms of the distance from the beginning of the item's segment. This distance is called the **offset**. In the preceding example, the current instruction was at the offset 1124 past 71A30, the latter being the location of the beginning of the code segment. Instruction addresses are given as offsets from CS; addresses of data items are given as offsets from DS.

The only restriction is that segments must begin at an address that is divisible by 16, i.e., one whose least significant digit in the hex representation is 0. (Compare this with base 10, in which a number is divisible by 10 if its least significant digit is 0.) In the foregoing example, the code segment began at address 71A30, whose least significant digit is indeed 0. Since the last digit is required to be 0, we do not even store it in the segment register. Thus, we would put 71A3 in CS, not 71A30. During execution, the 0 is automatically appended by the circuitry in the CPU, as if we had stored 71A30 instead of 71A3, so everything does work out correctly.

This procedure is followed for all the segment registers—CS, DS, SS, and ES (but not the other registers). A segment may begin at any address whose rightmost hex digit is 0, but that 0 is kept implicit as far as the segment registers are concerned— i.e., the 0 is not physically stored in those registers. Instead, the 0 is appended at the time the address computation is done. In the example, 71A3 is stored in CS, but at the time the CPU is ready to fetch the current instruction from memory (and thus needs to determine the address of that instruction), the circuitry in the CPU will automatically append a 0 to 71A3 before adding the resulting number (71A30) to c(IP) to form the address. So the value 71A3 in the CS register *means* that our code segment begins at address 71A30.

Note again that appending a 0 in hex—i.e., base-16 arithmetic—means multiplying by 16, just as appending a 0 in base-10 arithmetic means multiplying by 10. Thus, an address is always computed as

```
16*c(segment register) + offset value
```

The advantage of this segment-plus-offset design is that program size is conserved, since instructions need only 16 bits instead of 20 to specify an operand. Also, the Intel designers probably were worried about conserving space used by the circuitry in the CPU. A microcomputer CPU is constructed on a single **chip**, often smaller than the size of a dime. Since tens of thousands of electronic components must be stored on this chip, space is at a premium, and it was especially tight in the technology of the mid-1970's, when the first iAPX CPUs were designed, so tricks to save space were very valuable. Making segment registers and the resulting data paths only 16 bits wide instead of 20 may have saved some space.

In theory, the segment-plus-offset method for the iAPX family results in more compact programs—i.e., programs that take up less memory space. For example, suppose in a given program the data items all fit into one segment (see shortly). Then DS will have the same value throughout the execution of a program, so we can specify data operands using only four hex digits instead of five, such as is the case with 0002 versus 20052 in the earlier example. The situation is somewhat analogous to a phone directory, say, a directory of all the home phone numbers of the employees of a company. If all the employees live in the same telephone area code—or, in analogy to the DS register example here, the area code does not change as we go down the list of employee phones—we can omit the area code from the listings of phone numbers, displaying seven-digit numbers only. This would save space in the directory. But if employees live in more than one area code, we will need to list 10-digit numbers, including area codes, thereby using more space.

Offsets are limited to 16 bits (though for the iAPX 386/486 models, this is true only in real mode). Hence, the largest possible offset is FFFFH, which is 65535_{10}. In other words, the size of a segment is limited to about 65,000 bytes. This is written informally as **64K**, meaning 64 times 1,024; the value 1,024 is 2^{10}, and the "K" stands for "kilo" or thousand, which is close to 1,024.

Note that this limit on the segment size is just that—an upper limit. Consider a code segment, for example. As far as the hardware is concerned, the code segment encompasses all bytes from 16*c(CS) to 16*c(CS) + 65,535, but typically, only a portion of this is actually used. Thus, if, say, we place the data segment immediately following the last machine instruction in the code segment, it will appear to the hardware that the data segment overlaps the code segment.

Due to this 64K-byte limitation on the size of a segment, we might need multiple segments of a certain type, e.g., multiple code segments. For example, suppose our program's instructions take up about 82,000 bytes of memory. Then we will need two code segments, and we will have to change the value stored in CS whenever we switch from executing instructions in one segment to executing instructions in the other segment. Similarly, if our program has a large amount of data—say, very long arrays—we will need more than one data segment, and we will have to change DS every time we switch from using one data segment to using the other.

Note that offsets are interpreted as unsigned numbers, so that, for example, FFFFH is considered to be +65,535, not −1, as it would be as a 16-bit, two's-complement number.

The iAPX CPU family's segment-plus-offset representation of memory addresses sometimes creates problems that do not occur on "ordinary"—i.e., nonsegmented—machines. For instance, recall from Chapter 1 that the language C includes an operator **&** that means "address of." In the example from Program 1.2, &Y had the value 20052, since in that example we were assuming that the compiler had allocated that address for Y. This is certainly what would happen in non-iAPX machines, but what about iAPX machines?

As we have seen in the last few paragraphs, programs on iAPX machines specify addresses in segment-plus-offset form, instead of as a single value. In the example in Chapter 1, the variable Y is in the segment starting at 20050, and the offset is 0002. In translating a Pascal statement such as

```
X:=Y+4;
```

a compiler will create code whose first instruction is, roughly, "Add 4 to the contents of the word at offset 0002 in the data segment." DS will have been previously set to 2005 by this time, and thus, execution of this instruction will result in 16*2005H + 0002 = 20052H being placed in the MAR, so this code will work correctly.

Since the instructions will accordingly specify their data items using only the offsets of those items, rather than their full addresses, the offsets are in effect serving as the addresses. Then from the compiler's point of view, the "address" of Y on the iAPX machine in this example is 0002, not 20052, since the machine code specifies Y by 0002 instead of 20052. Accordingly, on iAPX machines, the compiler will ordinarily translate the expression &Y above to 2, not 20052.

Similarly, a C or Pascal **pointer** variable, which on most machines consists of an address, will be implemented only as an offset by compilers on iAPX machines.

But what about applications in which the C-language programmer needs to specify a full, 20-bit absolute address on an iAPX machine? How can this be done? One simple way involves using **far pointer** variables. As mentioned in the last paragraph, a C pointer on an iAPX machine ordinarily consists only of an offset, not a complete address. But a far pointer contains both the segment and offset value specifying an address. It is thus 32 bits long, with the more significant 16 bits containing the segment value (without the implied hex 0 at the right end) and the less significant 16 bits containing the offset.

Program 2.1 illustrates the use of a far pointer. The program writes the character 'A' to the first column in the second row on the monitor screen. What does this have to do with memory addresses? Well, on IBM (and compatible) microcomputers, the contents of the screen are stored in memory. We will see the details in Chapter 7 but can understand the basics quickly here. (Before continuing, the reader should note carefully that the following material applies only to IBM and compatible microcomputers, not computers in general, and not even all computers that use iAPX CPUs.)

The screen consists of 25 rows of 80 characters each. Let us number the rows 0, 1, ..., 24, starting from the top, and number the characters within any row 0, 1, ..., 79, starting from the left. Then character in row i and column j of the screen is stored at byte (not word) number

```
B8000H + 2 * (i*50H + j)
```

(For some monitors, the base location is B0000H instead of B8000H; if one value fails to work on your monitor, then try the other.) So if you wish to have a certain character appear in row i and column j on the screen, simply put the ASCII code for that character into memory location B8000H + 2 * (i*50H + j), and the character will appear immediately on the screen.

For example, to make the character 'A' appear in the first column in the second row of the screen, we would put 65, the ASCII code for 'A', at byte B80A0H, i.e., byte B800:00A0, of memory. Program 2.1 does this. (But after the program finishes execution, it will return to the operating system, printing out its familiar '>' prompt, thus scrolling the screen upward one line, so that the 'A' will appear in the first row, not the second.)

```
main()

{ char far *p;

   p = (char far *) 0xb80000a0;
   *p = 65;
}
```

Program 2.1

The '*' in the C statement

```
char far *p;
```

declares p to be a pointer. The keyword **far** is saying that we want p to be a far pointer, meaning that p will include both a segment and offset value. If we had written simply

```
char *p;
```

then p would still be a pointer to the **char** type, but p would only specify an offset.

The keyword **char** says that p points to a byte, not a full word. We want this here, since we want to write to *byte* B80A0H, not *word* B80A0H.

The line

```
p = (char far *) 0xb80000a0;
```

puts into p the hex value B80000A0. (Recall from Chapter 1 that '0x' means hex in C.) Since there are eight hex digits in this constant, it is 32 bits in length and thus of the C type **long**, a double-length integer. Hence, this is an example of type mixing, with the right-hand side of the statement having type **long** and the left-hand side being of type **char far ***, i.e., a far pointer to a character. As mentioned before, C is rather liberal about type mixing and will allow this. However, we put in the item

```
(char far *)
```

called a **cast**, in the statement in order to tell the compiler that we are conscious of our type mixing and are doing it deliberately. Thus, the statement

```
p = (char far *) 0xb80000a0;
```

says, "Treat the constant 0xb80000a0 as of type **char far ***, even though it is really of type **long**, so that we can assign it to the variable p, which is of type **char far ***."

Finally, the statement

```
*p = 65;
```

says to put 65—the ASCII code for 'A'—into the location pointed to by p. What address is that? Well, since p is of type **char far ***, the compiler will produce machine instructions that treat the first 16 bits of p as containing the segment value and the other 16 bits as being the offset—in this case, B800 and 00A0, respectively, exactly the location we want.

Seeing is believing! The reader is urged to run this program to make sure that he or she understands how it works. It will be much easier to understand the concepts in the program if you see the program in action.

The C language's ability to access specific numeric memory locations, as we have seen here, is one of the reasons for its popularity. It enables us to perform the "low-level" operation of accessing specific numeric memory locations from a "high-level" language. For this reason, C is sometimes called a "middle-level" language, combining the "best of both worlds." This flexibility is a major factor in its widespread, almost universal, usage in the modern computer industry.

Pascal lacks a feature such as this. However, most Pascal compilers written for single-user microcomputers do offer something like it. An example is Microsoft Pascal, which offers the Microsoft-specific, nonstandard Pascal features shown in the following Pascal analog of Program 2.1:

```
program a(input,output);
   var p : ads of char;
begin
   p.r:=16#00a0;  p.s:=16#b800;
   p^:='G'
end.
```

Those features of the program which are *not* standard Pascal, but are special to Microsoft Pascal, are the following:

- The **ads** type has the same meaning as a C far pointer;
- The notation '16#' is the equivalent of C's '0x'; i.e., it signifies a hex (base-16) constant;
- '.r' and '.s' mean the offset and segment portions of the address. (The letter *r* stands for "relative," since an offset is a distance relative to the start of the segment.)

The '^' *is* standard Pascal, corresponding to C's '*' operator, meaning "contents of." So the overall effect of this program is to put the ASCII code for 'G' into the memory byte at offset 00A0 of the segment that begins at B8000. That byte corresponds to the first column in the second row of the screen, resulting in 'G' appearing at that screen position.

Turbo Pascal offers something similar to these features of Microsoft Pascal, using an attribute called **Absolute**. Thus, various Pascal compilers for iAPX machines do allow us to write the equivalent of Program 2.1 in Pascal. However, a disadvantage is that the programs will not be **portable** across different compilers; that is, a program written for one compiler will not work on the others.

If we have a lot of far pointers, or calls to far procedures (intersegmental calls), it may be easier just to have the compiler implement all addresses as 32-bit segment-and-offset quantities. Most C compilers for iAPX machines offer this option, with different-sized **memory models**. The default is the **small** model, with a single code segment and a single data segment, resulting in 16-bit offset-only "addresses." In the **compact** model, there is only one code segment, but multiple data segments are allowed, and all data pointers, are 32-bit far pointers, as we just saw. Then there is the **large** model, and so on; see your compiler manual for details.

The segment-offset method that the iAPX family uses to specify memory addresses is sometimes a bit cumbersome, but it should be pointed out that the scheme has its advantages, too. In Chapter 8, we will see that it provides a very natural solution to problems concerned with **relocatability** and **code sharing**.

2.1.4 Motorola 68000 Family CPU Components

For comparison and contrast, let us very briefly discuss the register structure of the Motorola 68000 CPU. Again, it is basically similar to Figure 2.2. It has eight data registers, like the DRs in the figure; they are named D0 through D7.

The 68000 also has eight "address registers," A0 through A7. As the name implies, these registers hold addresses for various types of memory access.* For example, one type of memory access available in the 68000 is indexed addressing, and the function of Figure 2.2's XR can be performed by any of the registers A0 through A7. Recalling that indexing is useful for efficient access of array data structures (the details of which will be given in Chapter 6), we see that the 68000 allows us to efficiently access several arrays at once. This is not so for the iAPX family. Although CPUs in that family do have the four registers BX, BP, SI, and DI mentioned earlier that do certain kinds of indexing, they apply to different kinds of arrays, and only SI, DI, and BX may be used together. This problem of having too few registers is one of the drawbacks of the iAPX family.

Again, in defense of the iAPX family, it should be noted that the SI/DI pair is used to implement some extremely efficient array operations of a certain specialized nature. In some cases, a dramatic increase in program speed can be obtained, as an example in Chapter 6 will show. The 68000 does not have this feature. So each CPU has its advantages and disadvantages.

The 68000's version of PS is called the status register (SR). Keep in mind, though, that the difference is more than just in the names. For example, although some of the bits in the 68000's SR are similar in function to some of the bits in the iAPX family's FR, there are other bits in SR that have no counterparts in FR. This will become clearer in later chapters.

2.1.5 The CPU Fetch/Execute Cycle

After its power is turned on, the typical CPU pictured in Figure 2.2 will enter its **fetch/execute cycle**, repeatedly cycling through the following steps:

Step A.   The CPU will perform a memory read operation, to fetch the current instruction. This involves copying the contents of the PC to the MAR, asserting a memory-read line in the control bus, and then waiting for the memory to send back the requested instruction along the data bus to the MDR. While waiting, the CPU will update the PC, to point to the next instruction in memory, in preparation for step A in the next cycle.

Step B.   The CPU will copy the contents of the MDR to the IR, so as to free the MDR for further memory accesses. The CPU will inspect the instruction in the IR and **decode** it, i.e., decide what kind of operation this instruction performs—addition, subtraction, jump, and so on.

Step C.   Here the actual execution of the operation specified by the instruction will be carried out. If any of the operands required by the instruction are in memory, they will be fetched at this time, by putting their addresses into the MAR and waiting for them to arrive at the MDR. Also, if the instruction stores its result back to memory,

---

*As with most non-iAPX machines, these addresses will be linear, i.e., a single number, as opposed to the iAPX segment-offset pairs.

this will be accomplished by putting the result in the MDR, and putting the memory address of the word we wish to write to into the MAR.

After Step C is carried out, the next cycle is started, i.e., another step A, then another step B, and so on. Again, keep in mind that the CPU will continually cycle through these three steps as long as the power remains on. Note that all of the actions taken in these steps are functions of the *hardware*: the circuitry is designed to take these actions, while the programmer merely takes advantage of that circuitry, by choosing the proper machine instructions for his or her program.

A more detailed description of CPU operations would involve specifying their **microsteps**. These are beyond the scope of this book, however, and the three-step cycle just described will give sufficient detail for our purposes, although we *will* use microsteps to illustrate the term **clock speed** in Section 2.3.3.

The preceding generic description of a CPU's fetch/execute cycle needs to be modified only slightly to describe iAPX CPUs. First, in step A, instead of copying the PC to the MAR, what is copied to the MAR is $16*c(CS) + c(IP)$. Second, only the first byte of the instruction is fetched in step A. Recall that an iAPX 86 instruction can range from one to six bytes in length. (Actually, most non-iAPX CPUs have variable instruction lengths, too.) The CPU fetches the first byte of the instruction in step A and then, at the beginning of step B, inspects this first byte. By looking at the bit pattern contained in that byte, the CPU can tell whether there are any further bytes in the instruction; if so, the CPU fetches these other bytes from memory, until the entire instruction is in the IR. Note that in light of all this, we can see that the circuitry in the CPU will increment the IP by one in step A, and then in step B, if the circuitry discovers that the instruction is, say, k bytes long and that it must therefore fetch the remaining $k-1$ bytes, it will reincrement the IP by $k-1$.

To make these concepts concrete, let us look at a specific example. Suppose the state of the CPU just before step A in a certain cycle is as shown in Figure 2.4. In the figure, the notation "s.v." stands for "some value," meaning that some value is stored in that register—there is *always* some value stored in every register and memory byte in the machine, even if it is irrelevant "garbage." Values marked "s.v." will not play a role in this example; they are previously stored values that are of no concern to us. Again, the ALU does not have storage capability, so its box in the figure does not even have a label "s.v."

Here is what will happen during the fetch/execute cycle:

Step A. The CPU computes $21080 + 0002 = 21082$ from the CS and IP, copies the 21082 to the MAR, asserts MEMR in the control bus, and waits for memory to respond. Meanwhile, it increments the IP from 0002 to 0003, to point to the next byte in the code segment. Finally, the memory request is complete, and the requested byte is now in the MDR. Suppose this byte is 03H.

The state of the CPU will now be as shown in Figure 2.5.

Step B. The CPU copies the contents of the MDR to the IR and looks at the byte now in the IR, i.e., 03H. It recognizes (see Chapter 3 for details) that this particu-

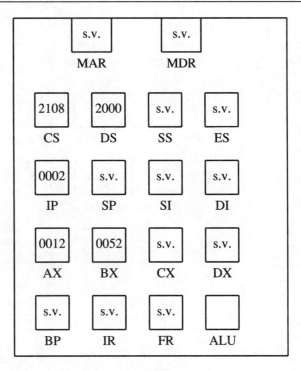

Figure 2.4

lar bit pattern is for a two-byte instruction, so it must fetch the second byte. It does this by copying the CS-plus-IP value, now 21083, to the MAR, and then asserting MEMR. While waiting for memory to service the request, the CPU again increments the IP, to 0004, so that it will point to the next instruction of the program. The IP always records "where we left off" in fetching from the stream of bytes in the code segment. If for example, the CPU had found that the current instruction was five bytes long, it would have fetched the remaining four bytes and thus would also have incremented the IP by four instead of one, so that it would again have pointed to the next sequential place in the code segment.

When the requested byte comes to the MDR, it is copied to the IR. Suppose this second byte is 07. Now the full instruction, 0307, is in the IR. Upon inspection of the IR, the CPU discovers that the instruction says to add to the AX register the contents of the data item whose offset is in BX.

The state of the CPU now will be as shown in Figure 2.6.

Step C. From step B, the CPU "knows" that the instruction says to add to the AX register the contents of the data item whose offset is in BX. So it "knows" that the

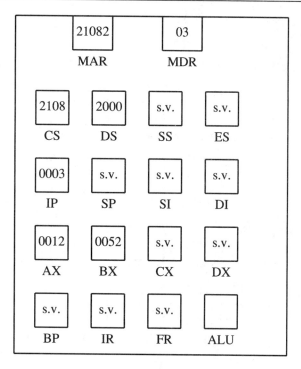

Figure 2.5

data item is at offset 52 in the data segment, i.e., at location 20052. Since we have to add this item to the value in the AX register, we must first fetch the item from memory. Thus, the CPU puts 20052 in the MAR, asserts MEMR, and waits for the result to appear in the MDR. Suppose this value turns out to be 15—i.e., c(20052) = 15. The 12 and the 15 are then fed into the ALU, producing 27, which is then stored back into AX, completing execution of the instruction. (If the instruction had said to store the result back into word 20052 in memory, instead of into AX, the CPU would have put the 27 into the MDR, put 20052 into the MAR, and asserted MEMW.)

The state of the CPU will now be as shown in Figure 2.7.

A new cycle will then begin. In step A, the instruction at memory location 21080+0004 = 21084 will be fetched. This makes sense: we just finished executing the instruction located at bytes 21082 and 21083, so the next instruction to be executed starts at the next byte, i.e., byte 21084. The reader should now go back and reread steps A and B, to verify that these steps did indeed increment the IP properly. The circuitry in the CPU has been arranged so that by the time step C ends (actually, even earlier, when step B ends), the IP has been incremented by exactly the number of bytes in the current instruction, so that it now points to the next instruction and is ready to fetch that instruction during step A of the next cycle.

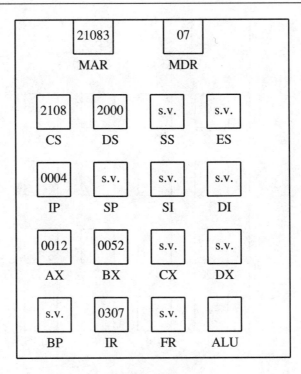

Figure 2.6

2.2 SOFTWARE COMPONENTS OF THE COMPUTER "ENGINE"

There are many aspects of a computer system that people who are at the learning stage typically take for granted as being controlled by hardware, but which are actually controlled by software. An example of this is the backspace action when you type the backspace key on the keyboard. You are accustomed to seeing the last character you typed disappear from the screen and the cursor moving one position to the left. You might have had the impression that this is an inherent property of the keyboard and the screen, i.e., that their circuitry was designed to do this. However, for most computer systems today, this is not the case. The bare hardware will not take any special action when you hit the backspace key. Instead, such action is taken by whichever **operating system** (OS) is being used on the computer.

The OS is software—a *program*, which a person or group of people wrote to provide various services to user programs. One of those services is to monitor keystrokes for the backspace key and to take special actions (move the cursor and put a blank where it used to be) upon encountering that key. When you write a program, say, in Pascal or C, you do not have to do this monitoring yourself, which is a tremendous

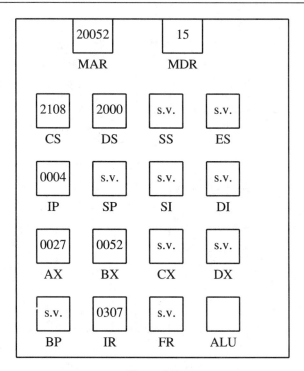

Figure 2.7

convenience. Imagine what a nuisance it would be if you were forced to handle the backspace key yourself: you would have to include some statements to check for the backspace key and to update the screen (move the cursor and put a blank where it used to be) if that character is encountered. Such a "do it yourself" approach is necessary in some applications, and you will learn that approach in Chapter 7. But, in general, it is much more convenient to let the OS do this work instead.

Processing backspaces is an example of one of the many services that an OS provides. Another example is maintaining a file system. Again, the theme is convenience. When you create a file, you do not have to burden yourself with knowing the physical location of your file on the disk. You merely give the file a name. The OS finds unused space on the disk to store your file and enters the name and physical location of the file in a table that the OS maintains. Subsequently, you may access the file merely by specifying the name, and the OS service will translate that into the physical location and access the file on your behalf. In fact, a typical OS will offer a large variety of services for accessing files.

A user program will make use of many OS services, usually by calling them as subroutines. For example, the built-in Pascal procedure **readln** (or its C-language counterpart, **scanf**) consists of calls to OS subroutines, along with some instructions that prepare the arguments for these calls. In terms of the "look under the hood" theme of this book, we might phrase this by saying that a look under the hood of a Pascal **readln** reveals calls to the OS. For this reason, the OS is often referred to as "low-level" software. Also, this reliance of user programs on OS services shows why the OS is included in our "computer engine" metaphor—the OS is indeed one of the sources of "power" for user programs, just as the hardware is the other source of power.

To underscore the notion that the OS services do form a vital part of the computer's "engine," consider the following example. Suppose we have a machine-language program—which we either wrote ourselves or produced by compiling from Pascal or C—for a Sun computer having a Motorola 68020 CPU. Can that program be run without modification on an Apple Macintosh having a Motorola 68020 CPU? The answer is probably no, assuming that the Sun is running the Unix OS and the Macintosh is running the Macintosh OS. The program will probably include a number of calls to OS services—recall that even reads from the keyboard and writes to the screen are implemented as OS services—and those services would be different under the two OSs. The services themselves would be slightly different, and at the very least, the form needed to call them from a user program would differ. In fact, even if the Macintosh were running Unix, there still might be some differences.

Thus, even though individual instructions of the program written for the Sun would make sense on the Macintosh since both machines would use the same type of CPU, some of those instructions would be devoted to OS calls, which would differ in the two systems. *Procedures* should be transferable, though, as long as they contain no OS calls and no references to input/output devices. For example, if we write a procedure for the Sun to sort an array of numbers into ascending order, that procedure should be directly usable on the Macintosh.

Since an OS consists of a program, written to provide a group of services, it follows that several different OSs—i.e., several different programs that offer different groups of services—could be run on the same hardware. For instance, this is the case for IBM microcomputers. The most widely used OS for these CPUs is MS-DOS (often simply referred to as DOS), developed by the Microsoft Corporation, but there are also several versions of Unix for IBM microcomputers, such as Xenix and Minix, and more recently, Microsoft has developed an elaborate extension of MS-DOS, called OS/2. On VAX hardware, one can run either Unix or VMS, the latter being an OS developed by the manufacturer of the hardware.

Conversely, the same OS—again, meaning the same set of services—can be written for several different machines. The major example of this is Unix, versions of which have been written to run on many different machines (cf. the previous paragraph). Unix is particularly easy to **port** to a new machine, since the bulk of it is written in a high-level language, C. Thus, if a C compiler has been written for the new machine, then most of a Unix version for that machine can be obtained simply by compiling the C-language parts of the Unix source code. All that remains then is to write the machine-dependent parts of Unix for the new machine, a much easier task than writing the entire system from scratch.

On the other hand, although the fact that Unix is written in a high-level language greatly enhances its portability among different machines, there is a disadvantage, too:

efficiency is sacrificed. As mentioned in the introduction, HLL programs are usually not very efficient: the machine code produced by a compiler from an HLL program will typically not make as efficient use of the hardware as will a hand-coded machine-language version of the same program. For example, a program running on a VAX under Unix—i.e., using the services Unix provides—will in general run less efficiently than it would running on the same VAX under VMS, using comparable services in VMS, since VMS was tailored for the VAX, while Unix was meant to be largely machine independent.

As mentioned, a user program avails itself of OS services by calling certain procedures of the OS program. These procedure calls are like procedure calls you have made in your own programs before; the only difference is that you made in*tra*program procedure calls, whereas the OS services are accessed via in*ter*program calls. Note carefully that this means that the user programs are the initiators here, not the OS: it is *not* the case that the OS is "watching over" the execution of the user program while the user program is executing and then "steps in and takes over" when it sees some particular situation occur. This would be impossible, because when a user program is running, no other program is running (assuming the computer has only one CPU), and thus, the OS is "dead" for the time being. We will return to this point in Chapter 4.

2.3 SPEED OF A COMPUTER "ENGINE"

What factors determine the speed of a computer "engine"? This is an extremely complex question that is still a subject of hot debate in both academia and the computer industry. However, a number of factors are clear and will be introduced here. The presentation will of necessity be an overview, and the interested reader should pursue further details in books on computer architecture and design. However, it is important to get some understanding of the main issues now—at the very least, enough to be able to understand newspaper PC ads! The discussion is aimed at that goal.

2.3.1 CPU Architecture

Different types of CPUs have different instruction and register sets. The iAPX family, for example, has a very nice set of character-string manipulation instructions, so it does such operations especially quickly. This is counterbalanced somewhat by the fact that CPUs in this family have fewer registers than do CPUs in some other families, such as those in the Motorola 68000 group. Since registers serve as local—and thus fast—memory, the more of them we have, the better, and thus, the iAPX family is at a disadvantage in this respect.

2.3.2 Parallel Operations

One way to get more computing done per unit time is do several things at one time, i.e., in parallel. Most modern machines, even inexpensive ones such as personal computers, include some forms of parallelism.

For example, most CPUs, including those in the iAPX family, perform **instruction prefetch**: during execution of the current instruction, the CPU will attempt to fetch one or more of the instructions that follow it sequentially—i.e., at consecutive increasing addresses—in memory. For concreteness, consider the example at the end of Section 2.1.5: during the time we are executing the instruction that starts at location 21082, the CPU might attempt to start fetching the next instruction, at 21084. The success or failure of this attempt will depend on the duration of the instruction at 21082. If the attempt is successful, then the major parts of steps A and B can be skipped in the next cycle—i.e., the instruction at 21084 can be executed more quickly.

Of course, the last statement holds only if we actually do end up executing the instruction at 21084. If the instruction at 21082 turned out to be a jump instruction, which moves us to some other place in memory, we will not execute the instruction at 21084 at all. In this case, prefetching of this instruction during execution of the one at 21082 would unfortunately turn out to be unused. The designers of the iAPX family might have tried to set up some elaborate system to predict whether the jump would occur, but this would be quite difficult to do well, and thus, it was not done. The prefetch mechanism *always* prefetches from the next sequentially higher address in memory, even though sometimes the prefetched instructions will not be used.

In iAPX CPUs, prefetched instructions are stored in the instruction queue (IQ) in the CPU. (The IQ is not shown in any of the figures in this text, and in fact, the MAR and MDR values shown in the example at the end of Section 2.1.5 assume, for simplicity, no prefetch.) The CPU will prefetch bytes sequentially past the current instruction at any time when the system bus is idle. The number of bytes fetched depends on how much bus idle time there is during execution of the current instruction and on whether the IQ has any room left for further prefetching. (The IQ in the 8088 CPU holds 4 bytes, the capacity is 6 bytes for the 8086 and 80286, and the 80386 has a 16-byte version.) Associated with the IQ are the instruction queue head and tail pointers (IQHP and IQTP), which record what range of instructions is currently resident in the IQ. If $c(IQTP) \leq c(IP) \leq c(IQHP)$ when step A starts, then we are in luck, and the CPU will skip ahead to step B (though it must still increment IP).

Actually, prefetching instructions is a special case of a more general form of parallelism, called **pipelining**. Pipelining treats the actions of an instruction as being like those of an assembly line in a factory. Consider an automobile factory, for instance. Its operation is highly parallel, with the construction of many cars being performed simultaneously. At any given time, one car, at any early stage in the assembly line, might be having its engine installed, while another car, at a later stage in the line, might be having its transmission installed. This operation is similar to the idea of prefetching instructions in a computer, in which one instruction is being fetched simultaneously with the execution of another instruction. Some complex CPUs, such as the more advanced members of the iAPX family, break down the processing of an instruction into several small stages and use an assembly-line approach so as to process several instructions at once.

Another form of parallelism is to design the computer to have several CPUs instead of just one. With n CPUs, we can execute n instructions at once, instead of one, thus potentially improving system speed by a factor of *n*. Typical factors in real applications are usually much less than *n*, due to such overhead as the need for the several CPUs to coordinate actions with each other. The hardware—especially the CPU and the bus—must be set up so as to allow such coordination to take place, by the way. The iAPX family, and most of the other major families, have features that support parallelism (e.g., the LOCK instruction prefix, described in Chapter 6).

2.3.3 Clock Rate

Recall from Section 2.1.5 that each machine instruction is implemented as a series of **microsteps**. Each microstep has the same duration, namely one **clock cycle**, which is typically set as the time needed to transfer a value from one CPU register to another. The term "clock cycle" is derived from the fact that the CPU is paced by a **CPU clock** (not to be confused with the **real-time clock** to be introduced in Chapter 7). Each pulse of the clock triggers one microstep.

Each instruction takes a certain number of clock cycles. For example, an addition instruction with both operands in CPU registers takes 2 clock cycles on an 80286 CPU, while a multiply instruction with these operands takes 21 clock cyles. Both cases assume that the instruction has been successfully prefetched, so that step A can be skipped. Also, if one of the operands is in memory, the time needed will increase beyond these values. The timing of these, and other, operations is listed in Appendix II.

The clock emits pulses at a regular rate, with each pulse acting as a signal for the next microstep to occur. On iAPX CPUs, this rate is typically in the range 4.77 to 33 **megahertz** (MHz), i.e., 4.77 to 33 million pulses per second, so that one clock cycle ranges from about 30 **nanoseconds** (ns), i.e., 30 billionths of a second, to 210 ns. Non-iAPX CPUs typically have clock rates in this range, too. By contrast, though, the Cray 2 supercomputer operates at over 200 MHz, i.e., with a clock cycle under 5 ns.

The time to execute a given instruction will be highly affected by the clock rate, even among CPUs of the same type. For example, as mentioned previously, a register-to-register addition instruction takes two microsteps on 80286 CPUs. A 16-MHz 80286 CPU will thus execute the add in 125 ns ($125 = 2 \times 1000 / 16$), while a 12-MHz 80286 will need 167 ns.

Within a CPU family, such as the iAPX family, the Motorola 68000 family, the VAX family, and so on, the later members of the family typically run a given program much faster than the earlier members, for two reasons:

(a) Due to advances in the fabrication of electronic circuitry, later members of a CPU family tend to have much faster clock rates than do earlier ones. We saw this earlier for the iAPX family, with the original 8088 having a clock rate of 4.77 MHz and some current 80386 models running at 33 MHz.

(b) Due to more clever algorithms, pipelining, and so on, the later members of a family often can accomplish the same operation in fewer microsteps than can the earlier ones. For example, a register-times-register multiplication took 113–118 cycles on the 8088, compared to the 21 cycles mentioned for the 80286. The 80386 is even faster.

A recent controversy has involved the effect of the complexity of the architecture on the achievable clock rate. Proponents of a **reduced instruction set computer** (RISC) architecture believe that by restricting the architecture so that it consists of a small, simple, and fairly uniform instruction set, a faster clock rate (and more efficient pipelining) can be achieved. A number of recently developed computers have adopted this philosophy.

2.3.4 Memory-Access Time

In recent years CPU speeds have been increasing at very impressive rates, but memory access speeds have not kept pace with these increases. There are a number of reasons for this, such as the fact that an electrical signal propagates more slowly when it leaves a CPU chip and the fact that control buses often must include **handshaking** lines, in which the various components attached to the bus coordinate their actions. These considerations are beyond the scope of this text, but the important point here is that memory-access speed is a major bottleneck in today's computers and, thus, that solutions to this problem are of great importance.

We have already seen two such solutions. One is prefetching instructions. This does not make memory access any faster physically, but it does something even better: it makes the memory-access time *appear* to be zero, since step A in the fetch/execute cycle is skipped by "hiding" the instruction fetch activity behind the execution of the previous instruction. Another solution is to include data registers, described earlier in this section, in the CPU. Most CPUs include a few data registers. These act like memory, but since they are internal to the CPU, they can be accessed quite quickly, avoiding the problems described in the previous paragraph.

If memory speed is not well matched to CPU speed (not uncommon among inexpensive machines), the CPU will often have to undergo **wait states** while waiting for memory to respond.

Bus size may affect memory-access speed, too, as we saw in the comparison of the 8088 and 8086 CPUs, and the 80386SX and the 80386 CPUs, in Section 2.1.1.

Finally, secondary memory speed plays a role in programs that use it. A slow disk drive, for example, will substantially impair the performance of programs that perform a lot of disk accesses.

2.3.4.1 Memory Caches.   An extension of the idea of coping with slow memory by storing things in registers is an area within the CPU designed to act as a **memory cache**. The cache functions as a temporary storage area for a *copy* of some small subset of memory, which can be accessed locally, thus avoiding a long trip to memory for the desired byte or word.

To create a memory cache, the memory is partitioned into **blocks**, say, of 512 bytes each. (Bytes 00000–00511 form block 0, bytes 00512–01023 form block 1, and so on.) The cache consists of a fixed number of slots, called **lines**. Each slot has room for a copy of one block of memory. The total number of lines varies with the computer; the number could be in the thousands or, on the other extreme, less than 10. At any given time, the cache contains copies of some blocks from memory, with different blocks being involved at different times. This implies that the cache also contains a table indicating which particular blocks currently have copies in the cache.

When the CPU needs to access an item in memory, it will check the cache first. If it is lucky enough for the item to be in the cache (a **cache hit**), it will access the item there, thus saving a time-consuming trip to memory for that access. If the item is not currently in the cache (a **cache miss**), the *entire* block containing that item is copied in from memory and placed in one of the lines in the cache. This of course means that whatever block is currently in that line must be removed from the cache to make room for the new block. What, then, becomes of the old block? Well, if at least one byte in that block had been written to during the block's residence in the cache, we will have to update the original copy in main memory. (Actually, the entire block will be written back.) On the other hand, if all accesses to that block during this time had been reads, we simply overwrite the old block in the given cache line. (There is also another variation of this, in which any byte written in the cache is immediately updated in memory, too, so that no writing back need be done when the block is replaced.)

It is important to note that, though both have the goal of avoiding memory access, data registers and a memory cache are very different in their "visibility" to the programmer. The programmer directly accesses data registers, by including instructions in his or her program to access them. A cache, on the other hand, is **transparent** to the programmer: the CPU does all the management of the cache—i.e., checking for a hit or miss and replacing the block upon finding a miss. As far as the programmer is concerned, it *appears* as if all memory accesses are to main memory.

An important issue in cache design is the **block replacement policy**. As mentioned, when a cache miss occurs, the cache must remove one of its current blocks to make room for the one that is the subject of the current memory-access request. Which block should be removed? Hopefully, the removed block will be one that will not be requested again for a long time into the future; since each block replacement is a time-consuming operation, we hope to postpone replacement as long as possible. But since future memory request patterns cannot be predicted, the designer of the cache must settle upon some policy that works "reasonably well" over a wide range of programs.

Most caches are designed to use a **least recently used** (LRU) policy, or a variation of it. As the name implies, this policy chooses for replacement whichever block has gone the longest time without being accessed, among all blocks currently in the cache. The motivation for this choice is an expectation that if a block has not been accessed for a long time, the probability is lower that it will be accessed in the near future, and thus, it can be "safely" replaced. Keep in mind, though, that the hardware is making this decision entirely on its own and carries out the replacement by itself, too. The programmer does not have to get involved with the process at all.

However, even though the actions of the cache are transparent to the programmer, it is sometimes helpful for the programmer to recognize the existence of a cache in designing his or her code. For example, consider the following two equivalent pieces of Pascal code, which both calculate the sum of all elements in a two-dimensional array declared to have m rows and n columns of integers:

Version I.

```
sum:=0;
for i:=1 to m do
    for j:=1 to n do
        sum:=sum+x[i,j];
```

Version II.

```
sum:=0;
for j:=1 to n do
    for i:=1 to m do
        sum:=sum+x[i,j];
```

Both versions are "correct"—i.e., will give the same answer. However, they access memory in completely different patterns, in different orders. Suppose, for simplicity, that the block size is 64 bytes, the cache has two cache lines, the compiler stores integers as two-byte items and uses row-major order, $m = 4$ and $n = 64$, and the compiler has placed the array x to begin at location C80H, i.e., 3200 in base 10, right at the beginning of block 50 (since 3200/64 = 50).

Now, if the cache is initially empty, then the reader should verify that version I of the code will result in eight cache misses, but version II will generate a lot more—256, a hit rate of 0%!* So two supposedly equivalent pieces of code might have very *different* run times. Once again, it does pay to "look under the hood."

Incidentally, it should be emphasized again that the cache is simply responding to a request for a specific memory location, not to a request for a named variable in Pascal, C, or some other HLL. In the preceding example, for instance, when the machine code for the line

```
sum:=sum+x[i,j];
```

*Here are the first few actions in the case of version II:

1. The cache is empty.
2. The program tries to access x[1,1], resulting in a cache miss.
3. The CPU loads the whole block containing x[1,1], which will be x[1,1], x[1,2], x[1,3], . . . , x[1,32], into the first cache line.
4. The program tries to access x[2,1], resulting in another cache miss.
5. The CPU loads the whole block containing x[2,1], which will be x[2,1], x[2,2], x[2,3], . . . , x[2,32], into the second cache line.
6. The program tries to access x[3,1], resulting in another cache miss.
7. The CPU loads the whole block containing x[3,1], which will be x[3,1], x[3,2], x[3,3], . . . , x[3,32], into the first cache line, since it is least recently used.
8. Etc.

is executed with i = j = 1, the author of that Pascal program thinks of the computer as accessing x[1,1]. But, as was emphasized in Chapter 1, the names in the program do not appear in the compiled machine language; all that will appear is the address, C80H. Thus, the cache is quite "unaware" of the fact that the block it fetches might bring in not only x[1,1] but also some other elements of that same array x; indeed, it does not even "know" that the words starting at the location C80H form an array. And on top of that, it does not "know" whether the program will be accessing other nearby elements in the near future.

In short, the cache simply is not "smart" at all. For example, in version II of the foregoing program, the cache is actually wasting its time bringing in a full block at each cache miss, since only one element in the block will actually be used before the block is replaced; but the cache will not "realize" this.

Nevertheless, experience shows that most programs tend to reuse memory items repeatedly within short periods of time; for example, instructions within a program loop will be accessed repeatedly. Similarly, most programs tend to use items that neighbor each other (as is true for the data accesses in version I of the earlier Pascal program), and thus, they stay in the same block for some time. For these reasons, it turns out that cache misses tend to be rare, on the order of 5% of all accesses.

The newest iAPX CPU, the 80486, has a built-in cache. The earlier iAPX models do not have one, though some computer manufacturers add one externally to the CPU. Computers such as the VAX typically have quite large caches. (Except where otherwise stated, we will ignore caches in any timing analyses we do in later chapters.)

2.3.5 OS Efficiency

At the end of Section 2.2, it was mentioned that Unix, though having the advantage of portability, is not very much tailored to a machine on which it runs. Thus, the software component of the computer's "engine" is a factor in the "engine's" speed: a call to a given OS service in Unix might be slower than a call to a similar service in another OS. Consequently, the same program running on the same hardware but under two different OSs might run faster under one OS than the other.

2.3.5.1 Disk Caches.   One of the services an OS might provide is that of a **disk cache**, which is a software analogue of the memory caches mentioned in Section 2.3.4.1. A disk is divided into **sectors**, which, on IBM microcomputers, are 512 bytes each in size. The disk cache keeps copies of some sectors in main memory. If a program requests access to a certain disk sector, the disk cache is checked first. If that particular sector is present in the cache, then a time-consuming trip to the disk, which is much slower than accessing main memory, can be avoided. Again, this action is transparent to the programmer: the program makes its request to the disk-access service of the OS, and the OS checks the cache and, if necessary, performs an actual disk access. (Note, therefore that the disk cache is implemented in software, as opposed to the memory cache, which is implemented in hardware.)

MS-DOS provides a disk cache whose size may be set via the BUFFERS command. For example, the command

```
> SET BUFFERS = 20
```

instructs MS-DOS to set aside enough memory for a 20-sector disk cache. Up to a point, the more buffers, the better, since the cache miss rate is reduced. But having too many buffers might actually degrade performance, since the OS may waste a lot of time searching for the requested sector in vain.

In Chapter 8, we will discuss **virtual memory**, which has some similarities to caches. It will turn out that a replacement policy is needed there, too. Thus, since two different OSs will have different replacement policies, and one might be much more efficient than the other, one OS may result in a faster "engine" than the other for the support of user programs.

We will return to the question of the factors affecting the speed of a computer "engine" frequently in the rest of this book. Keep in mind that, even though a computer engine may be capable of a certain speed, it is up to the programmer to make the most of this capability. This, too, will be a frequent topic in the book, with plentiful discussions as to how to achieve maximum capability.

ANALYTICAL EXERCISES

1. Consider the absolute memory address 529C8.
   (a) Give two possible segment/offset combinations that point to this absolute address.
   (b) What is the closest possible segment to 00000 for which the address 529C8 is still contained within that segment? In other words, let $x = c(DS)$; what is the smallest value of x for which 529C8 belongs to the current segment?

2. Devise and carry out an experiment to see whether your C or Pascal compiler allocates memory to variables exactly in the same order in which they are declared in the source file, as we saw in Table 1.1 in Chapter 1. Use C's & operator as your tool for investigation (or an analogous operator if your Pascal compiler offers one).

3. Conjecture as to what is the maximum length of an array of type **float** in C or type **real** in Pascal, under compilers for iAPX machines. Explain your reasoning carefully. Then devise and conduct an experiment to test your conjecture.

4. Consider versions I and II of the matrix-sum program in Section 2.3.4.1.
   (a) How would they compare in terms of numbers of cache misses if n = 4 and m = 7?
   (b) Write a program to do a general analysis of this setting, with general values for not only n and m, but also the block size b and the number of cache lines c.

5. Assuming the compiler does memory allocation as in the discussion surrounding Table 1.1, what would that table look like if our declaration of variables were the following?

```
int x,y,*z;
char far *p;
char *q,c,d;
```

6. Suppose a person writes a machine-language program whose instructions total 73 (base-10) bytes in length. She decides to have the code segment start at 256C0H and wants the data segment to start right after the code segment. Where will that be?

7. Suppose we were to try Program 2.1, which is designed for a PC, on an Apple Macintosh, without any changes to the C statements at all. Give a complete account of those aspects of the program which *will* not work and those which *may* not work.

8. Suppose we have a C program with declarations

```
int X,Y,Z,W[4];
char U,V,M,N;
float A,B,C;
int *Q,*R,*S;
```

Suppose also that the compiler allocates offsets for the variables as follows:

Variable	Offset
X	0050
Y	0052
Z	0054
W[1]	0056
W[2]	0058
W[3]	005A
W[4]	005C
U	005E
V	005F
M	0060
N	0061
A	0062
B	0066
C	006A

Let the space for Q, R, and S be allocated right after that for C. Suppose that when the program is loaded into memory for execution, the loader will set c(DS) to 5024—i.e., the variables shown in the table will be stored at the locations starting at 50290.

(a) What will be the five-hex-digit absolute addresses of each of the variables?

(b) Suppose the statements

```
Q = &X;
R = Q + 2;
S = (int *) ((int) Q + 2);
printf("%X %X %X %X %X %X\n",&X,&Y,&Z,Q,R,S);
```

are executed. What values will be printed out? To what variables will Q, R, and S now be pointing? Explain your answer very carefully, especially in the cases of R and S.

9. Answer the following questions about Program 2.1:
   (a) What numerical value will sizeof(p) have?
   (b) Suppose the declaration of p were to be changed to

   ```
   int far *p;
   ```

   (This assumption will not apply to parts (c) and (d) which follow.) Would the value of sizeof(p) be different from that in part (a)? If so, state what the new value would be; if not, explain why not.
   (c) After the line which assigns 65 to *p, suppose there were the following line:

   ```
   printf("%d %x %c\n",*p,*p,*p);
   ```

   What would be printed out?
   (d) State what change could be made to the program so that it will print a dollar sign in the second column of the second row of the screen (which will become the first row after scrolling).

10. Look at the example in Section 2.1.5, and suppose the instruction at 21082 had been one that subtracts BX from AX, i.e., performs AX ← AX − BX. Show what values would have appeared in Figure 2.7 in that case. (Assume Figure 2.4 remains the same.)

11. Suppose we have an 8088 machine with a cache added (external to the CPU). The cache has 2 lines, block size 4 bytes, and an LRU replacement policy. Consider a Pascal program that declares an array

    ```
    var z : array[1..100] of integer;
    ```

    which the compiler stores starting at location 0. Initially, the cache is empty, and then the program accesses the following variables, in the sequence indicated: $z[5]$, $z[6]$, $z[8]$, $z[4]$, $z[5]$, $z[1]$. Answer both of the following questions: How many cache misses will occur? In the end, which array elements will be in the cache?

12. Consider a Pascal program with declaration

    ```
    var c : array[1..60] of char;
    ```

    Suppose the program has an instruction that begins with

    ```
    if c[1] = 'G' then …
    ```

    Give IBM PC machine language up to but not including the first jump instruction, which the compiler might produce from this part of the statement. Assume that storage is like that of Table 1.1 and that the previous declaration is the only declaration in the entire program.

PROGRAMMING PROJECTS

1. In this problem, you will write a primitive picture-drawing program. The program will ask the user to input a *single* command to draw a *set* of vertical and horizontal lines on the screen, using asterisks ('*'). The background of the picture will be drawn using blanks.

Your program will consist of a main program and two subprograms, BlankOut and Draw-Line. The main program will read a set of coordinate pairs from the keyboard, ending with two −1's, which indicate the end of input, and then it will do some processing necessary for the calls to the two procedures. Both procedures must be written to access the screen by accessing the screen image in memory, as in Program 2.1, since this is much, much faster than using **writeln, printf** and so on.

The coordinate pairs will consist of the screen row and column numbers of the starting points and ending points of the lines to be drawn. For example, if the user types

```
5   4   5   12   8   20   16   20   -1   -1
```

this is a request for a line to be drawn from the point designated by row 5, column 4, of the screen to the point designated by row 5, column 12, and another line to be drawn from the point given by row 8, column 20, to the point denoted by row 16, column 20. Horizontal lines must have the left-hand point specified first, and vertical lines must be stated with the upper point first.

The subprogram BlankOut will put the character ' ' at all 2,000 positions on the screen, while the actual drawing of each *individual* line will be done by DrawLine.

Here is what BlankOut would look like in C:

```
BlankOut()

{  char far *p;
   int i;

   p = (char far *) 0xb8000000;
   for (i = 0; i < 2000; i++)  {
      *p = ' ';
      p += 2;              /* means the same as p = p + 2 */
   }
}
```

DrawLine is called by the main program, with a separate call for each line that you draw. The parameters for the procedure will take the following form:
- Starting Offset. This is the offset from B8000 (or, on some monitors, from B0000) at which your first '*' should go. For example, in the case of the user command given earlier, the first '*' goes at the point designated by row 5, column 4, on the screen, which is stored at offset 808 in base 10 (328H).
- Line Length. This is the number of characters in the line.
- Stride Size. This will be the number of memory positions between successive characters in the line, either 2 for horizontal lines or 160 for vertical lines. For example, consider the consecutive characters at columns 18 and 19 of row 1. The first of these two characters is stored at offset 00C4H and the second at offset 00C6H—a distance apart of 2 bytes, so the "stride" is 2. For vertical lines, that distance will be 160 bytes. By including this parameter, your procedure will not have to include separate code for the horizontal and vertical cases.

Here is an outline of the main program:

```
read in the user's command, storing the line coordinates in an array
    named Line and the number of lines in a variable named NLine
call BlankOut
for i = 1 to NLines do
    calculate the 3 parameters for DrawLine
    call DrawLine
```

Use either C or Pascal for this program. (It is essential that you review Program 2.1, in its C or Pascal version, before continuing.)

2. Write a C or Pascal program that will display a picture of a sailboat moving across the screen from left to right (and emerging from the left again after it disappears at the right edge). At the beginning of execution, the program will ask the user how fast ("slow," "medium" or "fast") the movement should be. Use a loop to control speed, looping around, say, 100,000 times doing nothing before making the boat move again. (More sophisticated methods exist using OS services, but this simple method is good enough here.)

3. Write a program to save the current contents, i.e., the 2,000 characters and their attributes, currently appearing on the monitor to a disk file. The program must also include code that will read such a file and restore the monitor screen as it appeared when previously saved to the file. There is an example of reading and writing files in C in Program 7.15; Pascal is less standardized, so you must consult your Pascal compiler manual if you wish to use Pascal for this program.

4. Add a code to Program 2.1 so that it will print out the value in DS, i.e., the location of the start of the data segment. Your code must print that value only, not with an offset.

3

Introduction to the iAPX Instruction Set and Addressing Modes

In this chapter, we will begin to learn the machine language for iAPX CPUs, which is the CPU family on which this book focuses. Although each type of CPU—iAPX, 68000, VAX, and so on—has its own machine language which varies in detail from machine to machine, the general principles are fairly similar across machines. Thus, someone who is proficient at programming in the machine language of one machine will be able quickly to learn to program on other machines.

Once again, keep in mind that machine language is what the computer executes; it does not execute Pascal, C, or any other high-level language. If we write a Pascal or C program on an IBM microcomputer (which we will often do in examples in this book), the compiler will translate our Pascal or C code to machine code such as that which will appear here. And, once that machine code is loaded into the computer's memory, the computer cannot tell whether it came originally from a Pascal source, or whether we wrote it directly in machine language ourselves.

3.1 AN INTRODUCTORY PROGRAM

We will write a simple program to calculate the sum of all the words stored in a given range of addresses in memory and put the sum in AX. The range of words to be summed will be specified by the BX and DX registers, with BX containing the offset of the start of the range and DX containing the offset of the end of the range. Since this range in memory will be used as the data for our program, rather than as the program's instructions, the offsets are relative to the value in the DS register, rather than the CS register.

The values in DS, BX, and DX will act as inputs to the program, supplied by the user. The user might wish to find the sums in several different memory ranges, and the program could be used to accomplish that goal, simply by running many times with different values in DS, BX, and DX. (In Section 4.1, you will see how the user can place the desired values into these and other registers before running the program.)

Our program's machine instructions must be entered into memory, but *where* in memory? The answer is that they can be placed anywhere in memory that is not in current use. This will be discussed further in later chapters, but for concreteness, let us suppose that we have decided to have our code segment begin at location 21080, and thus, we must initialize the CS register to 2108. (Again, you will see how to do this in Section 4.1.)

Note that we arbitrarily chose to use AX as the place at which we will store our sum. We could have used some other register instead. The same is true for the usage to which we will put DX in this program. On the other hand, though our usage of BX here could have been done with the DI or SI registers instead, you will see later that it could *not* have been done with any other register. And of course, CS and DS *must* be used to point to the beginning of the code segment and data segment, respectively, though our choice for the location of those segments was arbitrary. We will discuss the question of which registers can be used for which purposes in Section 3.3.

Suppose that in a particular run of the program, we will be interested in finding the sum of words 20050H, 20052H, and 20054H. In order to access these locations using BX and DX as just outlined, let us agree to set DS to 2000 and thus initialize BX to 50 and DX to 54. This scheme does work, since a value of 2000 in DS represents the location 20000 (recall that DS and the other segment registers suppress storage of an implicit 0 in the rightmost hex digit), and $20,000 + 50 = 20,050$ and $20,000 + 54 = 20,054$, as desired. Alternatively, we could set DS to, say, 2002, and then set BX and DX to 30 and 34, respectively. Obviously, lots of other combinations would work, too—i.e., would result in BX and DX pointing to the words 20050 and 20054, respectively.

Suppose then, that the contents of the aforesaid three words of memory are as shown in Table 3.1.

TABLE 3.1

Location	Contents
Word 20050	FFFD
Word 20052	0024
Word 20054	0100

Note carefully that we have emphasized that each of the items is a word in length. This is natural, because the adder in the ALU is designed to add operands of this size, but we wish to emphasize this for another reason as well. Look at the value in word 20052, which is the hex number 0024 (36 in base 10). Recall that *word* 20052 consists of *bytes* 20052 and 20053. The ALUs in iAPX machines are designed to work in what modern computer architecture terminology calls a **little-endian** manner. This means that when an ALU is performing, say, an addition operation, it assumes that the byte with the lower address contains the less significant part of the number (i.e., the less significant part is on the "little end" of the word). So, in the number 0024, the 24 is the less significant byte and is thus stored in the byte with the lower address (20052), while 00 is the more significant byte and is thus stored in the byte with the higher address (20053).

The format of Program 3.1 is that the hex number to the left of the '—' will be the address (offset measured from 21080 in the code segment) of the instruction, while the instruction itself will appear to the right of the '—'. On the far right will be some English, informally explaining what the instruction does. All numbers are in hex. (But keep in mind again that this is just a shorthand notation, with the actual storage being in 0's and 1's.)

```
0000 — 2BC0      subtract AX from itself (to make it 0)
0002 — 0307      add the word pointed to by BX to AX
0004 — 83C302    add 2 to BX (to point to the next word)
0007 — 3BD3      compare DX to BX
0009 — 79F7      if DX >= BX, then jump back to 0002
```

Program 3.1

Note that while most instructions in this program are exactly two bytes long (four hex digits), instructions do, in general, vary in length. It was mentioned in Chapter 2 that iAPX 86 instructions range in length from one to six bytes.

For example, the instruction at offset 0004, i.e., 83C302, is three bytes long. The first byte (at code segment offset 4, i.e., address 21084) contains 83, the second byte (offset 5) contains C3, and the third byte (offset 6) contains 02. This notation puts things in byte order—i.e., 83 is in byte 21084, C3 is in byte 21085 and 02 is in byte 21086. This is the custom when writing machine instructions on the printed page: as we go from left to right on the page, byte addresses increase. This is quite a contrast to the case we saw earlier, of writing integers on the printed page, in which byte addresses *decrease* as we go from left to right.

So the instruction at code segment offset 0 initializes AX to 0, for our sum, and then enters a loop, located at offsets 0002 through 0009. Each trip around the loop will increment BX by two, so BX will continue to advance successively through all the words in the desired range, which in this particular run of the program we have been assuming would be 20050, 20052, and 20054. The fourth line, the compare operation, is used to test whether we have hit the end point of the range; if not, the fifth line will make us jump back to the top of the loop, starting the next iteration.

Incidentally, a program, such as Program 3.1, consists of *instructions*. The reader should take care not to call them "commands." The term **command** is generally used to refer to things like operating system utilities; for example, MS-DOS's DIR command prints out file names on the terminal screen. DIR itself is a program, made up of instructions. This may seem like a small point, but it *is* an important one.

Let's look at the instructions of Program 3.1 in more detail, stepping through the first iteration. Before getting started, we will lay down a couple of ground rules for the pictures to be shown. First, we have to decide the size for the MDR. This size should be the same as the size of the data bus, which we will assume here is eight bits, as for the 8088 CPU. (By using this CPU as our example, we avoid complications beyond the scope of this book, such as the fact that on an 80286 CPU, words of even-numbered addresses are fetched whole, while words of odd-numbered addresses are fetched one byte at a time.) Second, to clarify the roles of the MAR and MDR registers, it will be assumed that no prefetching of instructions is done.

Before step A of the first instruction of the program, the state of the CPU is as in Figure 3.1. We use the same notation here as in Figures 2.4 through 2.7. However, notice that the label on the FR box has changed. This is because in this example we will be interested mainly in one particular bit of FR, bit 7, called the **sign flag** (SF), which

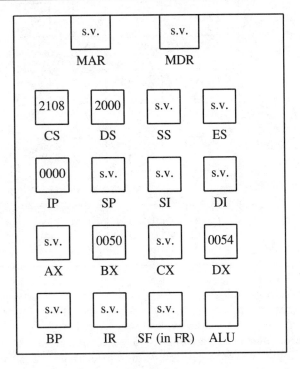

Figure 3.1

will be explained shortly. Now, let us look at how the CPU registers change as we execute the instructions of the program one by one.

2BC0.   This instruction subtracts AX from itself. (We will discuss *why* 2BC0 codes such an operation later, in Section 3.2.) Again, we have included this instruction in the program so that AX, the register in which we will be keeping our running total, will start out at 0.

After executing this instruction, the CPU state will be as in Figure 3.2. Note that not only have the contents of the the AX box changed, but so have the contents of the IP box. Remember, during each instruction, IP is incremented by as many bytes as the length of the instruction, so as to prepare for the next instruction fetch, in step A of the next cycle. At this time in the cycle, IP is pointing to offset 0002, which, from Program 3.1, we can see is indeed the location of the next instruction, 0307.

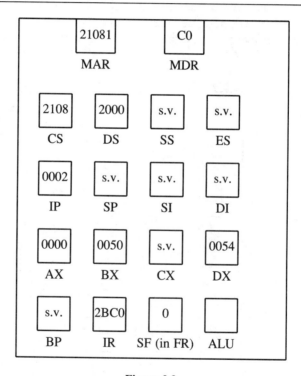

Figure 3.2

Furthermore, the figure now shows SF as being 0. To see why, first recall from Chapter 2 that in typical computers, the PS register records various aspects of the outcome of the most recent computation. Since computation—addition, subtraction, and so on—is done in the ALU, there are lines leading from the ALU to the PS register, so that each computation results in an immediate update of the PS. This was shown in Figure 2.2 (although only a single line was drawn there, for simplicity).

The iAPX family's PS register is the flags register, FR. The sign flag (SF) bit within that register is responsible for keeping track of whether the most recent computation resulted in a negative (i.e. "signed") number; c(SF) will be 1 if that result was negative, and it will be 0 if that result was nonnegative, i.e., positive or zero. Thus, value 1 means yes and 0 means no. So, c(SF) being 1, for example, means, "Yes, the result of the last computation was negative." Here, the computation in question was the subtraction of AX from itself, which of course resulted in a zero value, so c(SF) is 0 in Figure 3.2, and SF is saying, "No, the result of the last computation was not negative."

Bit 6 of the FR is the zero flag, ZF. Its contents are 1 or 0, depending on whether the result of the last computation was or was not zero, respectively. So, if Figure 3.2 were to show ZF (we omitted it from the picture to save space), it would show that c(ZF) is now 1.

Note that the MAR now contains 21081. The value in the MAR after step A was 21080, reflecting the fact that the first byte of the instruction was fetched; then, in step B, the remaining byte was fetched, which required putting 21081 into the MAR and which resulted in C0 being deposited by the memory into the MDR.

0307.   The decoding in step B will reveal that 0307 specifies an add operation, with the two operands defined as follows: the **destination** operand, i.e., the one whose value changes as a result of the operation, is AX, while the **source** operand, i.e., the other operand, is the memory word pointed to by BX. What "pointed to" means here is "whose offset is given by." Thus, 0307 specifies that we go to the memory location $20000 + 50 = 20050$ and add that value to the value already in AX.

Note that this operation is different from adding BX to AX, which corresponds to an instruction having the code 01D8. The source operand for the instruction 01D8 is BX itself, while for the instruction 0307, the source is the memory location *pointed to* by BX. Checking Figure 3.2 and Table 3.1, we see that the instruction 01D8 would add 50 to AX, while the instruction 0307 adds FFFD to AX.

We say that the instruction 0307 uses the **indirect addressing mode** to specify its source operand. This terminology stems from the fact that 0307 does not explicitly say where the operand is; it just says so indirectly, by saying the operand is wherever BX is pointing to.

Since c(AX) is 0000, the instruction 0307 will add FFFD to 0000, resulting in FFFD becoming the new contents of AX. Note that FFFD is a negative number, since its most significant bit is a 1 (recall Chapter 1); FFFD is the number −3. This information will be immediately relayed to the FR, and the new value of SF there will be 1.

The new CPU state is shown in Figure 3.3. You should take some time to examine the figure, making sure you understand the new contents of each box. Note that, unlike the aftermaths of the previous instructions, the MAR value here does not contain the address of the latest byte or word fetched from the instruction stream. This is because the latest memory access was to a data item, in location 20051 (which was the second byte of word 20050). Note again that this means that the contents of the MDR have become FF, not FD, due to the little-endian aspect discussed earlier.

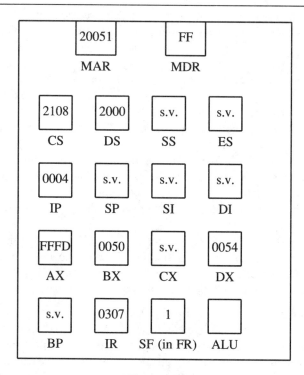

Figure 3.3

83C302. In step B, the CPU will discover that this instruction is another add operation, with the destination operand being BX, but with the source operand being specified by the **immediate addressing mode**. The latter means that the operand is actually contained within the instruction itself—in this case, as the *third* byte of the instruction (the 02—i.e., we will be adding 2 to BX).

The new CPU state is shown in Figure 3.4. Note that c(IP) is now 0007, whereas it previously was 0004; it has been incremented by three because it processed a three-byte instruction, and the new value of 0007 is just right, because it now points to the next instruction, 3BD3, as you can see in Program 3.1. Note also that c(SF) is now 0, because the result of the last computation, 52, was not negative.

3BD3. In step B, the CPU will discover that this is a compare operation, with source operand BX and destination operand DX. This operation subtracts the source from the destination; i.e., DX – BX will be calculated, *but the result will not be stored in either of these registers.* At first glance, it would seem that since neither the source nor the destination register is affected, then the instruction essentially does nothing! But this overlooks the fact that FR and, hence, SF are affected. Indeed, this is the point of the instruction; you will see that the next instruction, 79F7, makes use of the status of SF.

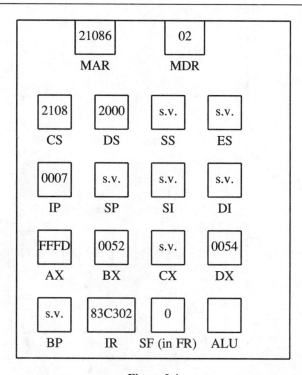

Figure 3.4

The new CPU state is shown in Figure 3.5.

79F7.   In step B, this instruction will be found to be a "jump if SF is not set" operation. The word "jump" here means to jump to another point in the program, as with a **goto** statement in Pascal or C. Another term used for "jump" with some types of CPUs is **branch**.

The description "if SF is not set" means "if c(SF) is not 1." (Recall from Chapter 1 that the terms **set** and **cleared** mean that a bit is 1 and 0, respectively.) SF reflects the result of the last computation—in our last instruction, the subtraction $DX - BX$, which had the value +2. This value is not negative, and as can be seen in Figure 3.5, c(SF) is indeed not 1. Thus, the jump will be made.

How does the CPU decide *where* to jump to? This is specified in the second byte of the instruction, F7 in this case. This quantity is to be interpreted as an eight-bit, two's-complement integer. Recall that the hex notation for the quantity, 11110111, is just a shorthand for a string of 0's and 1's. A quick conversion shows that this is the eight-bit two's-complement representation for −9.

What this means is that we should jump *backwards* nine bytes. The actual implementation of this jump is very simple: the circuitry of the CPU is designed to do the replacement

$$IP \leftarrow IP + displacement$$

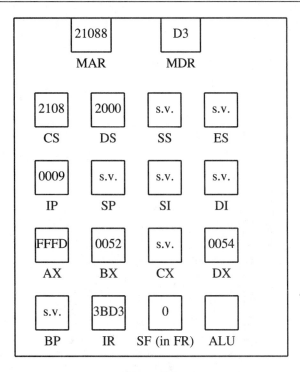

Figure 3.5

where **displacement** denotes the quantity in the second byte of the jump instruction, here F7 = –9. In steps A and B, IP has been incremented to 9 + 2 = BH, so adding –9 results in the value 2. Thus, we will jump back to offset 0002, which was the instruction 0307 (see Program 3.1)—exactly what we want, since this is the top of the loop.

The checking of SF and, if not set, the adding of the displacement to IP are done in step C. (Recall that step C is the step in which the actual execution of any instruction is done, including this instruction.) When the next step A comes, the CPU will look at c(IP) for its instruction fetch as usual and thus will use the new value put there during step C of the jump instruction.

If SF had been set, then the jump would not have been taken, and IP would not have been changed during step C. In that case, c(IP) would still be the value it was after step B, i.e., 000B. Then the next step A would execute the instruction at offset 000B. In other words, if a jump is not taken, then the next instruction to be executed will be the one sequentially following the jump instruction in memory.

Note that although the English description of the instruction 79F7 in the listing of Program 3.1 is "if DX >= BX, then jump back to 0002," this instruction does *not* actually deal with DX or BX. Nor does the instruction deal directly with the offset 0002. Thus, a more accurate English description would be "if SF is not 1, then add –9 to IP."

Whichever description we use, this instruction is called a **conditional jump**, because the jump is taken only under the condition that SF is cleared. There are several other conditional jumps in the core iAPX instruction set, such as "jump if ZF is not set." These are listed in Appendix II.

Figure 3.6 shows the new CPU state immediately after the conditional jump is executed. Note that c(SF) is 0. This is actually the value left over from the execution of the instruction 3BD3 at offset 0007. Jump instructions do not affect the FR register, since that register shows the outcome of the most recent *computational* instruction, which in this case is 3BD3, not 79F7.

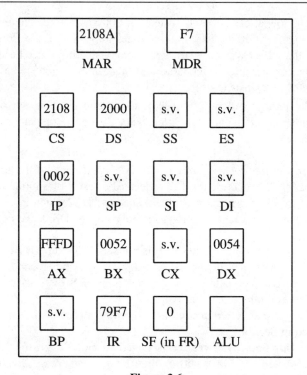

Figure 3.6

It is instructive to look at a certain variation of the program. The goal is the same in this version as before. The main difference in implementation is that instead of DX marking the end of the range of memory words to be summed, DX contains the *number* of words to be summed. In the example given, in which words 20050, 20052, and 20054 were summed, c(DX) would be 3. So, instead of looping until c(BX) passes c(DX), as in Program 3.1, we decrement DX by one in each iteration of the loop and leave the loop when c(DX) reaches 0. Program 3.2 is the new version of Program 3.1.

```
0000 — 2BC0      subtract AX from itself (to make it 0)
0002 — 0307      add the word pointed to by BX to AX
0004 — 83C302    add 2 to BX (to point to the next word)
0007 — 83EA01    subtract 1 from DX
000A — 75F6      if DX > 0 then jump back to 0002
```

Program 3.2

Note two things about the jump instruction:

(a) It is now at offset 000A, instead of 0009 as before. The reason is that the instruction now at offset 0007 is three bytes long, whereas in Program 3.1 the instruction at that offset was only two bytes long. This difference has in turn affected the displacement value, which is now F6 instead of F7; so we have to jump backward 10 bytes now, instead of 9.

(b) The jump instruction here is of the "jump if ZF is not set" type, instead of the "jump if SF is not set" type. Hex 79 coded the latter, and hex 75 codes the former.

Note also that no compare instruction is needed here: at the time the jump instruction at offset 000A executes, the FR reflects the result of subtracting 1 from DX—i.e., it reflects the positive, negative, or zero status of DX, which is exactly what we want. We *could* have put in an instruction here to compare DX to 0, but that would have been quite redundant.

In addition to the "jump if SF is not set" and "jump if ZF is not set" we have seen so far, the iAPX instruction set has a variety of other conditional jump instructions, such as the complementary instructions "jump if SF is set" and "jump if ZF is set" as well as several others listed in Appendix II.

There are also two unconditional jump instructions in the iAPX set, which will be described in Section 3.2.

At this point, the reader is urged to run Programs 3.1 and 3.2, in order to make concrete the ideas within them. To do so, read ahead in Section 4.1, which provides simple commands (E, R, G, T) that can be used to enter a program into memory and execute it. Don't worry about the fact that you will be reading this section out of sequence. The section is quite easy to read if you try the examples there on a real machine while you are reading.

3.2 A BRIEF LOOK AT INSTRUCTION FORMATS

In Program 3.1 and 3.2, why does 2BC0, the instruction at offset 0000, mean to subtract AX from itself? Actually, this question should be considered to be two questions, concerning two aspects of the iAPX coding scheme:

- Why does 2BC0 mean to perform a subtraction, as opposed to some other kind of operation?
- Why does it mean that both operands will be AX, as opposed to using other registers or memory cells for operands?

Clearly, the CPU's circuitry is designed to look at the 16 bits in 2BC0—i.e., 0010101111000000—and react by subtracting AX from itself. But the two questions above really concern individual bit fields:

- Which bits in the instruction indicate that it is a subtraction?
- Which bits indicate that the source operand is a register, rather than a word in memory? And how is AX specified as that register?
- Which bits indicate that the destination operand is a register, rather than a word in memory? And how is AX specified as that register?

We will discuss these questions here. They concern the idea of **instruction formats**, meaning the role that each set of bits plays in determining the meaning of an instruction.

The *full* answers to these questions for iAPX machines are *very, very* complex—conceptually simple, but with many, many special cases that would need to be enumerated. Fortunately, there is very little reason for learning the codings for all these cases, because starting with Chapter 4, we will use assembly language instead of machine language. For example, to indicate subtraction of AX from itself, we will use SUB AX,AX, instead of 2BC0. Clearly the form SUB AX,AX is much more convenient.

Still, one should at least be exposed to the concept of instruction formats, so we will discuss one of these formats here. We will call it register-to-register (RTR) format, to emphasize the fact that this format is for two-operand instructions in which both the source and destination operands are in registers. In Program 3.1, the instructions 2BC0 and 3BD3 are both of RTR form. The instruction 0307 is not of this type, since its source operand is in memory, not in a register.

The RTR format is shown graphically in Figure 3.7. Observe that RTR instructions are two bytes, i.e., 16 bits, long and that various bit fields are given names. For example, the first six bits, bits 15–10, are called the **op code** of this instruction. This

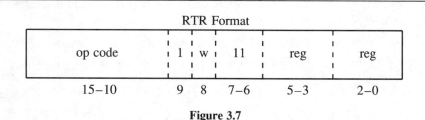

Figure 3.7

field, as you will see shortly, indicates what type of operation is to be done—addition, subtraction, and so on. In conjunction with the 1's in bits 9, 7, and 6, the op code field also indicates that the instruction is of the RTR type.

Let us look at these bit fields in a specific example, the instruction in offset 0007 of Program 3.1, which has the hex code 3BD3. Writing this out in binary, we have

```
0011 1011 1101 0011
```

Now let us group these 16 bits according to the fields defined in Figure 3.7. The result is shown in Figure 3.8.

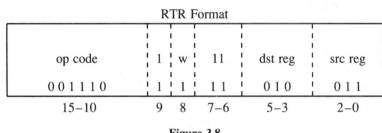

Figure 3.8

Let us examine each field in turn.

Op Code. For RTR instructions, the first six bits of the instruction code the operation; thus, we call these bits the "op code" field. In the instruction 0307, the bits are 000000 (the reader should verify this), indicating addition. The circuitry in the CPU is set up to recognize this. Similarly, in the instruction 2BC0, the first six bits are 001010, indicating subtraction. In 3BD3, the code is 001110, for the compare operation.

If we were to change the first six bits in 2BC0 from 001010 to 00000, resulting in the instruction 03C0, the instruction would mean to *add* AX to itself, rather than to subtract AX from itself.

If the first six bits in 2BC0 were to be changed to 001110, yielding 3BC0, the instruction would *compare* AX with itself (and would not be very useful).

If we were to change the first six bits of 2BC0 to 100010, yielding 8BC0, the instruction would do a **move** operation (abbreviated MOV in the chapters that follow). This copies the value of AX to itself (again, not very useful).

w. Bit 8 of an RTR instruction, denoted by "w" indicates whether the operands will be words (w = 1) or bytes (w = 0). For example, the instruction 3BD3 has w = 1. If we were to change this to w = 0, yielding 3AD3, the coding would mean to compare the *bytes* DL and BL, rather than the *words* DX and BX, as 3BD3 does.

Reg. Recall that RTR instructions are two-operand instructions in which both the source and destination operands are in registers. Recall also that the destination register is usually the one that stores the result of the operation (e.g., addition does $dst \leftarrow dst + src$, subtraction does $dst \leftarrow dst - src$, "move" does $dst \leftarrow src$, and so on). The reg fields indicate which specific registers are to be used.

The reg field for the destination register consists of bits 5–3, and the field for the source register is bits 2–0, using the system of codes shown in Table 3.2. (If w = 0, the registers AX, CX, DX, BX, SP, BP, SI, and DI should be replaced in the table by AL, CL, DL, BL, AH, CH, DH, and BH, respectively.)

TABLE 3.2

000	AX
001	CX
010	DX
011	BX
100	SP
101	BP
110	SI
111	DI

Again, let us use the instruction 3BD3 as an example. The destination reg field is 010, indicating DX, and the source reg field is 011, for BX. Thus, the instruction compares DX with BX, as we have seen in Section 3.1.

If we were to change the destination reg field to, say, 001, yielding 3BCB, then the instruction would compare CX with BX, rather than comparing DX with BX, as 3BD3 does.

If we were to change the source reg field to, say, 110, yielding 3BD6, then the instruction would compare DX with SI, rather than comparing DX with BX, as 3BD3 does.

Similarly, the instruction 2BC0 subtracts AX from itself. The reader should check that by changing the source reg field to BX, so that the instruction is 2BC3, the instruction would subtract BX from AX.

Note that bits 9, 7, and 6 in Figure 3.8 are set to 1; this is by definition of the RTR format.

Although the RTR format will be the only new format to be introduced here, it should be mentioned that we have already seen another format in Section 3.1, that of jump instructions. Recall the instruction 79F7 in Program 3.1. The first byte, 79, coded a "jump if SF is not set" instruction, and the second byte, F7, is the displacement, i.e., the distance to be jumped. The reader might realize in the present context that the 79 is actually the op code for this instruction. Then, in the instruction 75F6 in Program 3.2, the op code 75 means "jump if ZF is not set."

There are several other jump instructions, listed in Appendix II. One of them is an unconditional jump, with op code EB. Thus, EBF7 would mean to unconditionally jump backward nine bytes.

Note that the displacement field in the jump instructions we have seen so far is only one byte long. For example, the displacement F7 in the instruction 79F7 consists of two hex digits and thus one byte. Since the displacement field will be interpreted by the CPU as an eight-bit, two's-complement number, our jump range is limited to no further than 127 bytes forward (displacement = 01111111) and no further than 128 bytes backward (displacement = 10000000).

To allow for more flexibility than the EB and similar instructions provide, there is another unconditional jump instruction. It is a five-byte instruction consisting of the op code EA followed by a four-byte field that directly specifies the **target** of the jump, i.e., the place to which we want to jump. In the other jump instructions, the target was specified indirectly, as a *distance* from the position pointed to by IP. The EA instruction, on the other hand, directly specifies the offset value for the target in the second and third bytes of the instruction and the segment value for the target in the fourth and fifth bytes. (Recall from Chapter 2 that if a program is very big, we might need more than one code segment, and we might jump back and forth from one segment to another. Thus, it is necessary that an EA instruction specify both the offset *and* segment values of the target.)

For instance, suppose we wish to jump to offset 002D within the segment that begins at A4520. Then our instruction would be EA2D0052A4. Note that this instruction requires that bytes be reversed within the offset and segment fields—e.g., the offset 002D appears as 2D00.

Again, the iAPX instructions comprise a very large number of formats; the RTR and jump formats discussed here merely scratch the surface of this subject. The situation is further complicated by the fact that the register codings are not consistent across formats—e.g., the register codings given here for the RTR format do not hold for some other formats. The interested reader should consult one of the Intel programmer's manuals.

We have presented this sampling of instruction formats for the sake of "culture": anyone claiming to have some understanding of how computers work ought to understand the concept of an op code. Having done this, there is no reason to go further, dwelling on the tedious and largely irrelevant myriad of details involved in the iAPX family's many formats. Instead, we choose to move on, using assembly language, beginning in Chapter 4. This allows us to specify operations and operands in an English-like manner, with a special program doing the work of looking up op codes and register codes in tables.

Still, it is worthwhile making a brief remark about the variation in codings among different types of CPUs. It was stated at the beginning of this chapter that although each type of CPU—iAPX, 68000, VAX, and so on—has a different instruction set, there are enough similarities between instruction sets so that once you have learned to program one type of CPU, you can quickly learn to program other types. But keep in mind that in spite of this general similarity, each instruction set is different, and thus, a machine-language program for one type of CPU will be meaningless gibberish if one tries to run it on another type of CPU.

As an example, consider the instruction "jump if SF is not set" in Program 3.1. This instruction, 79F7, has a general form 79dd, where 'dd' denotes the displacement. The 68000 family of CPUs has a very similar instruction, but its coding is of the form 6Cdd. So even though the two types of CPU happen to have two instructions that work identically (in this case!), they still have different op codes. Furthermore, given any two types of CPU, each will have some instructions that the other lacks. Thus, you can see that a machine-language program written for one type of CPU has no hope at all of working on another type of CPU, since the two CPUs have different instruction sets, and even those instructions which have the same functions will have different encodings.

3.3 ALLOWABLE COMBINATIONS OF OPERATIONS AND OPERANDS

Look at Table 3.2. Does something seem to be missing? Something is indeed missing—the segment registers, CS, DS, SS, and ES. This produces some occasional inconvenience.

For example, suppose we need to produce code that will put the value 5,000 into the DS register. The operation would be **move** (i.e., copy), with op code 100010, mentioned earlier; the source operand would be the value 5,000, given in **immediate** addressing mode, just as the constant 2 was specified via this addressing mode in the instruction 83C302 in Program 3.1; and the destination operand would be the register DS. Unfortunately, as the use of the word "would" here implies, this instruction does not exist; instructions of such form—i.e., with the source being a constant and the destination being a register, use Table 3.2 to specify the register, and as we have seen, that table excludes the register DS!

We can still accomplish our goal of putting 5000 into DS, but instead of the single instruction

```
move 5000 to DS
```

we will need the two instructions

```
move 5000 to AX
move AX to DS
```

The first instruction is the ordinary **move** just mentioned, with op code 100010 and with AX being specified as 000, from Table 3.2. The second instruction is actually a different **move** instruction, with op code 10001110, which allows one of the operands to be a segment register. (The latter is coded as 00 for ES, 01 for CS, 10 for SS, and 11 for DS.)

The point is that not every operand is allowed to be combined with every operation. We say that those CPUs which allow more combinations of operands and operations than other CPUs are more **orthogonal** than those others. The iAPX family is considered to be less orthogonal than, say, the 68000 or VAX families.

In many senses, a low degree of orthogonality is a disadvantage; for example, it caused us to use two instructions instead of one in the previous example. However, it can also be a virtue. The designers of the iAPX family anticipated that certain combinations of operands and operations would be used so rarely that an occasional inconvenience (e.g., having to use two instructions instead of one) is a small price to pay for the program compactness that comes from disallowing these rarely used combinations.

One source of compactness is as follows. Again, look at Table 3.2. Eight registers are listed, using three-bit codings. Since those eight registers exhaust all possible three-bit coding patterns, we would need to use a four-bit coding scheme if Table 3.2 were to be extended to include the segment registers ES, CS, SS, and DS. This is only one extra bit, but it would in most cases be a wasted bit, since very few instructions would make use of the segment registers. So most two-operand instructions would be needlessly lengthened by two bits, more than a 10% increase over their typical length of 16 bits.

In some cases, instruction size would even be increased by three bits. For example, you will see in Chapter 6 that the iAPX instruction set includes a **loop** instruction designed to make program loops run faster. This instruction *requires* that its operand be in the CX register, and thus, no bits are used to specify a register. If any nonsegment register, rather than just CX, were to be allowed, then we would need a three-bit field to specify the register, and the **loop** instruction would be expanded from 16 bits to 19 bits—almost a 20% increase.

Since some programs use a large amount of memory, compactness of code can be very valuable; thus, the relatively nonorthogonal nature of the iAPX family can be advantageous. On the other hand, the need to allow for so many special cases does result in slower internal circuitry in the CPU. Furthermore, the use of an instruction such as the **loop** instruction ties up the CX register, and we cannot use CX for other purposes within the loop, which is a severe constraint in view of the fact that iAPX CPUs have so few registers anyway. So "nothing in life is free."

Appendix II lists all combinations of operands and operations. Note that we usually will not be very concerned with specific op codes or specific register codes, since we will begin using a code-free, more English-like method—assembly language— starting in the next chapter. But we still have to know which operands and operations may be used together.

Note carefully that once you start using assembly language, the "allowable operation/operand combinations" issue may arise frequently, especially in your first few programs. Unfortunately, the assembler error messages are often rather cryptic to the beginner, so if you encounter such a message, your first reaction should be that you probably have attempted an illegal operation/operand combination.

What can you do to check this supposition? Of course, you can check Appendix II or some equivalent, if you have it at hand. Another method is to try a quick experiment with the DEBUG program (or another debugger). However, the following rules of thumb work for most cases:

(a) Most one-operand instructions allow the operand to be either a nonsegment register or a memory location, but not a constant specified in immediate addressing mode.

(b) Most two-operand instructions allow both operands to be nonsegment registers.

(c) Most two-operand instructions allow one operand to be a nonsegment register and the other operand to be in memory.

(d) Most two-operand instructions allow one operand to be a nonsegment register and the other operand to be a constant specified in immediate addressing mode.

(e) No two-operand instructions allow both operands to be in memory.

Note that in these descriptions, the operands in memory might be specified via a register—e.g., in **indirect** addressing mode (see the instruction 0307 in Program 3.1). Note also, that the term "nonsegment register" means AX, BX, CX, DX, SI, DI, SP, and BP; the registers IP, IR, FR, MAR, and MDR (and of course, CS, DS, SS, and ES) are ineligible in this regard.

Whenever you find that an operation/operand combination that you wanted to use turns out to be invalid, you will have to use two or more instructions together to reach your goal. This was the case for the invalid instruction

```
move 5000 to DS
```

Instead, we had to resort to using the two instructions

```
move 5000 to AX
move AX to DS
```

ANALYTICAL EXERCISES

1. (a) Give the history of the contents of the MAR and MDR during the second execution of the instruction 0307 in Program 3.1. The steps to be covered are steps A, B, and C. Assume that all the numbers are the same as in the discussion of Program 3.1 in the text, except that

```
c(20050) = 514
c(20052) = 25
c(20054) = 3
```

and omit any effects on MAR and MDR of the prefetching of instructions that *follow* 0307.

   (b) In part (a), we specified the *second* execution of the instruction. Why would the answer to that part be less clear if we had asked for the *first* execution? (Hint: The answer involves the instruction prefetch mechanism, mentioned in Chapter 2.)

2. Consider the instruction SUB BX,5, whose machine-language form is 83EB05. Suppose the instruction starts at offset x (unspecified here; just refer to it as x) and that just before step A,

the values of various registers are as follows: CS = 2422, DS = 2020, BX = 4A, SS = F602, SP = 2300. (You will not need all of these.) For simplicity, ignore the effects of prefetching instructions.

(a) What is the value of IP just before step A?

(b) What will be the value of IP just after step C?

(c) Give the history of the values in MAR and MDR, as in Exercise 1.

3. It was mentioned in Section 1.2.5 that 742B is the code for an instruction to jump ahead 43 bytes. Verify that 43 is indeed the value specified in this code, and state the condition under which a jump will occur.

4. Suppose Program 3.1 has all the same initial values as described in Section 3.1, except that c(BX) and c(DX) are initialized to 0051 and 0052, respectively. What will be the final value in c(AX) after the program finishes execution?

PROGRAMMING PROJECTS

1. As explained in Section 3.2, we want to avoid getting bogged down in learning the myriads of instruction formats and thus will soon leave the world of machine language, using assembly language instead. But in order to get at least a "taste" of machine language, we will write one machine language program here.

Alter Program 3.1 so that it will count the number of negative numbers in the memory range specified by BX and DX. Here is an outline of such an altered program in "pseudocode":

```
        subtract CX from itself
    1 : ''move'' (i.e., copy) the word pointed to by BX to AX
        compare AX to 0
        if AX ≥ 0 go to 2
        add 1 to CX
    2 : add 2 to BX
        compare DX to BX
        if DX ≥ BX go to 1
```

Each of these instructions can be obtained by making slight alterations to one or more fields (e.g., the op code field) in one of the instructions in Program 3.1.

Most of the instructions needed will be either of the RTR format or of "jump format." However, four are of different formats. Three of those four are of what we will here call "ITR" (immediate-to-register) format, in which a constant specified in immediate addressing mode is added to a register. The instruction 83C302 in Program 3.1 was of the ITR form. Figure 3P.1 shows the general format for ITR instructions.

The op code in an ITR instruction for a given operation, say addition, is not the same as for an RTR instruction of the same operation. You can easily check that this is the case by looking at the difference between the two addition instructions in Program 3.1. For the compare operation, the ITR op code is 100000 (part 1) and 111 (Part 2).

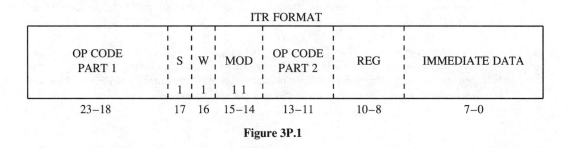

Figure 3P.1

The "reg" field in ITR instructions uses the codings in Table 3.2.

The fourth non-RTR instruction,

```
''move'' (i.e., copy) the word pointed to by BX to AX
```

is of yet another format. It will not be described in detail here. All you need to know is that (1) this format is the same one used for the instruction 0307 in Program 3.1; (2) the op code for this format is in the first six bits, just as with RTR format; and (3) the same op codes are used for this format as for RTR. Thus, a simple alteration to the 0307 instruction will give you the "move" instruction needed in the program here.

Demonstrate that your program works, by using DEBUG to (1) put the data that follow into consecutive words beginning at address 123A4H (use 30004 if this address turns out to be a conflict—i.e., if DEBUG does not load at that address); (2) load your program beginning at 20080H; (3) run the program; and (4) check the result. The test data are the base-10 numbers 5, −3, 12, 200, and −50.

Remember to use the DEBUG T and R commands extensively in your debugging. (Be sure to try these out on Program 3.1 first.)

2. Write a program in C or Pascal which lists on the screen any string of consecutive bytes requested by the user, essentially providing the same service as does the D command within DEBUG. Specifically, the user enters a command in the format

   xxxx yyyy n

i.e., four hex digits for a segment number, a blank space, four more hex digits for the offset within the segment, a blank space, and then a base-10 positive integer. The program will respond by reporting, in hex, the values of the n bytes beginning at address $16*xxxx + y$. (Note that if *yyyy* is sufficiently large, the segment starting at $16*xxxx$ will be exceeded, and your program must adjust to accommodate this case; it should print out n consecutive bytes in all cases, except for those in which the upper address limit of FFFFFH is exceeded.)

Use %x format if you write in C. In Microsoft Pascal, variables of type **integer** can be input with **read** or **readln** in hex by appending '16#' to the front of the value of the variable (e.g., 16#C007) when you type input to the program. For two-hex-digit output in Microsoft Pascal using **write** or **writeln**, append the characters '2:16' to the colon following the name (e.g., writeln(X:2:16)).

Test your program with DEBUG, by trying your program and DEBUG's D command on the same region of memory. But be careful—the loading of DEBUG itself may change some memory locations. Try some locations near absolute memory addresses FFFFFH, which are sure not to change. (They are in ROM and thus are not changeable.)

CHAPTER

4

Generating, Loading, and Executing Programs

As the title of this chapter implies, we will be interested in solutions to the following three problems:

- P1: How are a program's machine instructions generated?
- P2: How are the program's instructions and data loaded into main memory and the registers initialized properly?
- P3: How do we initiate *execution* of the program?

In Chapter 3, we went through a brief introduction to programming the iAPX family of CPUs. Program 3.1 was a program stored in offsets 0000 through 000A in a segment beginning at 21080. The program's function was to find the sum of all the words in a given range of the data segment, which we assumed began at location 20000, with the range defined by BX and DX.

That introduction to machine language showed one possible solution to the foregoing problem P1: we generate the instructions directly, by programming in the machine language directly. Section 4.1 will, then, address P2 and P3 for this context.

However, machine-language programming is quite tedious. We do not like to constantly have to look up op codes, register codes, and so on. Thus, in Section 4.2, we will discuss a much more convenient—yet still equivalent—solution to P1. This method consists of specifying op codes, register codes, and so on *indirectly*, using a system of English-like abbreviations, called **assembly language**. For example, the first instruction of Program 3.1, 2BC0, is specified in assembly language as SUB AX,AX.

'SUB' means the op code for subtract, and 'AX' is the register code for AX. A program called an **assembler** will do all the lookups of op codes, register codes, and so on in our behalf, thus alleviating us from a lot of tedium. In addition to discussing this more sophisticated approach to P1, Sections 4.2 and 4.3 will present a more sophisticated approach to P2 and P3, using the operating system's loader program to do the work.

Finally, in Section 4.4, we will go one step further and discuss the corresponding case for high-level languages (HLLs). In this case, we specify our program in the even more English-like manner of an HLL, and another special program, a **compiler**, has the job of generating the machine language, i.e., solving P1. We will compare and contrast the actions of assemblers and compilers and also note that, in the HLL context, we still use the same approach to P2 and P3 as in the assembly-language case.

4.1 USE OF DEBUG FOR LOADING AND EXECUTING PROGRAMS

On the early computers, there were switches and lights on the front of the computer that were used by a programmer to load or inspect individual memory locations and registers and to execute a program one instruction at a time. Modern computers generally have programs written to perform these functions, thus alleviating the programmer of the burden of dealing with unfriendly switches and lights. DEBUG is such a program for IBM microcomputers.

As its name implies, DEBUG is normally used as a tool to facilitate debugging of a user's program. We will use it later for that purpose too, but here we will use it only as a primitive method for loading and executing a user's program—i.e., as a solution to the foregoing Problems P2 and P3.*

Incidentally, more recent versions of DEBUG, called SYMDEB and CodeView, are extensions of the tool. They include the DEBUG commands that we will subsequently describe, and thus, the DEBUG material here will apply to SYMDEB and CodeView. On the other hand, SYMDEB and CodeView offer some very nice extra features. (Indeed, CodeView has so many such features that it seems unfair to describe it as a mere extension of DEBUG.) We will introduce these features, too, in Section 4.2 and in Chapter 5. Also, it should be noted that analogs of DEBUG exist in most operating systems; Unix (including Xenix on IBM microcomputers), for example, includes the 'adb' program, which is quite similar to DEBUG in function.

Keep in mind that DEBUG, SYMDEB and CodeView are all *programs*. Thus, they use the same general ingredients as Program 3.1—i.e., instructions to add, subtract, compare, jump, and so on. Their purpose is to help load, execute, or debug other programs, but this does not change the fact that they themselves are programs.

To use DEBUG, simply type DEBUG (and hit the carriage return key, i.e., the one labeled ENTER). DEBUG has many subcommands relevant to problems P2 and

---

*In Chapter 3, we asked the reader to skip ahead to this section, so as to learn how to use DEBUG for loading and executing Program 3.1. Thus, this section could have been presented in Chapter 3 instead of here in Chapter 4. However, we have placed it in Chapter 4 because of its relation to the theme of this chapter, namely, solving problems P1–P3.

P3. We will illustrate these using Program 3.1, so keep in mind the specific numbers we used there, e.g., the fact that we (arbitrarily) chose 21080 for the location at which our code segment will start.

First, what about P2? We just use the E ("enter") command. This command allows us to enter values into memory one byte at a time.

To enter our program's instructions, we type

```
E 2108:0000 2B C0 03 07 83 C3 02 3B D3 79 F7
```

Here, the 2108:0000 means to start entering bytes into the segment that begins at 21080 (again, the rightmost 0 digit is implicit, not explicit), at offset 0000 within that segment. The values to be entered are 2B, C0, 03, 07, 83, C3 02, 3B, D3, 79, and F7. Executing this command will result in these values being entered into bytes 21080, 21081, 21082, 21083, 21084, 21085, 21086, 21087, 21088, 21089, and 2108A, respectively.

As mentioned before, a segment/offset combination needed to specify a given address is not unique. Accordingly, you should make absolutely sure that you understand why the command, say,

```
E 2107:0010 2B C0 03 07 83 C3 02 3B D3 79 F7
```

would have exactly the same effect as the previous one.

Now the program is in memory. We can check this by using the D ("display") command. We enter

```
D 2108:0
```

which will display a number of memory bytes, starting with the one at 21080, on our screen.

```
2108:0000   2B C0 03 07 83 C3 02 3B-D3 79 F7 73 20 77 69 6C   +......;.y.s wil
2108:0010   6C 20 73 65 72 76 65 20-61 73 20 74 68 65 20 64   l serve as the d
2108:0020   61 74 61 00 B0 87 25 87-73 65 67 6D 65 6E 74 2C   ata...%.segment,
2108:0030   20 73 74 61 63 6B 20 73-65 67 6D 65 6E 74 20 61    stack segment a
2108:0040   6E 64 20 63 6F 64 65 20-73 65 67 6D 65 6E 74 20   nd code segment
2108:0050   6F 66 20 6F 75 72 20 70-72 6F 67 72 61 6D 2E 00   of our program..
2108:0060   B5 87 74 87 00 F5 87 B0-87 20 20 20 20 20 4E 6F   ..t......     No
2108:0070   77 20 67 65 74 74 69 6E-67 20 62 61 63 6B 20 74   w getting back t
```

Figure 4.1

The top row of Figure 4.1 shows bytes 21080 through 2108F, the second row bytes 21090 through 2109F, and so on. We see that the bytes 2B, C0, etc., are indeed in memory, in the proper locations. (This may not work on some machines, because by coincidence, 21080 might be within the location of the DEBUG program itself, in which case DEBUG will disobey your command, rather than letting itself be destroyed by obeying your command to change the contents of that region of memory! If so, choose some other location for your code segment, as well as your data segment if need be.)

On the right-hand side of the figure, any bytes that correspond to some ASCII code are displayed by the D command as the associated characters. For example, the first byte in the first row, 2B, happens to be the ASCII code for the character '+', so that character is displayed on the right-hand side. Of course, the fact that 2B is the ASCII code for '+' is just a coincidence; we are using 2B to represent a machine instruction (subtraction), not a character, and thus the '+' on the right-hand side is meaningless to us.

Note, however, that a lot of the other material on the right-hand side *is* meaningful, such as "will serve as." This is material left over from a previous usage of those bytes of memory. It is thus irrelevant to us here, but it does serve to remind the reader that there is always something stored in each byte of the machine and that if we do not change a byte, the byte will continue to store whatever was put into it long after we need it—actually, "forever," meaning until the power goes off or the machine fails.

We can enter our data using the E command, too. DEBUG doesn't "care" whether we are entering code or data; the E command is set up to load whatever we want into whatever memory location we want, without regard to our intentions.

Recall that the data for a particular run of our program were described in Table 3.1, which, for convenience, we will reproduce here as Table 4.1.

TABLE 4.1

Location	Contents
Word 20050	FFFD
Word 20052	0024
Word 20054	0100

We can now use the E command to enter these values into memory. This command can be used to enter any values into any memory location; again, the DEBUG program neither "knows" nor "cares" to what use we will put these values—e.g., whether they will serve as instructions or data in our program.

However, we have to be careful, because the E command, as mentioned earlier, expects us to enter data byte by byte. This was fine when we were entering instructions, because we usually write instructions in byte-order notation, so that we just use the same order for the E command. For example, recall from the discussion preceding Program 3.1 that the instruction 83C302 is indeed written in byte order, since 83 is in byte 21084, C3 is in byte 21085, and 02 is in byte 21086. Thus, we used the same order in our E command to enter the instruction.

By contrast, the data displayed in Table 4.1 is in *word* order, not byte order. (See the discussion of little-endian machines again in Chapter 3.) In the first line of

Table 4.1, in which the less significant byte is FD and the more significant byte is FF, the value FD will have the lower address (20050) and the value FF will have the higher address (20051). Thus, to use the E command in DEBUG, which demands that memory values be entered byte by byte in order of increasing address, we must enter the FD first and then the FF.

Accordingly, our E command to enter Table 4.1 into memory will be

```
E 2000:50 FD FF 24 00 00 01
```

rather than

```
E 2000:50 FF FD 00 24 01 00
```

even though it might feel "backwards." Apparently, a number of early users of DEBUG found this annoying. In response, the Microsoft Corporation, of course, could not change the hardware (specifically, the little-endian nature of the iAPX family of CPUs), but they could and did change the DEBUG software: DEBUG's newer versions, SYM-DEB and CodeView, include both EB ("enter by byte") and EW ("enter by word") commands to supplement the E command. To enter the first integer in Table 4.1, for example, we would type EW and then type FFFD, *not* reversing the bytes.

Again, we check our data loading using D, by typing

```
D 2000:50
```

though again, we must keep in mind that D will report memory values byte by byte, in order of increasing address.

Now let us see how to address the other part of P2, i.e., how to initialize register values. We invoke the R ("register") command, which is used to examine the contents of a register and, optionally, to load new contents. Since we put our code segment at location 21080, we must set c(CS) to 2108; we can do this by typing

```
R CS
```

The system will respond by writing to the screen the current value in the CS register. If we want to change that value (in this case, to 2108), we type in the value and hit the carriage return key; if not, we simply hit return right away. If you do want to load a value into that register, keep in mind that the R command, unlike the E command, expects the value to be entered in word form, not byte by byte. Thus to enter 2108, we type 2108, not 0821.

We can use this method to initialize the other registers in our example; we set IP to 0000, DS to 2000, BX to 0050, and DX to 0054.

If we type simply

```
R
```

then the contents of *all* the CPU registers will be displayed, including the flags in the FR register, which are displayed individually. Figure 4.2 shows what appears.

```
AX=0000  BX=0050  CX=0000  DX=0054  SP=FFEE  BP=0000  SI=0000  DI=0000
DS=2000  ES=15E1  SS=15E1  CS=2108  IP=0000   NV UP EI PL NZ NA PO NC
2108:0000 2BC0          SUB     AX,AX
```

Figure 4.2

Note that the values in FR are reported at the far right in the next-to-last line. The 'PL' means "plus," indicating that the SF flag is 0, and 'NZ'—i.e., "not zero"—means that the ZF flag is 0. If SF had been 1, the display would have had the notation 'NG' ("negative"), and if ZF had been 1, the report would have indicated that status with 'ZR' ("zero"). (The flags will be described in more detail in Chapter 6.)

The third line of Figure 4.2 indicates what the current instruction is, meaning the instruction pointed to by the current values of CS and IP. Since c(CS) = 2108 and c(IP) = 0000, that instruction is the one at 21080, which is 2BC0. This is no surprise, since we just loaded 2BC0 at that location and then set CS and IP to point to it.

Now, to solve P3, we can use either the G ("go") command or the T ("trace") command. For the former, we type

```
G n
```

which means to start execution at whatever instruction is currently specified by CS and IP (initialized using R, as we have done), up to but not including the instruction at offset *n*. Since the last byte of our program is at offset 000A, we type

```
G 000B
```

(The DEBUG commands G, T, D, and so on will use the current segment register value—CS for G and T, DS for D, etc.—if we do not specify a segment value. So in this case, G 000B is equivalent to, but takes less typing than, the commands G 2108:000B and G CS:000B.)

One can also type G alone, without specifying a place to stop. However, this would probably be a disaster in Program 3.1, because that program has no provision to stop! If we were to type just G alone, then when the CPU reached offset 000B, it would be ready to execute the "instruction" at that word of memory. Of course, we did not put an instruction there, and thus, the contents of that word will just be random "garbage." But the CPU will not "know" this, and it will proceed! In step A, it will fetch the contents of byte 000B and, then, in step B, decode them. If by chance the contents of that byte correspond to an op code of some instruction, then this instruction will be "executed." If the contents of byte 000B do not correspond to any op code, then the CPU will note an "illegal op code" error and return to the operating system, printing the '>' prompt to the screen and waiting for your next command. But if by chance the random bits in byte 000B and the bytes following it correspond to real op codes, your program could run for a long time, maybe even forever!

Instead of using G, our other option is to use the T command. Each time you type T, the system will execute the next instruction of your program, followed by an automatic R command, displaying the register values, and then stop and wait for your next command. Thus, you can watch the program "in action," seeing how various registers change after each instruction, in a manner similar to that of Figures 3.1–3.6. This ability to trace through the program step by step is clearly a very valuable debugging tool.

Figure 4.3 shows what appears on the screen if we use the T command at this point. The new values of the registers correspond to those shown in Figure 3.2, just as they should. Now, c(AX) is 0000 (though it was 0000 before, anyway), c(IP) has been incremented to 0002, and in the flags section, the 'NZ' in Figure 4.2 has been replaced by 'ZR', meaning "zero"; that is, ZF is now set, which it should be, since the result of the last computation was zero. And now the third line shows the new current instruction, 0307; if we type 'T', that instruction will be executed.

```
AX=0000  BX=0050  CX=0000  DX=0054  SP=FFEE  BP=0000  SI=0000  DI=0000
DS=2000  ES=15E1  SS=15E1  CS=2108  IP=0002   NV UP EI PL ZR NA PE NC
2108:0002 0307          ADD     AX,[BX]
```

Figure 4.3

In a short program such as Program 3.1, it is best to use the T command exclusively. However, in debugging a larger program, doing so would take too much time. For example, suppose you suspected that the bug was somewhere after the 50th instruction to be executed. Then it would be very inconvenient to keep hitting the T key 50 times to reach the area in which the bug is suspected to lie. It would be much easier to use the G command to reach that point quickly and then use the T command from there onward.

After executing our program, how can we check its "output," i.e., its result? This is very simple in the present context of running our program under DEBUG—just use the R command or D command, depending on whether the program's result is in a register or in memory. In Program 3.1, the sum is stored in AX, so we would type

```
R AX
```

to see our answer.

To leave DEBUG, just type Q ("quit").

You are very strongly urged to load and execute Program 3.1 as just described and verify the changes shown in Figures 3.1–3.6. The material in this book is very much of the "learn by doing" variety, and thus, you should try executing it as much as possible for yourself, in order to make the ideas concrete.

4.2 INTRODUCTION TO IAPX ASSEMBLY LANGUAGE

4.2.1 Hire a Clerk!

Programming in machine language is extremely tedious. It is quite inconvenient to work with the complicated set of codes for operations and addressing modes. A much better alternative to approaching problem P1 is using **assembly language**. Essentially, the assembly language for a given CPU is *equivalent* to the machine language for that CPU. The only difference is that the assembly language looks more like English and, thus, is much more convenient to use.

For example, consider the instruction 2BC0 in Program 3.1. This instruction subtracts AX from itself. The assembly-language version is

```
SUB AX,AX
```

which is considerably clearer than 2BC0!

In explaining assembly language, it is common to use the metaphor of a clerk. Imagine that you find the use of machine code tedious, and, as a solution, you hire a clerk. You and the clerk get together and agree upon some English-like symbols for the operations you want, e.g., SUB for subtract. You write your program on paper using this "English" symbolism and hand the paper to your clerk, and the clerk then enters the corresponding machine code using DEBUG. This way, you do not have to burden yourself with remembering or looking up the various op codes, codes for registers, and so on; the clerk does all of this for you.

These actions that would be taken by a human clerk are sufficiently mechanical that one could write a *program* to perform them. Such a program is called an **assembler**. An assembler takes a program written in the English-like form, such as SUB AX,AX, and produces machine code from it, such as 2BC0. The English-like form is called **assembly-language**.

The "English" symbols for the various codes are called **mnemonics**. In the assembly language instruction SUB AX,AX, the symbol SUB is the mnemonic for the subtraction op code and the symbol AX is the mnemonic for the AX register code.

In describing the translation that the assembler does from assembly language to machine language, we say that the assembler **assembles** a file of **source code** into a file of **object code**. (The same terminology is used for high-level language compilers: we say that a compiler compiles a source code file of, say, Pascal or C code into a file of object code.)

Here is an assembly-language version of Program 3.1:

```
        SUB AX,AX
LP:     ADD AX,[BX]
        ADD BX,2
        CMP DX,BX
        JNS LP
```

In this program, ADD, CMP, and JNS are the mnemonics for the add, compare, and jump-if-SF-is-not-set instructions. The symbol [ ] in the second line is the mnemonic for **indirect addressing mode**. In this mode,

```
ADD AX,[BX]
```

is an instruction that adds *the word pointed to by BX* to AX. By contrast, BX is used in **register addressing mode** in the instruction

```
ADD AX,BX
```

which adds *BX itself* to AX. In register addressing mode, the operand is in a register rather than in memory.

The symbol LP is a **label**; it gives the name LP to the place in the code segment occupied by the instruction ADD AX,[BX]. In this example, we have chosen the name LP to remind ourselves that this instruction is the beginning of a loop. The naming of this point in the code segment is a convenience to us, because we can then refer to it by name in the instruction JNS LP, instead of having to calculate the distance from this instruction to that point in the code segment, as we did in Chapter 3. The "clerk" will do this work for us, which is the whole point of having a clerk—to alleviate the burden of tedious work that we otherwise would have to do ourselves.

Here are the mnemonics of the other instructions we introduced in Chapter 3: MOV (move); JNZ (jump if ZF is not set); JS (jump if SF is set); JZ (jump if ZF is set); JMP (unconditional jump).

The DEBUG program includes a very simple assembler, in its A command. With this command, the user enters assembly-language instructions, and DEBUG not only translates them to machine code, but loads them into memory as well. For example, the user can type

```
A 2000:0060
```

followed by some assembly code, say,

```
ADD [BX],AX
ADD BX,2
```

The user hits the return key after each line and, after the last line, hits the return key twice as an "all done" signal to DEBUG. DEBUG will then produce the appropriate machine code from these lines and load them into memory starting at location $20000 + 0060 = 20060$.

The simple assembler in the DEBUG program is not very convenient. One of its major problems is that it does not allow labels. A jump, for instance, is specified by its target offset; thus, the instruction

```
JNS LP
```

would have to be specified instead as

```
JNS 0002
```

since LP is at offset 0002 (see Program 3.1). An intersegmental jump (op code EA, described near the end of Section 3.2), say, to offset 0024 in segment 45AC would be specified as

```
JMP 45AC:0024
```

For this and other reasons, DEBUG's simple assembler is convenient only for very short programs. A full assembler such as Microsoft's MASM or Borland's Turbo Assembler (TASM) is essential for general use.

4.2.2 A First MASM Example

Like DEBUG, MASM (or any other assembler) is just a program, consisting of instructions for addition, comparison, jumps, and so on, just as does Program 3.1.

To use MASM, we first use a text editor, say VI, to create the source file, whose name is required to have the suffix '.ASM'. In Program 4.1, this file will be named FIB.ASM, so we could type

```
> VI FIB.ASM
```

to create it. (The '>' prompt was typed by the operating system, to invite you to submit a command, in this case the VI command.) After that, we assemble the file by typing

```
> MASM FIB,FIB,FIB;
```

making sure not to forget the semicolon. This creates a file FIB.OBJ, which is the machine code produced by the assembly process. (The process also produces a file FIB.LST, which will be explained shortly.) Note that this command does not load the program into memory, so we can not yet run it at this stage. We must run the program through a **linker** first and then a **loader**, the details of which will be presented subsequently. Note, again that the linker and loader are *programs*, as are text editors such as VI.

Our main example in this section will be a program to compute **Fibonacci numbers**, defined as follows. Fibonacci numbers F_1 and F_2 are both equal to 1, and for $i \geq 3$, F_i is defined by

$$F_i = F_{i-2} + F_{i-1}.$$

Thus, $F_1 = 1$, $F_2 = 1$, $F_3 = 2$, $F_4 = 3$, $F_5 = 5$, $F_6 = 8$, and so on. This sequence of numbers is mainly of interest to mathematicians, but it provides a good example for our purpose here, which is to introduce MASM.

Program 4.1 is the file FIB.ASM for a program to compute the first *N* Fibonacci numbers. (Line numbers have been added to the display, even though the file itself does not include those numbers.) *Do not try to read the program yet!* Wait for the explanation that will follow Figure 4.4.

```
1
2
3    N EQU 10D
4
5    DSG SEGMENT
6        FIBNUM DW N DUP (?)
7        FHDR DB 'Fibonacci numbers:$'
8        SAVEBX DW (?)
9    DSG ENDS
10
11
12   SSG SEGMENT STACK
13       STK DW 100D DUP (?)
14   SSG ENDS
15
16
17   CSG SEGMENT
18
19   ASSUME CS:CSG,DS:DSG,SS:SSG
20
21   MAIN PROC FAR
22
23       ;   standard preamble to set DS
24       MOV AX,DSG
25       MOV DS,AX
26
27       ;   set F sub 1 and F sub 2 "by hand," to get started, and
28       ;       then set the remaining N-2 of them with a loop
29
30       ;   BX will serve as pointer to the Fibonacci currently
31       ;       being computed
32       ;   initialize to point to the place at which F sub 1 will be stored
33       MOV BX,OFFSET FIBNUM
34
35       ;   store F sub 1
36       MOV WORD PTR [BX],1
37
38       ;   move BX to point to F sub 2, and store F sub 2
39       ADD BX,2
40       MOV WORD PTR [BX],1
41
42       ;   point BX to F sub 3, to get ready for loop
43       ADD BX,2
44
45       ;   DX will always contain the number of Fibonacci
```

```
46      ;      numbers still remaining to be computed ;
47      ; so start it at N-2
48      MOV DX,N-2
49
50      ; here is the loop
51  LP1: MOV AX,[BX-4]  ;  get F sub i-2
52      ADD AX,[BX-2]  ;  add F sub i-1 to it, producing F sub i
53      MOV [BX],AX  ;  store F sub i
54      ADD BX,2  ;  point BX to the next one
55      SUB DX,1  ;  check whether loop done
56      JNZ LP1  ;  if not, go back to top of loop
57      ; end of loop
58
59      ; done with computation of all numbers, so now print them out
60
61      ; print out a header, using the DOS print-string service,
62      ;      Service Number 21/09
63      ; service is called by putting 9H in AH, pointing DX to the string
64      ;      (whose end is indicated by a '$'), and executing INT 21H
65      MOV DX,OFFSET FHDR
66      MOV AH,9
67      INT 21H
68      CALL PRCRLF ; go to a new line on the screen
69
70      ; a loop will print out the Fibonacci numbers, N iterations,
71      ;      using DI as the loop counter
72      MOV DI,N
73
74      ; BX will always point to the current number to be printed out,
75      ;      so initialize BX to the beginning of the array
76      MOV BX,OFFSET FIBNUM
77
78  LP2: MOV SAVEBX,BX  ;  save pointer value
79      MOV BX,[BX]  ;  get number
80      CALL DISPBX  ;  call display procedure to print out this number
81      CALL PRCRLF  ;  call procedure to print carriage return, line feed
82      MOV BX,SAVEBX  ;  restore pointer value
83      ADD BX,2  ;  point to next number
84      SUB DI,1  ;  done with loop?
85      JNZ LP2  ;  if not done yet, go to top of loop
86
87      ; standard code to return to DOS, using return-to-DOS service,
88      ;      Service Number 21/4C
89      MOV AH,4CH
90      INT 21H
91  MAIN ENDP
92
93  PRCRLF PROC  ;  print carriage return and line feed
94
95      ; use the DOS print-single-character service, Service Number 21/02
96      ; service is called by putting 2 into AH, putting the character
97      ;      in DL (which we have already done), and executing INT 21H
98      ; ASCII codes for CR and LF are 0DH and 0AH
```

```
 99
100        MOV AH,2
101        MOV DL,0DH
102        INT 21H
103        MOV DL,0AH
104        INT 21H
105
106        ;  all done, so return to caller
107        RET
108   PRCRLF ENDP
109
110   DISPBX PROC    ;   prints hex contents of BX to screen
111
112        ;  each nibble to be printed will be taken from bits 15-12 of BX
113        ;  so, we will keep rotating BX by 4 bits at a time, each time
114        ;     moving a new nibble into bits 11-8
115
116        ;  this will have to be done 4 times, for the 4 nibbles of BX,
117        ;     and we will use DH as the loop counter, starting at 4,
118        ;     then 3, 2, and 1
119        MOV DH,4
120
121        ;  the rotation of 4 bits will be indicated by CL, so put 4 there
122        MOV CL,4
123
124    LP: MOV DL,BH  ;  put a copy in DL, to work on it there
125
126        ;  prepare the nibble for printing
127        AND DL,0F0H  ;  put 0s in the lower 4 bits of DL, upper 4 unchanged
128        ROL DL,CL  ;  rotate so that the nibble is in bits 3-0 of DL
129
130        CALL PRNIB  ;  print that nibble
131
132        ROL BX,CL  ;  rotate BX to get to next nibble
133
134        ;  decrement loop count and check if done with all nibbles yet
135        DEC DH
136        JNZ LP
137
138        RET  ;  return to calling program
139   DISPBX ENDP
140
141   PRNIB PROC  ;  prints the contents of bits 3-0 of DL to the screen
142
143        ;  must convert numeric value in DL, in the range 0-F, to ASCII
144
145        CMP DL,9  ;  is it 0-9 or A-F?
146        JG A_F  ;  if so, go to the code to handle the A-F case
147        ;  if not, we are in the 0-9 case
148        ADD DL,30H  ;    ASCII codes for the characters '0'-9' are 30H-39H
149        JMP WR_CHAR  ;  OK, ready to write to screen
150   A_F: ADD DL,37H  ;    ASCII codes for the characters 'A'-F' are 41H-46H
151
```

```
152          ; here is where the actual writing to the screen takes place,
153          ;    using the print-single-character service, DOS Service 21/02
154          ; service is called by putting 2 into AH, putting the character
155          ;    in DL (which we have already done), and executing INT 21H
156  WR_CHAR: MOV AH,2
157          INT 21H
158
159          ; OK, nibble printed, so return to caller
160          RET
161  PRNIB ENDP
162
163  CSG ENDS
164
165  END MAIN
```

Program 4.1

As mentioned, inputting the file FIB.ASM of Program 4.1 to MASM will produce a new file FIB.OBJ containing the assembled code, i.e., the machine language produced by the assembler. Another file is produced by MASM at this time is FIB.LST, which will be very valuable in our understanding of what MASM does. This file is shown in Figure 4.4. (We have removed all comment lines and many blank lines from the file, so don't be alarmed that some line numbers are missing.)

```
 3 = 000A                         N EQU 10D
 4
 5 0000                           DSG SEGMENT
 6 0000   000A[                       FIBNUM DW N DUP (?)
 7            ????
 8                         ]
 9
10 0014   46 69 62 6F 6E 61            FHDR DB 'Fibonacci numbers:$'
11          63 63 69 20 6E 75
12          6D 62 65 72 73 3A
13          24
14 0027   0000                        SAVEBX DW (?)
15 0029                           DSG ENDS
16
17
18 0000                           SSG SEGMENT STACK
19 0000   0064[                       STK DW 100D DUP (?)
20            ????
21                         ]
23 00C8                           SSG ENDS
24
25
26 0000                           CSG SEGMENT
27
28                                ASSUME CS:CSG,DS:DSG,SS:SSG
```

```
29
30 0000                              MAIN PROC FAR
33 0000   B8 ---- R                    MOV AX,DSG
34 0003   8E D8                        MOV DS,AX
42 0005   BB 0000 R                    MOV BX,OFFSET FIBNUM
45 0008   C7 07 0001                   MOV WORD PTR [BX],1
48 000C   83 C3 02                     ADD BX,2
49 000F   C7 07 0001                   MOV WORD PTR [BX],1
52 0013   83 C3 02                     ADD BX,2
57 0016   BA 0008                      MOV DX,N-2
60 0019   8B 47 FC             LP1:    MOV AX,[BX-4]
61 001C   03 47 FE                     ADD AX,[BX-2]
62 001F   89 07                        MOV [BX],AX
63 0021   83 C3 02                     ADD BX,2
64 0024   83 EA 01                     SUB DX,1
65 0027   75 F0                        JNZ LP1
74 0029   BA 0014 R                    MOV DX,OFFSET FHDR
75 002C   B4 09                        MOV AH,9
76 002E   CD 21                        INT 21H
77 0030   E8 0055 R                    CALL PRCRLF
81 0033   BF 000A                      MOV DI,N
85 0036   BB 0000 R                    MOV BX,OFFSET FIBNUM
87 0039   89 1E 0027 R        LP2:    MOV SAVEBX,BX
88 003D   8B 1F                        MOV BX,[BX]
89 003F   E8 0060 R                    CALL DISPBX
90 0042   E8 0055 R                    CALL PRCRLF
91 0045   8B 1E 0027 R                 MOV BX,SAVEBX
92 0049   83 C3 02                     ADD BX,2
93 004C   83 EF 01                     SUB DI,1
94 004F   75 E8                        JNZ LP2
98 0051   B4 4C                        MOV AH,4CH
99 0053   CD 21                        INT 21H
100 0055                             MAIN ENDP
101
102 0055                             PRCRLF PROC
109 0055  B4 02                        MOV AH,2
110 0057  B2 0D                        MOV DL,0DH
111 0059  CD 21                        INT 21H
112 005B  B2 0A                        MOV DL,0AH
113 005D  CD 21                        INT 21H
116 005F  C3                           RET
117 0060                             PRCRLF ENDP
118
119 0060                             DISPBX PROC
128 0060  B6 04                        MOV DH,4
131 0062  B1 04                        MOV CL,4
133 0064  8A D7                LP:     MOV DL,BH
136 0066  80 E2 F0                     AND DL,0F0H
137 0069  D2 CA                        ROL DL,CL
139 006B  E8 0075 R                    CALL PRNIB
141 006E  D3 C3                        ROL BX,CL
144 0070  FE CE                        DEC DH
145 0072  75 F0                        JNZ LP
```

```
147 0074   C3                             RET
148 0075                          DISPBX ENDP
149
150 0075                          PRNIB PROC
154 0075   80 FA 09                  CMP DL,9
155 0078   7F 06                     JG A F
157 007A   80 C2 30                  ADD DL,30H
158 007D   EB 04 90                  JMP WR_CHAR
159 0080   80 C2 37               A_F: ADD DL,37H
165 0083   B4 02                    WR_CHAR: MOV AH,2
166 0085   CD 21                     INT 21H
169 0087   C3                        RET
170 0088                          PRNIB ENDP
171
172 0088                          CSG ENDS
173
174                               END MAIN
```

Figure 4.4

The .LST file essentially combines the .ASM and .OBJ files, putting the source code and object code side by side, so that we may see what object code the assembler has produced from our source code. Each line in Figure 4.4 has the following format:

```
<line number> <offset within data or code segment> <data or machine code> <source code>
```

For example, line 42 in FIB.LST is

```
42 0005   BB 0000 R                    MOV BX,OFFSET FIBNUM
```

This says that the assembly-language code MOV BX,OFFSET FIBNUM in FIB.ASM (see line 33 of that file) has been assembled into the machine code BB0000 and that the position of that code within the code segment will be at offset 0005.

It important to understand—and keep in mind—exactly what this last statement means. First, note the future tense, "will be." The machine code is not in memory yet. The clerk merely puts the code into the FIB.OBJ disk file. But later on, when we run the program, the code will be loaded into memory, and *at that time*, the instruction will be at offset 5 of the code segment. Second, when we say that the instruction is BB0000, remember that this hex notation is just "shorthand"; in the computer, everything is 1's and 0's, in this case 1011101100000000000000000.

Now let us discuss the assembly language program. *Since the file FIB.ASM is less cluttered than FIB.LST, and since FIB.ASM is the original source file—i.e., the one the programmer created—we will concentrate on Program 4.1. However, at times we will refer to the FIB.LST file, too, to make use of the additional information that it provides. (Unless stated otherwise, our references to line numbers will be to the file FIB.ASM.) If you flip ahead a few pages, you will see that the discussion of this program will be rather long and very detailed. But all of it concerns material that will be used repeatedly throughout the remainder of the book and that you yourself will often use as you write your own programs, so extra time spent now will be an excellent investment.*

First, there is an EQU ("equate") line at the top of the file, on line 3:

```
N EQU 10D
```

Let us look at the 10D first. The 'D' means decimal, i.e., base 10. Similarly, 'H' means hex. Recall again that every storage cell in the machine—memory, registers, disk space—stores items in terms of 1's and 0's. MASM will take care of any necessary conversion for us. For example, if we specify the number 52D, MASM will convert this to the proper bit string (110100) for us. Similarly, recall that hex is just a shorthand notation for bit strings anyway, so if we specify, say, 206H, MASM will create the bit string directly, namely, 1000000110.

EQU tells MASM that whenever it "sees" the symbol N in subsequent lines, it should act as if we had written 10D. For example, one of the effects of the EQU is that when MASM "sees" Line 72,

```
MOV DI,N
```

in Program 4.1, MASM will pretend that the line says

```
MOV DI,10D
```

An EQU line is very similar to one with a **const** declaration in Pascal or a **#define** in the language C.

MASM "remembers" that the symbol N means 10 by putting this information in its **symbol table**. This table is just an array in the MASM program. (Keep in mind again that MASM, DEBUG, editors such as VI, operating systems, and so on are all *programs* and thus have their own data structures such as arrays.) MASM uses this array to store all the symbols, such as N, during the time it is assembling a program.

We will be using N in this program as the number of Fibonacci numbers to be computed. So we will compute 10 such numbers; $F_1, F_2, F_3, \ldots, F_{10}$,

Next, line 5 says

```
DSG SEGMENT
```

Just as one must declare variables in Pascal or C, MASM requires that segments be declared too. This line's use of the reserved word SEGMENT shows that we are declaring a segment with the name DSG. Four lines later, at line 9, we see

```
DSG ENDS
```

which indicates the end of the segment named DSG.

A glance through the rest of the file shows that in addition to DSG, we have also declared two other segments, named SSG and CSG. The names can be arbitrarily chosen; here we chose the names DSG, SSG, and CSG to remind ourselves that these segments will serve as the data segment, stack segment, and code segment, respectively, of our program, but again, the names are whatever we choose them to be, just as is the case for choosing names of variables in Pascal or C. As the program shows, each segment declaration begins with a SEGMENT line and ends with an ENDS line. The file as a whole ends with an END line, in this case

```
END MAIN
```

The reserved word END indicates to MASM that MASM is now done with the work of assembly; there is nothing further left to assemble. (The word MAIN means something else, which we will explain later.)

Returning our attention to DSG, we next consider lines 6–8, which begin with FIBNUM, FHDR, and SAVEBX, respectively. These are all names of variables; in other words, we are declaring variables, just as we would in Pascal or C. Of course, again just as in Pascal or C, we should choose meaningful names that will help us remember what we are storing in each item. We chose the name FIBNUM, for instance, to help remember that this is where we are storing the Fibonacci numbers that we compute.

The format used in the variable declarations is

```
<name>  <size of each item>  <initial values>
```

For example, in the declaration of

```
FIBNUM DW N DUP (?)
```

FIBNUM is the name for this entry in the DSG segment. DW means "define word or words," so the items referred to are of size one word each. N DUP (?) means that we want the assembler to reserve N consecutive words, all having the duplicate initial value '?', a symbol that means "don't care"—i.e., we do not care what value these N words are initialized to.

Note carefully that the <initial values> portion of the declaration specifies not only initial values, but also how many items we wish the assembler to leave space for. This is important, because we want to set up an array of N words, just like an array in Pascal or C. (Indeed, arrays in Pascal and in C are in fact implemented by the compiler in the same way, i.e., as blocks of consecutive cells in memory.) So, in our declaration

```
FIBNUM DW N DUP (?)
```

we are telling the assembler the following:

> Please reserve space at this point in the data segment for N consecutive words, the first of which we will refer to henceforth by the name FIBNUM. We do not care what initial values these N words have, though.

When speaking in an informal manner in what follows, we will sometimes refer to the whole array as FIBNUM. However, keep in mind that technically speaking—i.e., from the assembler's point of view—FIBNUM is only the name of the *first word* in this array. Words following that will be specified using FIBNUM as a reference point: the second word is FIBNUM+2, the third is FIBNUM+4, and so on, since consecutive words differ in their offsets by two bytes.

Incidentally, we could have written this particular program without an array, but the logic would have been more complicated (after we finish discussing the program, the reader is urged to think about why this would be the case), and in any event, we wanted to present an early example of the use of arrays.

The next variable is FHDR, declared in line 7:

```
FHDR DB 'Fibonacci numbers:$'
```

As indicated by DB, we are talking about a byte or bytes, rather than a word or words as in the case of FIBNUM. A list of several initial values follows, indicating that we are defining a number of bytes here, not just one—i.e., an array of bytes. For initial values, we are telling MASM to initialize the first byte in this array, FHDR, to the ASCII code for 'F', the next byte, FHDR+1, to the code for 'i', the third byte, FHDR+2, to the code for 'b', and so on, up through the codes for 's' and ':'. Then the last byte is to be initialized to the ASCII code for a dollar sign. You can see the ASCII codes that MASM has produced from this in lines 10–13 of Figure 4.4. We will use this array as a header—i.e., a label—for our output.

Finally, in line 8, a single word is defined and named SAVEBX. As the name implies, we will use this as a place to save the value of the BX register.

Again, the names of variables can be arbitrarily chosen, but of course we chose FIBNUM, FHDR and SAVEBX to remind ourselves what each variable means in our program.

Now recall the discussion near Table 1.1 in Chapter 1, which mentioned that high-level language compilers will generally assign memory addresses to variables in the same order in which they are declared in the source file. The same is true for assemblers. Recalling that the offset is given as the second field within each line of the .LST file, we see from lines 6, 10, and 14 of the file FIB.LST that FIBNUM, FHDR, and SAVEBX will be in offsets 0000, 0014, and 0027, respectively, in the data segment. Thus, the assembler has indeed allocated space for these variables in the same order in which they were declared.

Since FIBNUM is the first variable declared, it will be assigned to the beginning of the data segment, so it makes sense that the .LST file tells us that the offset of FIBNUM will be 0000. The file also says that FHDR starts at offset 0014. We can see that this makes sense, too: FIBNUM, which consists of 10D words starting at offset 0000, will occupy offsets 0000, 0002, 0004, . . . , 0012H (the reader should verify this!), and the next word after 0012H is at offset 0014H, so that is where FHDR will start, as confirmed by line 10 of FIB.LST.

Since FHDR declares 19D bytes (count them!), which is 13H, the next variable, SAVEBX, will start at offset 0014H + 0013H = 0027H, which is shown in the second field in line 14 of FIB.LST.

MASM will enter the names FIBNUM, FHDR, and SAVEBX in its symbol table, along with their offsets. Then, for the remainder of the assembly process, whenever MASM sees FHDR, for example, it will consult its symbol table and see that FHDR is a name for offset 0014 in the data segment.

We will discuss stack segments in Chapter 5. But for now, just remember to have one in your program.

At the beginning of the segment CSG, on line 19, is the assembly directive,

```
ASSUME CS:CSG,DS:DSG,SS:SSG
```

This is meant to be information for MASM. It tells MASM to assume that, when the program is run, CS will be pointing to CSG, DS will be pointing to DSG, and SS will be pointing to SSG. Note that the ASSUME does *not* actually make these registers point to those segments; it is only telling MASM how to compute offsets. For example, the ASSUME is telling MASM that when MASM sees a reference to FIBNUM, the offset should be computed relative to DSG. This seems obvious in this relatively simple program, but in complex programs with several data segments it is less clear, and MASM essentially requires that you have it.

Note that several procedures are declared in CSG: MAIN, PRCRLF, DISPBX, and PRNIB (lines 21, 93, 110, and 141 in FIB.ASM). Each procedure begins with the reserved word PROC ("procedure") and ends with the reserved word ENDP ("end procedure"). For the time being, ignore the token FAR used in the declaration of MAIN. (It will be discussed in Chapter 5.)

The term **procedure** has the same meaning here as **procedure** and **function** do in Pascal and as **function** does in C. By the way, in MASM it is customary to consider even our main program as a procedure. We have named the main program MAIN in order to remind ourselves of the role we intend for it—i.e., as our "main" program— but we could have given it any name. Note also that we can declare the foregoing procedures in any order; we happen to have declared MAIN first, but we did not need to.

Observe in line 30 of the file FIB.LST that the assembler did not produce any machine language from line 21 of FIB.ASM.

```
MAIN PROC FAR
```

Nor, for that matter, did it produce any from line 19. Both of these lines in FIB.ASM were merely informational items for the assembler's benefit; they do not correspond to machine instructions, and as can be seen in lines 28 and 30 the assembler does not produce machine language from them, and thus puts nothing corresponding to them into the file FIB.OBJ.

Thus, the procedure MAIN actually starts on line 24 of FIB.ASM, which also explains why the offset column in FIB.LST does not increase from line 30 to line 33; both offsets are 0000. What the two lines say together is that MAIN will be our label for the instruction at offset 0000 of the code segment and that this instruction will be

```
MOV AX,DSG
```

Similarly, from lines 102–109 in FIB.LST, we can see that the first instruction in the procedure PRCRLF is

```
MOV AH,2
```

which will be at offset 0055 of the code segment, and that our label for that instruction will be PRCRLF.

Our discussion here will concentrate on MAIN. The other large procedure, DISPBX, as the name we have given it implies, displays the contents of the BX register on the screen. The program MAIN calls this procedure at line 80:

```
CALL DISPBX
```

In order not to introduce too many new instructions at this point, we will defer our discussion of the internal workings of DISPBX until Section 4.2.5. For now, just note that it may be used in the manner it is used here—i.e., to display c(BX) on the screen. You may wish to make use of DISPBX in your own programs. If you do, keep in mind that DISPBX changes the values of the registers AX, BX, CX, and DX. Accordingly, if your calling program has a "live" value in any of these registers at the time you call DISPBX, you should save the value before the call and restore it after the call, as we did with SAVEBX for other reasons.

You should, however, keep in mind that a CALL instruction includes a "jump" action. For example, look at line 89 of FIB.LST (all line numbers in this paragraph will refer to FIB.LST, not FIB.ASM). We will *not* immediately execute line 90. Instead, the CALL instruction will force a jump to line 119, where the procedure DISPBX starts. The procedure has offset 0060 within the code segment, and one can see this value within the machine code in line 89: E8 0060; the E8 is the op code, and the 0060 is the operand, which for a call instruction is the target of the jump. During step C of this instruction, the value 0060 will be placed into the IP register; the next step A will then fetch the instruction pointed to by IP, i.e., at offset 0060, so DISPBX will start running. During step C of the call instruction, the CPU will also save the place to return to after DISPBX finishes, i.e., offset 0042 (line 90), on the stack. Later, when step C of the RET ("return") instruction on line 147 is executed, the CPU will pull this value off the stack and put it in the IP register, thus forcing a return to line 90 and resuming execution of MAIN. We will discuss this process in much more detail in Chapter 5, but the reader should keep the "jump" nature of a CALL instruction in mind now.

Line 23 in the .ASM file,

```
;   standard preamble to set DS
```

is a comment. Just as comments in Pascal are indicated by

```
{   }
```

and those in C are given by

```
/*  */
```

in MASM anything to the right of a semicolon is a comment. Of course, comments are just as important in assembly-language programs as they are in HLL programs.

Next, lines 24 and 25 of FIB.ASM,

```
MOV AX,DSG
MOV DS,AX
```

point DS to DSG. (Recall that the ASSUME on line 19 does *not*.) Note that we cannot effect the move in just one instruction, i.e.,

```
MOV DS,DSG
```

because this is not a legal instruction, as we saw in Section 3.3.

Keep in mind that right now we are just discussing what happens at **assembly time**, the time during which MASM is producing the .OBJ machine-language file. (For an HLL source program, a **compiler** does the translation to the .OBJ file, and the time during which this is done is called **compile time**.) **Load time**, the time during which we will actually load the program into memory, and **run time**, the time during which we will actually run the program, will both occur later on. DS will not point to DSG until run time, when the MOV instructions on lines 24 and 25 are executed.

In fact, MASM has no idea where DSG will be. This is not decided until load time. At load time, the loader will find a place in memory for all the segments—DSG, SSG, and CSG—and then will load them there. But at assembly time, that place is unknown. Thus, MASM is faced with a problem: how can it assemble the instruction

```
MOV AX,DSG
```

without knowing where DSG will be? It solves the problem by only *partially* assembling the instruction, as you can see on line 33 of FIB.LST. The machine code produced is listed as B8----, with the ---- representing four as-yet-unknown hex digits for the address of DSG. MASM leaves a note in FIB.OBJ, saying essentially, "This is unfinished. Fill it in later, when the address of DSG is decided," and the loader will then do so at load time.

This, then, is how DS gets pointed to DSG. So how do CS and SS get pointed to CSG and SSG? Notice that there is no code for initializing them. Let us consider CS first. The very last line of FIB.ASM, line 165, is

```
END MAIN
```

This line carries two pieces of information:

(a) As mentioned earlier, the word END tells MASM that this is the end of the file; there is no more work left for MASM to do.

(b) The word MAIN tells MASM that when we execute our program in the future—again, currently we are just at assembly time, not run time—we want execution to start at the line labeled MAIN, i.e., line 21 in FIB.ASM. MASM will record this in a note in FIB.OBJ. The note will say that at run time we want the CS register to be initialized to the location of CSG (which will be known at that time, having just been decided by the loader) and we want the IP register to be initialized to 0000. These two values—the location of CSG and the value 0000—stem from the fact that MAIN is at offset 0000 of the segment CSG. (The note in the .OBJ file will not explicitly mention the name MAIN.)

By contrast, suppose the procedure PRCRLF had been declared first in CSG, with MAIN following it. Then PRCRLF would be at offset 0000, extending through offset 000A, and thus the line

```
END MAIN
```

would result in MASM's putting a note in FIB.OBJ which stipulated that the initial values of CS and IP should be CSG and 000B, respectively. (The reader should verify this claim.)

Similarly, since we used the reserved word STACK in our declaration of SSG, MASM will record this fact, too, so that at run time the loader can initialize SS to SSG. It will also initialize SP to the size of the stack segment, in this case 100D words, which is 0C8H bytes. Thus, SP will start out pointing to the end of the stack segment.

Lines 33 through 56 in FIB.ASM do the actual computation of the N Fibonacci numbers. The program logic here is similar to that of Program 3.1, but a few aspects are worthy of mention.

First, note from the comments that we are using BX as a pointer to the location of the Fibonacci number we are currently computing: F_1 will be at the location FIBNUM, F_2 will be at the location FIBNUM+2, F_3 will be at FIBNUM+4, and so on. Thus, when we are computing F_1, we will have BX point to FIBNUM, and then, to compute F_2, we will point BX to FIBNUM+2, etc.

To point BX to FIBNUM—i.e., to the word in which we will store F_1—we use the instruction

```
MOV BX,OFFSET FIBNUM
```

Recall that FIBNUM is at offset 0000 in the data segment. Thus, we could have accomplished the same thing with the instruction

```
MOV BX,0
```

But doing this would be less desirable. For example, if we later alter the program by adding a declaration in the segment DSG *before* FIBNUM, the latter instruction would not be correct anymore, whereas the former would. The same problem would occur if we were to combine DSG with another data segment that preceded it. (See the discussion concerning line 74 of FIB.LST.) By contrast, the instruction

```
MOV BX,OFFSET FIBNUM
```

would still be valid if such a change were to be made, and thus, this form is preferable.

MASM also offers an operator SEG to indicate the segment of an item. For example, the instruction

```
MOV BX,SEG FIBNUM
```

would have the same effect as

```
MOV BX,DSG
```

SEG is useful when we have more than one data segment or more than one code segment.

Incidentally, note that the instruction

```
MOV BX,OFFSET FIBNUM
```

is very different from the instruction

```
MOV BX,FIBNUM
```

To see the difference, compare the instructions

```
MOV BX,FHDR
```

and

```
MOV BX,OFFSET FHDR
```

The first would copy the contents of the word named FHDR to BX. From line 10 of FIB.LST, the contents are 46 and 69, the ASCII codes for the characters 'F' and 'i', respectively. By contrast, the second instruction would put 0014 into BX, since that same line 10 shows that FHDR starts at offset 0014.

People who are new to assembly language often make programming errors that are due to confusion between the address of a word and the contents of a word. Thus, the reader should spend extra time perusing the previous paragraph. People who are new to the language C often make the same kind of error, confusing, say,

```
x = &y;
```

with

```
x = y;
```

(The & operator in C was discussed in Chapters 1 and 2.) Once again, this illustrates the fact that one needs a good understanding of the world "under the hood" in order to be proficient in C.

The next instruction, line 36 of FIB.ASM,

```
MOV WORD PTR [BX],1
```

sets F_1 to 1. The brackets [ ] form the mnemonic notation that specifies indirect addressing. From Chapter 3, [BX] signifies that we move 1 to the memory location pointed to by BX, rather than to BX itself. Since BX is pointing to the beginning of FIBNUM, the result is that we are setting F_1 to 1, just as desired.

The role of the reserved words WORD PTR is interesting. In Chapter 3, we saw that some instructions have both word and byte forms. For instructions having RTR format, the status as word or byte is indicated by the 'w' bit, which is the last bit of the first byte of the instruction; this bit is 1 for the word form and 0 for the byte form.

The instruction we are considering here is not of RTR format, but its format does have a 'w' bit; thus, the instruction likewise has both word and byte forms. Since c(BX) = 0000, the word form of this MOV instruction would put 0001 into *word* 0000 in the data segment, while the byte form would put 01 into *byte* 0000. In other words, the word form would put 00 into byte 0001 and 01 into byte 0000, while the byte form would merely put 01 into byte 0000, leaving byte 0001 unchanged.

But if we simply wrote the instruction as

```
MOV [BX],1
```

it would be ambiguous; MASM would have no way of knowing whether we meant the word form or the byte form. So we use the words WORD PTR to tell MASM to produce machine code for the word form of the instruction. We would write BYTE PTR if we wanted the byte form, i.e.,

```
MOV BYTE PTR [BX],1
```

The ambiguity occurs only when immediate mode is used. For example, the phrase BYTE PTR is not needed in the instruction

```
MOV AL,[BX]
```

because the "clerk" notices that the destination, AL, is a byte instead of a word, and thus the programmer must have intended [BX] to signify the *byte* pointed to by BX, rather than the *word* pointed to by BX.

Another instruction that must be discussed is line 51,

```
LP1:   MOV AX,[BX-4]    ;    get F sub i-2
```

The destination operand specifier [BX−4] is similar to the form [BX] just discussed. It instructs the computer to copy the word pointed to by BX−4 to AX. Recall that consecutive Fibonacci numbers will be stored in consecutive words, two bytes apart. Hence, F_i and F_{i-2} will be four bytes apart, and since BX is pointing to F_i, BX−4 will point to F_{i-2}, as indicated in the comment "get F sub i−2."

This technique is called **based addressing mode**, in which a pointer to a memory location consists of a register value plus or minus a constant, in this case BX−4.

Again, the label LP1 in this instruction is extremely convenient for the programmer when specifying the branch target for the JNZ instruction in line 56. From line 60 of FIB.LST, LP1 denotes offset 0019 of the code segment. (Keep in mind again, though, that at assembly time the code is not yet loaded into memory. At that time, we are just planning what will go where at load time; e.g., the instruction labeled LP1 will be loaded into offset 0019 in the code segment.) As MASM assembles instructions one by one, it records the offsets that result. By the time it reaches LP1, it will have allocated the code segment up through offset 0018, so LP1 will be assigned to offset 0019. MASM makes a note of this fact by entering LP1 and its offset into the symbol table, so that it will recognize any subsequent reference to LP1 as meaning offset 0019. The instruction JNZ LP1 is such a reference. From line 65 of FIB.LST, this instruction gets assigned to offset 0027. Recall from Program 3.2 that the machine code of a JNZ instruction is 75dd, where dd is the displacement. If we were programming in machine language, we would have to calculate this displacement ourselves, but MASM does this for us. It "remembers" that LP1 is at 0019, and it "knows" that in step C of the JNZ instruction the IP value will already be incremented to $0027 + 2 = 0029$, so the required displacement is

```
19H - 29H = -10H = F0H.
```

So MASM translates JNZ LP1 to 75F0, as line 65 shows.

Features such as the last few we have been discussing make assembly language much more convenient than machine language. Not only can we use English-like abbreviations for operations, such as SUB for the subtraction op code, and refer to items in the data segment by name (e.g., FIBNUM) instead of by numerical offset, but we can also refer to items in the code segment by name instead of by offset. Again, the fact that we do not have to compute displacements in jump instructions is a major convenience, especially in large programs. In the case of Program 4.1, for example, we simply name line 51 LP1 and then put an instruction on line 56 to jump to LP1; the assembler worries about the offsets and the displacement for us.

At this point in the program, the computation of the Fibonacci numbers is complete, and we can print out the numbers to the monitor. First we will print a title, "Fibonacci numbers," which is accomplished by the instructions in lines 65–67:

```
MOV DX,OFFSET FHDR
MOV AH,9
INT 21H
```

As the comments on lines 61–64 assert, we will print out this title by calling the operating system's print-character-string service. All OS services exist as procedures that are called through the INT instruction. For those which have 21H as the operand of this instruction, the subservice number, 9 in this case, must be placed in the AH register. (Recall from Chapter 2 that AH is the high byte of the AX register, AL is the low byte of AX, BH is the high byte of BX, and so on.)

You will learn the details of the INT instruction in Chapter 8, but will make frequent use of it before then. Note again that the INT instruction, in a manner similar to that of a CALL instruction, includes a "jump" action. In line 67, for example, the execution of INT will result in a jump to some point within the operating system program; the latter will run for a while, performing the requested service, and then will return, via an IRET instruction (similar to RET) to resume execution of MAIN at line 68.

Service number 21/09 prints out the given string at the current cursor position on the screen and, of course, updates that position after writing out the string. The programmer indicates the end of the string by inserting a dollar sign (see the declaration of FHDR on line 7 in the DSG segment); the dollar sign itself is not printed out.

In requesting the OS service, we must specify which character string we want printed out. This is done by putting the data segment offset of the string into the DX register. In this case, the string is in the byte array FHDR, so we use the instruction

```
MOV DX,OFFSET FHDR
```

Note that in line 74 of FIB.LST there is an 'R' next to the machine code for this instruction. The machine code produced by the assembler is BA0014, with BA the op code and 0014 the immediate constant. (This instruction is another example of **immediate mode**.) The immediate constant is 0014, because that *is* the offset of FHDR, as can be seen from line 10 of FIB.LST. But it is possible that at link time we may wish to combine this data segment with some other one—say, one named DSEG. If DSEG is placed before DSG in the combined segment, then all the original offsets in DSG will be incorrect for the combined segment, and thus, instructions such as BA0014 would have to be changed by the linker. The assembler accordingly leaves a note (signified by the 'R') in the .OBJ file to warn the linker about this.

Next, in line 68, we call a procedure:

```
CALL PRCRLF
```

Again, this is like the call to DISPBX discussed earlier. After step C of line 68, we will not yet go on to line 72 (which is the next instruction, since lines 69–71 are just comment lines), but instead we will jump to line 93. Then, when we reach line 107, the RET instruction will make us jump back to line 72, resuming execution of MAIN at the point at which we were at the time of the call to PRCRLF.

The procedure PRCRLF sends the carriage return and line feed characters to the screen, so that we go to the next line on the screen. It does this in lines 100–104 with two calls to DOS service number 21/02, which prints a single character (contained in DL) to the screen.

Next comes the code for the actual printing of the Fibonacci numbers. Since there are N numbers, this printing will be done with a loop having N iterations. This loop starts at line 78, labeled LP2, and ends with line 85,

```
JNZ LP2
```

We will use the DI register to serve as a counter for the loop, just as we used DX in the loop at LP1. The reason for not using DX again is that we will be calling the procedure DISPBX, which uses DX itself, such as on line 119.

As with the loop labeled LP1, we will use BX to point to the current Fibonacci number—i.e., the current one to be printed. We again initialize BX to point to the first Fibonacci number by the instruction

```
MOV BX,OFFSET FIBNUM
```

in line 76, and you can see the by-now-familiar

```
ADD BX,2
```

in line 83, which makes BX point to the next consecutive Fibonacci number, in preparation for the next iteration of the loop.

As mentioned before, the printing will be done by the procedure DISPBX, which displays the number in BX on the screen. So, to prepare for the call to DISPBX, we must put the current number on BX, which is done by the instruction on line 79,

```
MOV BX, [BX]
```

Unfortunately, putting the current number in BX will destroy the old contents of BX, which were serving as a pointer to the current Fibonacci number. For example, suppose we are currently printing out F_4. This Fibonacci number has the value 3 and is stored at FIBNUM+6, i.e., offset 6 (since FIBNUM starts at offset 0). So c(BX) will be 0006 before execution of the instruction

```
MOV BX, [BX]
```

but it will be 0003 after execution! Since we want to be able to increment BX from 0006 to 0008 in preparation for printing F_5 in the next iteration of the loop, we need to *save* the value 0006 somewhere first.

This is done by the instruction on line 78,

```
MOV SAVEBX,BX
```

which saves a copy of BX in the word named SAVEBX in the data segment. This instruction is an example of **direct addressing mode**, the mode in which a memory location is specified directly within the instruction, as opposed to **indirect addressing mode**, which, we saw earlier, specifies a memory location indirectly by using a register as a pointer to that location.

After the call to DISPBX, we restore the old value of BX, using the instruction on line 82,

```
MOV BX,SAVEBX
```

The last instruction in the loop is JNZ LP2, on line 85. We will execute this instruction N times, once for each iteration of the loop. After the Nth execution, our work will be done! At that point, all N Fibonacci numbers will have been printed to the screen. So we will then want to return to the operating system, so that the OS will print out its familiar '>' prompt to the screen, waiting for our next command. To accomplish this return, we use another DOS service, the return-to-OS service. This is service number 21/4C, so we avail ourselves of it by the code

```
MOV AH,4CH
INT 21H
```

This service deallocates the memory that had been assigned to our program and returns control to the OS's command-reader portion, which, as mentioned earlier, will print out its familiar '>' prompt to the screen and wait for our next command, say, DIR or VI or whatever.

Note that even though we have declared three separate segments—for data, stack, and code areas—we do not necessarily have to do this. For example, we could have dispensed with the segment DSG, incorporating the declarations of FIBNUM, FHDR, and SAVEBX into the CSG segment. In fact, .COM files (which are like .EXE files but can be loaded into memory from disk more quickly) have this as a requirement. An example is Program 8.3, which has a DW declaration for a variable NTICKS right in the middle of code in a procedure! However, in most cases, declaring separate segments gives more flexibility and clarity.

The term **pseudo-op** deserves mention at this point. Remember that the format of .LST files is that each line contains a line number, then an offset, then data or machine code if any, and finally the original line from the .ASM file. However, line 30 of FIB.LST has an offset, 0000, reflecting the fact that MAIN is the first procedure within this segment (CSG), but no machine code. The reason is that the corresponding line in FIB.ASM, line 21,

```
MAIN PROC FAR
```

does not correspond to any machine instruction, e.g., an instruction to move, compare, add, jump, or any other instruction. For example, it is not like Line 33 of FIB.ASM, where a MOV instruction produced machine code, BB0000 (see Line 42 of FIB.LST). Instead, the line MAIN PROC FAR is a note to MASM from the programmer, just letting MASM know that this is the start of a procedure. Such notes are called **pseudo-ops,** or in many non-MASM assemblers, **directives**. From the absence of code in many lines of Figure 4.4, it is plain that there were many pseudo-ops in Program 4.1.

Recall the analogy of the assembler to a clerk. The analogy can be carried further for pseudo-ops. Imagine that you want a secretary to type a letter for you. You scribble out your letter by hand on a piece of paper. At various points on the piece of paper, you may write notes to the secretary, e.g., "Please skip two lines here." These notes are *not* to be included in the letter; they are just directions you are giving to the secretary.

Similarly, pseudo-ops are not to be included in your machine code; they are just directions to the "secretary," i.e., the assembler.

An important thing to remember is that MASM insists that a hex constant begin with a decimal digit, i.e., a digit between 0 and 9. Thus, MASM will claim an error if you write something like

```
ADD AX,FFF0H
```

The problem is that MASM might mistakenly "think" that FFF0H is the name of a variable in your data segment! Or it might confuse the constant BH (i.e., 11D) with the BH register, which you will recall is a name for the upper half of the BX register. So, in specifying hex constants that do not begin with a decimal digit, you must add a leading zero. Thus, you would write

```
ADD AX,0FFF0H
```

instead of the previous instruction, which will generate an error message from MASM ("symbol not defined").

Similarly, one must be very careful with hex constants that end in D. Suppose we wanted to move the hex constant 001D, i.e., the base-10 number 29, into BX. We might write

```
MOV BX,001D
```

but it would be wrong, because the assembler would treat the D as meaning decimal, i.e., base 10, so that the instruction would be treated the same as

```
MOV BX,1
```

which is not what we wanted at all! Instead, we would need to write

```
MOV BX,001DH
```

4.2.3 Command Sequence and Syntax for MASM and LINK

We stated earlier that we invoke MASM by typing

```
> MASM FIB,FIB,FIB;
```

This produces the files FIB.OBJ and FIB.LST. FIB.OBJ contains the machine-language version of our program and is "almost" ready to run. However, first it must be run through the **linker**, which in the Microsoft environment is a program named LINK. This program will produce yet another file, FIB.EXE, which is the executable file, i.e., the one that is actually run.

This process is similar for most operating systems. For example, Unix assembly language source files must have names ending with .s, as opposed to .ASM in MS-DOS, and the object files have names ending with .o, instead of .OBJ. A linker is used to create the analogues of .EXE files; the default name for such a file is a.out, though typically the user will choose a more meaningful name (e.g., 'vi' for the VI editor).

Some advanced operating systems allow **dynamic linking**, in which object files are linked in during the actual program run. OS/2, Microsoft's new powerful extension of MS-DOS, allows dynamic linking, adding much flexibility.

Note that neither the .OBJ file nor the .EXE file retains the symbol table that MASM formed during the assembly process (unless they were specially requested to do so). In the case of Program 4.1, for instance, these files will have no record at all of the names N, FIBNUM, FHDR, SAVEBX, STK, PRCRLF, DISPBX, PRNIB, LP1, LP2, LP, A_F, and WR_CHAR. Those names were only temporary objects and are just a temporary shorthand notation between the programmer and the assembler.

Consider, for example, lines 60 and 65 of FIB.LST, corresponding to lines 51 and 56 in the original source file FIB.ASM. MASM translates line 56 from JNZ LP1 to the machine code 75F0. In the latter, there is, obviously, no mention of the name LP1 at all! There does not need to be any such mention; that name has outlived its usefulness by this point. When MASM encounters the assembly language JNZ LP1, it does the following:

- Checks its symbol table, finding that LP1 denotes offset 0019;
- Calculates the distance to the LP1 instruction from the offset just past the JNZ instruction:

        0019H - (0027H + 2) = -10H = F0H;

- Produces the machine language instruction 75F0.

In other words, the whole point of labeling line 51 in FIB.ASM with the name LP1 is to enable MASM to calculate the **displacement** value, F0H, in the machine code assembled from line 56. That is the point of having MASM in the first place—we would prefer that MASM do this calculation instead of doing it ourselves, so that we can concentrate on other, less mechanical things. But once MASM has determined the value F0H, there is certainly no longer any need to retain the name LP1, and thus, that name will not appear in the file FIB.OBJ.

Similarly, when MASM encounters references to SAVEBX in assembling lines 78 and 82 of FIB.ASM, it will find from its symbol table that these are references to offset 0027 and thus put the value 0027 into the machine code. After producing that machine code, there is no longer any need to keep the name SAVEBX, and thus, this name will not appear in FIB.OBJ either—and, again, neither will any of the other labels (FIBNUM, LP2, and so on).

As the name implies, the main purpose of LINK is to combine several separate programs into one big one. The reason for this, as you will see in Chapter 5, is that it is often more convenient, or even necessary, to break a program into pieces, then produce separate .OBJ files for the pieces, and finally combine those .OBJ files together to form the executable .EXE file.

For Program 4.1, we have only one .OBJ file, but the linker must be run anyway, since it has other miscellaneous things to do, such as determining the ordering of the various segments (see shortly). To run the linker for this program, we type

```
> LINK /LI /MAP FIB,FIB,FIB;
```

Again, this produces the executable file FIB.EXE, together with a file FIB.MAP that we will discuss in Chapter 5. FIB.EXE will be almost exactly the same as FIB.OBJ, and it will include the notes left in FIB.OBJ by MASM and mentioned earlier, e.g., the fact that when run time comes along, we wish execution to begin at the line labeled MAIN.

As just stated, LINK will also determine the ordering of the various segments—in this case DSG, SSG, and CSG—within the file FIB.EXE, and, if the programmer requests it, LINK will even combine some of them together. There are a number of MASM pseudo-ops that the programmer can put into FIB.ASM to control this, and certain options can also be requested within the LINK command line itself. For example, one can stipulate that LINK order the segments alphabetically, meaning here that CSG would be first in the FIB.EXE file, then DSG, and then SSG.

These options are beyond the scope of this text. In the absence of such special requests, LINK will simply load the segments in the order you declare them, in this case first DSG, then SSG, and then CSG. Recall from Chapter 2, though, that segments must begin at addresses that are multiples of 16, i.e., that have a zero as their last hex digit. Thus, the segments DSG and SSG will start at such addresses (even though the *labels* DSG and SSG will suppress the final zero). Now here is the point: from Figure 4.4, lines 5 and 15, we see that DSG has size 29H = 41D bytes. This is *not* a multiple of 16, being 7 bytes short of the next higher multiple of 16, i.e., 48D. Thus, there are seven unused bytes between DSG and SSG in FIB.EXE.

For convenience, you can automate the assembly/linking process by making a DOS **batch** file, say, ML.BAT. The file name must end with .BAT, but otherwise any name can be chosen. We have chosen the name ML, for "MASM and LINK." Here is what the file would look like:

```
MASM %1,%1,%1;
LINK /LI /MAP %1,%1,%1;
```

The %1 means the first parameter (here, the only one). We would run this batch file by typing

```
ML FIB
```

and then DOS would run the command in ML.BAT with all instances of %1 being replaced by FIB. That is, it would run

```
MASM FIB,FIB,FIB;
LINK /LI /MAP FIB,FIB,FIB;
```

Then, if we had another program, say, ABC.ASM, we could type

```
ML ABC
```

and so on. (See also the idea of **make** files in Section 5.5.)

We can now describe the solutions to problems P2 and P3 set out in the first paragraph of this chapter. We type

```
> FIB
```

and in response, the operating system's loader program will load FIB.EXE into main memory from disk and will initiate execution of FIB.EXE. When the program is finished executing the familiar operating system prompt

```
>
```

will appear again, inviting you to submit your next command. Recall that the prompt does *not* occur automatically; it occurs because the program included the code

```
MOV AH,4CH
INT 21H
```

which called the OS's return-to-OS service.

It has been stressed several times that the various commands, such as VI, MASM, and LINK, are in fact *programs*. They are no different from the programs you write yourself and exist as .EXE files, just as does the FIB.EXE program. The reader should use the DIR command to verify that the files VI.EXE (or some other text editor), MASM.EXE, and LINK.EXE exist. (Type PATH to see which directories you should search for these files.) The respective files are what get executed when you use these commands.

If you write a high-level language program. OBJ and .EXE files are created, during the compiling and linking processes, respectively. The program VI, for example, was probably written in the language C. Running the C source file through the C compiler created an .OBJ file, that LINK then used to create the file VI.EXE. But whether the original source file was in a high-level language such as C, or whether it was in assembly language, the instructions in the .EXE file still consist of the basic iAPX machine instructions, such as move, compare, add, jump, and so on.

It should be noted that the default mode of MASM produces iAPX 86 code, so that such code can be used on any iAPX machine. If you want to use more advanced instructions—say, those available only in the 286 family and above—use the .286 or other pseudo-ops. Check your assembler manual for these.

4.2.4 Debugging Assembly-Language Programs

As the name implies, DEBUG was developed primarily as an aid to debugging user programs. Suppose, for example, that after assembling and linking Program 4.1 and then running the program by typing

```
> FIB
```

we got incorrect results. We can then use DEBUG, by typing

```
> DEBUG FIB.EXE
```

DEBUG will call the loader, which, as usual, will find an unused portion of memory for the program's segments, load the segments, and initialize CS and SS as described earlier. You will then be able to use DEBUG's commands to help debug the program, just as before.

Recall, for example, that DEBUG includes the T command, which allows you to execute your program one instruction at a time, watching how the register contents change along the way. This is a big help in pinpointing the locations of your errors.

Of course, before using the T command, you might want to use the G command, so as to quickly reach an area at which you suspect an error lies. If that area begins at, say, the 100th instruction in your program, you certainly do not want to type T 100 times before you can start to check for the bug!

Another situation in which you will want to avoid using T is when you reach a CALL or INT instruction that would force a jump to a procedure you already know to be free of bugs. Using T would mean that you would have to step through each of the called procedure's instructions individually, and since there may literally be hundreds of them, this would be a big waste of time if you knew that your bug was not among those instructions.

For example, in using DEBUG on Program 4.2 (see later), the author had the following appear on the screen:

```
AX=090D  BX=A00F  CX=0804  DX=0012  SP=00C8  BP=0000  SI=0000  DI=0000
DS=1411  ES=1401  SS=1452  CS=145F  IP=0018     NV UP EI PL ZR NA PE NC
145F:0018 CD21        INT    21
```

Remember, this is a call to a procedure in the operating system (which should be "reasonably" free of bugs). If one uses the T command at this point, one will step through that entire procedure, which might be quite long and thus extremely time consuming. Worse yet, the procedure might even include a CLI instruction, which, for reasons that will become clear in Chapter 7, will freeze up the keyboard, thus preventing further T commands that would execute the "antidote" instruction STI which usually follows CLI.

So instead of typing T in this kind of setting, we would type the command P, which would execute the procedure and stop only after returning from it, thus avoiding stepping singly through each instruction in the procedure.

In using DEBUG, you will find useful another DEBUG command not mentioned earlier: the U ("unassemble") command. This command allows you essentially to reverse the assembly process; U translates machine code back to assembly language. Typing

```
-U s:o
```

where 's' is the code segment and 'o' the offset, will display an assembly-language version of your code on the screen. For example, entering

```
U 3244:0502
```

will result in DEBUG looking at the machine code starting at memory location
$32440 + 0502 = 32942$ and displaying the code on the screen in assembly-language
form. This provides a convenient way to inspect code in memory.

A major drawback to using DEBUG in extensive debugging work is that it cannot
display any labels—e.g., LP1, SAVEBX, and so on in Program 4.1. In a sense, we can
hardly expect to see these labels, since they were discarded when MASM finished the
original assembly process (see Section 4.2.3). The labels will appear only as their
numerical offset values. For example, the instruction

```
JNZ LP1
```

in Program 4.1 will, after assembly by MASM, then linking, then loading via DEBUG,
and then unassembling using DEBUG's U command, appear as

```
JNZ 0019
```

(Lines 60 and 65 in Figure 4.4 show where the 0019 comes from.)

Other symbols that will be missing by the time you get to DEBUG are SAVEBX,
a word in the data segment, and the procedure name DISPBX (lines 14 and 119 in Figure 4.4). Suppose, for example, that we wish to start debugging at the line MOV
SAVEBX,BX in our program. From line 87 of Figure 4.4, we see that this instruction is
at offset 0039 in the code segment, so we type

```
-G 39
```

resulting in the response shown in Figure 4.5. (Recall that the line "Fibonacci
numbers:" is output from our program, not a message from DEBUG.) As is evident,
the instruction MOV SAVEBX,BX appears in the DEBUG display as

```
MOV [0027],BX
```

We then have to look at (line 14 of) the file FIB.LST again to see what is in offset 27
of the data segment. When we do, we discover that it is the word that we had named
SAVEBX. Similarly, if we now use DEBUG's T command twice, we get the response
shown in Figure 4.6, and again, we have to look at the file FIB.LST to see what procedure is in offset 60 of the code segment. When we do, we discover that it is DISPBX.

```
Fibonacci numbers:
AX=0924  BX=0000  CX=017A  DX=0014  SP=00C8  BP=0000  SI=0000  DI=000A
DS=1AFD  ES=1AED  SS=1B00  CS=1B0D  IP=0039    NV UP EI PL ZR NA PE NC
1B0D:0039 891E2700      MOV    [0027],BX
```

Figure 4.5

```
AX=0924  BX=0001  CX=017A  DX=0014  SP=00C8  BP=0000  SI=0000  DI=000A
DS=1AFD  ES=1AED  SS=1B00  CS=1B0D  IP=003F    NV UP EI PL ZR NA PE NC
1B0D:003F E81E00          CALL    0060
```

Figure 4.6

It is inconvenient to have to repeatedly refer to the .LST file in this manner, especially in a large program with hundreds of variables and procedures. It is thus much more convenient if our debugging tool can refer to these variables and procedures by their original names, rather than by their offsets. A **symbolic debugging tool** has this valuable capability.

The program SYMDEB is such a tool. It operates in exactly the same manner as DEBUG and includes all the same commands (T, G, etc., plus some new ones), but it also has the important capability of being able to deal with symbols instead of offsets. Of course, in order to do this, we must tell MASM not to throw away the symbol table during the assembly process.

How is the latter accomplished? We use the MASM pseudo-op PUBLIC. In the foregoing example, we would include a line

```
PUBLIC SAVEBX,DISPBX
```

at the top of the source file FIB.ASM. This commands MASM to make a note in FIB.OBJ that SAVEBX is a name for offset 0027 in the data segment and DISPBX is a name for offset 0060 in the code segment. (Similarly, we could save the label LP1, etc.) LINK will see this information in FIB.OBJ and copy the information to FIB.MAP. (The latter is produced by LINK along with FIB.EXE.) We then use a program called MAPSYM, typing

```
MAPSYM FIB
```

which in turn produces a file FIB.SYM that contains all the offsets of the symbols we declared PUBLIC in FIB.ASM.

So if we start debugging by typing

```
SYMDEB FIB.SYM FIB.EXE
```

we can use the same commands as in DEBUG. Typing G 39, as before with DEBUG, we get Figure 4.7 on the screen. So now we see that the word to which BX is copied is the one that we had named SAVEBX! This is much clearer than just referring to that word as offset 0027, as was the case in Figure 4.5.

Similarly, if we now type T twice, as we did with DEBUG, we get the display shown in Figure 4.8. Again, the description

```
CALL DISPX
```

```
Fibonacci numbers:
AX=0924  BX=0000  CX=017A  DX=0014  SP=00C8  BP=0000  SI=0000  DI=000A
DS=1B05  ES=1AF5  SS=1B08  CS=1B15  IP=0039   NV UP EI PL ZR NA PE NC
1B15:0039 891E2700        MOV     [SAVEBX],BX
```

Figure 4.7

```
AX=0924  BX=0001  CX=017A  DX=0014  SP=00C8  BP=0000  SI=0000  DI=000A
DS=1B05  ES=1AF5  SS=1B08  CS=1B15  IP=003F   NV UP EI PL ZR NA PE NC
1B15:003F E81E00          CALL    DISPBX
```

Figure 4.8

here is much clearer than the description

```
CALL 0060
```

that we got from DEBUG in Figure 4.6.

In the same way, you can use the D command to inspect variables—e.g., by typing

```
D SAVEBX
```

instead of the much less convenient

```
D 0027
```

Note again that if we had not declared SAVEBX and DISPBX to be PUBLIC (or if we had not used MAPSYM to create FIB.SYM), then SYMDEB would have produced the same results as DEBUG—i.e., we would get Figures 4.5 and 4.6 instead of Figures 4.7 and 4.8. Without the symbol table, SYMDEB would have been forced to use offsets for description.

CodeView is even more convenient than SYMDEB. For example, in addition to being able to pause for debugging at a particular line in the program, as with DEBUG's command

```
G n
```

one can specify a *time* at which to pause, say "Execute until the variable X equals 12." Also, CodeView uses a **window-based** mode for displaying its messages on the screen, which again makes debugging easier, and it also allows (but does not require) the use of a mouse to input many commands.

The reader is urged to use CodeView (or another advanced debugging tool, such as Turbo Debugger) if it is available. The best way to learn the tool is to experiment with the various commands; we will give only a short introduction here. (Different versions of CodeView may differ slightly from the description given next. Hit the F1 key for the on-line help facility if you need help.)

The basic setup of CodeView consists of two windows:

(a) The **display window**, which displays your program in its source file form or its DEBUG form. (The latter is like the output from DEBUG's U command, showing segments/offsets and machine and assembly code.) The display highlights the line containing the current instruction.

(b) The **dialogue window**, which accepts commands similar to those of DEBUG— e.g., the D command to display the contents of a block of memory.

The line-oriented "DEBUG-style" commands described in (b) are entered by typing the command. The following window-oriented CodeView commands are available through the function keys at the top (or the side) of your keyboard:

F1: Display help screen

F2: Display/remove window that lists register contents

F3: Change contents in display window from source to 'U' form or vice versa

F4: Display the "user screen," i.e., the screen the user would see if the program were run directly, without a debugging tool

F5: Execute until a breakpoint or end of program is reached

F6: Move cursor from dialog window to display window or vice versa

F7: Set a one-time-only breakpoint at line pointed to by cursor and execute to there

F8: Same as DEBUG T command

F9: Set/clear permanent breakpoint at line pointed to by cursor

F10: Same as DEBUG P command

The register window controlled by the F2 key is a narrow window on the right side of your screen that gives the same information as DEBUG's R command. The advantage over DEBUG, though, is that it allows you to watch the contents of registers change at the same time as you look at a whole screenful of your source file. By contrast, in DEBUG, you see only one line of your source file at a time during execution using T. Similarly, in CodeView your "output screen"—i.e., the screen you would see if you were running the program directly, without a debugging tool—is kept separate from the debugging screen, thus making things clearer; you can switch back and forth between the two screens by using the F4 key. By contrast, with DEBUG, debugging output is interspersed with program output (see Figure 4.5) and may be harder to follow.

Hitting the F8 key results in execution of one instruction in exactly the same manner as with T. The F10 key does the same thing as P, meaning that it will skip over procedure calls. That is, it will execute all the instructions of a procedure without stopping after each one. This is useful if the procedure is already debugged and you do not have the time or patience to step through each of its instructions individually.

If part of your program is in Pascal or C, even the F8 key has an advantage over its DEBUG counterpart, the T command: hitting the F8 key while the Pascal or C source is displayed will result in executing all the machine instructions corresponding to the current Pascal or C source statement. With the T command, you would have to execute these individually, which is slower and more tedious.

When you type a command of the form

```
G n
```

in DEBUG, the instruction at location n is called a **breakpoint**; it is a place where you want execution to pause, enabling you to "take a look around," inspecting the contents of registers and memory. In DEBUG, to specify the value n, you have to find segment and offset values for the line at which you want execution to pause. In CodeView, things are much more convenient: you simply use F3 to get to the display window and then use the up-arrow or down-arrow keys (or, to move screen by screen, use the PageUp and PageDown keys) to move the cursor to the line at which you want execution to pause; then you either hit F7, or hit F9 and then F5.

Again, you can display variables by name in CodeView, e.g.,

```
D SAVEBX
```

CodeView also allows you to *monitor* all changes to any variables you specify. In Program 4.2, for instance, if you submit the command

```
W? I
```

to CodeView, then CodeView will open a one-line window at the top of the screen. This window will display the current value of I, and each time I changes values, the change will be immediately reflected in the window. If you now type

```
W? N
```

then the window will expand to two lines, showing both variables, and so on. This feature is also accessible to Pascal and C programs.

Again, the best way to learn CodeView is to experiment with it. Try all of the commands just described at least once.

To run CodeView on, say, the Fibonacci number program, include the /ZI option at assembly time and the /CO option at link time:

```
> MASM /ZI FIB,FIB,FIB;
> LINK /LI /MAP /CO FIB,FIB,FIB;
```

You will not need to use the PUBLIC pseudo-op in your .ASM file. Also, append the string 'CODE' to your declaration of your code segment, e.g.,

```
CSG SEGMENT 'CODE'
```

Then type

```
> CV FIB
```

CodeView requires Version 3.6 or later of LINK, and full use of all CodeView features requires at least Version 5.0 of MASM, although most CodeView features can be used with earlier versions.

Whatever debugging tool you use—DEBUG, CodeView, Turbo Debug, or some other program—there are some common principles that will help you search for an error. For instance, quite often there is an error in the very line you are most sure is correct! Hence, if you are sure that at a certain point in your code the value in the AX register will be 0042H, verify it! Adopt a "confirmatory" approach: using the debugger, set a breakpoint at that place in the code, and check to see whether AX really does have the value 0042H. Or, if you are sure that certain code is being executed, even though the structure of the code does not guarantee this (e.g., it is in the midst of some if-then-else construct or in a procedure), then set a breakpoint there to confirm whether you are indeed reaching the code. In many cases, you will find that your error turns out to be in one of the lines that you were sure was correct. Don't underestimate the value of this seemingly simple debugging trick—it works!

So far, we have been concerned with debugging run-time errors. But what about assembly-time errors, i.e., errors displayed when you run MASM? The error messages from MASM are often rather cryptic, especially to the beginner. However, in trying to guess what these messages mean, note that they are often (especially for beginners' programs) telling you that you have made one of the following errors:

- You have used the wrong combination of operation and addressing mode. For example, if, in Program 4.1, instead of lines 24 and 25, we had the single "instruction"

```
MOV DS,DSG
```

  this would have been an invalid combination, since a MOV to a segment register cannot use immediate addressing mode. (See Section 3.3 and Appendix II.)
- You have a mismatch of operand sizes. For example, if you submit the "instruction"

```
MOV AL,BX
```

  MASM will give you an error message, since one operand is a byte and the other is a word. (On the other hand, the instruction

```
       MOV AL,[BX]
```

is legal and is *not* taken by MASM to be a type mismatch. The assembler takes this to mean "Move the *byte* pointed to by BX to AL," so that both operands are bytes.)

If you have an error such as this, fix it by using several instructions in place of one, as explained at the end of Section 3.3.

- You have an instruction that is ambiguous with respect to operand size. Ambiguity in operand size was discussed earlier, in connection with the WORD PTR and BYTE PTR, and is fixed by using one of those pseudo-ops.

- You have forgotten that hex constants must begin with a digit in the range 0–9. For example, if you specify the hex constant B888H, the assembler will complain with a message such as "symbol not defined"—because it thinks B888H is a symbol, rather than a numeric constant. This error is fixed by appending a 0 to the front of the constant, obtaining 0B888H.

- You have made a typing error somewhere. For example, suppose you declare a segment named PROGSEG, i.e.,

```
       PROGSEG SEGMENT
```

but then, at the end of the segment, you type

```
       PROGSEQ ENDS
```

The assembler will give a "block nesting error" message.

If you get an assembly error message you do not understand, check for the foregoing problems first.

In some cases, the assembler will not even be able to pinpoint which line of your source file is erroneous. It will simply give you an error message without mentioning a line number, or it will mention only the last physical line of the file. (In the latter case, the assembler was "expecting" to see something but had not found it by the time the end of the file was encountered.) In this situation, make an extra copy of the file and repeatedly remove lines from the file, reassembling after each deletion. (Remove about half of the remaining lines each time.) Eventually the error message will disappear, so you will know that the error was among the most recently removed lines. Applying the same technique to that set of lines, you will eventually determine which line was the source of the error.

Note that if you make a minor mistake in your command line with MASM or LINK, such as using a comma where you should use a space, MASM/LINK might not complain—but instead of complaining, it will produce wrong results! So check your spelling and punctuation very, *very* carefully. To minimize errors (and save typing), put your commands into .BAT files and use those.

4.2.5 Further MASM Examples

Program 4.2 finds prime numbers and displays them on your monitor. It reads in a number, MAX, which the user types at the keyboard, and then prints out all numbers less than or equal to MAX which are primes. Note that both input and output are in hex. (Note also that the input requires you to type leading zeros and that lowercase letters are used. For example, to input the value 26 (decimal), you type 001a (hex), not 1A.)

The reader is invited to write a decimal version of Program 4.2; only the procedures READBX and DISPBX would change. The *computational* part of the program would stay the same, since the computer can only do base-2 computation, regardless of what number base is used to *input and output* the numbers in the computation.

```
MAXPRM EQU 100D

DSG SEGMENT

        N DW (?)   ; the current number being tested for primeness
        MAX DW (?)   ; the largest number to be tested for primeness
        I DW (?)  ; potential divisor of N

        ; a couple of messages to print out:
        PROMPT DB 'enter MAX',0DH,0AH,'$'
        PRMLST DB 'prime list:',0DH,0AH,'$'

        ; as we find that a number is prime, we will record that fact
        ;    in the array PRIME, so that we can use this to help testing
        ;    primeness of subsequent numbers
        ; this saves work, since the prime testing will be done with
        ;    fewer potential divisors
        ; so byte PRIME+I will be set to 1 or 0, according to whether I
        ;    is prime or not
        PRIME DB MAXPRM DUP (0)

DSG ENDS

SSG SEGMENT STACK
        STK DW 100D DUP (?)
SSG ENDS

CSG SEGMENT 'CODE'

ASSUME CS:CSG,DS:DSG,SS:SSG

MAIN PROC FAR

        ; standard preamble to set DS

        MOV AX,DSG
        MOV DS,AX
```

```
        ; prompt user and read in MAX
        MOV DX,OFFSET PROMPT  ; prepare for DOS Service 21/9
        MOV AH,9
        INT 21H
        CALL READBX
        MOV MAX,BX

        ; print out title
        MOV DX,OFFSET PRMLST
        MOV AH,9
        INT 21H

        ; our first prime number is 2, which we process "by hand"

        ; first, record it
        MOV BX,2
        MOV SI,BX
        MOV BYTE PTR PRIME[SI],1
        ; now announce it
        CALL DISPBX
        CALL PRCRLF

        ; the rest of the numbers N, N = 3,..., MAX, will be tested in this loop
        MOV N,2
TOP:    ADD N,1  ; next N
        MOV BX,N
        MOV SI,BX
        CALL TESTPRM  ; test N for primeness
        MOV BYTE PTR PRIME[SI],AL  ; record the result
        CMP AX,1  ; this N prime?
        JNZ CHKDONE  ; if not, then skip the printing
        ; if so, print it out
        MOV BX,SI  ; restore value of BX, which TESTPRM destroyed
        CALL DISPBX  ; note: this destroys BX too
        CALL PRCRLF  ; go to next line on screen
CHKDONE: CMP SI,MAX ; done with loop yet?
        JNZ TOP  ; if not, test the next N

        ; standard code to return to DOS
        MOV AH,4CH
        INT 21H
MAIN ENDP

DISPBX PROC  ; prints hex contents of BX to screen

        ; each nibble to be printed will be taken from bits 15-12 of BX
        ; so we will keep rotating BX by 4 bits at a time, each time
        ;   moving a new nibble into bits 11-8

        ; this will have to be done 4 times, for the 4 nibbles of BX,
        ;   and we will use DH as the loop counter, starting at 4,
        ;   then 3, 2, and 1
        MOV DH,4
```

```
          ;  the rotation of 4 bits will be indicated by CL, so put 4 there
          MOV CL,4

   LP:  MOV DL,BH  ;  put a copy in DL, to work on it there

          ;  prepare the nibble for printing
          AND DL,0F0H  ;  put 0's in the lower 4 bits of DL, leaving upper 4 unchanged
          ROL DL,CL  ;  rotate so that the nibble is in bits 3-0 of DL

          CALL PRNIB  ;  print that nibble

          ROL BX,CL  ;  rotate BX to get to next nibble

          ;  decrement loop count and check if we are done with all nibbles yet
          DEC DH
          JNZ LP


          RET  ;  return to calling program
DISPBX ENDP


PRNIB PROC  ;  prints the contents of bits 3-0 of DL to the screen

          ;  must convert numeric value in DL, which is in the range 0-F, to ASCII

          CMP DL,9  ;  is it 0-9 or A-F?
          JG A_F  ;  if so, go to the code to handle the A-F case
          ;  if not, we are in the 0-9 case
          ADD DL,30H  ;   ASCII codes for the characters '0'-9' are 30H-39H
          JMP WR_CHAR  ;  OK, ready to write to screen
    A_F:  ADD DL,37H  ;   ASCII codes for the characters 'A'-'F' are 41H-46H

          ;  here is where the actual writing to the screen takes place,
          ;     using the print-single-character service, DOS Service Number 21/02
          ;  the service is called by putting 2 into AH, putting the character
          ;     in DL (which we have already done), and executing INT 21H
WR_CHAR: MOV AH,2
          INT 21H

          ;  OK, nibble printed, so return to caller
          RET
PRNIB ENDP


PRCRLF PROC  ;  print carriage return and line feed, to go to new line

          ;  use the DOS print-single-character service, Service Number 21/02
          ;  the service is called by putting 2 into AH, putting the character
          ;     in DL (which we have already done), and executing INT 21H
          ;  ASCII codes for CR and LF are 0DH and 0AH

          MOV AH,2
          MOV DL,0DH
          INT 21H
          MOV DL,0AH
```

```
        INT 21H

        ;  all done, so return to caller
        RET
PRCRLF ENDP

TESTPRM PROC
        ; tests N for primeness, returning 1 or 0 in AX, according
        ;    to whether N is found to be prime or nonprime
        ; method: for each I up to the square root of N, see if
        ;    I divides N
        ; if no such I divides N, then N is prime
        ; note, though, that we only try the prime I's, thus saving
        ;    work

        MOV I,2  ; 2 will be our first trial divisor
    PLP:
        ; if I isn't prime, don't bother trying it as a divisor of N
        MOV DI,I
        CMP BYTE PTR PRIME[DI],1
        JNZ NEXTI  ; if I not prime, skip it and try next I
        ; here I is prime, so try it as a divisor of N
        MOV BX,DI
        MOV AX,N
        DIV BL  ; divide c(AX) by c(BL), putting quotient in AL and remainder in AH
        CMP AH,0  ; is the remainder 0?
        JZ NOTPRM  ; if 0 remainder, then I divides N, so N is not prime
        ; should we try any further values of I, i.e., is I*I < N?
        ; to find out, use the MUL ("multiply") instruction, multiplying
        ;    c(AL) by c(BL), which puts the product in AX
        MOV AX,I
        MOV BL,AL  ; copy I to BL
        MUL BL  ; multiply c(AL) by c(BL), putting the product in AX
        CMP AX,N  ; I*I < N?
        JG PRM  ; if AX > N, we're done trying all I, and N has been found prime!
        ; otherwise prepare for next I
    NEXTI: INC I
        JMP PLP

  NOTPRM: MOV AX,0  ; report that N is not prime
        JMP DONE
    PRM: MOV AX,1  ; report that N is prime

    DONE: RET
TESTPRM ENDP

READBX PROC  ; reads a hex value from keyboard to BX

        ; note: must be a 4-digit number, so put in leading zeros if needed,
        ;       and must use lowercase for digits a-f

        ; method:
        ; set BX to 0, then loop around 4 times, once for each hex digit
```

```
        ; for each digit, multiply BX by 16, convert the ASCII to the numeric
        ;    version, and add to BX

        MOV DI,4  ; loop around 4 times, with DI being the loop counter
        SUB BX,BX  ; set BX to 0

    RLP:

        ; prepare to multiply c(BX) by 16D
        MOV AX,BX
        MOV CX,16D
        MUL CX  ; multiply c(AX) by c(CX), putting the result in AX

        MOV BX,AX  ; store back to BX, where we are accumulating the sum

        CALL READCHAR  ; read digit from keyboard

        ; have to convert the ASCII to numeric
        CMP AL,39H  ; 0-9 or a-f? ASCII for the character '9' is 39H
        JG LETTER  ; if a-f, go to a-f code
        SUB AL,30H
        JMP UPDATE
LETTER: SUB AL,57H  ; ASCII for 'a' is 61H, and 61H - 57H = 10D = 0AH

UPDATE: ; now add this to BX
        MOV AH,0  ; make sure nothing is in the high part of AX
        ADD BX,AX

        ; done with loop?
        SUB DI,1
        JNZ RLP  ; if not, go back to read another digit

        CALL PRCRLF  ; go to new line on screen

        ; all done, so return to caller
        RET
READBX ENDP

READCHAR PROC
        ; we will use DOS Service 21/01, which reads a single
        ;    character from the keyboard, placing it into AL
        ;    and echoing it to the screen
        MOV AH,1
        INT 21H
        RET
READCHAR ENDP

CSG ENDS

END MAIN
```

Program 4.2

Most of the code in the program centers around the creation and use of an array of numbers P_1, P_2, P_3,.... The array element P_i is set to either 1 or 0, according to whether i is found to be prime or nonprime. Once a number i is found to be prime, we use it in testing the primeness of later numbers. P_1 is at PRIME+1, P_2 is at PRIME+2, P_3 is at PRIME+3, and so on.

The reader should readily be able to read and understand the procedures MAIN and TESTPRM. They use the same constructs we have seen in earlier examples, with only a few new items, which we will now discuss.

First, both MAIN and TESTPRM use a new type of operand addressing, called **indexed addressing mode**. This is very similar to the based addressing mode we saw in Program 4.1. For example, in the instruction

```
MOV BYTE PTR PRIME[SI],1
```

which appears a few lines above the line labeled TOP in MAIN, PRIME[SI] simply means the location that is c(SI) bytes past the location labeled PRIME.

Note the pseudo-op BYTE PTR here, corresponding to the WORD PTR we saw in Program 4.1. Program 4.2 has been written so as to provide examples of instructions that manipulate byte operands.

The program uses the MUL (multiply) and DIV (divide) instructions, in the procedure TESTPRM. Here, it is the 8-bit versions of these instructions that are used: MUL multiplies by an 8-bit quantity and DIV divides by an 8-bit quantity.

To perform the multiplication $x*y$, x is specified by the programmer within the instruction itself (in this program, we have specified the BL register for that purpose), while y is only implicit; the iAPX instruction set insists that y be in the AL register, so we have placed it there. After execution of the instruction, the product $x*y$ is in the AX register (as a 16-bit quantity, since it is the product of two 8-bit numbers).

To compute the quotient u/v, the 16-bit quantity u must be in the AX register; again, the programmer has no choice here. The 8-bit quantity v can be in any 8-bit register specified by the programmer—here again, BL. The quotient u/v ends up in AL and the remainder in AH.

MUL and DIV also have 32-bit forms. To compute $x*y$, where x and y are 16-bit quantities, x is specified by the programmer but y must be in AX. The product $x*y$, which is 32 bits in size, will be put in DX and AX, with DX containing the more significant 16 bits and AX containing the lower 16 bits. To find u/v, the 32-bit quantity u must be in DX and AX, with the upper part in DX and the lower bits in AX, and v is specified by the programmer. The quotient and remainder will be found in AX and DX, respectively, after the instruction finishes execution.

DIV and MUL are discussed in more detail in Section 6.3.1, but the brief treatment here is sufficient for you to start using these instructions in your programs now.

Program 4.2 also uses the INC (increment) instruction, which adds 1 to its operand. The instruction

```
INC I
```

has the same effect as

```
ADD I,1
```

but is more efficient than the latter. The iAPX instruction set also has a corresponding DEC (decrement) instruction, which subtracts 1 instead of adding 1.

The code

```
JG PRM  ; if AX > N, we're done trying all I, and N has been found prime!
        ; otherwise prepare for next I
NEXTI:  INC I
    JMP PLP
```

implements the if-then-else programming construct familiar from Pascal or C. This is typical; such code will consist of at least one conditional jump instruction (JG in this case) and at least one JMP. The more deeply nested an if-then-else construct is, the more conditional and unconditional jumps there will be. And of course, this is true whether we program at the machine level directly, as we are doing here, or write Pascal or C code and the compiler produces the jumps.

Program 4.2 illustrates how other programming constructs you have used in Pascal or C are implemented at the machine level. For example, the procedure MAIN contains a 'for' loop (MAIN in Program 4.1 had two of them), and it has a 'while' loop in the procedure TESTPRM.

Armed with at least an introductory exposure to MASM, let us now look at the details of the procedure DISPBX used in Programs 4.1 and 4.2 and the procedure READBX used in Program 4.2. Recall that the goal of DISPBX is to display on the screen the contents of BX in hex form and the goal of READBX is to read a hex number from the keyboard into BX.

A glance at the code in DISPBX shows that there is a loop, starting at the line LP and ending with the line

```
JNZ LP
```

You can see that the loop counter is the DH register and that there are four iterations of the loop, one iteration for each of the four hex digits that are to be printed out.

Recall that each hex digit in turn corresponds to a four-bit field, called a **nibble**. In the following discussion, we will number the nibbles in a 16-bit register, with nibble 3 being bits 15–12, nibble 2 being bits 11–8, nibble 1 being bits 7–4, and nibble 0 being bits 3–0. For an eight-bit register, such as AL, we will call the more significant four bits nibble 1 and the less significant four bits nibble 0.

Now, BX has four nibbles, and each iteration of the loop processes one of them. The first three lines,

```
LP: MOV DL,BH  ;  put a copy in DL, to work on it there

;  prepare the nibble for printing
AND DL,0F0H  ;  put 0's in the lower 4 bits of DL, leaving upper 4 unchanged
ROL DL,CL  ;  rotate so that the nibble is in bits 3-0 of DL
```

consist of preparation (see shortly) for the main action, which is the printing of a nibble to the screen, the latter being accomplished by the call

```
CALL PRNIB
```

Right after that call, note the instruction

```
ROL BX,CL
```

ROL is the "rotate left" instruction. It "rotates" the bits in the destination operand, BX, by the amount shown in the source, CL—here, four bits. In the "rotate" operation, nibble 3 will become nibble 0, nibble 2 will become nibble 3, nibble 1 will become nibble 2, and nibble 0 will become nibble 1.

The reason for using the ROL instruction is that we want to arrange things so that the nibble currently being processed is always in the nibble 3 position of BX. So each time around the loop, we rotate BX left by four bits, so that a new nibble is in the nibble 3 position and is ready to be printed.

The way the nibble currently in the nibble 3 position of BX is printed is as follows. BH is copied to DL (line LP), resulting in BX's nibble 3 being copied to nibble 1 of DL. Next, DL itself is rotated so that it swaps its nibbles 1 and 0, with the result that the copy of BX's nibble 3 is now at the nibble 0 position of DL, as required by PRNIB.

The AND instruction does what is indicated in the comment, i.e., "erase" nibble 1 of DL, so that nibble 0 is isolated for the computation done by PRNIB. We will go into the details of this operation in Chapter 6.

The PRNIB procedure contains no new instructions, but an example will help clarify its operation. Suppose that upon entry to PRNIB, c(DL) = 00000011, i.e., we desire to print the nibble 0011 to the screen in hex form. That would mean printing the character '3'. Thus we need to convert the *number* 3, i.e., 11, to the *ASCII character* 3, i.e., 00110011. The code here does this, after differentiating between the cases 0–9 and a–f, since those two sets of characters occupy noncontiguous parts of the ASCII table.

Now let us turn our attention to the READBX procedure. Its function is to read in four hex digits and place the corresponding four nibbles in BX. Its algorithm for doing so relies on the fact, pointed out in Section 1.1, that the hex notation for a number also is the base-16 representation for that number. For instance, the example given for this in Section 1.1 concerned the string

```
1001110010101110
```

which is the base-2 representation of the base-10 number 40,110. Grouping the 16 bits of the string into nibbles and hex notation, we have 9CAE, and 9CAE does indeed turn out to be the base-16 representation of 40,110:

$$9(16^3) + 12(16^2) + 10(16^1) + 14(16^0) = 40,110$$

Thus, the main loop of READBX has the outline

```
set BX to 0
for i = 1 to 4 do
  multiply BX by 16
  read a digit
  convert the digit from a character to a numeric value
  add the numeric value to BX
```

The actual code is a direct implementation of this outline. Note that the reading of the character is done by a call to another procedure, READCHAR, which is in turn a call to DOS service number 21/01.

4.2.6 Tools Developed So Far

Programs 3.1, 3.2, 4.1, and 4.2, though rather simple, provide the reader with a fairly wide-ranging introduction to the iAPX architecture—i.e., the iAPX instruction set and addressing modes—and to MASM and techniques for programming in it. We have already accumulated the following powerful core of tools with which we can write programs.

Instructions.

```
MOV, ADD, SUB, CMP, JNZ, JNS, JZ, JS, JG, JMP, CALL, RET, INT, DIV,
MUL, ROL, ROR, INC, DEC
```

Addressing modes.

```
register, indirect, direct, based, immediate, indexed
```

MASM pseudo-ops.

```
EQU, SEGMENT, ENDS, PROCEDURE, ENDP, END, PUBLIC, DW, DP, DUP,
ASSUME, OFFSET, SEG, WORD PTR, BYTE PTR
```

Programming constructs.

```
for/while loops, if-then-else, arrays, procedure call
```

DOS services.

```
21/01, read single character from keyboard; 21/02, write single
character to monitor; 21/09, write character string to monitor;
21/4C, exit to DOS
```

"Homegrown services".

```
READBX, read four-digit hex value from keyboard into BX; DISPBX,
display contents of BX on monitor in hex; PRCRLF, print carriage
return and line feed
```

In other words, although we have not presented all of these tools in full detail yet, the reader now has the tools with which a large variety of programs can be written. In Chapter 6, we will introduce more advanced instructions and addressing modes and treat the foregoing instructions and addressing modes in more detail, but the reader is *already* in a good position to start writing many complex programs, some of which are suggested in the exercises at the end of the chapter.

4.3 MORE ON PROGRAM LOADING AND TRANSFER OF CONTROL

Let us take a closer look at the approach to problems P2 and P3 described at the beginning of the chapter. We will do so in the context of the main example in that section, in which we submitted the commands

```
> VI FIB.ASM
> MASM FIB,FIB,FIB;
> LINK /LI /MAP FIB,FIB,FIB;
> FIB
```

These commands run four programs: VI.EXE, MASM.EXE, LINK.EXE, and FIB.EXE. In between these programs, and before and afterwards, the operating system (OS) runs, printing out the '>' prompt to invite the user to submit a command.

The four programs VI.EXE, MASM.EXE, LINK.EXE, and FIB.EXE must be loaded into memory in order to run. The OS does this loading. Thus, before going further, we should discuss how the OS itself gets loaded into memory. Again, the OS is a *program*. In fact, it is the first program to run when we first turn on the computer (except for a brief run of the small program discussed in the next paragraph). Thus, our first order of business before discussing the question of how the OS loads *other* programs into memory is to ask how the OS program *itself* is loaded. The answer is as follows. (Our description here is for IBM microcomputers, but the principles are similar on most other machines.)

The circuitry of the CPU is designed so that on powering it up, CS and IP will automatically be set to FFFF and 0000, respectively, and the fetch/execute cycle—Step A, Step B, Step C, Step A, Step B, . . . , will be started. Thus, the program at memory location FFFF0 + 0000 = FFFF0 begins executing. The fabricators of the computer knew that this would happen, so they placed a program in ROM—read-only memory, whose contents are stored permanently, even when the power is off—at address FFFF0. This program, the **boot loader program**, is a relatively short program whose main function is to read a part of the OS, which we will call Part I, from disk and load it into memory at some location. The last instruction of the boot loader is a JMP to the latter location; this gets Part I of the OS running. Part I of the OS then reads the rest of the OS, which we will call Part II, from disk.

The boot loader program is written to read in the OS from a specific place on the disk (sector 0, in terminology which will be explained in Section 7.1). So whatever OS is stored at that place on the disk will be the one loaded. Most owners of IBM microcomputers today use the MS-DOS OS, so the disks they use will have MS-DOS stored at sector 0, but if one uses a disk that has another OS, say Minix, stored in that portion of the disk, Minix will be loaded and will be the OS used.

This whole process is usually described informally as "booting up the system." Note how it is crucial that the boot loader program be in ROM, so that it is stored permanently, even when the power is off.

Once the OS has been loaded and is running, it performs various initializations and then starts its **command reader** (CR). The CR portion of the OS prints out the '>' prompt, inviting the user to submit a command. When the user does submit a command, say,

```
VI FIB.ASM
```

CR will load VI or whatever other program is requested. (A few of the more simple commands, such as DIR, are actually part of the CR, and those do not have to be loaded.) Here is what will happen in MS-DOS for a general program X.EXE, when we type the command

```
> X
```

1. The OS looks in its disk directory for the location of the file X.EXE on the disk.

2. The OS looks in its memory usage table, to find a currently unused area of memory at which it can load X.EXE.

3. The OS then loads X.EXE at that place, at the same time recording the locations at which it loads the individual segments of X.EXE. The segments will be loaded consecutively and contiguously in whatever order they have in the file X.EXE. As the OS does its loading, it also completes the formation of whatever instructions were only partially specified back at assembly time, such the one on line 33 of Figure 4.4.

Note that the loading location determined in step 2 will depend on the circumstances at the time, i.e., on what other programs happen to be in memory at the time that loading takes place. Thus, each time we run X, it may be loaded into a different memory location. This reinforces the point that completion of the assembly of line 33 in Figure 4.4 must be done by the loader, not by the assembler or the linker.

4. The OS looks in the X.EXE file to determine at what instruction execution should begin, according to the programmer's request. Recall that, for example, in the program FIB.ASM (Program 4.1), the programmer made such a request by including the line

```
END MAIN
```

Upon seeing a similar line in X.ASM, MASM left a note in X.OBJ, which was seen by LINK and passed on in X.EXE, which is where the OS now gets this information.

5. The OS now uses the information from step 4—i.e., the information as to what instruction execution should begin with—together with the information, obtained in step 3, about the memory address of the segment that contains this instruction. Together, these two pieces of information determine what the initial values of CS and IP should be.

However, the OS does not put these values in CS and IP yet. Say, for example, the values of CS and IP are supposed to be 5000 and 0000, respectively. Suppose the OS were to use the instructions

```
MOV AX,5000
MOV CS,AX
```

to load CS. For concreteness, suppose this code starts at offset 1044 of the OS's own code segment, which itself starts at, say, B1140. Then, at the end of step B of the instruction MOV CS,AX, the IP register would contain the value 1044+5 = 1049, since the two MOVs occupy five bytes. During step C , the value in CS would change from B114 to 5000. So in the next step A, the CPU would fetch the instruction at offset 1049 of the code segment starting at 50000. In other words, the program X.EXE would start running! Not only would this be premature—because SS is not yet set to the proper value—but also, we would start running X at the wrong place in X, that is, at offset 1049 instead of at offset 0000. Accordingly, all that is done for now is to *determine* what the initial values of CS and IP should be.

6. From the information recorded during step 3, the OS determines the initial values for SS and SP.

7. The OS is now ready to initiate execution of X. The OS accomplishes this by a long jump (or by another instruction that is similar) to the start of the program, i.e., to the place determined in step 5. The jump instruction's step C (in the A, B, C cycle) of course involves setting CS and IP to the two values that were determined, so at the next step A, the program X will be running! (This way, the values of both CS and IP are set together, avoiding the problem discussed in step 5.)

Now, since only one program at a time can run (if there is only one CPU, which is still the case for most computers today), the OS is *not* running at this time; it is "dead." The only way that the OS will be "revived" is if X voluntarily relinquishes control, using an INT 21H instruction to call an OS service, or if it is forced to give up control, by an external signal sent along a wire leading to the CPU. (This signal is a "cousin" of INT that we will learn about in Chapter 7.)

Note that the CPU is "unaware" that it is now running a different program—i.e., that it has stopped running the OS and started running X; the CPU just "minds its own business," pacing through steps A, B, C, A, B, C, A, etc, and it doesn't "notice" that one of those step C's resulted in a transfer of control from one program (the OS) to another (X). Indeed, the CPU "has no idea" that the OS and X are separate programs anyway; from its point of view, they are both part of one huge program.

8. Eventually, X will finish execution. Then, if, like FIB.ASM, X.ASM includes the code

```
MOV AH,4CH
INT 21H
```

which is a request for the OS's return-to-OS service, then this will be executed, causing a transfer of control back to the OS, and the OS will then print out its '>' prompt, waiting for the user's next command, say, DIR or VI, or whatever command (including X again) the user has at his or her disposal. When the user submits that command, step 1 is initiated again.

Note that if X.ASM does *not* include code such as the foregoing, the CPU will not "complain" at all. On the contrary, it does not "know" that our program is done. The only thing it does "know" is to continually execute its step A, step B, step C, step A, etc., cycle, and that is exactly what it will continue to do. So if, for example, we leave out the preceding MOV and INT instructions at the end of a program, the CPU will simply continue its cycle and execute whatever instructions follow the last instruction of our program. In the case of Program 4.1, this would result in an extra, unwanted execution of DISPBX and, eventually, execution of "garbage" instructions. (See the related discussion on using the G command, but *not* in G n form, in Section 4.1.)

By the way, recall now that DEBUG is a *program*, which runs when you type commands to it. The DEBUG program has its own values in CS and the other registers. Thus, when you use the R command to put, say, 2108 into CS for you, it cannot literally be true that DEBUG obeys this command—for the same reason as we observed in step 5 for the OS. For example, suppose the code segment for DEBUG is at 40CD0. Then if DEBUG were really to obey your command to put 2108 into CS, DEBUG itself would stop running! Your program would be running, but prematurely if you have not yet set IP or the other registers to the values you want. And if you tried to set IP before setting CS, you would force an unwanted jump to some random point in DEBUG, which of course you do not want either!

So how can DEBUG implement commands like R? In fact, the problem is more general than that. Let us consider a general debugging program, which we will call DBG. How can DBG implement a command like R? The answer is to save the values the user requests for CS and IP, for use in a later jump (or similar) instruction when the user submits the G command.

For example, suppose the user asks DBG to put 2108 into CS, 0200 into IP, and 1FA2 into AX. DBG would *not* immediately obey those commands. Instead, it would merely record that they are the wish of the user. Then, when the user types

```
G n
```

DBG could simply put 1FA2 into AX and do a far JMP instruction to 2108:0200.

But what about the 'n' in this case? What would make the CPU return control to DBG when we reach address n? The answer is again quite simple: before acting on the

"G n" command, DBG can replace the user program's instruction at location n by a JMP instruction that jumps to the proper point in DBG! (Other, more advanced methods could be used for this too, but the point is that this simple method will work.)

Again, it is important to keep in mind that DEBUG, the OS, etc., are just ordinary programs. They do not have "magical powers." DEBUG, for example, is not hovering over the CPU, watching the user program run, and then stepping in and halting that program when it reaches address n—that would be impossible, since DEBUG is not even running (nor is any other program) when the user program is running. DEBUG is just an ordinary program with ordinary capabilities, and thus, it relies on ordinary instructions such as JMP (or some equivalent) to transfer control back and forth between it and the user program.

4.4 LOADING AND EXECUTING PROGRAMS DERIVED FROM HLL SOURCES

Let us take a step back from the details presented in Sections 4.1 and 4.2 and pause to recall what their purpose, and that of this chapter as a whole, is—describing solutions to Problems P1–P3:

> P1: How are a program's machine instructions generated?
>
> P2: How are the program's instructions and data loaded into main memory, and the registers initialized properly?
>
> P3: How do we initiate *execution* of the program?

As we have learned, the answer to P1 in the HLL case is that we specify our program in HLL and a special program called a **compiler** generates the machine language from it. But the reader should avoid drawing too close an analogy between assemblers and compilers and between assembly language and HLLs.

True, both assemblers and compilers generate machine code from English-like source files. However, an assembly language for a given machine is tied quite tightly to that machine—it specifies instructions directly in that machine's instruction set—whereas an HLL is *machine independent*. Thus, the same Pascal source file can be compiled on any machine, and of course, the machine language generated from that program on, say, a VAX will be completely different from that generated on an IBM PC.

Furthermore, there is a more subtle difference here. Suppose we compile the same Pascal program on the same IBM PC, once using a Microsoft compiler and once using the Borland Corporation's Turbo compiler. The two machine-language programs thereby produced will both "work," in the sense that they will do what the programmer has asked for in the Pascal source. However, the two machine-language programs will probably be different; they will both consist of instructions from the iAPX set, of course, but they will probably differ in which instructions they use from this set and in which order they execute them. As a result, one of the programs may be more efficient than the other (e.g., one may run faster than the other). By contrast, in assembly language, the programmer specifies which machine instructions he or she wants, so the same instructions will be generated no matter which assembler is used.

We also might get different machine-language programs from the *same* compiler on the *same* machine. Consider the iAPX family, for example. As mentioned in Chapter 2, the newer CPUs in this family are upwardly compatible with the older ones—i.e., programs running on the older models will work on the newer ones, too. But the converse is not necessarily the case, since the newer CPUs include some extra machine instructions not available in the older CPUs. However, to make sure that a program works on *all* iAPX CPUs, a compiler might restrict itself to the "lowest common denominator"—i.e., it might produce machine code that uses only the instruction set available on the oldest CPU in the family. As an example, the Microsoft C compiler does this, generating iAPX 86 machine code as its default, and not using the advanced instructions available in for instance, the iAPX 286 family. If the latter are desired, a special request must be made for them, via the /G2 option in the CL command.

Turning our attention back to problems P1–P3, what happens after code generation in the HLL case? The typical approach is identical to what we saw in Section 4.2. If, for example, we have a Pascal source file Y.PAS, the Pascal compiler will generate machine code and store it in Y.OBJ, just as an assembler will produce X.OBJ from a file X.ASM. We then use LINK, as usual, to produce Y.EXE. (Microsoft Pascal and C allow the link and compile steps to be combined, using the PL and CL commands.)

Furthermore, the situation concerning the locations of variables is the same in the HLL case as for the case of MASM files: variables are assigned only offsets, not full addresses, by the compiler, with the data segment they reside in not being decided until load time.

Note that once we obtain an .EXE file, there really is no way to tell what form the original source file had, i.e., assembly language versus HLL. The instruction 2BC0, for example, will have the *same* function—to subtract AX from itself—regardless of whether the original source file was written in assembly language or in an HLL.

We execute the .EXE file by simply typing

```
> Y
```

When Y finishes execution, it will return control to the OS via

```
MOV AH,4CH
INT 21H
```

(or some equivalent), just as we have done in our assembly-language programs. The only difference is that in the HLL case the compiler puts in the call to DOS, whereas in the assembly-language case we do this ourselves.

ANALYTICAL EXERCISES

1. In Program 4.1, which instructions are guaranteed not to be prefetched even during their first execution? In other words, for which instructions in that program can we be sure that step A

of the fetch/execute cycle will not be skipped? (Be sure not to include pseudo-ops. They are not instructions, and they are not in the executable .EXE file, and thus, it is nonsense to talk about prefetching them.)

2. Consider FIB.ASM in Program 4.1. Suppose I run MASM and LINK and then type FIB to execute my program. The operating system reads FIB.EXE from disk, and my program starts running.

   (a) Assume that the operating system's loader has initialized CS to 3200. What will be the contents of byte 32062 in memory?

   (b) Suppose that before assembling and linking I had made a certain change to *one* line of the file FIB.ASM. Suppose also that at load time the operating system initialized IP to 0019. What line in FIB.ASM did I change, and what was the change? Explain your answer *carefully*.

3. In Program 4.1, which lines are pseudo-ops?

4. Consider the instruction MOV [BX],AX in line 53 of Program 4.1. What will be the values in MAR and MDR at the very end of step C of the third execution of this instruction? Use the c () notation to denote any values that you are unable to find from Figure 4.4.

5. In general, which is the bigger file, X.ASM or X.OBJ? Explain why, using the instruction

       ADD AX, [BX]

   and state the number of bytes corresponding to this instruction in both files.

6. Suppose that parts of a file X.ASM are as follows:

```
X           SEGMENT
A           DB 3 DUP (?)
B           DB 5 DUP (?)
            .
            .
            .
X           ENDS
            .
            .
            .
Y           SEGMENT
            CMP DX,BX
            JZ T
            ADD AX,[BX]
        T:  MOV AX,OFFSET B
            .
            .
            .
Y           ENDS
            .
            .
            .
```

   Suppose we use MASM on this file, then LINK, and type DEBUG X.EXE. Then we type U.

   (a) In the response to the U command, what will be the assembly-language portion of the line corresponding to JZ T?

(b) Answer (a) for the case of T : MOV AX,OFFSET B.

(You should be able to answer these questions without actually running the program on a real machine.)

7. Do some "detective work" and give the first few instructions of the boot loader program on your machine. Use DEBUG to try to change the first instruction to MOV CX,52H. Check to make sure that it did indeed change. What went wrong?

8. In Program 4.1, what is the maximum possible value we can set for N in the EQU pseudo-op and still get meaningful Fibonacci numbers?

9. Suppose that in Program 4.1 each Fibonacci number F_i was stored in one byte of the array FIBNUM instead of one word. What changes would need to be made to the program? Assume that no changes will be made to DISPBX.

10. In Section 4.2.3, it was mentioned that unless the programmer makes special requests to either MASM or LINK, the ordering of the segments in the .EXE file will be the same as the order in which the programmer declared them in the original .ASM file. Verify this by adding code to the beginning of Program 4.1 that will print to the screen, in hex form, the values the loader has chosen for CSG, DSG, and SSG. Verify also that a predictable number of bytes are wasted—e.g., there are seven unused bytes between DSG and SSG.

11. Suppose the segment DSG in Program 4.1 is loaded starting at address 4C080 of memory.

(a) At what addresses will SSG and CSG be loaded?

(b) Suppose the programmer had accidentally written

```
MOV AX,CSG
```

instead of

```
MOV AX,DSG
```

for line 24 of the program. Then, the program would still work, except for a minor malfunction. What aspect of the results will be incorrect? Be very specific in your answer. (Figure 4.4 should be useful here.)

(c) Continue to assume the programming error in (b). If N were to have a large enough value, the program *would* fail. What is the smallest value of N that would make this happen?

12. Consider a data declaration

```
X DW 420CH
```

Give an equivalent declaration for X using DB instead of DW.

13. Suppose we had inadvertently omitted lines 89 and 90 from Program 4.1. What would happen after execution of the last iteration of the loop in lines 78–85? Specifically, what will occur on the monitor screen after the Nth Fibonacci number is printed out?

14. In Program 4.1, suppose the label to be printed at the top of the output were "Fib. numbers:" instead of "Fibonacci numbers."

(a) What hex value would be in the byte at offset 0017H of the data segment?

(b) At what offset would SAVEBX be?

15. In Program 4.1, look at the instruction labeled LP1. In the following questions, do not include the blank characters, or carriage returns or line feeds, even if applicable to a question.

(a) How many bytes will the instruction occupy in FIB.ASM?

(b) How many bytes will the instruction occupy in FIB.OBJ?

(c) How many bytes will the instruction occupy in FIB.LST?

16. In Program 4.1, suppose we were to attempt to change the instruction JNZ LP2 (line 85) to JNZ PRCRLF. Would this be a valid instruction, i.e., one acceptable to the assembler? If so, give the resulting machine code; if not, state very clearly why not.

17. In Program 3.1, suppose we want the program's final action to be to force a reboot of the system. Give machine language code that could be put into offset 000B of this program's code segment to make this occur.

PROGRAMMING PROJECTS

> Note: In all programming projects from this point on, run your programs by typing their names, e.g.,
>
> ```
>     > FIB
> ```
>
> for Program 4.1. Do *not* use DEBUG to run your programs; use it for debugging only.

1. **(a)** Write and test an assembly-language program that will report whether the base-10 number 15,392 is evenly divisible by 7.

   (b) Modify and test your program in (a) so that it will input positive numbers N and K from the keyboard and report whether N is evenly divisible by K. The two numbers will be input in hex form, with no intervening spaces, carriage returns, or other characters, using the procedure READBX from Program 4.2.

2. Write and test an assembly-language program that will write to the screen the cubes, i.e., third powers, of all of the base-10 integers between 1 and 20. The cubes will be written to the screen in hex, using the procedure DISPBX from Program 4.1.

3. Write and test an assembly-language program that will input a single character and report the ASCII code for that character. Use the procedure READCHAR from Program 4.2 to input the character and the procedure DISPBX from that same program to report the ASCII code.

4. Write and test an assembly-language program that will input a base-10 number between 1 and 127 and report the character whose ASCII code is that number. For the unprintable characters (i.e., those with base-10 codes 1–31), display a message which reports that they are unprintable. Use the procedure READBX from Program 4.2 to input the code, in hex form, and DOS services for the output to the screen.

5. Write and test an assembly-language program that will input three numbers X, Y, and Z and report which one is largest. Use the procedure READBX from Program 4.2 to read in these numbers, in hex form, with no intervening spaces, carriage returns, or other characters. Treat all three numbers as unsigned.

6. Write a procedure DISP10 which will display the contents of BX in base 10, to be used in place of the procedure DISPBX in Programs 4.1 and 4.2, which displayed the contents of BX in hex form. Here is an outline:

Since a 16-bit string can code unsigned numbers ranging from 0 to 65,535, the base-10 contents of BX will have as many as five decimal digits, which we will call d_4, d_3, d_2, d_1, and d_0 (from left to right).

Use the following outline to get the d_i:

> Divide BX by 10,000 to get d_4.
> Divide the remainder by 1,000 to get d_3.
> Divide the remainder by 100 to get d_2.
> Divide the remainder by 10 to get d_1.
> The remainder will be d_0.

Use the DIV instruction to do your division, as explained after Program 4.2. For example, to do the first of the foregoing divisions, i.e.,

> Divide BX by 10,000 to get d_4.

you might use the following code:

```
MOV DX,0
MOV AX,BX
MOV CX,10000D
DIV CX
```

To print a digit, first convert the digit from numeric to character form by adding 30H, and then invoke DOS's print-character service, number 21/02, by using the following code:

```
Put the ASCII code of the digit into DL
MOV AH,2
INT 21H
```

Test DISP10 by using it in place of DISPBX in Program 4.1, so that your modified version of that program will still *compute* the same Fibonacci numbers, but will *display* them in base 10 instead of hex. In Program 4.1, just replace line 80 by

```
CALL DISP10
```

and replace lines 110–139 by your DISP10 procedure.

7. Write a procedure READ10 that will read a five-digit base-10 number from the keyboard and store it in BX, just as the procedure READBX did in hex form in Program 4.2. Use the following outline:

```
Put 0 in BX
For i = 1 to 5 do
    Read in a digit, using DOS service number 21/01
    Multiply BX by 10D
    Subtract 30H, to convert the digit from character to numeric form
    Add the digit
```

Test your procedure by using it in Program 4.2 in place of READBX.

8. Program 4.1 consists first of a computation phase, in which it computes all its Fibonacci numbers, and then a separate printing phase, in which it displays all the numbers it has computed. In the meantime, it stores the numbers in an array. Modify the program so that it does not use an array. Instead, it simply maintains variables FI1 and FI2 which store the last two Fibonacci numbers found and updates these two variables each time a new Fibonacci number is calculated. Here is an outline in pseudocode:

```
For i = 3 to N do
   Begin
   Compute the ith number
   Print it out on the screen
   End
```

9. Write an assembly-language procedure CONVERT that will take a signed integer stored in AX in two's-complement form and convert it—if possible—to signed magnitude form (again in AX). Your procedure will also return an error code in BX (1 for an error, meaning that AX contained an unconvertible negative number, and 0 for a nonerror).

Test your procedure by calling it on the following decimal numbers: −29; 200; 0; −32,767; −32,768. Declare these numbers in your data segment as

```
Z DW -29D,200D,0,-32767D,-32768D
```

Use DISPBX from Program 4.1 and OS service number 21/09 to aid in your output.

Here is an outline that you can use:

```
Set BX to 0
For i = 1 to 5 do
  Get the element at Z + c(BX) and put it in AX
  Call CONVERT
  If error then write out error message (using DOS service 21/9)
  Call DISPBX
  Add 2 to BX
```

You can use Program 4.1 as a model for much of the detail, such as how to set up a 'for' loop, and how to do the "get the element" operation. Note that you will also need something similar to Program 4.1's SAVEBX.

(Hints for the code for CONVERT: If the number in AX is found to be negative, first change it to its positive form—say, by subtracting it from a zero value placed in some other register—and then use an ADD instruction with a well-chosen constant.)

10. Suppose we want to implement the following pseudocode:

```
If c(AX) > 0 then set BX to 1
Else if c(AX) = 0 then set BX to 0
Else if c(AX) < 0 then set BX to -1
```

Write an assembly-language procedure to do this and an assembly-language main program to test it.

11. Write an assembly-language program that will act as a "hex calculator," performing addition, subtraction, multiplication and division of numbers entered in hex form and displaying the results in hex. Input is of the form *xxxxyzzzz*, where *xxxx* and *zzzz* are hex constants and *y* is one of +, −, *, and /. Note that in the case of *, the product will consist of eight hex digits, not just four, and in the case of /, both the quotient and remainder should be reported. Make use of the procedures READBX and DISPBX in Program 4.2: call READBX to read *xxxx*, then call DOS service 21/01 to read *y*, then call READBX again to read *zzzz*, and finally, use DISPBX to print out the results.

12. Write an assembly-language program that will report the prime factorization of a user-specified number. For example, the prime factorization of the number 504 is

$$504 = 2^3 \, 3^2 \, 7$$

The program will output one prime factor per line, with '**' denoting exponentiation. For example, if the user inputs 504, the output will be

```
2**3
3**2
7
```

You may want to use Program 4.2 as the foundation for this program, a basis from which you will make modifications.

13. Write a program which, when executed, will force the system to reboot. (To avoid the need for the advanced use of segment declarations, load your program by hand, using DEBUG's A command (a simple assembler).)

CHAPTER

5

Modular Programming: Subprograms, Linkers, and Macros

In the introductory programming courses you took, you probably were taught about **modular** and **top-down** programming, each of which involves breaking a program into a number of essentially self-contained pieces. Typically, the main program should be fairly short, perhaps a page, and should consist in large part of calls to subprograms—**procedures** and **functions** in Pascal, **functions** in C, etc. The goal is to organize one's thinking better during the original programming process and to make future maintenance and revision of the program easier.

The notion of modular programming will also be very important for us here, for several reasons:

- Assembly-language programming can benefit from the top-down approach, just as programming in high-level languages does. In MASM, the term used for subprograms is **procedures**, as seen in Chapter 4. (In assembly languages for non-iAPX machines, the usual term is **subroutine**, sometimes abbreviated to **routine**.)

- In some settings it is convenient, or even necessary, to write our program as a mixture of two or more languages. For instance, we might write most of a program in Pascal or C, but write part of it in assembly language or FORTRAN. Sometimes one of the subtasks that our program must perform has already been written by someone else in a language other than our favorite one. If so, we will write most of our program in our favorite language, but will incorporate the other person's program into ours, again resulting in a mixed-language program.

Mixed-language programs are automatically modular to some degree—e.g., there might be a Pascal module and an assembly-language module, with the machine-language translations of the two modules combined to produce the final program.

- Some frequently used operations are coded into efficient procedures and then stored in files or directories called **libraries**, so that many different programs can make use of them. ("Why reinvent the wheel?") This, too, results in increasing modularization.

- Even if we work purely with a single high-level language, the "look under the hood" theme of this book implies that it is important to know how compilers translate calls to subprograms in high-level languages. For example, it is important to know that the top-down philosophy, though good from the point of view of human efficiency, has a harmful effect on machine efficiency, actually slowing execution speed to some degree.

Knowing how compilers translate calls to subprograms is absolutely crucial to the mixed-language programming approach.

5.1 STACKS

A **stack** is an area in main memory that we use for temporary storage. We introduce the idea here because it will play a central role in procedure calls. The stack we use for this purpose is sometimes called the **run-time stack** and, most often, "the" stack; we will adopt the latter terminology.

The stack can be *any* contiguous block of words in memory, fixed at one end (the **base**) and movable at the other end (the **top**). Just as the CS register points to the beginning of the memory area we are using for code storage, and DS points to the beginning of our data storage area, SS points to the beginning of the memory area we are using for the stack—i.e., it points to the beginning of the stack segment. The stack itself is some subregion of the stack segment.

Similarly, just as the SS register plays a role analogous to CS for the stack segment, the SP register plays a role analogous to IP: SP contains the distance from the beginning of the stack segment to the current top of the stack, in the same way that IP contains the distance from the beginning of the code segment to the current instruction.

The base and top of the stack are defined as follows:

(a) The base is defined to be the address that is the sum of the value in the SS register and the *initial* value of the SP register.

(b) The top is defined to be the address that is the sum of the value in the SS register and the *current* value of the SP register.

(Recall that the word "sum" in these definitions means that before the sum is computed, a zero is appended to the right end of the segment register value.)

For example, suppose we initialize SS to 5000 and SP to 74. Suppose we then **push** the values 57, 4, and 12 onto the stack, in that order. Then the stack would be as shown in Figure 5.1. (Twenty-bit memory addresses appear on the left, their contents in the next column, and comments on the far right.) Also, at this time, c(SP) will be 006E. Note that the stack grows toward 0000; each item that is pushed onto the stack makes c(SP) decrease by two. Note also that there *is* something in 50074, but as far as the stack is concerned, it makes no difference what it is.

```
5006E          12       top
50070          4
50072          57
50074          ____     base (not used for stack storage)
```

Figure 5.1

To remove the top item from the stack, we say that we **pop** the stack. If we pop the stack in Figure 5.1, we get the situation shown in Figure 5.2. At this time, c(SP) will be 0070; it had been 006E, but the pop *added* two to it, just as a push *subtracts* two. Note that the value 12, which had been at the top of the stack before, is still there—i.e., c(5006E) is still 0012—but this item is no longer considered to be part of the stack.

```
50070     4     top

50072     57

50074     ...
```

Figure 5.2

iAPX CPUs, and most other modern CPUs, include instructions and addressing modes that make the push and pop operations more efficient. For example, suppose we wish to push the value 22H onto the stack. There are both primitive ways and advanced ways to do this. We will usually use the advanced way, but a discussion of the primitive way will help deepen our understanding of stack operations.

The primitive way of pushing a value onto the stack is illustrated in Program 5.1. Here, the BP register is used for what appears to be indirect addressing, just as BX was used in the examples in Chapters 3 and 4. However, things are a bit different for BP.

```
SUB SP,2;     update the stack pointer for the new top
MOV BP,SP;    copy SP to BP
MOV WORD PTR [BP],22H;    push 22H
```

Program 5.1

Indirect addressing on iAPX machines is limited to specifying operands in the data segment (unless one uses a **segment override**, to be discussed in Chapter 6). We, however, are discussing operands that are in the stack segment, not the data segment. Thus, instead of using indirect addressing mode, we use **based addressing mode**, which was also mentioned in Chapter 4 in the context of operands in the data segment. Based addressing mode in the stack segment uses the BP register. In other words, the circuitry of the CPU is set up so that the use of BX in based addressing will be interpreted as an offset in the data segment, while in the case of BP, the offset is taken to be in the stack segment.

Recall that in indirect addressing mode, the register contains the segment offset of the operand. In based addressing mode, this offset is determined by adding the register contents to a constant specified in the instruction.

For example, in Program 4.1, there was an instruction

```
MOV AX, [BX-4]
```

The constant in this case is -4. The offset of the operand is then $c(BX) - 4$, and since BX is being used, this offset is interpreted as an offset in the data segment. Thus, the actual address of the operand is $16 * c(DS) + c(BX) - 4$.

In Program 5.1, there is an instruction

```
MOV WORD PTR [BP],22H
```

The constant x in the form $[BP \pm x]$ here seems to be missing, but it is zero, and the assembler allows us to write nothing in this case. The offset of the operand is then $c(BP) + 0$, and since BP is involved, this is an offset in the stack segment. The full operand address is thus $16 * c(SS) + c(BP) + 0$.

Since BP is the *only* register that can be used for based addressing within the stack segment, we cannot write the foregoing code as shown in Program 5.2. There is a much easier option, using a special iAPX instruction whose MASM mnemonic is PUSH. Program 5.3 shows how to use this instruction in the preceding context.

```
SUB SP,2
MOV WORD PTR [SP],22H
```

Program 5.2

```
MOV AX,22H
PUSH AX
```

Program 5.3

Note that PUSH is an instruction, just as ADD, JMP, CALL, etc., are instructions. It has an op code (01010 in the format in which the operand is a register) and goes through the step A–step B–step C sequence just as any instruction does. Even though PUSH combines the *actions* of a SUB and two MOVs (compare Programs 5.1 and 5.3), you should not think of PUSH as "consisting of several instructions." PUSH is an instruction in its own right. It can be used in register mode, as we have done here, and in most other addressing modes, except for immediate mode.

Program 5.3 is not only easier to program and clearer to read than Program 5.1, but equally importantly, it is more efficient:

- It is time efficient, since only two instructions must be fetched and decoded, rather than three.
- It is space efficient: its two instructions take up a total of 4 bytes in memory, while the three instructions of Program 5.1 take up 10 bytes.

There is also a POP instruction. Be careful of its syntax, though. For example, consider the instruction

```
POP BX
```

The syntax makes it look like the BX register is the object that is getting "popped." That is not true. What is getting popped is the *stack*, not BX. BX is merely the place where we put the value that gets popped off the stack.

Since the stack is part of memory, you should allocate space for it, using a special segment declaration, such as

```
X       SEGMENT STACK
        DB 100 DUP (?)
X       ENDS
```

We do not need to initialize SS and SP in our program, since the operating system will do so for us, as mentioned in Chapter 4. SS will be automatically initialized to whatever address in memory the segment X has been assigned by the loader, and SP will be initialized to the end of X. For instance, the initial contents of SP in the segment X above will be 100H = 256D.

Note that this automatic initialization means that we must be sure that the height of the stack in bytes (that is, twice the excess of PUSHes over POPs) will not at any time during the execution of our program get any larger than 256. Otherwise, the stack could extend into areas of memory that are being used for something else, since the loader will allocate contiguous memory areas for the various segments of a program.

In order to illustrate this and several other concepts, suppose the error in the preceding paragraph does occur. Suppose the segment X is followed in the .ASM source file by several large segments Y, Z, and so on. Then, if the excess of pushes over pops ever reaches 128, c(SP) will at that time have the value 0000, having started at 256D but having been decremented by two 128 times. If there is then another push, c(SP) will be decremented by two once again, yielding FFFE. In other words, SP will be pointing to the spot FFFEH = 65,534 bytes past the beginning of X. If the segment Y is large enough, SP will be pointing to a place in Y! And if not Y, then it will be pointing to a place in Z or to something past Z, again depending on the sizes of Y and Z. So pushing something onto the "stack" here may actually destroy some item in Y or Z, or in a segment that follows them. If we are lucky, the word written to will be in some unused part of memory, but clearly, it need not be.

Note that the hardware, at least if it is in the iAPX 86 subfamily, is not watching out for such a disaster. If the stack exceeds its boundaries in this manner, the CPU will simply continue to execute instructions, "unaware" of the problem. Thus, the *software* must check for this situation and react to it. This means that in programming in assembly language, the programmer must include code such as

```
CMP SP,0
```

if there is any chance of such an event occurring. If, instead, we are programming in a high-level language, the compiler must include such code. Either way, the software has the responsibility here, since the hardware does not do these kinds of checks. We will see that CPUs in the iAPX 286/386/486 subfamilies do include hardware that performs the appropriate checks, if the CPU is running in **protected mode**. However, even for these machines, the software must take advantage of the hardware, by including machine instructions that will move the CPU into protected mode. The MS-DOS operating system does not do this. So even if you have a 286/386/486 machine, if you are using MS-DOS, then these hardware checks are not being done. (And if you have a CPU from the more primitive iAPX 86 family, which does not include such hardware, those hardware checks *cannot* be done.)

From Chapter 3, we do need to mention SS in an ASSUME pseudo-op:

```
ASSUME SS:X,...
```

In the next section, we will see the primary motivation for discussing stacks in this chapter: procedure calls. But before moving to that topic, it should be mentioned that another common use of the stack is as a temporary storage place.

5.2 PROCEDURES

Suppose we have a main program M that will call a procedure S. Both M and S are in memory, of course; for simplicity, let us assume for now that M and S are both in the same code segment.

Let us denote by C the point within M at which S is called. The idea is that at C, we will do a JMP (or something similar) to wherever in memory S starts and thus execute S. The last instruction of S will be another JMP, so that we will come back to point C or, speaking more precisely, come back to D, the instruction following C. We then resume execution of M.

It is crucial to note that S must have some way of knowing where D is, so that the JMP back from S can be done. One way of achieving this would be to save the necessary information, called the **return address**, on the stack, as is done in Program 5.4.

```
C:      MOV AX, OFFSET D    ; load address (offset within code seg) of D to AX
        PUSH AX        ; address of D is now on stack
        JMP S          ; JMP to procedure S
D:      ...            ;  instruction that follows the call
        ...                   .
        ...                   .
        ...                   .
S:                     ; start of S
        ...            ; body of S (maybe many instructions)
        POP AX         ; pop saved return address (D) back to AX
        JMP AX         ; JMP to the address pointed to by AX, i.e., back to D
```

Program 5.4

Incidentally, the reader might wonder why we do not simply arrange the return from S with the code

```
JMP D
```

instead of

```
MOV AX,OFFSET D
PUSH AX
```

in M and

```
POP AX
JMP AX
```

in S. That would work fine, but it would be far too restrictive: we might want to call S from *several* different points in our program, not just from C. Thus, we indicate the return address via a stack entry instead.

Note that the saving of return addresses on the stack in this manner is perfect for procedure calls, due to the stack's **last-in, first-out** (LIFO) property. In a sequence of **nested** procedure calls (e.g., M calls S, S in turn calls T, etc.), the last return address pushed onto the stack is the first one we want to pop.

Thus, saving a return address on the stack is a good idea. However, there is a better way to do this than the one used above in Program 5.4. Just as there is a primitive way and an advanced way to do pushing and popping, there is also a primitive way and an advanced way to do procedure calls. The more advanced (and more efficient) way of saving a return address on the stack inheres in the fact that the iAPX instruction set, as well as those of most other CPU families, includes a CALL instruction. Accordingly, we could write

```
CALL S
```

instead of

```
C:        MOV AX, OFFSET D
          PUSH AX
          JMP  S
```

in Program 5.4. Then, when CALL S is executed, it will perform the following two operations:

(i) Save the return address on the stack—i.e., it will push the code segment offset value of the instruction following the call, in this case the offset of D.

(ii) Jump to S.

As was the case with PUSH, the CALL instruction is more efficient than the set of several more primitive instructions that it replaces, both in terms of execution time and memory space. It is also clearer than those instructions.

Thus, the code in Program 5.4 would be

```
C:   CALL S
D:   ...
```

Again, CALL S will save the return address—i.e., the offset of D—on the stack. This is easy to accomplish: by the time step C of the CALL instruction starts, c(IP) has already been incremented to point to the next instruction, i.e., the one at D. Thus, the CALL instruction simply saves the *current* value of IP on the stack.

Similarly, there is an easier way to return from S back to M (to D) than by using POP and JMP: the RET ("return") instruction. RET will pop the previously saved IP value off the stack and put it into the IP—so we jump back to D, as desired. Again, this is more efficient and clearer than the primitive instructions it is intended to replace.

A more concrete example of the use of CALL and RET is in Program 4.1. In Figure 4.4, the .LST file for that program, the call to DISPBX is on line 89, and the DISPBX procedure itself starts on line 119 (actually on line 128, since lines 119–127 are just pseudo-ops and comments). Think about what happens in step C of the CALL instruction. First, the current IP value—which is 0042, having been incremented from 003F during steps A and B—is pushed onto the stack. Then a jump is made to offset 0060, i.e., line 128, so that DISPBX will start execution. Eventually, DISPBX will reach line 147 and execute the RET instruction. Step C of that instruction will simply pop the stack and place the popped value into the IP register. Since the CALL had pushed the value 0042 onto the stack earlier, the RET will pop that value back off the stack. And since the register into which RET places that popped value is IP, the result is that IP will contain 0042. Then step C ends and step A starts. Since c(IP) is now 0042, the new step A will fetch the instruction from line 90–which is precisely what we want; i.e., we will resume execution of MAIN at the point immediately after the CALL instruction.

Note that in effecting the jump to S, the CALL instruction will put the address of S into the IP. But what if CS must be changed, too—i.e., what if S is in a different segment of memory than M? Actually, this situation can be handled easily, because there are really two kinds of CALL instructions. They both use the assembly-language mnemonic CALL, but they differ in their machine codes:

(a) The ordinary kind of CALL, just described, is known as a **near** call. The first byte of its machine code is its op code, E8. Its second and third bytes contain the distance in bytes from the CALL to S.

Execution of this kind of CALL will first push the current value of IP onto the stack, for return purposes, as described. Then the jump to S is accomplished by adding to the IP the 16-bit value contained in the second and third bytes of the instruction. Since the assembler, at assembly time, had originally set these two bytes to be the distance between the current IP and the offset value for S, the addition will result in the new IP value's being the offset for S—i.e., we will jump to S, as desired.

(b) The second kind of CALL is known as a **far** call. Its first byte is 9A. Since S is allowed to be in a different segment in this case, we must specify S by both an IP value and a CS value. Thus, the second and third bytes of the machine code for this kind of CALL instruction will contain the offset value for S, and the fourth and fifth bytes will contain the CS value for S.

Execution of this kind of CALL will first result in pushing the current CS value, and then the current IP value, onto the stack; since we are jumping to a different segment, *both* of these values are needed to specify the proper return point. Then the second and third bytes of the instruction will be copied to IP, and the fourth and fifth bytes will be copied to CS; i.e., we will jump to S.

Even though the mnemonic for both instructions is the same, the assembler will "know" whether to produce machine code E8*xxxx* or 9A*xxxxyyyy*. The way it "knows" is that it looks at the declaration of S in the source code file; i.e., it checks whether you have declared S as

```
S     PROC NEAR
```

or

```
S     PROC FAR
```

In the former case, the assembler will translate a CALL instruction to E8*xxxx*, i.e., code for a near call, while in the latter case it will produce a far call, with code of the form

9A*xxxxyyyy*. If you omit the keyword NEAR or FAR, the assembler will use a default of NEAR, as long as the called procedure is in the same segment as the call.

Once again, let us use the call to DISPBX in Program 4.1 to illustrate the difference between near and far calls. Figures 4.6 and 4.8 are DEBUG/SYMDEB output from that program. The call to DISPBX has the machine code E81E00. Let us see whether that makes sense. The first byte, E8, is the op code for a near call, so that's fine. The second and third bytes, 1E and 00, then indicate that the distance from the instruction following the call to DISPBX is 001E. (There is a "little-endian" byte reversal.) Let us verify this. The instruction following the call is at offset 003F + 3 = 0042, since the call is a three-byte instruction. Then, computing 0042 + 001E, we get 0060, which indeed is the location of DISPBX, as seen in line 119 of Figure 4.4. (On the other hand, line 89 of that figure shows the "machine code" to be E8 0060, which is incorrect, since it shows the location of the called procedure instead of the distance to that procedure. The designers of the .LST file wrote the file that way so that it would be easier to read.)

Clearly, a near call is more efficient. It has faster execution, since it pushes only one item onto the stack instead of two and takes up less memory, three bytes instead of five. On the other hand, if S is too far away from C—i.e., more than 64K bytes away—then we will be forced to use a far call. If we do try a near call and the procedure is too far away, then MASM or LINK will let us know, at assembly time or link time.

A similar situation obtains for RET. The "near" RET, which is the one we have described, has the machine code C3, while the "far" RET has the code CB. The far RET will pop the stack, into IP, and then pop the stack *again*, into CS. The assembler will know whether to produce C3 or CB by looking at the declaration of the procedure S. (Actually, even if such information is absent, the programmer can force things by using CALLF and RETF to indicate a far call and far return, respectively.)

Note that the pushing and popping and the jumping back and forth involved in procedure calls makes the program run a little slower. So in terms of *machine* efficiency, procedures are detrimental. However, their role in helping to clarify the human thought process, as embodied in the philosophy of top-down design, is quite beneficial in terms of *human* efficiency. Thus, except in programs or program sections in which execution speed is crucial, the use of procedures is on the whole beneficial.

Recall now that subprograms in high-level languages typically have **parameters**. (An alternative term is **arguments**.) For example, suppose we are writing a subprogram to sort an array of integers. Then there would be two parameters: one to indicate which array is to be sorted and another that specifies how many numbers are to be sorted.

In Pascal, the declaration of such a subprogram might be

```
procedure Sort(var X : ArrayType; N : integer);
```

and a call to the subprogram might look like

```
Sort(Y,M);
```

Here, the **actual parameters** Y and M listed in the call will play the roles of the **formal parameters** X and N in the procedure declaration.

When a compiler encounters a subprogram call in a high-level language program, such as the preceding call, the compiler will produce the machine-language equivalent of

```
CALL SORT
```

But what will the compiler do with the parameter portion of the call, e.g., the Y and M in the foregoing example? Phrased in the terminology commonly used in the computer industry, how can a calling program **pass** the parameters to the called subprogram? And of course, we also will want to know how parameter passing should be done if one is programming in assembly language directly.

As an example, let us adapt Program 3.1 into a procedure, whose name will be SUM. Recall that this program finds the sum of the contents of the individual words in a range of memory. The new procedure's parameters are the starting location of the array and the ending location. (The reader might wish to review Program 3.1 before proceeding further.)

In our first subexample, we will pass the parameters in registers. Specifically, we will write the code in SUM under the assumption that the calling module will, before the CALL SUM instruction, put the values of the parameters in registers, with c(BX) equal to the array starting location and c(CX) equal to the array ending location. (We use CX instead of DX for the latter, just for the sake of variety.) Program 5.5 shows the desired code. (Keep in mind that the first and last lines are pseudo-ops.)

```
SUM      PROC NEAR
         SUB AX,AX
TOP  :   ADD AX,[BX]
         ADD BX,2
         CMP CX,BX
         JNS TOP
         RET
SUM      ENDP
```

Program 5.5

The calling module would *prepare* BX and CX prior to the CALL SUM, as follows. Suppose that in this particular call to SUM, we want to sum the 10 words beginning at the location Z. Then the call would be as shown in Program 5.6.

```
MOV BX,OFFSET Z
MOV CX,OFFSET Z+12H
CALL SUM
```

Program 5.6

Note that Program 5.6 is not a complete program; only the lines near the call are shown. Of course, Z would be an array defined in the data segment. (The reader should verify that Z+12H is indeed the 10th word of the array, where Z+0 is the first word, Z+2 is the second, and so on.)

If one person writes SUM and a different person writes the calling module—as is often the case in practice—then the one who writes SUM must tell the one who writes the calling program how the parameters will be passed—e.g., in BX and CX, as in the preceding example, or on the stack, as in the examples that follow.

Another example of passing parameters in registers is DOS service number 21/02 in Program 4.1, which prints a character to the screen. Though DOS services are invoked using the INT instruction instead of the CALL instruction, you will see in Chapter 8 that INT is very close to CALL, and the DOS services *are* procedures. DOS service number 21 is a group of services, so one parameter in the call is the subservice number, 02 in Program 4.1. The code for DOS service number 21 has been written to look for this parameter in the AH register, and subservice number 02 looks for the second parameter, the character to be printed to the screen, in the DL register. The reader should verify this usage in the calls to service number 21/02 from within the procedure DISPBX in Program 4.1.

Using registers to pass parameters is fine if we have a small number of parameters. If we have more, then we must put them in some area of memory instead, especially since iAPX CPUs have only a few registers. Often, the most convenient way to do this is to use the stack (which, recall, *is* part of memory). This approach is shown in Program 5.7. As we have occasionally seen in earlier programs, we are constrained a little here by limitations on what operations and operands can be used together. We would like to have an instruction, say,

```
PUSH OFFSET Z
```

but unfortunately, the PUSH instruction does not allow the use of the immediate addressing mode. (The immediate constant would be OFFSET Z.) Thus, we have to use the MOV and PUSH together.

```
MOV AX,OFFSET Z
PUSH AX
MOV AX,OFFSET Z+12H
PUSH AX
CALL SUM
```

Program 5.7

Now, to see how SUM must be written in this case, we first must look at the state of the stack that will occur upon entry to SUM, i.e., at the very end of step C for the CALL instruction. This is shown in Table 5.1. In examining the table, keep in mind "who did what." The two parameters (the beginning and ending offsets of the memory block to be summed) were pushed onto the stack as a result of the two PUSH instructions. The return IP value was pushed as one of the operations performed by the CALL instruction. Program 5.8 shows what SUM might look like, written with Table 5.1 in mind.

TABLE 5.1

top	return IP value
top + 2	2nd parameter
top + 4	1st parameter

```
SUM     PROC NEAR
        SUB AX,AX
        MOV BP,SP;
        MOV BX,[BP+4];          copy start address to BX
        MOV CX,[BP+2];          copy end address
TOP :   ADD AX,[BX]
        ADD BX,2
        CMP CX,BX
        JNS TOP
        RET
SUM     ENDP
```

Program 5.8

The reader should study Programs 5.7 and 5.8 and Table 5.1 with the utmost care before moving on to more complex cases. Understanding the structure of the stack during a procedure call is absolutely vital: if even one item is not set up correctly, the program will fail! Again, as mentioned at the beginning of this chapter, procedure calls play a major role in almost all real-world applications, so extra time devoted to understanding stack structures will be well spent indeed.

Next, we turn to the question of linking the .OBJ files coming from several different source files. A very common situation is that in which the calling program and the subprogram are developed separately, in separate source files. For instance, our calling program may consist of a single procedure MAIN, consisting partially of the code in Program 5.7, in a file M.ASM. Our subprogram SUM may be in a file S.ASM. In that case, they are assembled separately, producing, e.g., M.OBJ and S.OBJ, and then LINKed together to form the executable .EXE file. There are two main reasons why this situation is common:

(a) Suppose we have already developed and debugged SUM, but we are not finished debugging MAIN. In our debugging process, we will have to use the MASM command many times, which is time consuming, especially with real-world programs that might be hundreds or even thousands of lines long. We can make things a little less time consuming by using MASM on MAIN alone, not on MAIN and SUM together; that way, MASM will have to do less work each time we use it. The point is that SUM is already debugged, so why keep wasting time repeatedly re-assembling it?

(b) Either MAIN or SUM might be written in a high-level language. For instance, we might write MAIN as a Pascal program, say, in a file M.PAS, and write SUM in assembly language, in a file S.ASM. As mentioned in the introduction to the text, this is a common situation, combining "the best of both worlds": we write *most* of the program in a high-level language, for convenience, but write certain crucial portions of the program in assembly language, for extra efficiency. In such mixed-language situations, there is an automatic separation into modules—here, M.PAS and S.ASM.

With multifile programs, certain modifications are needed to link the .OBJ files. To see what these modifications are, let us see what the whole program would look like if we did *not* have MAIN and SUM in different files. Then we would have only one source file, say W.ASM, which would be as shown in Program 5.9. Note that we have chosen to use the "stack method" for parameter passing here, but could have used the "register method" instead.

```
SSG     SEGMENT STACK
        DB 100 DUP (?)
SSG     ENDS

DSG     SEGMENT
        Z       DB 100 DUP (?)
DSG     ENDS

CSG     SEGMENT

MAIN    PROC FAR
        ASSUME SS:SSG,CS:CSG,DS:DSG
        MOV AX,DSG
        MOV DS,AX
        misc. code here, e.g., that stores stuff in Z
        MOV AX,OFFSET Z
        PUSH AX
        MOV AX,OFFSET Z+12H;   2*10-2 = 18 = 12H
        PUSH AX
        CALL SUM
        more misc. code here, e.g., using the results of call to SUM
        MOV AH,4CH
        INT 21H
```

```
MAIN      ENDP

SUM       PROC NEAR
          SUB AX,AX
          MOV BP,SP
          MOV BX,[BP+4]
          MOV CX,[BP+2]
TOP :     ADD AX,[BX]
          ADD BX,2
          CMP CX,BX
          JNS TOP
          RET
SUM       ENDP

CSG       ENDS


END MAIN
```

Program 5.9

On the other hand, suppose we put the main program and SUM in separate files M.ASM and S.ASM. Program 5.10 shows what we would need in M.ASM. Observe that in the first line of the file, we have EXTRN SUM : FAR. This is a pseudo-op that warns the assembler that SUM will be in another source file, so that when the assembler sees CALL SUM but no SUM procedure in this source file, it won't "panic." The line with EXTRN says that SUM will be defined externally, i.e., in another file. When the assembler produces the machine code file M.OBJ, it will also leave a "memo" to LINK in M.OBJ, saying that M.OBJ contains a yet-to-be-resolved reference to SUM.

```
          EXTRN SUM : FAR
SSG       SEGMENT STACK
          DB 100 DUP (?)
SSG       ENDS
DSG       SEGMENT
Z         DB 100 DUP (?)
DSG       ENDS
CSG       SEGMENT
MAIN      PROC FAR
          ASSUME SS:SSG,CS:CSG,DS:DSG
          MOV AX,DSG
          MOV DS,AX
          misc. code here, e.g., that stores stuff in Z
          MOV AX,OFFSET Z
          PUSH AX
          MOV AX,OFFSET Z+12H;  2*10-2 = 18 = 12H
          PUSH AX
          CALL SUM
          more misc. code, e.g., using the results of call to SUM
```

```
            MOV AH,4CH
            INT 21H
MAIN        ENDP
CSG         ENDS
            END MAIN
```

Program 5.10

Meanwhile, the assembler only partially assembles the line CALL SUM, just as the line

```
MOV AX,DSG
```

was only partially assembled in line 33 of FIB.LST in Figure 4.4. Since we have stated in the line with EXTRN that SUM will need a far call, the code produced by MASM will be 9A--------. (Review the material on the instruction format for far calls.) The -------- will be filled in later, once the offset and segment values for SUM become known.

Program 5.11 shows the contents of the other file, S.ASM. We have called the code segment in S.ASM SUMCSG in order to avoid confusion with the code segment CSG in M.ASM. However, this distinction is not required.

```
            PUBLIC SUM
SUMCSG      SEGMENT
            ASSUME CS:SUMCSG
SUM         PROC FAR
            SUB AX,AX
            MOV BP,SP
            MOV BX,[BP+6]
            MOV CX,[BP+4]
TOP :       ADD AX,[BX]
            ADD BX,2
            CMP CX,BX
            JNS TOP
            RET
SUM         ENDP
SUMCSG      ENDS
            END
```

Program 5.11

The line PUBLIC SUM at the top of the file has another pseudo-op, PUBLIC, and is the counterpart of the line with EXTRN in the other file. As we saw in Section 4.2.4, PUBLIC tells MASM not to discard the specified symbols at the end of the assembly process. Thus, MASM will respond to the line PUBLIC SUM in S.ASM by including a note in S.OBJ to the effect that offset 0000 in the segment SUMCSG is named SUM. (It is offset 0000 because it is the first line in S.ASM; if in doubt, remember that you can confirm the offset by looking at S.LST.) Without the pseudo-op PUBLIC, this information would *not* be recorded and the name SUM would be thrown away.

At link time, LINK will see a "memo" in M.OBJ saying that the line CALL SUM was not fully assembled, due to a lack of knowledge of the location of SUM, and LINK will also see a "memo" in S.OBJ saying that SUM is offset 0000 in that file. The first memo is reporting a problem, but the second memo is providing the information on how to solve that problem. LINK will thereupon go ahead and resolve the problem. However, as you will see shortly, LINK can only achieve a partial resolution.

Incidentally, the line

```
SUM PROC FAR
```

indicates that the procedure SUM will be called using a far CALL, so the assembler, in assembling the RET instruction, will produce machine code for a **far** RET. The reader should confirm this by assembling Program 5.11 and looking at the .LST file.

To use the LINK option in this setting, we enter

```
> LINK /LI /MAP /CO M S,M,M;
```

(Omit the /CO option if you do not use CodeView.) This is essentially the same as what we had in Chapter 4, except that now two symbols, M and S, appear in front of the first comma. This means that we will have two .OBJ files, M.OBJ and S.OBJ, which we are asking LINK to combine into one executable file. That latter file will be named M.EXE. To execute M.EXE, we simply type

```
> M
```

as before.

As mentioned earlier, at assembly time, MASM produces the partially assembled instruction 9A--------, with the -------- to be filled in by the offset and segment values of SUM. Now, at link time, LINK knows the offset value: SUM is at offset 0000 of the code segment SUMCSG in S.OBJ. However, LINK does not know where this segment will be loaded at load time. Thus, all LINK can do is fill in a little more of the partially assembled instruction. Accordingly, what was 9A-------- in M.OBJ will now be 9A0000---- in M.EXE. The remaining part of the instruction will not be filled in until load time, when the loader knows where in memory it will load the code segment SUMCSG.

With the changing of SUM into a **far** procedure, MASM will translate CALLs to SUM as **far** calls, and Table 5.1 will change. With the **far** version of SUM, the state of the stack upon entry to SUM will be as shown in Table 5.2. In accordance with that table, the references [BP+4] and [BP+2] in Program 5.9 are replaced by [BP+6] and [BP+4] in Program 5.11.

TABLE 5.2

top	return IP value
top + 2	return CS value
top + 4	2nd parameter
top + 6	1st parameter

Note the END in the very last line of S.ASM in Program 5.11, compared to the line

```
END MAIN
```

in M.ASM. Recall that an END line does two things, not one. First, it lets the assembler know that it is the last line of the file. Second, it lets the assembler (which passes the information on to LINK, etc.) know at what point in the program we wish to begin execution, in this case at the line labeled MAIN. Obviously, there can be only one such **entry point** in a program, so LINK requires that only one file can have a line of the form

```
END x
```

All other END lines must consist of the keyword END alone.

Although it would not really matter in this particular example, it is good practice to "clean up" the stack—that is, remove the two parameters from the stack—when a procedure finishes execution. For example, after the line

```
CALL SUM
```

in Program 5.10, we should do something like either

```
POP CX
POP CX
```

or, better,

```
ADD SP,4
```

in order to remove the parameters from the stack. (Again, keep in mind that the values are not "removed" from memory; we are merely removing them from the *stack*, by moving the SP away from that area of memory.)

Why should we "clean up" the stack? Well, again, in this program it will not make any difference, but if we had a program that had a very large number of procedure calls, the stack would continue to grow with these "leftover" parameters after each call. If the stack grew to the point at which it filled our entire stack segment, problems would arise, as discussed at the end of Section 5.1.

Worse yet, suppose the procedure SUM itself calls a procedure, say, GY, with, say, three parameters. In other words, suppose SUM were to include the lines

```
MOV AX,1st parameter
PUSH AX
MOV AX,2nd parameter
PUSH AX
MOV AX,3rd parameter
PUSH AX
CALL GY
```

Then just before the RET instruction within GY, the stack would appear as shown in Table 5.3, assuming that the call from SUM to GY was of type **near**.

TABLE 5.3

top	SUM's return IP value
top + 2	GY's 3rd parameter
top + 4	GY's 2nd parameter
top + 6	GY's 1st parameter
top + 8	MAIN's return IP value
top + A	MAIN's return CS value
top + C	SUM's 2nd parameter
top + E	SUM's 1st parameter

After GY executed the RET, the stack would appear as shown in Table 5.4. Subsequently, when SUM executed *its* RET, the CPU would pop the top two (since it is a **far** RET) elements of the stack, placing them into IP and CS. Thus, IP and CS would contain two of the parameters SUM had sent to GY—meaningless "garbage," since what we *want* in IP and CS are the offset and code segment values for the return point in MAIN. This would be a disaster: we wouldn't return to MAIN, but would be executing "code" at some random place in memory.

TABLE 5.4

top	GY's 3rd parameter
top + 2	GY's 2nd parameter
top + 4	GY's 1st parameter
top + 6	MAIN's return IP value
top + 8	MAIN's return CS value
top + A	SUM's 2nd parameter
top + C	SUM's 1st parameter

Consequently, we would *have to* clean up the stack after the call to GY in SUM. Here is what the code surrounding the call to GY would be:

```
MOV AX,1st parameter
PUSH AX
MOV AX,2nd parameter
PUSH AX
MOV AX,3rd parameter
PUSH AX
CALL GY
ADD SP,6
```

Another "good practice" along the lines of cleaning up the stack after a procedure call is to minimize **side effects** that result from such calls. The procedure SUM in Program 5.11, for example, makes changes to the registers AX, BX, CX, and BP. If the calling program, at the point of the call to SUM, has values in any of these registers that it will use after the return from SUM, the calling program would have to save those values. For example, the calling program could save and restore BP's value before and after the call to SUM, with, say, a PUSH before the call and then a POP after the call.

But it would be much nicer to deal with the problem within SUM itself. That way, the procedure would be self-contained, and the writer of the main program (if different from that of the procedure, again a very common situation in the real world) would not have to be burdened by saving and restoring any values that might be changed by SUM.

Recall that the DOS services are essentially procedures, called with an INT 21H instruction. Fortunately, almost all of them follow the practice of the last paragraph. Thus, the user need not worry about saving register values before a DOS call (see Section 8.1).

Almost all modern CPUs—VAX, Motorola 68000 family, and so on—implement procedure calls in the manner we have described here for the iAPX family: a stack is maintained, return addresses are saved there by CALL instructions, and return addresses are popped off by RET instructions. The only differences between iAPX and the other machines in this regard are those due to the segment-plus-offset nature of iAPX address formation: whereas the stack in iAPX machines is pointed to jointly by SS and SP, in non-iAPX machines there is only SP; and whereas iAPX machines must have two types of CALL and RET instructions, one NEAR and the other FAR, non-iAPX machines have only one type.

5.3 MACHINE-LEVEL ASPECTS OF PROCEDURES IN HIGH-LEVEL LANGUAGES

As mentioned earlier, a multilingual program may reside in several, separate files. This setting will be the central focus of Section 5.3.2, but we will need as preparation the more general material in Section 5.3.1.

5.3.1 What the Compiler Produces from HLL Procedure Calls

Program 5.12 is a program written entirely in Pascal. Let us see how the compiler translates this program's procedure calls. The program does very little, but its simplicity will be a virtue in introducing some important concepts.

```
program Td(input,output);

   var V,W :integer;

   procedure Trade(var X,Y : integer);
      var Temp : integer;
   begin
      Temp:=X;
      X:=Y;
      Y:=Temp
   end;

begin
   V:=12;   W:=15;
   Trade(V,W);
   writeln(V,W)
end.
```

Program 5.12

The central part of the program is a procedure, Trade, which exchanges the values of its two parameter variables. The main program sets up these variables, calls the procedure, and prints out the results.

Note that in the declaration of Trade, the two formal parameters are declared with the keyword **var**, which is the Pascal manner for specifying that parameters are of the **call-by-reference** type. Without the keyword **var**, the parameters would be of the **call-by-value** type.

In Pascal, one should declare parameters to be of call-by-reference type if the subprogram is going to change the values of the parameters back in the calling program. This is the case in Program 5.12, of course, since both V and W will be changed during the execution of Trade. Even in cases in which a parameter is not changed, it might be more efficient to make it a call-by-reference parameter anyway. Now, let us take a "look under the hood" to see why call-by-reference parameters are necessary or desirable in these settings.

The key difference between call-by-reference and call-by-value parameters is in the machine code produced by a Pascal compiler. The compiler passes call-by-reference parameters in the form of the *address* of the variable and passes call-by-value parameters in the form of the *value* of the variable.

To make this distinction concrete, let us look at the code produced from Program 5.12 by the Microsoft Pascal compiler. Suppose the source file is named T.PAS. Then the first command we type is

```
> PAS1 T,T,T,T
```

This command says that we wish to produce a machine code file T.OBJ, a list file T.LST, and a file T.COD, which we will explain momentarily.

Next, we type

```
> PAS2
```

and then

```
> PAS3
```

At this point, the production of the files T.OBJ, T.LST, and T.COD is complete. Finally, we employ LINK in the form

```
> LINK /LI /MAP /CO T,T,T;
```

which produces the executable file T.EXE and the map file T.MAP. If your directory path is not set up to search for the Pascal **library** (which contains various Pascal built-in procedures, e.g., **sqrt**), the linker will tell you which ones you are missing. Then you must insert them, too:

```
> LINK /LI /MAP /CO T,T,T,library file name(s);
```

If you need several library files, separate them with spaces and do not forget to include the drive name, e.g.,

```
> LINK /LI /MAP /CO T,T,T,C:\LIB\LIBPAS7.LIB;
```

Again, we could do the same thing with a batch file, say, PC.BAT:

```
PAS1 %1,%1,%1,%1
PAS2
PAS3
LINK /LI /MAP /CO %1,%1,%1;
```

We would then type PC T and could type PC with other file names for other programs. This approach would save us a lot of typing if we compile many different Pascal programs.

As before, we run the source program by typing

```
> T
```

Our goal is to look at the machine code produced by the compiler from the Pascal source code. A convenient way to do this is to look at T.COD, which contains an assembly-language version of the machine code, along with the code segment offset of each instruction. Figure 5.3 shows the file T.COD.

```
L9:

Procedure/Function : TRADE

    ** 000001    PUSH    BP
    ** 000002    MOV     BP,SP
    ** 000004    SUB     SP,0002H
L10:
    ** 000008    MOV     DI,[BP].06H
    ** 00000B    MOV     AX,[DI]
    ** 00000D    MOV     [BP].FEH,AX
L11:
    ** 000010    MOV     SI,[BP].04H
    ** 000013    MOV     AX,[SI]
    ** 000015    MOV     [DI],AX
L12:
    ** 000017    MOV     DI,[BP].04H
    ** 00001A    MOV     AX,[BP].FEH
    ** 00001D    MOV     [DI],AX
I3:
    ** 00001F    MOV     SP,BP
    ** 000021    POP     BP
    ** 000022    RET     0004H
L15:

Procedure/Function : TD

    ** 000025    PUSH    BP
    ** 000026    MOV     BP,SP
    ** 000028    SUB     SP,0004H
    ** 00002C    PUSH    DI
    ** 00002D    PUSH    SI
    ** 00002E    MOV     STKBQQ,BP
L16:
    ** 000032    MOV     V,000CH
    ** 000038    MOV     W,000FH
L17:
    ** 00003E    MOV     AX,@@V
    ** 000041    PUSH    AX
    ** 000042    MOV     AX,@@W
    ** 000045    PUSH    AX
    ** 000046    CALL    TRADE
L18:
    ** 000049    MOV     AX,@@OUTFQQ
    ** 00004C    PUSH    AX
    ** 00004D    PUSH    V
```

```
      ** 000051    MOV      AX,7FFFH
      ** 000054    PUSH     AX
      ** 000055    PUSH     AX
      ** 000056    LCALL    WTIFQQ
      ** 00005B    MOV      AX,@@OUTFQQ
      ** 00005E    PUSH     AX
      ** 00005F    PUSH     W
      ** 000063    MOV      AX,7FFFH
      ** 000066    PUSH     AX
      ** 000067    PUSH     AX
      ** 000068    LCALL    WTIFQQ
      ** 00006D    MOV      AX,@@OUTFQQ
      ** 000070    PUSH     AX
      ** 000071    LCALL    WTLFQQ
I4:
      ** 000076    POP      SI
      ** 000077    POP      DI
      ** 000078    MOV      SP,BP
      ** 00007A    POP      BP
      ** 00007B    LRET
```

Figure 5.3

In the file T.COD, the labels beginning with 'L' indicate line numbers in the original Pascal source file. For example, the label 'L16' denotes line 16 of Program 5.12 (there were two blank lines at the top of that program), and we see, from lines starting at the one labeled L16 in T.COD, that the compiler has translated line 16 of the source file to

```
L16:
      ** 000032    MOV      V,000CH
      ** 000038    MOV      W,000FH
```

which makes sense since the source line was "V = 12; W: = 15;" and $12_{10} = C_{16}$ and $15_{10} = F_{16}$. Note that the compiler has assigned these two MOV instructions to offsets 32H and 38H of the code segment.

Since the procedure Trade is declared in T.PAS before the main program Td (this latter name comes from the **program** line—i.e., the top line—in T.PAS), the code for Trade occupies the earlier portion of the code segment, and the code for Td comes afterward. In the left-hand column, values are shown which are offsets within the code segment.

The code for Trade looks very similar to that of Program 5.11, in the sense that there are a lot of references to BP. This is because the compiler passes parameters on the stack, just as Program 5.11 does. Incidentally, the format [BP].x means the same as [BP+x]; for example, [BP].06H is just an alternative mnemonic for [BP+6].

We see that the compiler has assigned to offsets 1 and 21 code to save and restore BP. This code was not needed in Program 5.11, because Program 5.10, which called

Program 5.11, did not use BP. However, in Program 5.12, the compiled code in the main program does use BP, as is plain from the Td portion of Figure 5.3. Thus, it is crucial that Trade not destroy the value of BP, so the compiler has put in PUSH and POP instructions to save that value upon entry to Td and restore it to BP upon exit from Td.

The Microsoft Pascal compiler always uses BP in the main program, so any subprogram must save and restore its value. This will be important to keep in mind when you write your own assembly-language subprograms to interface with Pascal main progams, as we do later.

On the other hand, the values of the registers AX, BX, CX, DX, SI, and DI do not have to be saved and restored by Trade, even though Trade uses AX, SI, and DI. The reason for this is that the Microsoft Pascal compiler arranges things so that the nonsegment, non-BP registers never have an "active" value at the time of a call. To see what this means, consider AX. Figure 5.4 shows that, just before the call to Trade, the compiler did produce code that uses AX. However, by the time we reach offset 46, the value in AX has outlived its usefulness. AX had only been used as a mechanism to get @@V onto the stack and is now no longer needed. Thus, subprogram Trade is free to use AX itself, as in offset B, without saving the main program's value of AX first.

```
**   00003E    MOV      AX,@@V
**   000041    PUSH     AX
**   000042    MOV      AX,@@W
**   000045    PUSH     AX
**   000046    CALL     TRADE
```

Figure 5.4

The token @@ is just an alternative way of indicating OFFSET. Thus, the instruction

```
MOV AX,@@V
```

is identical to (i.e., will have the same machine code as)

```
MOV AX,OFFSET V
```

The reason we need the offsets of V and W here, rather than the values in V and W, is that the corresponding formal parameters, X and Y in the declaration of Trade, were declared as parameter type **var**, i.e., as reference parameters, and as mentioned earlier, reference parameters are passed by address. (Recall that on iAPX machines, the role of the address of a variable is typically played by the offset of the variable within the data segment.) If the declaration of Trade had made X and Y value parameters instead of reference parameters—i.e., if the declaration were

```
procedure Trade(X,Y : integer);
```

then the code produced for the call to Trade would have been that shown in Figure 5.5.

```
**  00003E    MOV      AX,V
**  000041    PUSH     AX
**  000042    MOV      AX,W
**  000045    PUSH     AX
**  000046    CALL     TRADE
```

Figure 5.5

The code in Figure 5.4 pushes the data segment *offsets* of V and W, which can be found from T.LST (not shown) to be 54 and 56; by contrast, the code in Figure 5.5 pushes the *contents* of V and W, which, from Program 5.12, are 12 and 15.

It is common for compilers to store not only parameters on the stack, but local variables as well. This can be seen in Trade. Trade has one local variable, Temp. Instead of storing Temp in the data segment, Trade stores it in the stack. Temp is of type **integer**, so it is of size two bytes. Hence, to allocate space for Temp, the compiler expands the stack by two bytes:

```
**  000004    SUB      SP,0002H
```

Later, in offset D, the code produced from the compiler for the Pascal statement Temp:=X is

```
**  00000D    MOV      [BP].FEH,AX
```

Since FEH is the eight-bit two's complement representation of –2, [BP].FEH, or equivalently, [BP+0FEH], does indeed point to this newly allocated top of the stack where Temp resides.

So the procedure call will result in parameters, return addresses, and local variables being put onto the stack. These objects are collectively referred to as the **stack frame** for the call.

Note that not all of the machine code in the .EXE file appears in the .COD file: the .EXE file has what we will call "preparation code" that first performs various initializations, e.g., for the stack, and then calls our program Td as if it were a procedure. Then, at the end of Td, at offset 7B, an LRET ("long" return, i.e., far return) instruction takes us back to the "preparation code." That code ends with a call to our familiar DOS service 21/4C that we have been using in our assembly-language programs. This service takes us back to the operating system, which will then display its '>' prompt, inviting us to submit another command.

Even the code visible in the .COD file contains some initializations, in offsets 25 through 2E. The translation of the Pascal code itself does not start until offset 32.

The code starting at L18 corresponds to the call to **writeln** in the Pascal source program. Recall that **writeln** is a built-in procedure supplied by the compiler instead of being written by the user; all the user has to do is make the call to **writeln** and the compiler will produce the proper code, which we see here in offsets 49–71. Apparently, the compiler-supplied procedure WTIFQQ is **writeln**. The material before the call to **writeln** is apparently preparation for that call. For example, you can see V and W being pushed onto the stack as parameters to that call, which makes sense since the call in the Pascal source file is

```
writeln(V,W);
```

The language C has a natural, "do it yourself" analog of Pascal's **var** construct for subprogram parameters. As we have seen here, **var** is merely a device the programmer uses to let the Pascal compiler know that he or she wishes to pass the *address* of a variable, rather than the variable itself. (Recall that on iAPX machines, the compiler typically passes the offset, and not the full address; but we will loosely speak of addresses in this sense in what follows.) For example, in the procedure Trade of Program 5.12, by declaring X and Y to be of type **var**, we signaled the compiler to produce code that pushed the addresses of X and Y, as we subsequently saw.

But in C, things are much more direct. Instead of the programmer implicitly asking the compiler to push the value, instead of the address of a variable, the programmer explicitly states which one he or she wants. Suppose the variable is Q. Then the programmer would write either Q or &Q, depending on whether the value or address is needed. (Review Program 2.1 before continuing.)

In the present example, the C-language call to Trade would be

```
Trade(&V,&W);
```

and the procedure Trade itself would be

```
void Trade(XP,YP)
    int *XP,*YP;
{   int Temp;

    Temp = *XP;
    *XP = *YP;
    *YP = Temp;
}
```

The keyword **void** says that Trade will be like a Pascal **procedure** rather than a Pascal **function**—i.e., Trade will not return a value. The declaration

```
int *XP,*YP;
```

says that both XP and YP are pointers to integers, and the expressions *XP and *YP denote the contents of the integers pointed to by XP and YP.

As another example, consider a C version of the Pascal procedure Sort that we mentioned briefly in Section 5.2. Its declaration in Pascal was

```
procedure Sort(var X : ArrayType; N : integer);
```

Note that the parameter X is of type **var**, but N is not. This makes sense, since the array X will be changed by the procedure—it is getting sorted—but N will *not* change and thus does not have to be of type **var**. So, again, when the compiler translates a call to Sort—say, for the array Y of M elements, i.e.,

```
Sort(Y,M)
```

it will produce machine code that pushes the *address* of Y onto the stack, but pushes the *value* of M.

In C, the programmer would handle things directly. The declaration of Sort would be

```
Sort(XP,N)
    int *XP,N;
```

where the first parameter is a pointer to (i.e., an address of) an integer, but the second parameter is itself an integer, not a pointer to one.

The call would be identical to

```
Sort(Y,M);
```

in Pascal. Yet it may seem strange—isn't there a type mismatch between the actual parameter Y and the formal parameter XP? The answer is no, because in C, any array *name*, say, Y here (but *not* an array *element*, say, Y[2]), is treated as the address of the beginning of the array. In other words, any array name is treated as a pointer to the start of the array. Thus, Y and XP here are quite consistent with each other. If you insist, you can write the call as

```
Sort(&Y,M);
```

The compiler will accept this form, but give you a polite message telling you that the '&' is redundant.

Incidentally, the Intel people who designed the iAPX 286, 386, and 486 CPUs added ENTER and LEAVE instructions to the instruction set of the iAPX 86 family, with an eye toward facilitating the setting up and dismantling of stack frames in Pascal and C. ENTER pushes the BP value onto the stack, allocates room on the stack for local variables by subtracting from SP the number of bytes specified by the programmer (as the first operand of the ENTER instruction), and finally points BP to the stack frame it has just created. ENTER is used at the beginning of a procedure, and the LEAVE instruction undoes all of what ENTER has done at the end of the procedure.

Clearly, ENTER and LEAVE save the programmer some work and make a procedure run faster. The reader is invited to explore whether his or her compiler avails itself of these two useful instructions. For example, with Microsoft C, one can use the /G2 option in the CL compile command, telling the compiler that one desires the compiler to produce code using iAPX 286 instructions. One can then check the .COD file to see whether the compiler has taken advantage of ENTER and LEAVE. In an example the author examined, the compiler did use the LEAVE instruction, but did the actions similar to ENTER "by hand," i.e., by using several primitive instructions in sequence. The compiler did this because it called its internal function **chkstk**, which checked for stack overflow before actually expanding the stack.

5.3.2 Mixed-Language Programming

Now that we have learned the basics of the machine-level aspects of procedure calls in high-level languages, we look at the question of mixed-language programming, particularly when one of the languages is assembly language. As our main example, we return to the example of Section 5.2. We will still have the procedure SUM, which finds the sum of a set of consecutive words in memory, in an assembly language file S.ASM, but now our main program will be in a Pascal file M.PAS or a C file M.C.

5.3.2.1 Mechanics of the Interfacing of Languages.   Suppose, just as a very simple example, that we wanted to fill the array Z with squares of integers and then call SUM to find the total of those squares. The file M.PAS would look like that shown in Program 5.13.   Note that the function Sum is missing from this file: it is declared, but with no body. The reason is that this function is in the assembly-language file S.ASM. Note also the keyword **extern** in the declaration of sum. It is similar in intention to EXTRN in assembly language, telling the compiler not to worry that the function body is missing!

```
program Mn(input,output);

    type AryType : array[1..10] of integer;
    var Z : AryType;
        I,S : integer;

function Sum(var First,Last:integer) : integer; extern;

begin
    for I:=1 to 3 do
        Z[I]:=I*I;
    S:=Sum(Z[1],Z[3]);
    writeln(S)
end.
```

Program 5.13

The 'extern' function doesn't have to be written in assembly language, although it is here. Instead, it could be another Pascal file, for instance, or C or FORTRAN.

We compile M.PAS, assemble S.ASM, and link as in Section 5.2:

```
> PAS1 M,M,M,M
> PAS2
> PAS3
> MASM S,S,S;
> LINK /LI /MAP /CO M S,M,M;
```

(Again, add in a library file field to your LINK command if necessary, as explained earlier.) In other words, we compile the Pascal code and assemble the assembly language, producing two .OBJ files, and then link them into a single executable .EXE file, M.EXE. Again, to run this file, we type

```
> M
```

As before, the PAS3 command is optional, but extremely valuable, since it produces a file M.COD, which shows an assembly-language version of the machine code the compiler has produced from the Pascal source M.PAS. Most compilers offer this kind of service; for example, in the Unix operating system, the Pascal compiler pc and the C compiler cc both offer this service, under the -S option.

Figure 5.6 shows the contents of M.COD. Pay particular attention to the call to SUM, in offsets 2F through 3C:

```
** 00002F     MOV      AX,@@Z
** 000032     PUSH     AX
** 000033     MOV      AX,@@Z+4
** 000036     PUSH     AX
** 000037     LCALL    SUM
** 00003C     MOV      S,AX
```

The call to SUM is written here as LCALL, to emphasize that it is a **far** ("long") call. Microsoft Pascal makes all calls to external subprograms of type **far** by default.

```
L10:
Procedure/Function : MN

     ** 000001     PUSH     BP
     ** 000002     MOV      BP,SP
     ** 000004     SUB      SP,0004H
     ** 000008     PUSH     DI
     ** 000009     PUSH     SI
     ** 00000A     MOV      STKBQQ,BP
L11:
     ** 00000E     MOV      I,0001H
  I6:
```

```
L12:
        **  000014    MOV       DI,I
        **  000018    SHL       DI,1
        **  00001A    MOV       AX,I
        **  00001D    IMUL      AX
        **  00001F    MOV       Z-2[DI],AX
I4:
        **  000023    MOV       AX,I
        **  000026    INC       AX
        **  000027    MOV       I,AX
        **  00002A    CMP       AX,0004H
        **  00002D    JNE       I6
I5:
L13:
        **  00002F    MOV       AX,@@Z
        **  000032    PUSH      AX
        **  000033    MOV       AX,@@Z+4
        **  000036    PUSH      AX
        **  000037    LCALL     SUM
        **  00003C    MOV       S,AX
L14:
        **  00003F    MOV       AX,@@OUTFQQ
        **  000042    PUSH      AX
        **  000043    PUSH      S
        **  000047    MOV       AX,7FFFH
        **  00004A    PUSH      AX
        **  00004B    PUSH      AX
        **  00004C    LCALL     WTIFQQ
        **  000051    MOV       AX,@@OUTFQQ
        **  000054    PUSH      AX
        **  000055    LCALL     WTLFQQ
I3:
        **  00005A    POP       SI
        **  00005B    POP       DI
        **  00005C    MOV       SP,BP
        **  00005E    POP       BP
        **  00005F    LRET
```

Figure 5.6

In Program 5.13, the main program puts values into the first three elements of the array Z and then calls SUM to find the sum of those three elements. Recall from Section 5.2 that SUM takes as parameters the locations of the first and last words to be summed. Thus, our Pascal program needs to supply the offsets of Z[1] and Z[3]. This is accomplished in Program 5.13 by declaring Sum's formal parameters, First and Last, to be of type **var**, i.e., to be reference parameters instead of value parameters. As code segment offsets 2F and 33 of Figure 5.6 show, this does achieve the desired effect: the assembly code produced by the compiler pushes @@Z, i.e., the offset of Z, and since our first array element is Z[1], this is the offset of Z[1]. Similarly, @@Z+4 is the offset of Z[3].

Again, without the keyword **var**, the *value* of a variable, not the *location* of the variable, gets pushed onto the stack before a call. If the variable happens to be an array, then the entire array is pushed onto the stack—a very time-consuming process if the array is lengthy. For this reason, it is good practice to use **var** for array parameters, even if the arrays will not be changed by the subprogram.

Program 5.14 shows what the file S.ASM looks like. The code is modified slightly from that in Program 5.11. (Keep in mind, this is still code which we wrote ourselves in assembly language, as in Section 5.2. It is not a .COD file, such as Figure 5.6, which shows "compiler-produced" machine code.)

```
SUMCSG    SEGMENT
          ASSUME CS:SUMCSG
          PUBLIC SUM
SUM       PROC FAR
          PUSH BP
          SUB AX,AX
          MOV BP,SP
          MOV BX,[BP+8]
          MOV DX,[BP+6]
 TOP  :   ADD AX,[BX]
          ADD BX,2
          CMP DX,BX
          JGE TOP
          POP BP
          RET 4
SUM       ENDP
SUMCSG    ENDS
END
```

Program 5.14

The first instruction of the .ASM file, PUSH BP, saves the old value of BP on the stack, and the next-to-last instruction, POP BP, restores that value when we leave the procedure. (This was explained earlier, in the analysis of Program 5.12.) These two instructions must be kept in mind when writing any assembly-language procedure to interface with Microsoft Pascal or C. If the BP value used by the Pascal main program is destroyed by the procedure, then the program will not work properly upon return from the procedure. (In fact, the reader is urged to compile, assemble, link, and then run the program without PUSH BP and POP BP in the procedure SUM and then observe how the system "locks up" as a result.)

A consequence of adding the instruction PUSH BP at the beginning of SUM is that Table 5.2 must be revised again, to the configuration shown in Table 5.5. A glance at Table 5.5 shows why the references [BP+6] and [BP+4] in Program 5.11 are replaced in Program 5.14 by [BP+8] and [BP+6].

TABLE 5.5

top	old BP value
top + 2	return IP value
top + 4	return CS value
top + 6	2nd parameter
top + 8	1st parameter

At this point, the reader is urged to compare the [BP+x] forms used in Programs 5.8, 5.11, and 5.14, to facilitate his or her understanding of the concepts presented.

Note that if Sum were to change any of the parameter values fed into it, it would again have to do so by using the form [BP+x]. For example, we could have declared Sum as a **procedure** instead of a **function**:

```
procedure Sum(var First,Last,Total:integer); extern;
```

The call to Sum would then be

```
Sum(Z[1],Z[2],S);
```

and in that case, Program 5.14 would be modified to the following (changed lines contain a comment):

```
SUMCSG    SEGMENT
          ASSUME CS:SUMCSG
          PUBLIC SUM
SUM       PROC FAR
          PUSH BP
          SUB AX,AX
          MOV BP,SP
          MOV BX,[BP+0AH]  ; one more parameter now, so each one is deeper in the stack
          MOV DX,[BP+8]  ; one more parameter now, so each one is deeper in the stack
  TOP  :  ADD AX,[BX]
          ADD BX,2
          CMP DX,BX
          JGE TOP
          MOV BX,[BP+6]  ; get address of the parameter Total
          MOV [BX],AX  ; return sum in that parameter
          POP BP
          RET 6  ; three parameters to pop
SUM       ENDP
SUMCSG    ENDS
END
```

Another difference between Programs 5.11 and 5.14 is the RET instruction, which in the latter becomes RET 4. To see what this does, note that if the instruction were an ordinary RET instruction, then after its execution, the stack would now look like Table 5.6 instead of Table 5.5.

TABLE 5.6

top	2nd parameter
top + 2	1st parameter

As mentioned earlier, we should "clean up" the stack after the call to SUM. This could be done by putting code like

```
ADD SP,4
```

right after the call, i.e., at offset 3C in Figure 5.6. However, this is impossible, since the code in that figure came from the compiler and we cannot really control what code the compiler will produce.

For this reason, the advanced version of the RET instruction, written using the mnemonic RET x, is quite helpful. RET x instructs the computer to perform an ordinary RET, but then also add x to SP, to remove the parameters from the stack. In the case shown here, RET 4 is what is needed.

A Pascal function subprogram produces a return value, e.g., the one placed in S in the statement

```
S:=Sum(Z[1],Z[3]);
```

in Program 5.13. The compiler expects this value to be returned via AX, as can be seen in the instruction

```
MOV S,AX
```

in offset 3C of Figure 5.6. (In this case the return value was of the type **integer**. Other conventions, followed for other data types, are delineated in the compiler manual, although one can always just inspect the .COD file to see where the compiler is expecting a return value to appear, as we have done here.) Fortunately, the code in S.ASM already does what the compiler expects: ever since Program 3.1 in Chapter 3, we have been using AX to store the sum in this sample program. If not—say, if we had been using CX to store the sum—then we would need a line

```
MOV AX,CX
```

just before RET 4.

Observe that we have declared SUM as a **far** procedure in Program 5.14:

```
SUM  PROC FAR
```

The reason is that, as already mentioned, the code in M.OBJ produced by the compiler from M.PAS will include a **far** call to SUM. This FAR pseudo-op in S.ASM will then cause MASM to produce a **far** return from the RET 4 line, thus matching the **far** call.

Keep in mind that the compiler will create a data segment in which to store the global variables declared in M.PAS. Thus, upon entry to the procedure S.ASM in the preceding examples, DS will be pointing to the data segment of M.PAS. If we had declared a data segment—named, say, SUMDSG—in S.ASM, then we would need to include code at the beginning of S.ASM to save the old value of DS, point DS to our new data segment, and then, before returning to the calling program, restore the calling program's value of DS.

For example, we might have the code

```
PUSH DS
PUSH AX
MOV AX,SUMDSG
MOV DS,AX
POP AX
```

at the beginning of S.ASM and, at the end of that file, have

```
POP DS
```

Of course, the references [BP+8] and [BP+6] in the procedure SUM in Program 5.14 would have to be revised to [BP+0AH] and [BP+8], since pushing DS would have expanded the stack.

Things are similar, but not identical, in the language C. Let us look at the same example as just described, but in C instead of Pascal. Our main program will then be in a file M.C, the contents of which are shown in Program 5.15.

```
extern int far SUM( int * , int * );

int Z[3],I,S;

main()

{

    for (I = 0; I < 3; I++)
        Z[I] = (I+1)*(I+1);
    S = SUM(Z,Z+2);
    printf("%d\n",S);
}
```

Program 5.15

For readers who are not familar with C, C's **for** loop is similar to that of Pascal, but is more flexible. In this program, the three fields within the **for** statement say the following. The first field, I = 0, obviously says to initialize I to 0. The second field, I < 3, is clear too: keep iterating while I < 3. The last field, I++, says to increment I by 1 each time the bottom of the loop is reached.

Again, arrays in C automatically start with the index 0, so the declaration

```
int Z[3]
```

allocates three integers, Z[0], Z[1], and Z[2].

The line

```
extern int far SUM( int * , int * );
```

says that the function SUM will be in another file. This file will of course be the assembly-language file S.ASM in here, but it could be a file in C or some other language instead. The arguments in the declaration are both of type **int ***, meaning a pointer to an integer. Since a pointer in Pascal, C, or whatever is an address of an item, the declaration is saying that the two parameters in the call to SUM will both be addresses of integer variables—which is exactly what the keyword **var** indicates in the Pascal version of this program (Program 5.13).

We have chosen to declare SUM as **far**. Unlike the Microsoft Pascal compiler, the Microsoft C compiler will assume by default that an external function is **near**. Thus, to minimize the number of changes made to SUM from Program 5.14, we have made SUM **far**.

As mentioned earlier, in the language C an array name is treated as a pointer to the beginning of the array. Thus, in the context of the call to SUM,

```
S = SUM(Z,Z+2);
```

what do Z and Z+2 really mean—what will the compiler interpret them as?

(a) As mentioned earlier, an isolated array name without a subscript, in this case Z, is considered a pointer to the beginning of that array. Thus, Z denotes the address of the first element of Z, namely, Z[0]. (Recall that all C arrays have a starting subscript of 0.)

(b) The expression Z+2 is taken to signify pointer arithmetic. Recall from Chapter 1 that in the general declaration

```
q *P
```

P is a pointer to objects of data type q. For any integer m, $P+m$ then denotes the object that is m objects past the one pointed to by P. In other words, $P+m$ points to the object m*sizeof(q) bytes past where P is pointing to. Since, in the foregoing, Z is a pointer to an integer—specifically, the integer Z[0]—$Z + 2$ points to the integer that is two integers past that point, i.e., to Z[2].

So, "once all the dust settles," the net effect is that the call to SUM will pass as parameters the addresses of the first and third elements of the array Z—just what was desired, since we want to sum up the first three words of the array.

Program 5.16 shows the file S.ASM, which is only slightly modified from Program 5.14. The two coding changes that need to be made are the following. First, the references [BP+8] and [BP+6] have been exchanged. This was necessary, because C compilers pass parameters in reverse order. Thus, the parameters Z and Z+2 in Program 5.16, are passed in the order Z+2 and then Z. The reader can verify this reversal in the file M.COD in Figure 5.7.

```
SUMCSG     SEGMENT
           ASSUME CS:SUMCSG
           PUBLIC _SUM
_SUM    PROC FAR
           PUSH BP
           SUB AX,AX
           MOV BP,SP
           MOV BX,[BP+6]
           MOV DX,[BP+8]
   TOP  : ADD AX,[BX]
           ADD BX,2
           CMP DX,BX
           JGE TOP
           POP BP
           RET
_SUM       ENDP
SUMCSG       ENDS
END
```

Program 5.16

Second, RET 4 in Program 5.14 is now back to simply RET. The reason for this is that, unlike the Pascal compiler, the C compiler produces code in the calling program that "cleans up the stack," i.e., removes parameters after a call. In Figure 5.7, the instruction in offset 3E,

```
ADD SP,4
```

coming right after the call to SUM, shrinks the stack by two words, which were the words containing the two parameters. By contrast, in Figure 5.6, the .COD file for the Pascal version of this program, there was no such "cleanup" instruction following the call, so we needed to do it ourselves, with a RET 4 at the end of SUM.

Another difference, *small but crucial*, is that the symbol SUM is now called _SUM, with an underscore and capital letters, to be consistent with typical C usage. Also, note that it is *required* that SUM be named with all capital letters in the C program.

To create an executable file M.EXE, we would first run S.ASM through MASM as before (don't forget to use the /ZI option), producing S.OBJ. Then we would use the CL ("compile and link") command, which combines the compile and link steps into one command (later versions of Microsoft Pascal also allow this, through the PL command):

```
> CL /Fc /Zi M.C S.OBJ
```

The /Fc option says that we wish to produce a .COD file, and the /Zi option says that we wish to retain the symbol table so that we can use CodeView. Again, if you are missing any library files, or any **include** files, the compiler will tell you which ones you are missing, and you can modify your command line to

```
> CL /I include file name(s) /Fc /Zi M.C S.OBJ /link library file name(s)
```

The CL command compiles the C-language source code and links it to S.OBJ to produce M.EXE. Figure 5.7 shows the .COD file also produced.

```
; | ***
; | ***
; | *** extern int far SUM( int * , int * );
; | ***
; | *** int Z[3],I,S;
; | ***
; | *** main()
; | ***
; | *** {
; Line 11
        PUBLIC  _main
_main   PROC NEAR
        *** 000000      55                          push    bp
        *** 000001      8b ec                       mov     bp,sp
        *** 000003      33 c0                       xor     ax,ax
        *** 000005      e8 00 00                    call    __chkstk
        *** 000008      56                          push    si
; | ***
; | ***    for (I = 0; I < 3; I++)
; Line 13
        *** 000009      c7 06 00 00 00 00           mov     WORD PTR _I,0
        *** 00000f      eb 04                       jmp     SHORT $F106
                                        $FC107:
        *** 000011      ff 06 00 00                 inc     WORD PTR _I
                                        $F106:
        *** 000015      83 3e 00 00 03              cmp     WORD PTR _I,3
        *** 00001a      7d 15                       jge     $FB108
; | ***       Z[I] = (I+1)*(I+1);
; Line 14
        *** 00001c      8b 36 00 00                 mov     si,WORD PTR _I
        *** 000020      46                          inc     si
        *** 000021      8b c6                       mov     ax,si
```

```
        *** 000023      f7 ee                    imul    si
        *** 000025      8b 1e 00 00              mov     bx,WORD PTR _I
        *** 000029      d1 e3                    shl     bx,1
        *** 00002b      89 87 00 00              mov     WORD PTR _Z[bx],ax
        *** 00002f      eb e0                    jmp     SHORT $FC107
                                     $FB108:
;|***      S = SUM(Z,Z+2);
; Line 15
        *** 000031      b8 04 00                 mov     ax,OFFSET DGROUP:_Z+4
        *** 000034      50                       push    ax
        *** 000035      b8 00 00                 mov     ax,OFFSET DGROUP:_Z
        *** 000038      50                       push    ax
        *** 000039      9a 00 00 00 00           call    FAR PTR _SUM
        *** 00003e      83 c4 04                 add     sp,4
        *** 000041      a3 00 00                 mov     WORD PTR _S,ax
;|***      printf("%d\n",S);
; Line 16
        *** 000044      50                       push    ax
        *** 000045      b8 00 00                 mov     ax,OFFSET DGROUP:$SG110
        *** 000048      50                       push    ax
        *** 000049      e8 00 00                 call    _printf
        *** 00004c      83 c4 04                 add     sp,4
;|*** }
; Line 17
        *** 00004f      5e                       pop     si
        *** 000050      8b e5                    mov     sp,bp
        *** 000052      5d                       pop     bp
        *** 000053      c3                       ret

_main   ENDP
_TEXT   ENDS
END
;|***
```

Figure 5.7

C-language .COD files are a little nicer than Pascal's .COD files, because they intersperse the original C code with the compiled assembly code. For example, in offsets 1C through 2F, there is the assembly code compiled from

```
Z[I] = (I+1)*(I+1);
```

which appears just above those offsets in the .COD listing.

In the language C, even the main program, main( ), is treated as a subprogram—i.e., in C terminology, as a **function**. Accordingly, local variables are stored on the stack, just as was the case with the variable Temp in the procedure Trade in Program 5.12. Again, in C, this is even true for main( ). Thus, if in Program 5.15 the variables Z, I, and S had been declared as local to main( ), i.e., with the code

```
main()

{  int Z[3],I,S;

   for (I = 0; I < 3; I++)
      etc.
}
```

then the compiler would have stored Z, I, and S on the stack and would have referred to them via BP, with BP–2, BP–8 and BP–0AH pointing to Z, I, and S, respectively. Compare this situation with what we see in Figure 5.7, where these variables are specified via offsets in the data segment, since Program 5.15 declares them to be global. (Unfortunately, the .COD file does not show these offsets in the machine-code part of the file, which always shows offset 0000.)

One thing to note if you are interfacing an assembly-language subprogram with a C-language main program is that although the C compiler automatically makes all the global variables in the main program available to other modules, including the assembly-language subprogram, accessing these variables requires knowledge of the segment structure set up by the C compiler. If your assembly-language routines need access to the global variables of your main program and you do not want to pass their addresses as parameters, as we have done in the foregoing example, you will need to consult your compiler manual.

Incidentally, one possible use for mixed-language programming is to give your HLL code access to DOS services, since HLLs do not give direct access to the INT instruction, or to the AH or other registers needed for the parameters of the calls. However, most compilers for DOS systems make some provision for such access. For example, Microsoft C offers built-in functions such as **int86** for this purpose. Again, check your compiler manual for details.

5.3.2.2 Debugging Mixed-Language Programs.
DEBUG, SYMDEB, CodeView, and other software tools can all be used to greatly speed up the debugging process in mixed-language environments. As noted in Section 4.2.4, though, it is annoying to use DEBUG, since it does not use the symbols from the original source file. To remedy the situation, one can just use SYMDEB or CodeView instead of DEBUG, and, in addition, perform the crucial step of telling the compiler not to throw away the symbol table. We will show how to do the latter for Microsoft compilers, but most others have features that are similar. For example, Unix compilers allow the -g option on the command line, which tells the compiler to save the symbol table. (If you only have DEBUG on your computer, see the note a little later on that tells you how to expedite getting to your assembly-language module.)

Suppose, for instance, we wish to use SYMDEB with Programs 5.13 and 5.14. Again, we use PUBLIC in Program 5.14 to save any labels from the .ASM file and use the analogous token **[public]** in Program 5.13, in the declaration section:

```
var [public] Z : AryType;
        I,S : integer;
```

The compiler then saves the symbols Z, I, and S in the machine-code file it produces, M.OBJ, in the same way that MASM saved the symbols SAVEBX and DISPBX in the example in Section 4.2.4. Otherwise, no symbols would be saved.

As before, we use LINK and then MAPSYM and SYMDEB in the same way as in the example in Section 4.2.4:

```
> MAPSYM M

> SYMDEB M.SYM M.EXE
```

The latter command will put us at the preinitialization part of our program. To get to the actual start of the program, which is named Mn (see the source listing, Program 5.13), we type

```
-G MN
```

(Recall what the G command does in DEBUG/SYMDEB.) At this point, we can either single-step using the T command or use G again. For example, if we suspect that an error is in the assembly-language procedure SUM itself and want to go there quickly instead of painfully single-stepping with the T command, we type

```
-G SUM
```

Even with only DEBUG on your machine, there is still a "quick and dirty" way to get to SUM: include, for the duration of the debugging process, an INT 3 instruction at the beginning of the procedure SUM in the file S.ASM (Program 5.14). (Make sure to reassemble, link, etc., if you make this change.) Upon entry to DEBUG, just type

```
-G
```

The program will then execute without stopping, until it gets to the line INT 3, which will force a return to DEBUG. At that point, IP will be pointing to the line INT 3, which you want to skip; so, since INT 3 is a one-byte instruction, just add 0001 to IP, using DEBUG's R command. You can then use T, or G in its 'G n' form, from there.

With SYMDEB or CodeView, we can refer to the variables by name, just as we saw in Section 4.2.4. For example, using the command D on the variable I in Program 5.13, i.e.,

```
-D I
```

allows us to view the current value of I. This is also a quick way to find the offset of a variable. Typing the command for the variable I yields

```
3816:4030  .. .. .. .. 4D 41 58 50-52 4D 20 45 51 55 20 31
3816:4040  30 30 30 44 0D 0A 0D 0A-44 53 47 20 53 45 47 4D
```

The current value of I is then 414DH, and it is stored at offset 4034 of segment 3816. (Blanks are displayed in the first four bytes, which are offsets 4030, 4031, 4032, and 4033.)

As we saw in Section 4.2.4, CodeView provides even more features than does SYMDEB, and if at least part of your program is in Pascal or C, the advantages of CodeView over DEBUG/SYMDEB are particularly strong. (Though, if you have an older version of the Pascal compiler, some of CodeView's features cannot be used.) For example, the F3 key allows you to switch the display window back and forth between displaying your Pascal/C source code and the assembly-language view of the machine code the compiler produced from the Pascal/C code. This feature is particularly useful in mixed-language programs; if you have CodeView (or some other advanced debugging tool, such as Turbo Debugger) available, its use is strongly recommended.

In CodeView, we can also have a window continuously monitor the value of one or more Pascal/C variables, using the W? command introduced in Section 4.2.4. For example, if, in Program 5.15, we wish to monitor the value of the C variable I, we type

```
-W? I
```

The usage of CodeView is the same as described earlier; for the example here, we would simply type

```
> CV M
```

Following are some specific tips for finding your bug. Note that many of them deal with the stack; do not attempt mixed-language programming until you thoroughly understand the role played by the stack. Note also that the "confirmatory" approach mentioned in Section 4.2.4 is quite prominent in the tips that follow, too.

- Using either the F3 key in CodeView, or tracing through to the call with SYMDEB, or else looking at the .COD file, examine the machine code that the compiler has produced from your calls to procedures in other files. Has the compiler set up the parameters in the way you expected?

- Set a breakpoint at the first instruction within a procedure. Do this for two reasons—first, to make sure that the procedure is actually reached, and second, to check the stack: upon entry to the procedure, are the elements of the stack exactly *what* you expected, and are they *where* you expected them to be? Check these by typing

```
-D SS:SP
```

in SYMDEB or CodeView. Actually, this is the very first thing you should check, since errors here are so common.

- If your calling program is in the language C, make sure that your **extern** statement and your calls use all capital letters for the name of the procedure and that in the procedure itself, the name is preceded by an underscore, '_'.

- Make sure that your calls and the procedures they invoke match in terms of being near or far and in terms of call by value versus call by reference.

- At various points in your code, make sure that the variables have the values you think they should have.

- As mentioned in Section 4.2.4, Microsoft assemblers, compilers, and linkers are overly tolerant of errors in spelling, punctuation, and syntax. Indeed, in some cases, they do not even complain about such errors, but produce incorrect results instead! Double-check the accuracy of your commands. To reduce the probability of typing errors, put your commands in .BAT files or, better yet, in MAKE files (see Section 5.5). Not only will doing so reduce errors, but it is also much faster and saves typing. Since in a typical debugging section you will probably reassemble, recompile, and relink dozens of times, using MAKE relieves you of the tedium of repeatedly typing the associated commands, allowing you to concentrate fully on the debugging task itself.

- If your procedure has its own data segment, make sure that you have saved the calling program's value of DS properly and that you restore it properly when leaving the procedure. In the case of reference parameters that are changed by the procedure, you will have to restore the caller's DS value before making such changes, since those parameters are in the caller's data segment.

5.4 MACROS

A *macro* is another form of subprogram that is best explained by example. Suppose there are 12 places in a program in which we wish to put the sum of AX, BX, and CX in DX. Of course, this would be a natural situation in which to write a procedure, but we could also use a macro. Let us compare the two possible versions of the subprogram, which we will call ADDREGS.

Declaration. For the procedure version of ADDREGS, we would declare the procedure as we have done earlier. This is shown in Program 5.17.

```
ADDREGS PROC FAR
        SUB DX,DX
        ADD DX,AX
        ADD DX,BX
        ADD DX,CX
        RET
ADDREGS ENDP
```

Program 5.17

On the other hand, the macro version of the program would have what is shown in Program 5.18 at the top of the .ASM file.

```
ADDREGS MACRO
        SUB DX,DX
        ADD DX,AX
        ADD DX,BX
        ADD DX,CX
        ENDM
```

Program 5.18

Call.   For the procedure version of the program, at each of the 12 spots at which the operation is to be performed, we would have

```
CALL ADDREGS
```

For the macro version, we would instead have

```
ADDREGS
```

without the word 'CALL'.

Action of Assembler.   For the procedure version, the assembler would translate the call into a CALL instruction, i.e., a machine instruction with the CALL op code.

For the macro version, the assembler would replace the line

```
ADDREGS
```

by the code

```
SUB DX,DX
ADD DX,AX
ADD DX,BX
ADD DX,CX
```

and assemble that code along with the other code that surrounds it. We say that the assembler **expands** the macro at the line ADDREGS.

For example, suppose one of the 12 spots at which ADDREGS is to be called looks like this:

```
ADD BX,2
ADDREGS
CMP DX,5
```

The resulting .OBJ file—i.e., machine-language code—produced would be identical to what would have been produced if this code fragment had instead been

```
ADD BX,2
SUB DX,DX
ADD DX,AX
ADD DX,BX
ADD DX,CX
CMP DX,5
```

Plainly, then, a macro is simply a generalization of the EQU pseudo-op we saw in Chapter 4.

What are the relative advantages and disadvantages of macros, compared to procedures? The main disadvantage of macros is *space*; for instance, in the above example, the machine code for ADDREGS will be duplicated 12 times, making the .OBJ and .EXE files larger than they would be with a procedure. More importantly, the increased size of the .EXE file means that the program will use more space in main memory when we run it.

However, an advantage of the macro is *speed*: the program with the macro will run faster than the one with the procedure. The CALL instruction takes extra time: the current IP value must be pushed onto the stack, a new IP value must be obtained, and, of course, there is a corresponding delay for the RET instruction. Of course, this assumes a NEAR call; a FAR call would result in even more delay. The macro version has no such delays.

In general, the shorter a procedure is, the more benefit we can obtain by converting it to a macro, since the stack-operation overhead of a procedure call and return is proportionally greater for shorter procedures. The procedure READCHAR in Program 4.2 is a good candidate for conversion to a macro.

Another advantage of macros is that a macro can do some things that a procedure cannot. For example, say we have a procedure W, the call to which requires passing three parameters on the stack. Suppose all three parameters are words in memory and we wish to pass their addresses—i.e., their offsets within the data segment. If the three locations are named, say, A, B, and C, then we could let the following code precede the CALL:

```
MOV AX,OFFSET A
PUSH AX
MOV AX,OFFSET B
PUSH AX
MOV AX,OFFSET C
PUSH AX
CALL W
```

However, a neater alternative—i.e., one that is clearer (as well as that saves typing)—is to use a macro. We could name the macro PUSHPAR and name its formal parameter R:

```
PUSHPAR    MACRO R
           MOV AX,OFFSET R
```

```
        PUSH AX
        ENDM
```

Then, just before the CALL to W, we would have the code

```
    PUSHPAR A
    PUSHPAR B
    PUSHPAR C
    CALL W
```

The final result (the .OBJ and .EXE files) would be identical to what would have been produced if the .ASM file had contained

```
    MOV AX,OFFSET A
    PUSH AX
    MOV AX,OFFSET B
    PUSH AX
    MOV AX,OFFSET C
    PUSH AX
    CALL W
```

but the use of the macro, as mentioned makes for a much clearer source file and saves typing.

A useful variation of macros is the **conditional macro**. Suppose we are writing a program that uses floating-point numbers. The program is supposed to be able to run on any iAPX machine. Some such machines are equipped with floating-point **coprocessors**—special-purpose CPUs whose instruction sets deal mainly with floating-point operands. For example, the FADD instruction does floating-point addition, as opposed to the integer addition done by ADD. These coprocessors in effect extend the instruction set of the machine's main CPU.

On iAPX machines that do not have such coprocessors, we can still do floating-point operations by writing our own procedures for them. The code would include integer-operand instructions, logical instructions, and shift instructions.

Now, we want our program to be able to take advantage of a floating-point coprocessor in machines that have it, but also, to be able to run on other machines. How can we write our program so that it will work on either kind of system?

The answer is that we can use a conditional macro. This macro would have the form, say,

```
    IF FP_CO_CPU
        FADD _____
    ELSE
        a call to a floating-point addition procedure would go here
    ENDIF
```

At the top of the file, the user would insert a line

```
    FP_CO_CPU = TRUE
```

or

```
FP_CO_CPU = FALSE
```

depending on whether the coprocessor was present or not. Then, when the program was assembled, the assembler MASM would see the conditional macro and act accordingly: If FP_CO_CPU had been defined to be TRUE at the top of the file, then MASM would respond to the macro by putting the machine code for

```
FADD _____
```

in the .OBJ file; otherwise, MASM would put in the call to the floating-point addition subroutine.

5.5 MAKE: A MAINTENANCE UTILITY FOR PROGRAM MODULES

In the preceding sections of this chapter, we have strongly emphasized the fact that the source code for a program is typically scattered in several files. In some cases this scattering is due to the mixed-language nature of the source, and in almost all cases it is also due to the fact that good software engineering practice requires breaking down a program into a number of separate modules.

It was also stressed that when debugging or revising a program, it makes no sense to recompile or reassemble all the program modules when just a few changes are made to only some of the modules. Instead, recompilation or reassembly should be done only for those modules which contain changes, with the old .OBJ files being retained for the other modules. LINK, of course, is then used to link all the .OBJ files together into the executable .EXE file.

In the real world of software engineering, the source code for a single program is often scattered in dozens and even hundreds of source files! Maintenance of these files then becomes a nontrivial matter. If we make a few changes to a few files, we must recompile or reassemble each of these files before using LINK. In the frenzy of debugging, with changes constantly being made, it becomes difficult to keep track of which files we have changed and, among those, which ones we have remembered to recompile or reassemble.

To help deal with this kind of dilemma, MS-DOS provides a program called MAKE that automates the process of recompiling and reassembling. (The name "MAKE" comes from the Unix utility of the same name. Many other similar programs are available commercially.) The key to MAKE's operation is that it checks the **time stamp** of each file—the time of the last modification to the file, which is information that MS-DOS maintains for any file. (This information is printed out when you type the DIR command, for example. It is available to a program—e.g., MAKE—via DOS service number 21H/57H.)

The point of checking time stamps is to flag program modules for which the source module is newer than the associated object module. If the source file has a later date/time than its object file, that is a sign that the object file does not reflect the most recent changes made to the source file and that it must be updated—i.e., the source file needs to be recompiled/reassembled. MAKE can handle all of this, plus any neccessary linking, automatically, according to instructions we provide it.

The instructions left for MAKE are in a file whose suffix is .MAK. As an example, we have named the following SUM.MAK, corresponding to the program whose source code consists of Programs 5.13 and 5.14:

```
S.OBJ:    S.ASM
     MASM /ZI S,S,S;

M.OBJ:    M.PAS
     PAS1 M,M,M,M
     PAS2
     PAS3

M.EXE:    M.OBJ S.OBJ
     LINK /LI /MAP /CO M S,M,M;
```

The first two lines,

```
S.OBJ:    S.ASM
     MASM /ZI S,S,S;
```

tell MAKE that the file S.OBJ has as its source the file S.ASM and that if MAKE finds that the latter file is newer than the former, MAKE should reassemble S.ASM using the command

```
     MASM /ZI S,S,S;
```

Similarly, the next four lines,

```
M.OBJ:    M.PAS
     PAS1 M,M,M,M
     PAS2
     PAS3
```

tell MAKE that M.OBJ comes from M.PAS, and if MAKE determines that the latter is newer than the former, it should recompile M.PAS using the Pascal compile command sequence indicated.

Lastly, the lines

```
M.EXE:    M.OBJ S.OBJ
     LINK /LI /MAP /CO M S,M,M;
```

tell MAKE that the file M.EXE comes from the files M.OBJ and S.OBJ and that if at least one of them is newer than M.EXE, they should be relinked using LINK as indicated.

We would create the file SUM.MAK just once, and then each time we make a change to one or both of the source files, we simply type

```
MAKE SUM.MAK
```

and MAKE will automatically administer whatever recompiling or reassembly and linking are needed. For example, suppose we change the next-to-last line of Program 5.13 to

```
writeln('the sum is ',S)
```

MAKE will notice that S.ASM does not need to be reassembled, so it will skip that action, but it will see that M.PAS is newer than M.OBJ and, thus, will recompile that file. It will then perform the indicated link.

The MAKE file for a C source file would be similar to that for the previous Pascal source file and would have the following instructions:

```
S.OBJ:   S.ASM
         MASM /ZI S,S,S;

M.OBJ:   M.C
         CL /c /Fc /Zi M.C

M.EXE:   M.OBJ S.OBJ
         LINK /LI /MAP /CO M S,M,M;
```

The only new item here is the /c option in the CL command, which means "compile only," i.e., do not link.

MAKE (and other commercial products that are similar) is considered an indispensable tool, used daily by many software engineers. Even in the relatively simple settings of this book, it can save you time and just plain make life easier! The reader is urged to use it freely.

ANALYTICAL EXERCISES

1. Suppose we look at a file W.ASM that someone else has written and have no idea what the program is supposed to do. However, we do notice that a certain section of code in which there are four consecutive lines of POP AX is inefficient. Give more efficient code that we could *safely* substitute for those four lines. State whether your code is more efficient in speed, number of bytes of memory used, or both.

2. Suppose we have a program that is the result of separately assembling files X.ASM and Y.ASM and then linking. Suppose the *entire* file X.ASM, except for EXTRN and/or PUBLIC pseudo-ops, is as follows:

```
CSG     SEGMENT
        T PROC FAR
```

```
        ASSUME CS:CSG
        MOV AX,DSG
        MOV DS,AX
        MOV AX,0
        ADD AX,A
        ADD AX,B
        ADD AX,C
        RET
        T ENDP
CSG     ENDS
        END
```

Show what EXTERN and/or PUBLIC pseudo-ops are needed in X.ASM, and then do the same for Y.ASM.

3. Suppose we are in the process of writing an assembly-language program. We notice that the same seven-line code segment will appear in four different places in the source file G.ASM. This segment, we see, will assemble to 20 bytes of machine code. Consider the following alternatives: (1) Make the seven-line segment a macro. (2) Make it a NEAR procedure. (3) Do nothing special; that is, let the segment appear in four different places in G.ASM.

   (a) Compare the sizes of the three resulting versions of G.OBJ, specifying numerical differences in bytes. Your answer should be of the form (for example) "(1) will be 60 bytes smaller than (2), and (2) will be the same size as (3)." Remember to tell how many bytes smaller or larger each version is relative to the others.

   (b) Compare the running times of the three resulting versions of G.EXE, *without* specifying numerical differences. Your answer should be of the form (for example) "(1) will run at the same speed as (2), and both will be faster than (3)."

4. Consider a C-language file G.C that consists of the three functions, main( ), a( ) and b( ). There are several different lines in the source file G.C at which b is called. The first few lines of b are as follows:

```
b()

{  int x;

   printf("%d\n",&x);
```

During the execution of G.C, the printf line will be executed several times. State *exact, specific* conditions under which the values printed out will not all be identical. You should be able to do this problem without actually running the program on the computer.

5. Write a few lines of code that will do the equivalent of POP BX, without using the POP instruction.

6. In the main example given in Section 5.4, in that we are assuming 12 calls to ADDREGS, how many bytes larger would the program be if it implements ADDREGS as a macro instead of as a procedure? Assume that in the procedure version ADDREGS would be called as NEAR.

7. What machine code would the compiler produce from the RET instruction in Program 5.11? You should be able to answer without actually assembling the program.

8. Give a few lines of assembly code that would produce the same effect as a near RET instruction, without using the RET instruction.

9. In Program 4.1, suppose that the loader has loaded the SSG segment starting at location 60440 in memory. What will be the contents of the stack just prior to execution of line 154 of Figure 4.4? Give your answer in address/contents form, as in Figure 5.1.

10. Suppose we have a file X.ASM containing a procedure P that is to be called from a Microsoft Pascal main program in the file A.PAS. We assemble X.ASM and compile A.PAS, producing X.OBJ and A.OBJ, respectively, and then link these two object files to make the final executable file. Suppose subsequently we have a Microsoft C program in a file B.C and would like to call that same procedure P from this C program, without changing P; we will just use the same file X.OBJ that we produced earlier. Why might this be impossible? State the exact conditions under which it *would be* possible.

11. Suppose we are on an Intel machine and want to make a separate stack, separate from the one pointed to by SS/SP. This new stack will be in our data segment, declared as follows:

```
NEWSTK DB 20H DUP (?) ;  stack space
TOPSTK DW DUP (?) ;  stack pointer
```

Suppose we wish to have the stack grow in the direction of increasing, not decreasing, addresses. Give assembly-language code that could be used to push the hex value A05B onto this stack.

12. What is the smallest size we could give STK in Program 4.1 without damaging other segments?

PROGRAMMING PROJECTS

1. Write an assembly-language FAR procedure named MAX with two parameters, which we will refer to here as X and Y. The procedure will determine which of X and Y is larger, and will place the larger value in the AX register before returning. Write and test two versions of the program:

    (a) A simple version that is callable from an assembly-language main program in the same file.

    (b) A version that is callable from a Pascal or C program.

2. Write a NEAR assembly-language procedure whose parameters we will refer to here as N and A. The procedure will input a series of four-digit hex numbers, placing them in consecutive words beginning at offset A of the current data segment. The numbers will be separated by a single space and will all be on one line of input. Use the procedure READBX from Program 4.2. Test your procedure by writing a main program that will reside in the same file as the procedure.

3. Write an assembly-language FAR procedure named DISP10 that is callable from an assembly-language module *in a separate file*. DISP10 will have one parameter, which we will refer to as X, and will display on the screen the base-10 version of X, considering X a 16-bit signed integer. DISP10 will first check to see whether X is negative. If so, it will print a '−' sign to the screen and then will replace X by −X; the latter is now positive, and DISP10 will continue with the algorithm for positive numbers.

    Write an assembly-language main program (again, in a separate file) that tests DISP10, calling it twice, once with the value 402CH and once with 0B888H. Pass the parameters on the stack. For the core of DISP10, use the algorithm outlined in Programming Project 6 of Chapter 4, which does division by 10000D, then 1000D, etc. However, in order to exercise some new skills, put the following into your code:

(i) Use a loop, with four iterations.

(ii) One approach to dealing with the divisors 10000D, 1000D, 100D, and 10D would be to initialize some register to 10000D and divide it by 10D in each iteration of the loop. However, division is a time-consuming operation, and anyway, the goal of this problem is to exercise some new skills, so put these divisors in an array, say DVSR. This array is required to be stored in DISP10's own data segment, not in the main program's data segment. Any other variables that DISP10 uses—say, a variable I to act as a loop counter—must be declared here, too; in other words, DISP10 is not allowed to use any variables in the calling program's data segment at all. (This restriction is so that DISP10 can be general, i.e., usable from any program.) Note that this means that at the beginning of DISP10 we must save the old value of DS on the stack, put into DS the value of DISP10's own data segment, and at the end of DISP10 pop the saved value of DS back to DS.

(iii) DISP10 must save and later restore any other registers it uses; we do *not* want to burden the calling program with this work.

(iv) DISP10 will suppress the printing of any leading zeros. For example, if c(BX) = 0024D, then only '24' will be printed. (If c(BX) = 0000, then just '0' will be printed.)

4. Write an assembly-language procedure, callable from C or Pascal, which finds the minimum and maximum values in a given array of (signed) integers. The procedure will have four parameters, namely, the starting address of the array, the number of elements in the array, and the minimum and maximum values of the array. The first, third, and fourth parameters must be of the reference type, but the second need not be and is in fact easier to implement as a value parameter. Write a calling program in C or Pascal to test your procedure.

5. Write a subprogram that will display to the screen the memory location—i.e., segment and offset—from which it is called. Write two versions, one a procedure and the other a macro. Write an assembly-language main program to test your subprograms, running it with DEBUG so as to verify easily that the correct location is reported.

6. Rewrite Program 5.14 so that it can be used with a modified version of Program 5.13, in which the function Sum is now declared as

```
function Sum(Z:AryType; N:integer) : integer; extern;
```

The array parameter is now of the call-by-value type, and the line containing the call to it is

```
S:=Sum(Z,3);
```

Test this new version of SUM by modifying Program 5.13 as specified and compiling, assembling, linking, and running.

7. In Section 5.3.2, it was pointed out that if a procedure P is to have its own data segment, separate from that of the calling program C, the location of C's data segment must be saved and restored by P, so that upon return to C, C will be able to access its data segment properly. Write a macro to facilitate this task. Your macro will have one parameter D and will push the current value of DS on the stack and put the address of D in DS; D, of course, is intended to be the name of P's data segment. Write a main program to test your macro. Also, explain why implementing this task as a procedure would be more complicated than implementing it as a macro..

8. Write a procedure that will **concatenate** two character strings, producing a third one. The procedure will have three parameters, which are the offsets of the first bytes of each of the three strings (which are all assumed to be in the current data segment). All strings are terminated with null characters, i.e., a byte whose bits are all zeros. Write a program to test your procedure.

9. Write procedures GETM and PUTM that will fetch from and store to any absolute memory address (five hex digits) specified by the programmer. For GETM, there will be two parameters, the first containing the first four hex digits of the address and the second containing the fifth digit, in bits 3–0. The procedure will fetch the contents of the address and return them in AX. For example, to fetch the contents of word 2A338, we would use the following code:

```
MOV AX,2A33H
PUSH AX
MOV AX,0008H
PUSH AX
CALL GETM
```

After the call, AX would contain c(2A338). PUTM will work the same way, with its first two parameters specifying the address of the word to which we want to store some value and the third parameter being the value to be stored. Write an assembly-language main program to test both procedures, and run it using DEBUG to verify that the indicated memory location really has the contents it should have.

10. Write an assembly-language macro EXCGDATA that will exchange the values of two labeled words in the current data segment, as did the Pascal procedure Trade in Program 5.12. For example, if the data segment contains the declarations

```
Q DW (?)
W DW (?)
```

then the macro call

```
EXCGDATA Q,W
```

would result in the values of Q and W being exchanged. Use the stack for temporary storage. Make your procedure as efficient as possible.

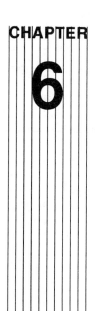

CHAPTER

6

A Further Look at the iAPX Architecture

The **architecture** of a computer is generally defined to be the view of the machine as seen by an assembly-language programmer. As such, it consists of the CPU's register set, instruction set, and set of addressing modes. It does not include the CPU's internal implementation structure, e.g., the number of internal buses that connect CPU components to each other.

In previous chapters, we learned about a number of features of the iAPX architecture. We now take a further look at that architecture, occasionally making brief comparisons to some non-iAPX architectures.

6.1 A FURTHER LOOK AT THE iAPX FLAGS REGISTER

Recall from Chapter 3 that iAPX CPUs include a flags register, FR. It was mentioned in that chapter that the FR contains bits which indicate the status of the most recent computation done by the ALU. The line leading from the ALU to the FR in Figure 3.2 shows that the result of any computation is immediately reflected in updated values of the computation-status bits in the FR.

So far we have been concerned with two of these bits, the sign flag, SF (bit 7), which indicates whether the computation had a negative result, and the zero flag, ZF (bit 6), which indicates whether the computation had a zero result. We will now discuss two more computation-status bits: the carry flag, CF (bit 0) and the overflow flag, OF (bit 11).

204

6.1.1 The Carry Flag

To see the importance of the CF, recall the discussion in Chapter 1 of data representation in n-bit strings. In the iAPX 86 and 286 family of CPUs (and in the 386/486 families, in 16-bit mode), we have 16-bit words and thus work mainly with 16-bit strings. In particular, the ALU works on 16-bit quantities.

It was mentioned in Chapter 1 that strings of this size cannot represent unsigned integers larger than 65,535 or signed integers outside the range –32,768 to +32,767. If we have an application that requires larger integers, we will have to store each integer in more than one word. Furthermore, in order to do arithmetic with such multiword integers, we will need to feed them into the ALU one word at a time. The CF plays an important role in this operation.

For concreteness, let us assume that all integers in a certain application can be represented in 32-bit strings—i.e., each integer is storable in two words. Suppose we have one such integer stored at X and another at Y, which are names of places in the data segment. For example, we might have

```
DSG   SEGMENT
      X DW  2 DUP (?)
      Y DW  2 DUP (?)
DSG   ENDS
```

Again, note that X and Y are each two-word arrays, not single words. Incidentally, we will assume that the 32-bit numbers are being interpreted here as unsigned integers; if the application were to interpret them as signed, the code shown in Program 6.1 would become more complex.

We will store a 32-bit integer at X, with the more significant word at X and the less significant word at X+2. Another 32-bit integer will be stored at Y and Y+2 in the same manner. Suppose we wish to add these two 32-bit integers together and store the result back in Y. Program 6.1 shows code that will do this.

```
      ; get the two halves of X into registers
MOV AX,X+2
MOV BX,X
      ; add the lower half of X to the lower half of Y
ADD Y+2,AX
      ; account for the carry, if any
JNC G
INC BX
G:    ; add the upper half of X (and carry, if any) to the upper half of Y
ADD Y,BX
```

Program 6.1

Mainly, the program just adds the word at X+2 to the word at Y+2, and the word at X to the word at Y. But it also accounts for the fact that there may be a carry out of bit 15 when the word at X+2 is added to the word at Y+2; this carry must be added into the sum of the word at X and the word at Y.

To accomplish the monitoring of a carry, we use the JNC instruction. If a carry out of bit 15 occurs during the execution of the instruction

```
ADD Y+2,AX
```

then the CF in the FR will be set; otherwise CF will be cleared. The JNC instruction, of course, is a "jump if CF is not set" instruction.

The code in Program 6.1 can be made compact by using the iAPX instruction ADC, as shown in Program 6.2. ADC adds together its two operands and adds one to them if CF is set. (There is also an SBB ("subtract with borrow") instruction to do the analogous operation for subtraction.) The use of ADC has thus replaced three instructions by one, saving code space and increasing execution speed.

```
      MOV AX,X+2
      MOV BX,X
      ADD Y+2,AX
G:    ADC Y,BX
```

Program 6.2

It was mentioned in Chapter 1 that the C language includes a **long** integer type, which is generally twice the size of an ordinary **int** integer type. For example, the Microsoft C compiler for iAPX 86 and 286 machines allocates **int** variables as one word and **long** variables as two words. Again, given the 16-bit ALU of these machines, this means that a sum involving two **long** variables will need to be compiled into something like Program 6.1 or 6.2. To investigate this operation, let us write a C program and look at the .COD file produced by the compiler. Program 6.3 shows the C file.

```
long X,Y;

main()

{   scanf("%ld%ld",&X,&Y);
    Y += X;
    printf("%ld\n",Y);
}
```

Program 6.3

From before, the **scanf** function is like Pascal's **read**, **printf** is like Pascal's **write**, and the '%' signs indicate what kind of format the data will be read or written in, with 'd' meaning integer format. The prefixed 'l' stands for "long," so %ld denotes a long-integer format. Since X and Y will be changed by the execution of **scanf**, these two parameters must be passed as reference parameters (review the term in Chapter 5 if needed), so we have to use the '&' operator. The assignment Y += X is a short notation for Y = Y + X.

Incidentally, as mentioned earlier, the language C has far fewer "safety checks" than the reader might be accustomed to. For example, if, in the **printf** statement, we had used %d instead of %ld, then only the integer value represented by the less significant 16 bits of Y would have been printed out, even though the compiler "knows" that Y is a 32-bit quantity. Similarly, if we had forgotten an & in the **scanf** call, the compiler would not have objected in this case either, resulting in disaster: if X were at offset 20 and currently contained the value 544, and the user of the program were to input 12 as the new value of X, then, instead of putting 12 into offset 20, **scanf** would put 12 into offset 544!

Figure 6.1 shows a few lines from the .COD file produced from Program 6.3, related to compiling the instruction Y += X;. As is evident, the compiler did indeed take advantage of the instruction ADC. As is also evident, the compiler is storing the more significant word at a higher address, the opposite of what we did in Programs 6.1 and 6.2. Either way is fine, as long as all operations are consistent. For example, the code in C's **printf** function must be consistent with the storage approach. And, if we were to write an assembly-language procedure to manipulate these 32-bit integers in response to a call from a C program, we would have to write code using this order, too.

```
; |***     Y += X;
; Line 11
        *** 00001a a1 00 00              mov     ax,WORD PTR _X
        *** 00001d 8b 16 02 00           mov     dx,WORD PTR _X+2
        *** 000021 01 06 00 00           add     WORD PTR _Y,ax
        *** 000025 11 16 02 00           adc     WORD PTR _Y+2,dx
```

Figure 6.1

In the display of register values in DEBUG/SYMDEB/CodeView, the condition c(CF) = 1 is indicated by 'CY' ("carry") and c(CF) = 0 by 'NC' ("no carry").

6.1.2 The Overflow Flag

In the introduction to the text, it was mentioned that in the Pascal statement

```
Sum:=X+Y;
```

where X, Y, and Sum are of type **integer**, the resulting value of Sum could be negative even if X and Y are positive. In Chapter 1, a specific example was given in which X = 28,502, Y = 12,344, and the resulting value of Sum was –24,690. The reason for this anomaly is that the true sum, 28,502 + 12,344 = 40,846, cannot be represented as a 16-bit, two's-complement number. The circuitry in the ALU is designed to sense this situation, called an **overflow**, and if it occurs, the OF flag in the FR will be set to indicate that it has occurred. *However*, the machine will not halt or take any sort of special action; it will simply continue with its step A, step B, step C, step A, etc., cycle, sequentially executing the instructions that follow the one that produces the overflow.

So it is up to the *programmer* to include code that takes special action in the event of an overflow. Just as there is a JNS instruction that jumps if SF is not set, and corresponding instructions JNZ and JNC for ZF and CF, there is a JNO instruction—"jump if OF is not set"—for the OF flag. (There are also JS, JZ, JC, and JO instructions, for "jump if SF is set," "jump if ZF is set," and so on.)

As an example of an overflow situation, let us look at code produced by the Microsoft Pascal compiler, shown in Program 6.4. If you compile and run this program with the values X = 28,502 and Y = 12,344, the value –24,690 will be printed out for Y—with no warning message of any kind! This result is not surprising when one examines the machine code produced by the compiler. The relevant lines from the .COD file are given in Figure 6.2. As the figure shows, following the instruction ADD Y,AX, there is no JNO or other instruction which checks the OF flag. (Recall from Chapter 5 that the instruction MOV AX,@@OUTFQQ is part of the code compiled from the call to **writeln** in the Pascal source code and, thus, has no relation to the ADD instruction that precedes it.) Thus, no error is reported.

```
program OvrFlo(input,output);

    var X,Y : integer;

begin
    readln(X,Y);
    Y:=X+Y;
    writeln(Y)
end.
```

Program 6.4

```
L9:
        ** 000043    MOV    AX,X
        ** 000046    ADD    Y,AX
L10:
        ** 00004A    MOV    AX,@@OUTFQQ
```

Figure 6.2

Microsoft Pascal does allow the programmer to make a special request directing the compiler to include code that checks for overflow. This is done by adding a comment

```
{ $mathck+ }
```

in the program source file, say, after the **program** declaration at the top of the file. After modifying Program 6.4, so as to include this comment and running the program with the same input, we get the error message

```
? Error: signed math overflow
  Error Code 2054
PC = 2B78: 000A; SS = 161D, FP = 1212, SP = 176A
```

Again, this happened, not by magic, but at our request: the compiler put in the new code to check OF and take proper action if OF is set. We can see this code in the *new* .COD file:

```
L11:
     ** 000043    MOV      AX,X
     ** 000046    ADD      Y,AX
     ** 00004A    JNO      $+3
     ** 00004C    CALL     I4095
L12:
     ** 00004F    MOV      AX,@@OUTFQQ
```

Immediately after the ADD instruction, the compiler has placed a JNO instruction. In the event of an overflow, a compiler-supplied procedure named I4095 is called, and, of course, it is this procedure which prints out the error message. Otherwise, we jump to the MOV instruction three bytes down from the JNO and proceed as usual.

Note that the procedure I4095 includes the code

```
MOV AH,4CH
INT 21H
```

(or will jump to such code), so that the program is terminated and we return to the operating system (OS), which will then print out its usual > prompt and wait for your next command. The key point is that your user program is voluntarily relinquishing control to the OS. As discussed in Section 4.3, the OS *cannot* "watch over" your program while your program is running—when your program is running, the OS is *not* running, and thus, the OS cannot do anything at all then. In particular, checking the OF flag has to be done by your program itself, not by the OS.

Again, it is important to distinguish between the roles of hardware and software here. The hardware does check for overflow and records such an event in the OF flag, but the software—the machine code produced by the compiler in these examples—does not check it, unless we ask the compiler to produce OF-checking code.

It is likely that the compiler on which you first learned programming produced code to watch for such errors, regardless of whether or not the programmer asked for it. Thus, you might be quite surprised to see that the default policy of the compiler here is *not* to produce code to check for overflow (although an earlier version had the opposite default value). However, this policy is very common. For example, the 'pc' Pascal compiler available with the Unix operating system has the same default: no code for checking overflow will be produced, unless the programmer explicitly requests it, through the −C option. The advantage of not including overflow-check code, of course, is increased speed, although in this example the increase in speed is very minor.

Furthermore, in many C compilers, such checks are not even available as options. Neither the Microsoft C compiler nor the Unix 'cc' compiler is capable of producing code that checks for overflow. Thus, in cases in which this protection is needed, the programmer will need to write portions of the program in assembly language and then link them to the C main program, as in Chapter 5.

The problem of overflow also occurs with instructions such as CMP. Consider, for instance, the instruction

```
CMP BX,DX
```

which computes the quantity DX − BX and sets up flags accordingly. We might follow this instruction with

```
JS Z
```

Looking at this code, it appears that we want to jump to Z if c(BX) < c(DX). But wait a minute—are these supposed to be unsigned or signed quantities? Suppose, for example, c(BX) = 7FFFH and c(DX) = 8000H. If we intend these as unsigned integers, then c(BX) < c(DX), but if we mean them to be signed, then c(BX) > c(DX)! (The reader should verify this.) In *both* cases, the SF flag will be set, so we now see that using a simple JS is not good enough.

For that reason, the iAPX instruction set includes other conditional jump instructions, which check various flag settings. To illustrate, consider the following C program (a very simple example, but one that suffices for our purpose):

```
main ()

{  int x,y;   unsigned int a,b;

   scanf("%d %d %u %u",&x,&y,&a,&b);
   if (x < y) x++;
   if (a < b) y++;
}
```

Let us look at the .COD file to see what machine code the compiler produced from the comparisons in the two **if** statements:

```
; |***     if (x < y) x++;
; Line 8
        *** 000023 8b 46 f8                   mov     ax,WORD PTR [bp-8]    ;y
        *** 000026 39 46 fa                   cmp     WORD PTR [bp-6],ax    ;x
        *** 000029 7d 03                      jge     $I108
        *** 00002b ff 46 fa                   inc     WORD PTR [bp-6] ;x
; |***     if (a < b) y++;
; Line 9
                        $I108:                                             -
        *** 00002e 8b 46 fc                   mov     ax,WORD PTR [bp-4]    ;b
        *** 000031 39 46 fe                   cmp     WORD PTR [bp-2],ax    ;a
        *** 000034 73 03                      jae     $I109
        *** 000036 ff 46 f8                   inc     WORD PTR [bp-8] ;y
; |*** }
```

Clearly, the machine code produced by the compiler for the two **if** statements is identical, except for the conditional jumps used: for the comparison of the signed quantities, the compiler has used the JGE (jump if greater than or equal to) instruction, which jumps if c(SF) = c(OF); for the unsigned case, it has used the JAE (jump if above or equal to) instruction, which jumps if c(CF) = 0.

In the display of register values in DEBUG/SYMDEB/CodeView, the condition c(OF) = 1 is indicated by 'OV' ("overflow"), and c(CF) = 0 is indicated by 'NV' ("no overflow").

6.1.3 Other Flags

Three other flags in FR are the following:

DF: Direction Flag (bit 10).   This is used for special string instructions that will be described later in the chapter.

IF: Interrupt Flag (bit 9).   This is used to control whether the CPU will check to see if some I/O device needs attention. The IF will play a central role in Chapter 7.

TF: Trap Flag (bit 8).   This is the mechanism which allows single-step tracing for debugging programs—e.g., the T command within DEBUG. If an instruction sets this flag, then after each subsequent instruction, the CPU will perform the equivalent of INT 1—that is, a call to service 3. This service is actually not part of DOS (which allocates space for it but just puts an empty routine there); instead, it is usually user written and is part of a debugger such as DEBUG. When we invoke the T command, DEBUG sets bit 8 and does a jump to the instruction we wish to execute. Since the trap flag is set, there will be an automatic return to DEBUG. (You will see how the INT instruction works in Chapter 8.)

There are also an auxiliary carry flag (AF, bit 4) and a parity flag (PF, bit 2) in FR. We will not discuss these here.

Most, but not all, instructions affect most, but not necessarily all, flags. Appendix II shows which flags are affected by each instruction.

A number of special iAPX instructions can be used to set or clear the flags. STC, STD, and STI set CF, DF, and IF, respectively, while CLC, CLD, and CLI clear those flags. CMC will perform a **complement** operation on the carry flag, changing 1 to 0 and vice versa.

In addition, there are instructions to make copies of the flags' values. LAHF loads copies of bits 7–0 of FR to the AH register. SAHF stores copies of these bits from the AH register. Also, PUSHF pushes the entire FR onto the stack, and POPF pops the stack and places the popped value into FR. Section 6.3.2 gives an application of these two instructions.

As mentioned in Chapter 2, most types of CPU have something like the iAPX family's FR. In the 68000 CPU family, for instance, the analogue of FR is called the status register (SR), which includes as a subset the condition code register (CCR). The CCR contains bits named N (negative), Z (zero), V (overflow), and C (carry), corresponding to the iAPX FR's SF, ZF, OF, and CF, respectively. The SR also has a T (trace) bit, basically the same as FR's TF. The CPUs in the 68000 family also have bits corresponding to FR's IF.

6.2 A FURTHER LOOK AT iAPX ADDRESSING MODES

In Chapter 3, we introduced several addressing modes; since then, we have used a couple of others. We will now look at all these modes in a more organized way and discuss some new modes. Again, keep in mind that these are modes that are specific to the iAPX family, although the modes in other machines are usually quite similar.

6.2.1 Register Mode

In register addressing mode, the operand is stored in a register. For example, the instruction

```
SUB AX,BX
```

has both of its operands specified via register addressing mode, while

```
SUB CX,6
```

has only its destination operand specified in register addressing mode. (Its source operand is specified in immediate addressing mode.) Any nonsegment register can be used for register addressing mode.

Storing an operand in a register is much better than storing it in memory, since access to a register (which is internal to the CPU) is faster than access to memory (which is external). Unfortunately, a CPU—especially in the iAPX family—will have only a few registers. Thus, we can only store in registers the items which we anticipate to be most frequently accessed—e.g., we store our sum in AX in Program 3.1. And if we work in a high-level language, hopefully our compiler will be "smart" enough to guess which variables will be most frequently accessed and will put those in registers rather than in memory.

The latter point motivates the C language's **register** attribute. For example,

```
register int G;
```

not only declares G to be an integer variable, but also is a "hint" from the programmer to the compiler that G would be a good candidate for allocation in a register instead of a memory word. The compiler is not required to comply; assignment of G to a register is at the compiler's discretion, especially if one declares more **register** variables than the machine has registers! However, if the compiler *is* able to allocate G in a register, we might achieve some increased code speed.

The following C program is a simple example of register addressing mode:

```
int x[100];

main()

{   int i,s;
    register int rs;

    s = 0;
    for (i = 0; i < 100; i++)
        s += x[i];

    rs = 0;
    for (i = 0; i < 100; i++)
        rs += x[i];
}
```

Upon inspection of the .COD file after compilation of the program, we find that the compiler has indeed granted our request that it try to store the variable rs in a register. The lines corresponding to the C code

```
    s = 0;
```

and

```
    rs = 0;
```

are

```
    *** 00000a    c7 46 fe 00 00        mov   WORD PTR [bp-2],0
```

and

```
    *** 00002d    2b f6                 sub   si,si
```

The compiler has stored s in main( )'s stack, but rs in the SI register.

Unfortunately, C's **register** type is of limited usefulness, especially in a machine using an iAPX CPU, since iAPX CPUs have rather few registers. In fact, the Microsoft C compiler is even more restrictive, since it only uses the SI and DI registers for this purpose and thus has a limit of only two **register** variables.

6.2.2 Immediate Mode

In immediate addressing mode, the operand is a constant stored in the instruction itself. For example, as mentioned earlier, the source operand 6 in the instruction

```
SUB CX,6
```

is specified via immediate addressing mode.

Since it was stated that all addressing modes other than register addressing mode specify operands somewhere in memory, this must be the case for immediate addressing mode, too. This is indeed true: an immediate operand is part of the instruction itself, and since the instruction is stored in memory, it follows that the immediate operand is in memory.

Since an immediate operand is in memory instead of in a register, we run the risk of increased execution time for any instruction that uses immediate addressing mode. However, this is usually not a problem, since iAPX CPUs prefetch instructions. Recall from Chapter 2 that these CPUs will always prefetch upcoming bytes in the instruction stream whenever the bus is free and the instruction queue (IQ) has room. (The capacity of the IQ ranges from 4 bytes in the 8088 to 16 bytes in the 80386.) Thus, since immediate operands are part of the instructions, an immediate operand might already have been prefetched into the IQ before the instruction cycle reached step A; in this case, access to this operand will be just as fast as in register mode.

For example, the instruction SUB CX,6 happens to be a three-byte instruction. If we are reasonably lucky, all three bytes of the instruction will previously have been prefetched before step A of the instruction cycle. If so, they will be ready for us in the IQ, and thus, the 6 will be accessed just as quickly as if it had been specified in register mode.

6.2.3 Direct Mode

In the direct addressing mode, the operand is in memory and the offset of the operand is specified within the instruction itself. The offset is taken to be relative to the current data segment—i.e., the segment currently pointed to by DS.

For example, in the instruction

```
LP2: MOV SAVEBX,BX
```

in Program 4.1, the source operand, BX, is specified via register mode, but the destination operand, SAVEBX, is given in direct addressing mode. Looking at line 87 of Figure 4.4, we see that this instruction has been assembled to 891E 0027. The last four hex digits, 0027, give the location of SAVEBX, as confirmed on line 14 of the figure. So the location of the operand is indeed being specified explicitly within the instruction itself.

Of course, we can always specify a location in direct address mode *numerically*, instead of using a label. If so, however, we must use brackets. For example, the assembly-language line

```
MOV [0027],BX
```

would have *exactly* the same effect as the line

```
MOV SAVEBX,BX
```

in Program 4.1: MASM would assemble either of these lines to the machine instruction 891E 0027.

6.2.4 Indirect Mode

In contrast to direct addressing mode, in which the instruction *explicitly* indicates the data-segment offset of the operand, indirect addressing mode specifies that offset "indirectly," by telling the CPU that the desired offset value is contained in a given register. For instance, the instruction

```
TOP: ADD AX,[BX]
```

in Program 5.5 says that the source operand's offset is the value contained in BX.

Any of the registers BX, SI, and DI may be used with this mode, with brackets being used for mnemonics. Incidentally, it is unfortunate that the designers of MASM (and Intel before them) used brackets both for denoting indirect mode, as we see here, and for denoting direct mode with a numerically specified offset, as we saw in Section 6.2.3. However, we can avoid confusion by remembering that if the brackets enclose a register name, then either indirect, indexed, or based mode is being used, whereas if the brackets enclose a constant—either a numeric constant such as 0027 or a label constant like SAVEBX—then direct mode is being used.

Indirect addressing mode is useful when working with arrays, as in Program 5.5, particularly if one is accessing the arrays sequentially, as in that program. For random access of arrays, indexed addressing is more efficient, as we will see momentarily.

6.2.5 Indexed Addressing

In the indexed addressing mode, the offset of the operand is specified as a constant plus the contents of a register, with the constant specified within the instruction itself. The assembly-language mnemonic for indexed addressing mode is

```
const [reg]
```

where 'const' is either a numeric constant or a label constant and 'reg' is either SI or DI. (In fact, the names of these two registers stem from the fact that they are designed for use in indexed mode—source index (SI) and destination index (DI).) The data-segment offset of the operand is then

```
const + c(reg)
```

For example, suppose we have an array named SALARY (which, say, contains the hourly salaries for a group of employees) that starts at offset 120 of the data segment. Suppose also that we want to add the ith element of the array to CX, where the value of i is in register AX. We could then use the code shown in Program 6.5.

```
;   ith element is at SALARY + (2i - 2)
;       so double AX and subtract 2
ADD AX,AX
SUB AX,2
MOV SI,AX
ADD CX,SALARY[SI]
```

Program 6.5

The expression SALARY[SI] in the last instruction of the program is an example of indexed addressing mode, i.e., of the form

```
const [reg]
```

In this example, 'reg' is of course SI and 'const' is the offset of SALARY. (The latter can be seen more clearly in the machine-language version of the program, which includes the constant 0120.) The net effect is that the address of the source operand is OFFSET SALARY + c(SI).

Compilers usually use indexed addressing mode when translating HLL array accesses. For example, recall the Pascal statement

```
Z[I]:=I*I;
```

in Program 5.13. From the lines following L12 in the .COD file in Figure 5.6, we can see that the compiler translated the statement to

```
; put 2*I in DI
MOV DI,I
SHL DI,1

; put I*I in AX
MOV AX,I
IMUL AX
```

```
; finally, copy AX to Z[I]
MOV Z-2[DI],AX
```

As you will see later, SHL DI,1 multiplies DI by two, and IMUL is the signed version of the MUL instruction we have used earlier. Our focus will be on the last instruction,

```
MOV Z-2[DI],AX
```

Here, the role of 'const' in the general form for indexed mode is played by Z-2, meaning the offset of the array Z, minus two. Thus, the address of the destination operand is

```
OFFSET Z - 2 + c(DI)
```

The reader should verify that this is exactly where Z[I] is, keeping in mind the fact that the compiler stores Z[1] at Z, Z[2] at Z+2, Z[3] at Z+4, and so on.

Use of the indexed addressing mode is more efficient than use of the indirect mode in this case. If we used indirect addressing mode, Program 6.5 would instead look like Program 6.6. In comparing the two programs, we see that the use of indexed mode reduces the code from five instructions to four, again resulting in advantages in memory storage and program speed.

```
ADD AX,AX  ;  i-th element is at X+(2i-2)
SUB AX,2
MOV SI,AX
ADD SI,OFFSET SALARY
ADD CX,[SI]
```

Program 6.6

A glance at some .COD files shows that compilers almost always use indexed addressing mode for accessing arrays. At this point, it is worth mentioning again, as we did in the discussion concerning Program 6.4, that there is no "little man" inside the computer, "watching over things" to make sure that nothing goes wrong. In the present context, this means that indexed addressing mode (or any other related mode) does *not* check the ranges of array subscripts.

```
program Ix(input,output);

    type AryType = array[0..10000] of integer;

    var X,IAry : AryType;
        J,I,Sum : integer;

    procedure time(var s:string); extern;

    procedure prtime;
```

234 A Further Look at the iAPX Architecture   Chap. 6

```
        var y : string(40);
    begin
        time(y);
        writeln(y)
    end;

begin
    {code to prepare X and IAry would go here}
    prtime;
    for J:=1 to 100 do
        begin
        {additional code might go here}
        Sum:=0;
        for I:= 1 to 10000 do
            Sum:=Sum+X[IAry[I]]
        {additional code might go here}
        end;
    prtime
end.
```

Program 6.7

Program 6.7 sums up selected elements of an array X, with the element indices them-selves coming from the array IAry. (There are also two calls to a procedure named 'prtime', which prints out the time, which we will use later on.) Since both arrays have subscript ranges of 0 to 10,000, it will be a violation of the range of the array IAry if I < 0 or I > 10,000 (though it is clear in this particular program that this will not occur) and a violation of the range of X if IAry[I] is below 0 or above 10,000. However, the compiler will not produce code to check for these violations, unless we specifically ask it to, just as we found in Section 6.1 that the compiler will not produce code to check for overflow unless we ask it to.

This absence of any code to check for overflow is clear from the .COD file, the relevant lines of which are shown in Figure 6.3. For example, consider the fetch of IAry[I]. First, I is copied to the DI register. Then, DI needs to be doubled, since element I of IAry is at IARY + 2*I. This doubling could be done by the instruction ADD DI,DI, though it is done here by the SHL instruction (see Section 6.3). But the point is that nowhere is DI checked to make sure that it is in the range 0..10,000.

```
L26:
    **  00005B    MOV    DI,I
    **  00005F    SHL    DI,1
    **  000061    MOV    DI,IARY[DI]
    **  000065    SHL    DI,1
    **  000067    MOV    AX,X[DI]
    **  00006B    ADD    SUM,AX
```

Figure 6.3

The situation can be remedied by giving the compiler a specific command to check ranges:

```
{ $indexck+ }
```

As with the example in Section 6.1, this command can be placed right after the **program** statement at this top of the Pascal source file. Figure 6.3 will then become Figure 6.4. Note that there are now two calls to RCIEQQ, a built-in procedure supplied by the compiler. This procedure checks ranges and takes appropriate action—issuing an error message and terminating the program—if a range violation is discovered. It has two parameters, which of course are the lower and upper bounds of the array index—0 and 10,000 here. The figure shows that both parameters are being pushed onto the stack before the call. The 0 could be generated by the instruction SUB AX,AX, although here the compiler uses the XOR instruction instead. The 10,000 is also pushed; in hex form, it is 2710H.

```
L28:
     ** 00005B    PUSH     I
     ** 00005F    XOR      AX,AX
     ** 000061    PUSH     AX
     ** 000062    MOV      CX,2710H
     ** 000065    PUSH     CX
     ** 000066    LCALL    RCIEQQ
     ** 00006B    XCHG     AX,DI
     ** 00006C    SHL      DI,1
     ** 00006E    PUSH     IARY[DI]
     ** 000072    XOR      AX,AX
     ** 000074    PUSH     AX
     ** 000075    MOV      AX,2710H
     ** 000078    PUSH     AX
     ** 000079    LCALL    RCIEQQ
     ** 00007E    XCHG     AX,DI
     ** 00007F    SHL      DI,1
     ** 000081    MOV      AX,X[DI]
     ** 000085    ADD      SUM,AX
```

Figure 6.4

Again, the default policy of the Pascal compiler is *not* to generate code to check array ranges, because omission of such code produces a faster program. But how much faster? The answer in this case is very interesting.

The procedure 'prtime' in Program 6.7 prints out the current time of day, in hours, minutes, and seconds. It calls a procedure Time that is provided by the compiler. That procedure in turn calls the operating system's print-time-of-day service, service 21/2C. (It would be instructive for the reader to compile and run Program 6.7 using DEBUG (or some other debugger) to trace through the code until this call to the operating system is reached, to verify that the service is indeed called.) Incidentally, whenever looking at the run time for a program, keep in mind the notion of machine dependence: after compiling the program, the resulting machine code in .EXE can be run on any iAPX machine, but there will be major variations in timing from one system to another, as explained in Chapter 2.

Note that there is an outer loop in Program 6.7—the "for J" loop. Thus, the effect of whatever slowdown is introduced by adding range checks will be multiplied 100 times. This illustrates the fact that in most cases in which we wish to improve the execution speed of a program, the most fertile areas for improvement lie within loops.

The result is quite remarkable: the program takes 8 seconds to run in the version that omits range checks and 93 seconds to run in the version that includes range checks! In other words, we are paying a heavy price for the safety bought with range checks.

The reason for the high overhead of range checks is that the two PUSH instructions, the CALL to RCIEQQ, etc., do take time, and since the Pascal loop consists of only a single statement, this overhead is proportionally quite large. Accordingly, we might opt for doing our own range checks in the Pascal source, rather than rely on the compiler. The modified Pascal source code would then be as follows:

```
for J:=1 to 100 do
    begin
    Sum:=0;
    for I:= 0 to 10000 do
        begin
            if (I < 0) or (I > 10000) then goto 999;
            IA:=IAry[I];
            if (IA < 0) or (IA > 10000) then goto 999;
        Sum:=Sum+X[IA]

        end
end;
```

(We put a writeln for an error message at label 999.)

The result is a big improvement: run time will be 15 seconds. This is still double the 8-second time for the original code, but far better than the 93-second time that resulted from the code produced by the compiler for checking ranges.

As with the example concerning overflow in Section 6.1, the situation with range checks is not restricted to Pascal or Microsoft compiler products. The Unix 'pc' Pascal compiler also has a default policy of no range checking, and neither the Microsoft C compiler nor the Unix 'cc' C compiler even offer range checking as an option, let alone as the default.

The iAPX 286, 386, and 486 models include a BOUND instruction, which speeds up the implementation of a test such as

```
if (I < 0) or (I > 10000)
```

This instruction effectively combines two CMP instructions and associated jumps into one instruction. It has two operands. The first is the subscript value to be tested, e.g., I here. The second operand is the name of a two-word block of memory in which the programmer has put the bounds, e.g., 0 and 10,000 here. If a violation of bounds is found, the CPU will execute the equivalent of an INT 5 instruction. Of course, the procedure corresponding to the INT call must be prepared beforehand, either by the operating system or by the author of the program.

6.2.6 Based Mode

In the based addressing mode, the offset of the operand is expressed as the contents of a register plus a constant, just as in indexed mode. The register must be BX for operands in the data segment and BP for operands in the stack segment, as we saw in Section 5.1.

The assembly-language mnemonics for based mode are

```
[reg ± const]
```

and

```
[reg].const
```

and

```
const[reg]
```

These are all equivalent, in the sense that MASM will produce exactly the same machine code from any of them.

Recall from the last section that in typical uses of indexed mode, the operand is a variable distance from a fixed reference point. For instance, in the instruction

```
ADD CX,SALARY[SI]
```

from Program 6.5, SALARY was the name of an array, and the source operand was c(SI) bytes from the start of that array. As we vary SI, we access different elements of the array SALARY. Thus, the operand is a *variable* distance, c(SI), from a *fixed* reference point, SALARY.

In typical uses of based mode, the idea is essentially just the opposite of that of indexed mode: the operand is a *fixed* distance from a *variable* reference point. For instance, we used based addressing mode in Program 4.1, in the instruction

```
LP1:   MOV AX,[BX-4]
```

There, we were fetching the Fibonacci number F_{i-2}. We had arranged things so that BX would always be pointing to F_i, the current Fibonacci number. Thus, F_{i-2}, which is two words behind F_i, is four bytes behind, so that BX − 4 points to it. So as i changes, BX points to different locations, but F_{i-2} is always a distance of four bytes behind BX. In other words, the operand is a fixed distance away from a variable reference point.

Another example of the use of based addressing mode is **record** structure from Pascal (or **struct** in the language C). A Pascal record type is just a collection of several variables, which are referenced collectively.

For example, we might define a type PartRec in a warehouse program, as in Program 6.8. This "packaging" of the part number, quantity, and price of a given part can lead to a substantial improvement in program clarity.

```
type PartRec = record
          PartNum : integer;
          Quantity : integer;
          Price : integer
        end;
```

Program 6.8

We might then have declared several variables of the type PartRec:

```
var CurrPart,NewPart,TempPart : PartRec;
```

For instance, CurrPart ("current part," the one currently under consideration) has CurrPart.PartNum as its part number, CurrPart.Quantity as the number of parts of this type in stock, and CurrPart.Price as its price.

A Pascal compiler could take advantage of the based addressing mode we have introduced. Suppose our Pascal program includes the code fragment shown in Program 6.9. The compiler must produce machine code from this fragment. On an iAPX machine, a compiler could take advantage of based addressing, say, as shown in Program 6.10. Consider, for instance, the instruction MOV P,[BX+4]. BX points to the record CurrPart in the fragment, but at other places in the program it might point to the record NewPart or TempPart. Nonetheless, no matter whether we are accessing CurrPart, NewPart, or TempPart, the Price field will be a fixed distance—four bytes—from the beginning of the record. So we have a variable reference point, i.e., the record, but a fixed distance, four bytes, from that point—again, the operand is a fixed distance from a variable reference point.

```
if CurrPart.PartNum = 125 then
    CurrPart.Quantity:=12
else
    CurrPart.Quantity:=5;
P:=CurrPart.Price;
```

Program 6.9

```
            MOV BX,OFFSET CURR_PART
            CMP [BX],125D
            JNE E
            MOV [BX+2],12D
            JMP O
     E:     MOV [BX+2],5D
     O:     MOV P,[BX+4]
```

Program 6.10

Of course, this technique is equally useful for the C language's **struct** type, which is the analogue of Pascal's **record** type. In C, the Pascal declaration in Program 6.8 would look like Program 6.11, and the Pascal code in Program 6.9 would look like Program 6.12 in C. Again, the compiler would translate this C source code to something like Program 6.10.

```
struct PartRec   {
        int PartNum;
        int Quantity;
        int Price;
        } CurrPart,NewPart,TempPart;
```

Program 6.11

```
if (CurrPart.PartNum == 125)
   CurrPart.Quantity = 12;
else
   CurrPart.Quantity = 5;
P = CurrPart.Price;
```

Program 6.12

6.2.7 Combined Indexed and Based Modes

The iAPX family also includes addressing modes in which the offset of the operand is given by

```
c(reg1) + c(reg2) + const
```

where reg1 is either BX (to specify an operand in the data segment) or BP (to specify an operand in the stack segment) and reg2 is either SI or DI. For example, this mode is used to specify the destination operand in the instruction

```
MOV [BX+SI+420],CX
```

Just as indexed addressing mode is useful in accessing one-dimensional arrays, combined indexed and based modes are useful for accessing two-dimensional arrays.

6.2.8 Use of the Addressing Modes in JMP and CALL Instructions

The various addressing modes can be used with JMP and CALL instructions. For example, the following are all legal, and have various effects:

```
JMP BX
JMP [BX]
JMP FAR PTR Z
JMP DWORD PTR Z
```

One can get MASM to generate a variety of JMP or CALL instructions this way, varying near and far aspects, as well as presence and absence of indirection. For example, JMP FAR PTR Z will produce a far jump to Z, while JMP DWORD PTR Z will produce a far jump to the place *pointed to* by the contents of Z and Z + 2 (containing the offset and segment of the jump target, respectively). The reader is invited to experiment with these, using DEBUG or some other debugging tool, to see the actions taken.

6.2.9 Segment Override

Suppose, in a certain assembly-language program, that one of our instructions needs, for some reason, to copy the contents of the absolute address 2AD46 to BX. Keep in mind that this is an absolute address, not an address relative to DS. If, for example, we knew that DS had the value 2020, then the instruction

```
ADD BX, [0AB46H]
```

would accomplish our goal, since

```
16*2020 + AB46 = 20200 + AB46 = 2AD46
```

But this kind of knowledge is unrealistic, since we would usually not know at the time we write the program what value will be in DS—i.e., where the loader will load our data segment. Thus, there is no guarantee that the location 2AD46 will fall within the data segment. So how can we access that location?

One way, of course, would be to change DS temporarily to point to a region near 2AD46. We could use code like that shown in Program 6.13. In default form, direct addressing mode supplies an offset that is interpreted relative to the current value of DS. In this case, that value is 2AD4, so that the instruction

```
MOV BX, [0006]
```

moves to BX the contents of absolute address 2AD40 + 0006 = 2AD46, as desired. (Of course, we could have used other segment-offset combinations, such as putting 2AD2 in

DS and then using an offset of 0026 in the MOV instruction; this would still result in address 2AD46 being accessed.)

```
PUSH DS  ;  save old value of DS
MOV AX,2AD4
MOV DS,AX  ;  location 2AD46 is now at offset 0006
MOV BX,[0006]  ;  [ ] is mnemonic for direct addressing mode in numeric form
POP DS   ;    restore DS
```

Program 6.13

A better way to accomplish the move is given in Program 6.14. The **instruction prefix** ES: in the instruction MOV BX,ES:[0006] tells the assembler to append a **segment override byte** at the beginning of the machine code for this instruction. This byte tells the CPU *not* to use the default register DS as the segment value from which the offset is measured, but instead to use ES. You can now see where the name comes from: the segment override byte *overrides* the default *segment* register for an instruction. The name ES stands for "extra segment." Instead of undergoing the nuisance of constantly changing the value of DS, as in Program 6.13, we can keep DS pointed to the "main" data segment and use ES to point to an "extra" segment, which is much handier. It is like having an extra hand when working with shop tools. Imagine having a hammer in one hand and pliers in the other hand—wouldn't it be nice to have a "third hand" in that situation? The ES register gives us an "extra segment" to use, in that same spirit.

```
MOV AX,2AD4H
MOV ES,AX
MOV BX,ES:[0006]
```

Program 6.14

Segment override works the same way with other registers. For example, consider the instruction

```
MOV CX,[BP+2]
```

in Program 5.8, which is a procedure called from a main program. This instruction retrieves a parameter from the stack. By default, the use of BP in based addressing mode refers to the stack—i.e., c(BP) is treated as an offset from the SS register. That is why the instruction

```
MOV CX,[BX+2]
```

would *not* retrieve the parameter from the stack, since, by default, BX is used to specify offsets from DS, not SS. But if we do want to use BX here, we can use segment override, to override the default segment for that register. If we had earlier set c(BX) to c(SP), the instruction

```
MOV CX,SS:[BX+2]
```

would produce the same effect as MOV CX,[BP+2] does in Program 5.8. It tells the CPU to ignore the default segment register for BX, which is DS, and use SS instead. Of course, since we are already using BX for other purposes in Program 5.8, the use of segment override would actually complicate, rather than simplify, our lives (we would have to save and restore BX with PUSH and POP), so we probably would not choose to use the technique. But the point is that it is technically possible, and sometimes desirable, to use segment override with registers other than ES.

6.3 A FURTHER LOOK AT THE iAPX INSTRUCTION SET

6.3.1 Other Arithmetic Instructions

So far, the main arithmetic instructions we have used are ADD, SUB, MUL, and DIV. Let us take a closer look at the last two and introduce some others.

To describe MUL, recall that in the multiplication $x*y$, x is called the **multiplier**, y is called the **multiplicand**, and $x*y$ is called the **product**. The MUL instruction allows the programmer freedom only in specifying the multiplier; the multiplicand *must* be in AX, and the product *must* go into DX and AX (see shortly). MUL is an example of the nonorthogonal nature of the iAPX instruction set.

Since we are multiplying two 16-bit numbers together, the product is a 32-bit quantity, with DX and AX storing the more significant and less significant 16-bit portions, respectively.

For example, to multiply 2025H by the quantity in BX, we would use the code

```
MOV AX,2025H
MUL BX
```

The product would then be in DX and AX, as just described. Again, the multiplier and product locations are implicit in the operation—i.e., AX and DX are not mentioned in the mnemonics MUL BX, since we have no choice for these registers.

The MUL instruction affects the OF flag, but in a somewhat different way from the way the ADD instruction does. If we multiply two 16-bit numbers together, we get a 32-bit product, and since this can fit into the DX,AX pair that MUL uses for its products, there is no possibility of overflow in the sense we saw for the ADD instruction. However, if, in some particular application, the product is supposed to be a 16-bit number, a nonzero c(DX) after MUL would mean an error. Thus, the designers of the iAPX CPUs set up the circuitry for MUL so that it sets OF if c(DX) turns out to be nonzero.

Division basically is done in the same setting as multiplication. Recall that in the division x/y, x is called the **dividend**, y is called the **divisor**, and x/y is called the **quotient**. The DIV instruction has an implicit 32-bit dividend in DX and AX, with DX containing the high 16 bits and AX the low 16 bits, while the divisor is specified explicitly in the instruction. The quotient is implicitly AX, and the remainder after division is implicitly DX.

For example, suppose we want to divide 2025H by the number in BX. We could use the code shown in Program 6.15. After execution of this code, the quotient and remainder will be in AX and DX, respectively.

```
MOV AX,2025H
MOV DX,0
DIV BX
```

Program 6.15

Note that we had to put 0 into DX, even though in this example our dividend was only a 16-bit number. The CPU circuitry that implements DIV does not "know" that the dividend happened to be small enough to fit into 16 bits, and thus, DIV will assume that DX contains the upper word of the dividend. Had we not set DX to 0, whatever "garbage" happened to be in DX would be used by DIV, giving us a grossly incorrect answer.

MUL and DIV do multiplication and division, respectively, of unsigned numbers. Their counterparts, IMUL and IDIV, handle the signed case. However, one must be a bit more delicate in using IDIV. Suppose, for example, that, in using IDIV, we want our dividend to be the number –6, which is FFFA as a 16-bit hex number. Then we do *not* want to put 0 in DX, as we did in Program 6.15. In bit form the dividend –6 is

```
1111111111111010
```

If we put 0 into DX, then the 32-bit DX,AX dividend would be

```
00000000000000001111111111111010
```

which, as a 32-bit string, codes 65,530, not –6. The latter has the code

```
11111111111111111111111111111010
```

So instead of the instruction MOV DX,0 we should use MOV DX,0FFFFH. (Recall that when we include an immediate constant in an instruction—in this case, the constant FFFFH—MASM insists that the constant begin with a numeral, so we must prefix the 0 here.)

Accordingly, for the general case of a 16-bit dividend in, say, BX, divided by CX, we could use the code shown in Program 6.16. However, the instruction CWD ("convert word to double word") shown in Program 6.17 would do the job more conveniently and efficiently. CWD has no explicit operands; its implicit operands are AX and DX. It copies bit 15 of AX to all bits of DX. As is evident from Program 6.16, that is exactly what we need here. So CWD enables us to replace four instructions by one, which will result in less space used for machine code and faster execution.

```
        MOV AX,BX
        JS N  ;  jump if SF set
        MOV DX,0
     JMP  D
N:   MOV DX,0FFFFH
D:   IDIV CX
```

Program 6.16

```
    MOV AX,BX
    CWD
    IDIV CX
```

Program 6.17

Recall from Chapter 3 that some instructions have byte forms as well as word forms. This is also the case for IMUL, MUL, IDIV, and DIV. If your multiplier and multiplicand are both 8-bit quantities, use MUL or IMUL in 8-bit form, say, by specifying the multiplier via an 8-bit cell such as the BH register. Similarly, if you have a 16-bit dividend and an 8-bit divisor, use IDIV or DIV in 8-bit form.

Just as there are special instructions for addition and subtraction by one, there also are special instructions for multiplication and division by powers of two. For example, the instruction SAL ("shift arithmetic left") will perform multiplication efficiently by powers of two. Thus, if you wanted to multiply the contents of AX by $8 = 2^3$, you could use the code shown in Program 6.18. The SAL instruction will **shift** AX by three bit positions to the left. The old contents of bit 0 will go into bit 3, the old contents of bit 1 will go into bit 4, and so on, with the old contents of bit 12 going into bit 15. Meanwhile, the vacated bits—bits 2, 1, and 0—will be filled with zeros.

```
    MOV CL,3
    SAL AX,CL
```

Program 6.18

As an example, suppose c(AX) originally was 5, which is

```
0000000000000101
```

in binary. After shifting left three bit positions, AX will look like this:

```
0000000000101000
```

This is binary for 40, which indeed equals 8*5. The process is very similar to the base-10 case: if we shift a base-10 number three digits to the left, appending three zeros at the right end, we multiply the number by 1,000, which is 10^3. In base-2 arithmetic, shifting three bits to the left multiplies the number by 2^3.

As with other arithmetic operations, we must watch for overflow when using SAL. For example, suppose c(AX) is 4,099. In binary form, this is

```
0001000000000011
```

If we shift left by three bits, we get

```
1000000000011000
```

Since the most significant, i.e., leftmost, bit has changed from 0 to 1, the number has changed from positive to negative—an error, since both operands in the multiplication were positive. The problem is that 8*4,099 = 32,792, which is beyond the upper bound for 16-bit signed numbers, namely, 32,767. The circuitry in the ALU will detect this error and set the OF flag to indicate it. Of course, it is still the programmer's responsibility to include code such as JNO to check OF.

The use of SAL for multiplication can result in a substantial increase in execution speed. The instruction

```
SAL BX,CL
```

where c(CL) has been set to b, takes $5 + b$ clock cycles on iAPX 286 machines. By contrast, the equivalent instruction

```
MUL BX
```

where c(AX) = 2^b, takes 21 cycles. So, if one needs to do, for example, multiplication by eight, one will find that SAL is about 2.5 times faster than MUL.

What about multiplication by something other than a power of two—say, multiplication by nine? We could use SAL to get $8x$ and then use ADD to produce $9x$. Since a register-to-register ADD instruction only takes two clock cycles, this combination of two instructions would still be faster than MUL alone.

Similarly, division by powers of two can be performed efficiently by the SAR instruction, which shifts to the right. To divide the contents of AX by eight, for example, we could use the code shown in Program 6.19. The SAR instruction will shift bit i to bit $i-3$, for $i = 14, 13, \ldots, 3$. Bits 2–0 are lost. (They comprise the remainder upon division by 8.) Bits 15–12 will be filled by copies of the old value of bit 15, which is necessary for the operation to work correctly for negative dividends.

```
MOV CL,3
SAR AX,CL
```

Program 6.19

To illustrate how the SAR instruction works with negative dividends, suppose AX contains the value –2, i.e.,

```
1111111111111110
```

and suppose we want to divide by two. Division by two should mean a shift to the right by one bit. But if this were to be done naively to the preceding bit string, the result would be

```
0111111111111111
```

which is +32,767, not –1, which we would expect to get! But if the shift to the right is accompanied by the copying of bit 15 as just described, then the result is

```
1111111111111111
```

which is –1, the correct value.

If we are working with unsigned numbers, we can use SHR instead of SAR. SHR simply puts zeros into the left-hand bits that are vacated by the shift to the right. The assembler will also recognize the mnemonic SHL, but it is translated to the same op code as SAL, since shift-left operations are identical for unsigned and signed numbers.

A related pair of instructions is ROL ("rotate left"), which was introduced in Chapter 4, and its rightward counterpart ROR ("rotate right"). The key difference between a rotation and a shift is that, although, in a rotation, shifting is done, no bits are lost, either off the left end for a left shift or off the right end for a right shift. Instead, the bits are rotated around to the other end, to fill vacated positions.

```
MOV CL,3
ROL AX,CL
```

Program 6.20

Program 6.20 illustrates the ROL instruction. This instruction will move bit 0 to bit 3, bit 1 to bit 4, and so on through bit 12 to bit 15. Bits 13, 14, and 15 are moved to bits 0, 1, and 2, respectively. If the original contents of AX were

```
1011010100001100
```

then the new contents will be

```
1010100001100101
```

All of SAR, SAL, SHR, SHL, ROR, and ROL can be used in either word or byte form. If more than one bit needs to be shifted, as in the preceding examples, the number of bits to be shifted must be in CL; it is not allowed to be specified in any other register. In the case of shifting by only one bit, CL is not specified in the assembly-language mnemonics. For example,

```
SAR BX,1
```

specifies a shift of BX to the right by one bit position. (At the machine level, the multi-bit and single-bit versions of SAR have different op codes.)

Except for the 486 model, the iAPX architecture does not include instructions that do floating-point arithmetic. However, Intel produces **coprocessor** chips—named 8087, 80287, and 80387—that do provide such instructions and thus supplement the capabilities of the CPU. For example, there is an FADD instruction to add two floating-point numbers in the 32-bit format discussed in Section 1.2.2. (The coprocessor can also handle a 64-bit version.) Without this supplemental instruction, we would have to use a combination of more primitive instructions to do the same thing—e.g., we might use AND (see Section 6.3.2), SHR, and SHL to separate the mantissa and exponent fields of the number in question, use more shifts to equalize the exponents so that the mantissas can be added, add the mantissas using the ordinary integer ADD instruction, and so on. A coprocessor will do all this in a single instruction and, moreover, is implemented to do many of the steps in parallel. Thus, a floating-point add operation using FADD is *much* faster than it would be using primitive instructions.

There are, of course, floating-point operations for subtraction, multiplication, division, comparison, and so on, and the 387 chip even has instructions such as FSIN, which computes the trigonometric sine of an angle. Thus, a coprocessor can bring about a tremendous increase in the speed of a program that does a lot of floating-point computation. Many computers using iAPX CPUs include sockets in which such a coprocessor can easily be inserted if purchased separately. Incidentally, even if a coprocessor is present, one needs to take positive action to use it. For example, a compiler needs to be informed of the presence of the coprocessor. If a Pascal program has a statement

```
X:=X+Y;
```

where X and Y are declared of type **real**, we want the compiler to generate an FADD instruction, instead of a call to a procedure that does floating-point addition using primitive instructions. Thus, we must inform the compiler that our system has a coprocessor chip. Check your compiler manual for details.

If you have a coprocessor, such as any of those in the 80x87 series, the main processor must actively coordinate its actions with the coprocessor. ESC and WAIT can be used for this task. The operation is fairly delicate, and we will not go into it any further here.

The new iAPX 486 CPU incorporates FADD and the other floating-point instructions as part of its own instruction set. Thus, no coprocessor is necessary.

The arithmetic instructions in non-iAPX architectures are generally similar to what we have seen here. There are some noteworthy exceptions, however. For example, **vector architectures**, such as that of the Cray machines, include instructions for **scalar** operations, as we have seen here, *and* instructions for **vector** operations, i.e., operations dealing with arrays as their basic operands. Thus, in addition to an ordinary ADD instruction, such a machine will have a VADD instruction, which adds two arrays together, element by element. In other words, suppose we have the Pascal code

```
for i:=1 to n do
   x[i]:=x[i]+y[i];
```

where n is within the size of arrays that our machine can handle with the VADD instruction. The compiler could implement this Pascal loop with a single machine instruction, instead of setting up a loop of several machine instructions. This not only would allow a lot of steps A and B to be skipped, but also would enable parallelism in the form of **pipelining**, in which, say, a beginning stage of the action

```
x[125]:=x[125]+y[125]
```

might be done simultaneously with an advanced stage of

```
x[124]:=x[124]+y[124]
```

Vector instructions such as VADD comprise one of the major sources of speed for machines such as the Cray, although, of course, it only applies to applications that are **vectorizable**. (Machines of this class typically also have an extremely fast clock rate, which helps almost any application.)

In another interesting departure from iAPX architecture, in some architectures, even some basic *integer* operations are "missing." For example, although most modern machines have MUL and DIV instructions such as those we have discussed, some RISC architectures (see Chapter 2), such as the SPARC from Sun Microsystems, do not have such instructions. Instead, these operations must be synthesized by using several primitive instructions. The designers of SPARC felt that by omitting these and certain other instructions, a much faster architecture could be designed.

6.3.2 Logical (Boolean) Operations

In many applications, we are interested in manipulating one or more bits in a memory word or in a register. We might wish to **set** a group of bits, i.e., make all the bits in the group 1's, or **clear** the group of bits, i.e., make them all 0's. Or we might need to test whether a certain bit pattern is in a given field of a word. For example, you will see in Chapter 7 that input/output devices such as keyboards and printers are controlled by setting or clearing certain bits in **interface registers**, which attach a device to the bus.

To set bits, we use the OR instruction. This instruction performs the **or** operation, which operates on the set {0,1} as shown in Figure 6.5. The word "or" here is borrowed from the logical **or**, such as the Pascal keyword **or** and the C symbol ‖. The value 0, then, plays the role of **false** and 1 represents **true**. Note that **or** also operates like addition, except that 1 "+" 1 = 1.

```
0 or 0 = 0
0 or 1 = 1
1 or 0 = 1
1 or 1 = 1
```

Figure 6.5

Figure 6.5 can be written in the compact form shown in Figure 6.6, in which x can be either 0 or 1. The figure shows the central usefulness of the **or** operation for bit manipulation: if we **or** any bit with 0, that bit is unchanged; if we **or** any bit with 1, that bit is changed to a 1. Thus, the **or** operation can be used to change specified bits to 1's, by **or**-ing with 1's, while leaving the other bits in the word unchanged, by **or**-ing with 0's.

```
x or 0 = x
x or 1 = 1
```

Figure 6.6

Suppose, for instance, that we wish to set bits 3 and 8 in BX—i.e., make these bits 1's—but leave the other bits in BX unchanged. Then we simply **or** BX with

```
0000000100001000
```

This bitstring has 1's at bits 3 and 8, so Figure 6.6 tells us that if we **or** BX with that number, bits 3 and 8 of BX will become 1's and all other bits in BX will be left unchanged, just as desired. So the instruction we would use is

```
OR BX,0108H
```

As another example, suppose we wish to set the trap flag, bit 8 in the FR (see Section 6.1.3), but do not want to disturb the other flags in the FR. We could use the code

```
PUSHF   ; push FR onto stack (will not affect FR)
MOV BP,SP   ; prepare to use OR on the stack
OR WORD PTR [BP],0100H   ; set bit 8, not changing the other bits
POPF   ; get the new set of values of the flags back into FR
```

To clear bits—i.e., put zeros in them, we use an AND instruction. The **and** operation is analogous to Pascal's **and** and C's **&&** and is shown in Figure 6.7. The operation works the same as multiplication.

```
0 and 0 = 0
0 and 1 = 0
1 and 0 = 0
1 and 1 = 1
```

Figure 6.7

Figure 6.8 shows the compact form of **and**; according to it, **and**ing a bit with a 0 will clear that bit, while **and**ing with a 1 will leave the bit unchanged. For example, if we wished to clear bit 14 of AX but not change any of the other bits in AX, we could **and** AX with the quantity

```
1011111111111111
```

To do this, we would use the instruction

```
AND AX,0BFFFH
```

```
x and 0 = 0
x and 1 = x
```

Figure 6.8

Both OR and AND affect the flags register, just as the arithmetic operations, such as ADD and SUB, do. For instance, by checking the ZF flag after using the proper AND instruction, we can test whether certain bits contain zeros. Suppose we wished to test whether bits 2 and 15 of BX are both zeros, and if they are, we will jump to a place named Q. The code shown in Program 6.21 would accomplish this task. Observe that after the AND is executed, the result will be 0000H if and only if the *original* bits 15 and 2 were both zero—which is exactly what we wanted to check. If the result is 0000H, the ZF flag in FR will be set and will be noticed in the JZ instruction.

```
MOV AX,BX    ;   make a copy of BX, so as not to destroy it
AND AX,8004H;   copy bits 15 and 2 and make all the rest zeros
JZ Q    ;     if both bits are zero, jump to Q
```

Program 6.21

In Program 6.21, BX is copied to AX so as not to destroy BX with the AND operation. No such copy would have been necessary if we had used TEST instead of AND, as shown in Program 6.22. The TEST instruction performs the same action as AND, but does *not* store the result back to the destination operand. Instead, the result is simply discarded. The goal, of course, has still been achieved: the flags in FR— particularly, ZF—have been updated. In this sense, the relationship of TEST to AND is analogous to that of CMP to SUB.

```
TEST BX,8004H
JZ Q
```

Program 6.22

Another logical operation is NOT, which changes 0's to 1's and vice versa. If, for example, DX contains

```
1101001011101101
```

then, after execution of the instruction

```
NOT DX
```

DX will contain

```
0010110100010010
```

In terms of high-level language operations, **not** is like Pascal's keyword **not** and C's symbol '!'.

Yet another commonly used logical instruction is XOR (exclusive or). In mathematical logic, the term **exclusive or** means "one or the other, but not both." In other words, the truth of the logical expression x-exclusive–or-y implies that one of x and y is true, but not both. So, in terms of 0's and 1's, again with 0 meaning false and 1 meaning true, x-exclusive–or-y for *bits* x and y would have the value 1 if exactly one of x and y is 1 and would have the value 0 otherwise. An alternative way of viewing the operation is that x-exclusive–or-y is equal to $x + y$ mod 2.

A common usage of XOR is to make a quantity zero. For example,

```
XOR AX,AX
```

will produce the same effect as

```
MOV AX,0
```

Program 6.23 illustrates many of the concepts presented in the last few subsections. It uses logical operations and shift/rotate instructions to implement what are called **packed arrays** in Pascal. The idea is to save memory space by "packing" several items in a word of memory.

For example, we might have a Pascal declaration, such as

```
var Y : packed array[1..40000] of 0..3;
```

Each element of the array takes on the value 0, 1, 2, or 3. Accordingly, every value in this range can be stored in a two-bit string, and thus, eight values can be stored in one word. The array Y, then, would take up only 40,000/8 = 5,000 words, rather than 40,000. (An additional benefit, with some compilers, is that we would be allowed to use such a long array in the first place. Recall Analytical Exercise 3 in Chapter 2.)

Unfortunately, many Pascal compilers only partially implement or even completely ignore the **packed** attribute. However, if the attribute is needed, we can write our own assembly-language procedures to manage a packed version of an array and, as in Chapter 5, interface these procedures to our Pascal program. Program 6.23 shows this could be done. It inputs values from the keyboard, stores them into the packed array, and retrieves the values at the user's request. (Of course, the program would also *use* the values—say, for various computations—but we have not done so here.)

```
program P(input,output);

     type AryType = array[1..5000] of integer;

     var X : AryType;    {all elements will be packed here}
         Index1,   {index from user's point of view}
         Index2,   {index within X}
         BitPos    {starting bit position of this element}
              : integer;
         Done : boolean;
         Command : char;

     procedure Store(V,I2,BPos:integer; var A:AryType); extern;
```

```
function Vl(I2,BPos:integer; var A:AryType) : integer; extern;

procedure FindI2BPos;
    var Remain : integer;
begin
        {finds I2 and BitPos}
    Index2:=Index1 div 8 + 1;
    Remain:=Index1 mod 8;
    if Remain <> 0 then
        BitPos:=17-2*Remain
    else
        begin
        Index2:=Index2-1;
        BitPos:=1
        end
end;

procedure AccessAry;
    var Val : integer;
begin
    writeln('enter index');
    readln(Index1);
    FindI2BPos;
    if Command = 's' then
        begin
        writeln('enter value to be stored');
        readln(Val);
        Store(Val,Index2,BitPos,X)
        end
    else
        writeln('the value is ',Vl(Index2,BitPos,X))
end;

begin
    Done:=false;
    repeat
        writeln('store, retrieve, or quit?');
        readln(Command);
        if Command = 'q' then Done:=true
        else AccessAry
    until Done
end.
```

Program 6.23

To illustrate how the program operates, suppose the user wishes to put the value 3 into Y[10]. If the compiler had been one that obeys packing, we could have declared Y as

```
var Y : packed array[1..40000] of 0..3;
```

and the code would have looked something like

```
Y[Index1]:=Val;
```

where earlier code had read 10 and 3 into Index1 and Val, respectively. But here we are assuming that the compiler does not obey the **packed** attribute (Microsoft Pascal does not fully implement this attribute), and thus, we will do packing on our own, by writing some assembly-language procedures to supplement the Pascal program. First, note that there is no array Y in the program. Instead, the array name is X, and we will pack our "Y" into it. In particular, each element of Y will take up two bits, and we will pack eight elements of Y into each element of X. Thus, Y[1] through Y[8] will be in X[1], Y[9] through Y[16] will be in X[2], and so on. We see, then, that Y[10] will go into X[2], in the second field, i.e., bits 13 and 12, of that word. In terms of the variables in Program 6.23, this means that

Index1 is 10
Val is 3
Index2 is 2
BitPos is 13

From the code in Program 6.23, the actual storage of 3 into Y[10]—i.e., into bits 13 and 12 of X[2]—will be done by the procedure Store. This procedure, as well as its counterpart function Vl, which retrieves a previously stored value, is an assembly-language procedure in a file PCKD.ASM, shown in Program 6.24. Let us trace through STORE in the .ASM file. First, there is a call to the macro PREPREGS. This was made a macro because both STORE and VL use its code. (The reader should rewrite PREPREGS as a procedure to see why a macro is so much better. The problem is that a procedure call would affect the stack.) PREPREGS first executes the code

```
PUSH BP
MOV BP,SP
```

which was mentioned in Chapter 5 to be necessary when interfacing to Pascal or C.

```
PUBLIC STORE,VL

PREPREGS  MACRO
; prepares BP, BX, CL, AX for either STORE or VL:
;        --    set BP to SP, as usual
;        --    point BX to the word that contains the requested bit field
;        --    set CL to the number of bits to be rotated (see AX, next line)
;        --    get the word pointed to by BX, put it in AX, and rotate so that
;              the requested bit field is on the right end
; set up BP:
PUSH BP
MOV BP,SP
```

```
;  set up BX:
;  first get I2
MOV BX,[BP+0AH]
;  convert I2 to a distance from the beginning of array
ADD BX,BX
SUB BX,2
;  now determine offset of the word within the data segment
ADD BX,[BP+6]
;  set up CL
MOV CL,[BP+8]
DEC CL
;  set up AX
;  get the word from memory
MOV AX,[BX]
;  rotate the requested bit field to the right end
ROR AX,CL
ENDM

ACSG    SEGMENT
ASSUME CS:ACSG

STORE PROC FAR
PREPREGS
AND AX,0FFFCH   ;  blank out the field
;  now store the value in our AX copy
ADD AX,[BP+0CH]
;  rotate back to position
ROL AX,CL
;  OK, copy back to storage word
MOV [BX],AX
POP BP
RET 8
STORE ENDP

VL PROC FAR
PREPREGS
AND AX,0003H
POP BP
RET 6
VL ENDP

ACSG    ENDS
END
```

Program 6.24

Next, we determine the distance of our word from the beginning of the array. X[1] is at X, X[2] is at $X + 2$, X[3] is at $X + 4$, and so on, so, in general, the distance we want is $2*I2 - 2$. Our code adds this distance to the beginning offset of the array—which was the parameter pointed to by $BP + 6$—to get the offset of our word. The code then stores this offset in BX.

The next action is to copy our storage word to AX and rotate the field of interest to the right end, i.e., to bits 1 and 0 of AX. For Index1 = 10, etc., this will mean copying the word at X + 2 and rotating it 12 bits to the right (from bit 13 to bit 1). The number of bits to be rotated comes from subtracting 1 from the parameter BPos. This parameter is the one pointed to by BP + 8.

We are now ready to store the value 3 into AX. Keep in mind, though, that AX still contains copies of all the other bits of our storage word, not just the bit field at which we will be storing a new value. What we are going to do is put that value into that bit field in AX, rotate AX back to its original order, and then finally write AX back to our storage word. In doing all this, we must be careful to preserve those bits which are not supposed to be changed.

With this latter aim in mind, examine the instruction

```
AND AX,0FFFCH
```

This instruction put zeros in bits 1 and 0 of AX, while leaving bits 15–2 unchanged. We then store our value—the parameter pointed by BP + CH—into bits 1–0 by a simple add instruction:

```
ADD AX,[BP+0CH]
```

Finally, we rotate back—i.e., rotate 12 bits to the *left*, so that our field is back at bits 13 and 12 again—with the instruction

```
ROL AX,CL
```

and write AX back to the storage word:

```
MOV [BX],AX
```

The procedure VL, which *retrieves* a previously stored item, is very similar to STORE. We copy the storage item to AX, rotate the field of interest around to bits 1–0, and then **and** AX with the bit string

```
0000000000000011
```

Accordingly, all bits are cleared to 0 except bits 1 and 0, which comprise the field we wanted to retrieve. Thus, we have isolated that field and can return its value to the Pascal calling program. (Recall that Pascal and C expect the value to be returned via AX, which is fine, since it is already in that register.)

Program 6.24 would be linked to Program 6.23 in the manner presented in Chapter 5.

As mentioned previously, some Pascal compilers ignore the **packed** attribute. If we have such a compiler on our machine, we can use assembly-language supplements to do our own packing, as we have just done. The case of the language C is quite different. On the one hand, C does not even have an attribute like Pascal's **packed**. On the other hand, it has enough other features that allow us to do our own packing without resorting to writing procedures in assembly language. In fact, C has a number of features that are analogues of the machine instructions AND and OR and the various shift instructions. That is why we can often avoid resorting to the use of assembly language if we are writing in C.

Program 6.25 is a C-language analogue of Programs 6.23 and 6.24. The main program and the functions FindI2BPos and AccessAry are almost exactly the same as those of the Pascal version in Program 6.23. Note, though, that all arrays in C start at element 0. Thus, the array X consists of X[0], X[1], ... , X[4999], and our "imaginary" array Y consists of Y[0] through Y[39999]. Y[0] will be stored in bits 15–14 of X[0], Y[1] will be stored in bits 13–12 of X[0], and so on.

```c
#define TRUE 1
#define FALSE 0


int X[100];   /* all data will be stored here */


int Index1,   /* index from user's point of view */
    Index2,   /* index within the array X */
    BitPos;   /* starting bit position */


char Command,   /* user command (sTORE,rETRIEVE,qUIT) */
     CR;   /* carriage return */


void Store(V,I2,BPos)
   int V,I2,BPos;
{ unsigned int Mask;

   /* set up a mask with 0's at the bit field of interest, 1's elsewhere */
   Mask = 0xffff - (0x0003 << BPos-1);
   /* AND the element of X with the mask, putting 0's into the bit field of interest */
   X[I2] &= Mask;
   /* now add in V at that bit field, by shifting V and adding it to X[I2] */
   X[I2] += V << BPos-1;
}


int Vl(I2,BPos)
   int I2,BPos;
{ unsigned int XI2;   /* need unsigned, since it will be shifted */

   XI2 = X[I2];
   /* shift left, to get rid of bits 15, 14, ..., BPos+1 */
   XI2 <<= 15 - BPos;
```

```
/* shift right, to get the field in bits 1 and 0, with 0's in bits 15-2 */
XI2 >>= 14;
/* the value of interest is now in XI2 */
return(XI2);
}


void FindI2BPos()
{  int Remain;
   Index2 = Index1 / 8;
   Remain = Index1 % 8;
   BitPos = 15 - 2*Remain;
}

void AccessAry()
{  int Val;
   printf("enter index0);
   scanf("%d%c",&Index1,&CR);
   FindI2BPos();
   if (Command == 's')  {
      printf("enter value to be stored0);
        scanf("%d%c",&Val,&CR);
        Store(Val,Index2,BitPos);
      }
   else
      printf("the value is %d0,Vl(Index2,BitPos));
}


main()

{  char Done;  /* Boolean */

   Done = FALSE;
   do  {
      printf("store, retrieve, or quit?0);
        scanf("%c%c",&Command,&CR);
        if (Command == 'q')
           Done = TRUE;
        else
           AccessAry();
      } while (!Done);
}
```

Program 6.25

___

If you are new to the C language, note that in reading characters, it is not possible to skip over the end-of-line character (there is no analogue of Pascal's **readln**), so that character must be read, too. Otherwise, it would be read as the next user "command." Note also the **#define** lines at the top of the file. These are the C analogues of Pascal's **const** declaration. The keyword **void** in the declarations of Store, FindI2BPos, and

AccessAry means that these functions have no return value—i.e., they are like Pascal procedures instead of Pascal functions; in C, all subprograms are called functions. The **!** symbol in the **while** statement is the same as Pascal's **not**. Also, in the function FindI2BPos, note that / plays the role of Pascal's **div** and % is the same as Pascal's **mod**.

Now we will be able to implement our own packing by taking advantage of some special features of the language C. The two main features used here will be the left-shift and right-shift operators, << and >>. The operator << performs the same operation as SHL/SAL (and, of course, the C compiler translates C statements using this operator to SHL/SAL machine instructions, as you can check by examining the .COD file or running a debugger). The operator >> performs an SAR operation on variables of the C type **int** and an SHR operation on variables of the C type **unsigned int**. The **&** operator in C performs an AND operation, and OR and other logical operators are available, too. C also provides a type of **struct** that operates on **bit fields** within a word. We could have used this construct as an alternative to the approach taken here.

Now let us take a look at the Store function, which typifies these bit-level operations:

```
void Store(V,I2,BPos)
   int V,I2,BPos;
{  unsigned int Mask;

   /* set up a mask with 0's at the bit field of interest, 1's elsewhere */
   Mask = 0xffff - (0x0003 << BPos-1);
   /* AND the element of X with the mask, putting 0's into the bit field of interest */
   X[I2] &= Mask;
   /* now add in V at that bit field, by shifting V and adding it to X[I2] */
   X[I2] += V << BPos-1;
}
```

As an example, suppose we wish to store the value 2 into "Y[9]". The location for this storage will be X[1], bits 13−12; i.e., I2 is 1 and BPos is 13. (The reader should verify that these are the proper values.) Our first step will be to put zeros into that bit field. In assembly language, we would do this by ANDing with the hex value CFFF. Since, as mentioned earlier, C does allow ANDing, all we have to do is construct that hex value. This is accomplished by the C statement

```
   Mask = 0xffff - (0x0003 << BPos-1);
```

Recall that '0x' is C notation for hex constants. Since BPos is 13, we are shifting the hex constant 0003H leftward by 12 bits, yielding 001100000000, i.e., 3000H. Subtracting that from FFFFH yields CFFFH, exactly what we wanted.

We can now AND CFFFH with X[I2]:

```
   X[I2] &= Mask;
```

The **&** is the analogue of the AND operator. The preceding statement is just an abbreviation for

```
X[I2] = X[I2] & Mask;
```

just as C allows us to abbreviate

```
W = W + 6;
```

as

```
W += 6;
```

if we wish to. (The designers of C intended this shorthand as a hint to the compiler: informing the compiler that the operand on the left and right sides of the equal sign refer to the same location might allow the compiler to produce more efficient machine code.)

Now we have zeros in the bit field in which we will store "Y[9]". So all we have to do is add the shifted version of V to X[I2]:

```
X[I2] += V << BPos-1;
```

Let us step back from the details for a moment and again bring up the point that it is these special features of the C language that have allowed us to write the entire program in C, without resorting to assembly language. Even though C is considered a high-level language, its bit-manipulation features allow access to low-level aspects of the machine. We have already seen that C also allows (even requires) one to work with machine addresses, such as when we have call-by-reference parameters. For these reasons, C is sometimes called a "middle-level" language, combining the convenience of a high-level language with at least some of the machine-level access capabilities of assembly language. Again, the latter feature sometimes enables us to avoid, or at least minimize, the usage of assembly language. This, more than anything else, is the source of C's huge popularity as a systems programming language today.

Program 6.25 reinforces an earlier remark made back in the introduction to the text: phrased in terms of the title of the book, C programming does require a good understanding of what is "under the hood." The reader might wonder whether we would be able to take the same approach in Pascal as we have done in Program 6.25, again avoiding writing any assembly language. For example, even though Pascal has nothing like C's operator >> , we know that a right shift is the same as division by a power of two. A right shift of three bits, for instance, is the same as division by $2^3 = 8$. But as we saw in Section 6.3.1, this has different meanings for signed versus unsigned numbers. Pascal (at least the standard version) offers only signed integers, and thus, division by eight is the same as an SAR shift by three bits, *not* an SHR shift by three bits. This is bad, because if bit 15 contains a 1 before the shift, it will be replaced by a 1, not a 0, as we want in the Vl function of Program 6.25, for example. There are ways to fix this up, but it would be much easier just to use assembly language in this case.

Logical operations play a vital role in many applications. Almost any architecture, not just that of the iAPX family, offers instructions to perform such operations.

6.3.3 String Instructions

The two groups of iAPX instructions discussed so far in this chapter—arithmetic and logical operations—have analogues on other types of CPUs, and the same is true for the stack manipulation and procedure call/return instructions introduced in Chapter 5. However, the iAPX instructions to be discussed next, which do string manipulation, do not exist on many CPUs, and they are in fact one of the most powerful features of the iAPX family.

To introduce the subject, suppose we have two arrays, X and Y, declared in our current data segment DSG, consisting of 100D bytes each, and suppose that at some point in our program, we want to copy X to Y. We could do this by setting up a loop, which uses an ordinary MOV instruction to do the copying byte by byte (or word by word), but the following code would execute much faster:

```
MOV AX,DS  ;  set ES to point to DSG
MOV ES,AX
MOV SI,OFFSET X  ;  MOVSB uses SI and DI, so prepare them
MOV DI,OFFSET Y
MOV CX,100D  ;  the REP form of MOVSB uses CX, so prepare it
CLD  ;  move through memory in a positive direction
REP MOVSB  ;  OK, go ahead with the string copy
```

The instruction MOVSB copies the byte at DS:SI to the byte at ES:DI, and after doing this, it also increments SI and DI so as to be ready to copy the next byte. The increment is +1 here, but can be −1 if desired. The sign of the increment is controlled by the **direction flag** DF, which is bit 10 in the FR (see Section 6.1). The CLD ("clear direction" flag) instruction clears this bit, making the increment +1; the STD flag would set the bit, making the increment −1. There is also a word form of the instruction, MOVSW, which copies whole words and thus increments by either +2 or −2. MOVSB and MOVSW copy from a place in the data segment, pointed to by SI, to a place in the extra segment, pointed to by DI. Since, in this example, both X and Y are in our current data segment, we needed to point ES to that data segment first.

Incidentally, since these instructions copy *from* the place pointed to by SI *to* the place pointed to by DI, you can see where the names of the SI and DI registers come from: 'S' stands for "source" and 'D' stands for "destination."

The REP instruction before MOVSB indicates that the MOVSB operation should be *repeated*, decrementing CX during each repetition and continuing until CX reaches zero. In this way, all 100 bytes of X will eventually be copied to all 100 bytes of Y. The programmer does not need to set up an explicit loop, and, more importantly, the code will be *much* more efficient.

The use of MOVSB, especially in conjunction with REP, is an extremely fast-executing technique for copying one array to another. It is an excellent example of how hand coding to take advantage of special hardware features can improve the performance of a program. To demonstrate the technique, suppose we have a program that at some point must copy 10,000 characters from one array to another. Suppose further that the copy operation is contained as part of a larger loop. (As mentioned before, timing considerations are seldom worth addressing unless the operation involved is part of a loop.) Program 6.26 is just such a program. It copies the array S1 to S2. It also reports the time, by calling 'prnttime' twice. This function, in turn, calls _strtime, which is an internal C function provided by the compiler. The function _strtime is essentially the same as the procedure 'time' provided by the Pascal compiler (see Program 6.7). In order to use it, we need to insert the line

```
#include <time.h>
```

The file time.h contains miscellaneous material needed to call _strtime and the other time functions provided by the C compiler. The #include directive tells the compiler to include the file named as part of the source file currently being compiled—in our case, Program 6.26.

```
#include <time.h>

char S1[10000],S2[10000];

void prnttime()
{   char t[9];
    _strtime(t);
    printf("%s\n",t);
}

main()

{   int i,j;

    for (i = 0; i < 9999; i++) S1[i] = 'G';
    prnttime();
    for (j = 0; j < 1000; j++)   {
       /* other code would go in here */
       for (i = 0; i < 9999; i++) S2[i] = S1[i];
       /* other code would go in here */
       }
    prnttime();
}
```

Program 6.26

Program 6.26 takes 56 seconds to run on a particular machine with CPU in the iAPX 286 family. Let us see how much this can be improved. First, the language C is well known for its efficient use of pointers, so one could try to rewrite the program using pointers. This is shown as Program 6.27. Here, p1 and p2 are pointers to characters. We initialize them to point to S1 and S2, respectively. (Again, recall that in C an array name without a subscript points to the starting address of the array. Thus,

```
    p1 = S1;
```

is fine. It would be redundant to write

```
    p1 = &S1;
```

although most compilers would accept it.)

```
    #include <time.h>

    char S1[10000],S2[10000];

    void prnttime()
    {   char t[9];
        _strtime(t);
        printf("%s\n",t);
    }

    main()

    {   int i,j;
        char *p1,*p2;

        for (i = 0; i < 9999; i++) S1[i] = 'G';
        prnttime();
        for (j = 0; j < 1000; j++)  {
            /* other code would go in here */
            p1 = S1;  p2 = S2;
            for (i = 0; i < 9999; i++) *(p2++) = *(p1++);
            /* other code would go in here */
            }
        prnttime();
    }
```

Program 6.27

The symbol ++ in C means that the associated variable is to be incremented, either before or after accessing it, depending on whether the symbol appears before or after the variable, respectively. For example, suppose M and N are integer variables. Then the assignment statement

```
    M = N++;
```

would assign the current value of N to M and *then* add 1 to N, while the statement

```
    M = ++N;
```

would add 1 to N *first* and then copy the *new* value of N to M.

The assignment statement

```
*(p2++) = *(p1++);
```

in Program 6.27, with the C symbol * in this context meaning "contents of," performs the following operations:

```
find x, the contents of the location currently pointed to by p1
increment p1
put x in the location currently pointed to by p2
increment p2
```

Note that since p1 and p2 point to the **char** type, which has a **sizeof** value of 1, increments to p1 and p2 have the value 1 also, i.e., they advance by one byte.

So does the use of pointers speed up Program 6.26? Unfortunately, the change to pointers does *not* help at all. In fact, it *hurts* performance: the run time for Program 6.27 is 76 seconds, an *increase* from Program 6.26's time of 56 seconds. The reader is urged to compile the code and analyze the .COD file, to see why the version with pointers is actually slower.

Most C compilers offer string manipulation functions that the user can call, just as we have done with the function _strtime in Programs 6.26 and 6.27. One of these is **strcpy**, whose name comes from "string copy." Since these string functions are meant to be efficient, one would guess that **strcpy** uses the MOVSB or MOVSW instruction, each of which, as mentioned, is extremely fast. Program 6.28 is a version of Program 6.26 that uses **strcpy**. In tracing through its execution with CodeView (DEBUG would work, too, of course), one can see that **strcpy** does indeed use MOVSB. Thus, we should expect a substantial improvement in speed of execution. In practice, this turned out to be the case, with Program 6.28 taking only 10 seconds to run, compared to Program 6.26's 56 seconds. So the use of **strcpy** produced more than a fivefold increase in execution speed.

```
#include <time.h>

char S1[10000],S2[10000];

void prnttime()
{  char t[9];
   _strtime(t);
   printf("%s\n",t);
}

main()

{  int i,j;

   for (i = 0; i < 9999; i++) S1[i] = 'G';
   prnttime();
   for (j = 0; j < 1000; j++)  {
```

```
            /* other code would go in here */
            strcpy(S2,S1);
            /* other code would go in here */
            }
        prnttime();
    }
```

Program 6.28

However, one still might expect that a hand-coded assembly-language version of **strcpy** would work even better. The .ASM file of such a version, named _MYSC, is given as Program 6.29. By now, the reader should be a veteran in programming assembly-language procedures that are to be linked to Pascal or C main programs, so most of this code should look familiar. The only new feature is the use of REP and MOVSW, together with the attendant preparation, e.g., setting up ES and executing CLD.

```
    ACSG    SEGMENT

    ASSUME CS:ACSG

    PUBLIC _MYSC

_MYSC PROC FAR
        PUSH BP
        MOV BP,SP
        PUSH ES
        MOV AX,DS
        MOV ES,AX
        CLD
        MOV CX,5000D
        MOV SI,[BP+8]
        MOV DI,[BP+6]
        REP MOVSW
        POP ES
        POP BP
        RET
_MYSC ENDP

    ACSG    ENDS
    END
```

Program 6.29

Program 6.29 is linked to the C-language main program as usual. The main program now looks like Program 6.30. (Note the **extern** declaration of MYSC.)

```
#include <time.h>

char S1[10000],S2[10000];

extern void far MYSC( char * , char * );

void prnttime()
{   char t[9];
    _strtime(t);
    printf("%s\n",t);
}

main()

{   int i,j;

    for (i = 0; i < 10000; i++) S1[i] = 'G';
    prnttime();
    for (j = 0; j < 1000; j++)  {
        /* other code would go in here */
        MYSC(S2,S1);
        /* other code would go in here */
        }
    prnttime();
}
```

Program 6.30

Run time of the combined Programs 6.29 and 6.30 was only three seconds! This is more than a threefold increase in speed over Program 6.28, which itself was already dramatically better than Program 6.26.

Another example of the use of MOVSW arises in Pascal Program 6.31. This program does very little; it is just a shell to illustrate a principle, namely, the following. Note that the array parameter X in the procedure P is not declared to be of the type **var**. It was mentioned in Chapter 5 that this practice is generally not recommended, even if the procedure does not change the array, because non-var parameters must be copied to the stack. Now, in Program 6.31, the Pascal programmer, knowingly or not, has asked the compiler to produce code to copy 1,000 words to the stack—a very time-consuming operation. But in those cases in which words must be copied to the stack, for whatever reason, it is of interest to know whether the compiler will produce *efficient* code to do this. In the case of Program 6.31, it has; Figure 6.9 shows the .COD file, which reveals that the compiler has produced code to copy the 1,000 (= 03E8H) words to the stack using REPZ and MOVSW, instead of setting up a loop, which would be inefficient.

```
program NV(input,output);

    type Ary = array[1..1000] of integer;
```

```
        var A : Ary;

        procedure P(X:Ary);
        begin
        end;

    begin
        P(A)
    end.
```

Program 6.31

```
    L13:
            ** 00001B    MOV      SI,@@A
            ** 00001E    MOV      CX,03E8H
            ** 000021    SUB      SP,07D0H
            ** 000025    MOV      DI,SP
            ** 000027    CLD
            ** 000028    PUSH     SS
            ** 000029    POP      ES
            ** 00002A    REPZ
            ** 00002B    MOVSW
            ** 00002C    CALL     P
```

Figure 6.9

In addition to MOVSB and MOVSW, the iAPX family has several other instructions for string manipulation. For example, STOSB and STOSW are similar to MOVSB and MOVSW, except that the source operands are in AL and AX, respectively; this arrangement is useful if one needs to store the same value in each of several consecutive bytes or words in memory. Other examples are CMPSB, which will compare two strings, and SCASB, which will scan a string, searching for a particular character specified as an operand in the instruction.

Again, the instructions discussed in this subsection do not have direct counterparts in many other CPU types. (The VAX does have a MOVC instruction that is similar to MOVSB.) Thus, these instructions are very important features of the iAPX family.

6.3.4 Loop Instructions

iAPX loop instructions are intended to speed up the implementation of loops. Recall the second loop in Program 4.1, centered around the line labeled LP2:

```
        MOV DI,N
        MOV BX,OFFSET FIBNUM
    LP2: PUSH BX
        MOV BX,[BX]
```

```
CALL DISPBX
POP BX
ADD BX,2
DEC DI
JNZ LP2
```

(We have replaced two of the instructions in the original program by PUSH and POP, which had not yet been introduced in Chapter 4. Similarly, we have replaced a SUB instruction with a DEC instruction.)

We can accomplish the same thing using the LOOP instruction:

```
      MOV CX,N
      MOV BX,OFFSET FIBNUM
LP2: PUSH BX
      MOV BX,[BX]
      PUSH CX
      CALL DISPBX
      POP CX
      POP BX
      ADD BX,2
      LOOP LP2
```

The LOOP instruction first decrements the contents of the CX register by 1; then, unless that action resulted in the zero flag (ZF) being set, a jump to the indicated target, in this case LP2, is performed. (Note that we initialized CX to N before entering the loop, just as we had done for DI in the original version of the program.) In other words, the *single* loop instruction is doing the work that was formerly done by the *pair* of instructions

```
DEC DI
JNZ LP2
```

This at first sounds like a "win," i.e., a reduction in execution time and memory usage. But in fact, it is not the case.

First of all, LOOP is only slightly faster than the pair of instructions it replaced. For example, in the iAPX 86 family, loop takes 8 clock cycles (if the jump is taken), while the DEC and JNZ instructions take $2 + 7 = 9$ cycles, not much longer. Second, in this particular example, we had to add a PUSH and a POP instruction to keep the loop counter in CX from being changed by the procedure DISPBX. (The latter changes the CL register.) In other words, the LOOP instruction has not helped at all to eliminate code.

Unfortunately, the latter is a general problem with both LOOP and its "cousins," LOOPE, LOOPNE, LOOPZ, and LOOPNZ and is a prominent disadvantage of the **nonorthogonal** nature of iAPX architecture (see Section 3.3). These instructions are all constrained to use CX, and no other register. By contrast, VAX architecture has an SOB ("subtract one and branch") instruction that is quite similar to LOOP but can use any of several registers for its loop counter. (The same problem arises in a number of other iAPX instructions. For example, the reason DISPBX uses the CX register is that DISPBX includes the ROR and ROL instructions, which again are constrained to using CX (via CL, the lower half of CX).)

Thus, loop instructions are not nearly as advantageous as the string instructions we examined in the previous subsection. This is borne out in another way by inspecting the .COD files produced by Microsoft compilers; these compilers do *not* make use of loop instructions.

Note that loop instructions would be of limited use anyway, even if they could be used with registers other than CX. Most programs have a lot of loops, but the overhead involved in "administering" a loop—incrementing or decrementing some value and jumping back to the top of the loop unless some condition holds—comprises only a small proportion of the loop's execution time, except in very **tight** loops, i.e., loops consisting of only a small number of instructions.

6.3.5 Miscellaneous Instructions

A few instructions do not fit into any of the previously mentioned categories but are useful also.

6.3.5.1 LEA.   The LEA ("load effective address") instruction is similar in effect to the OFFSET pseudo-op but is much more flexible. To illustrate, the instruction

```
LEA AX,G
```

would have the same effect as

```
MOV AX,OFFSET G
```

But LEA can also compute "fancier" offsets, such as

```
LEA CX,Z[BX]
```

which would be equivalent to, but more efficient than

```
MOV CX,OFFSET Z
ADD CX,BX
```

6.3.5.2 XLAT.   The XLAT instruction was included in the iAPX architecture with the intention of expediting table lookups. XLAT copies the value at offset c(BX) + c(AL) to AL. This operation could be performed with an ADD together with a MOV, but XLAT does all of it in one instruction, thus saving time and memory space.

6.3.5.3 XCHG.   The XCHG ("exchange") instruction lives up to its name, exchanging the contents of its two operands. Such an exchange is useful because of the shortage of registers in iAPX CPUs. We would like to store as many items as possible in registers, but there just are not enough of them to do this, especially since many of the iAPX registers have special roles. For example, BX is used for data segment offsets, BP for stack segment offsets, CX for the LOOP instruction, and so on. Thus, we may have to juggle some items back and forth between, for example, memory and registers.

To illustrate, the code

```
XCHG BX,CX
```

would be a more efficient substitute for the equivalent but slower

```
PUSH BX
PUSH CX
POP BX
POP CX
```

XCHG allows us to use only one instruction instead of four.

6.3.5.4 LOCK. The LOCK instruction prefix is useful in a **shared-memory multiprocessor** system. Such a system has several CPUs sharing the same memory; instead of having just the memory and CPU connected to the bus, the memory together with *several* CPUs are connected to the bus. The idea, of course, is to reduce the execution time of an application, by partitioning its task into several subtasks that can be done in parallel, each by a different CPU.

The problem with such an arrangement is that there may be **shared variables**. For example, consider an airline reservation system. Suppose the variable NLEFT stores the number of seats remaining in a given flight. (Ignore the airlines' practice of over-booking here!) The program used by a telephone reservation clerk might have code such as the following:

```
CMP NLEFT,0  ; is NLEFT > 0?
JE ALLGONE   ; if no seats left, tell customer
; else some seats are left, so book one
DEC NLEFT  ; reduce NLEFT by 1
CALL TAKEINFO  ; enter the customer's name and other information for this seat
```

A serious problem can arise with this code. Suppose two customers call two clerks, say, X and Y, at roughly the same time. The two clerks then type a command to query the reservation data base. Suppose they are running the preceding program on two different CPUs. Then they will both execute the CMP instruction, but one of them, say clerk X, may be a fraction of a second earlier than the other. If so, then they will both execute the DEC instruction, which will mean trouble if the two executions overlap. Suppose NLEFT has the value 5—that is, there are five seats left on this flight. Recall from Chapter 2 that DEC, just like any other instruction, consists of a set of microsteps. Then if the two executions of DEC overlap, the following sequence could occur:

X's CPU fetches NLEFT into its MDR, getting a value of 5
Y's CPU fetches NLEFT into its MDR, getting a value of 5

X's CPU subtracts 1, and puts the result, 4, back into its MDR

Y's CPU subtracts 1, and puts the result, 4, back into its MDR

X's CPU does a memory write, resulting in NLEFT having the value 4

Y's CPU does a memory write, resulting in NLEFT having the value 4

So NLEFT will end up having the value 4, instead of the correct value, 3. And further, if the value of NLEFT had originally been 1, so that only one seat had been left, the clerks will promise that one seat to two customers, a serious error on the part of the airline (again, unless it deliberately overbooks). Finally, in the procedure TAKEINFO, the variable NLEFT may have been used as an index into the table that records passenger information. If so, that procedure would make an entry at line NLEFT + 1 of the table. But then both customers will think they have reserved a seat on the flight when in fact only one of them has done so. (The one who will get the seat is Y's customer, since Y will execute TAKEINFO after X does, thus overwriting what X entered for X's customer.)

The iAPX architecture's LOCK instruction prefix enables us to avoid this calamity. To see how it works, note that the troubles which occurred in this hypothetical situation all stemmed from the fact that the two executions of the DEC instruction overlapped, with their microsteps interleaved. The LOCK prefix prevents this overlapping from occurring, by locking the bus for the duration of execution of the instruction that follows it. For example, if we had written

```
LOCK DEC NLEFT
```

then clerk X, who started executing DEC slightly earlier than clerk Y, would actually be able to complete all of DEC's microsteps before Y started executing them. Thus, there would be no overlap, and the final value of NLEFT would be correct—two less than before, instead of one less.

Note, however, that the problem would then only be shifted to the CMP instruction, and a LOCK prefix would not help here. So we solve the problem by setting up another variable, as in, say,

```
PASSKEY DB (?)
```

which restricts access to the shared variable NLEFT. A PASSKEY value of 1 will mean that some other clerk is currently accessing NLEFT, and thus, we must stay away from it for the time being; a value of 0 will mean that we can proceed. Here is the new code:

```
    MOV AL,1
CHECKREADY:
    LOCK XCHG AL,PASSKEY
    CMP AL,1
    JE CHECKREADY  ; not ready yet, keep checking
    CMP NLEFT,0  ; is NLEFT > 0?
    JE ALLGONE  ; no seats left, tell customer
```

```
; seats are left, so book one
DEC NLEFT  ; reduce NLEFT by 1
MOV PASSKEY,0  ; now let others access NLEFT
CALL TAKEINFO  ; enter the customer name and other information for this seat
```

The reader is invited to verify that the foregoing code works. Be forewarned, though, that this kind of programming tends to be confusing to novices. On the other hand, the idea of variables such as PASSKEY is central to almost all multiprocessor applications.

6.3.5.5 HLT. HLT ("halt") stops the cycle of step A, step B, step C, and so on, putting the CPU to "sleep" until "awakened" by an externally generated electrical signal called an **interrupt** (see Section 7.2). HLT is also useful in a multiprocessor system. Suppose one of the CPUs is waiting for input from some external device. We *could* set up a loop in our program to wait for that input, but this would still result in instruction fetches and thus add to bus traffic. The latter would be a problem, since it would reduce access to the bus by the other processors. To resolve the difficulty, we could have the CPU in question execute an HLT instruction, so that it does not get in the way of the other processors.

ANALYTICAL EXERCISES

1. Suppose, in Program 6.15, that we had forgotten to put 0 in DX and that the contents of DX were 10D. If c(BX) = 5, what would result? What value *should* be there?

2. Following Program 6.3, there is a short explanation of the C language's **%ld** format for the **scanf** and **printf** functions, for 32-bit quantities. Review that explanation, and answer the following question. Suppose, in Program 6.3, that we used the **%ld** format in the call to the **scanf** function but forgot to do so in calling **printf**, using **%d** for the latter. If the value 100000D is read in for both X and Y, what value for Y will be printed out instead of 200000D?

3. Devise and conduct an experiment, similar to those in this chapter, to investigate how much execution time can be saved by using a LOOP instruction instead of implementing the loop operations "by hand."

4. Suppose Microsoft Pascal were to make available a variable type **short integer**, implementing signed eight-bit integers. Suppose further that in Program 5.13, AryType had been defined as

```
    array[4..10] of short integer;
```

and the **for** statement had been

```
    for I:=6 to 10 do
```

What would change in offsets 14 through 1F in Figure 5.6?

5. As indicated in Section 6.3.1, in some cases we can do multiplication by a constant faster by using SHL and ADD than by using the MUL instruction itself. How would we do this for

multiplication by 21D? How much faster would the operation be if the multiplicand is in a register?

6. In Program 4.2, how much could the value of MAXPRM be increased without making other changes to the program and still produce correct results for all values of MAX up to MAXPRM?

7. At the end of Section 6.1.2, a .COD file is shown for a C-language program that includes comparisons of both signed and unsigned integers, with the compiler using a JGE instruction to implement the former and a JAE instruction to implement the latter. Show specific numerical values for the variables x, y, a, and b in the C program for which JGE and JAE produce different actions. Explain in detail which of the relevant flags are set or cleared.

8. Suppose we have a C source file, G.C, in an iAPX/MS-DOS environment:

```
int x[5],y,z,*p,*q;

main()

{ p = &y; q = p; }
```

(Of course the program would probably have more statements, but for our purposes here, suppose this is the entire program.) Suppose we compile and link the program, and then type

```
DEBUG G.EXE
```

Say, in order to be able to look at code produced by the compiler, we used DEBUG's 'U' command to view an assembly language version of that code. Give assembly-language code that might appear, corresponding to the pair of assignment statements. (Assume storage similar to that of Table 1.1 in Chapter 1.)

PROGRAMMING PROJECTS

1. Rewrite Programs 6.23 and 6.24 so that they will pack integers in the range 0..15 instead of 0..3.

2. Write an assembly-language procedure having parameters O, B1, B2, and V that places the value V into bits B1 through B2 of the word at offset O of the current data segment. (This is a generalization of the procedure STORE in Program 6.24, and the reader may want to use that program as a model for the one here.) Write an assembly-language main program to test your procedure.

3. Write an assembly-language procedure having parameters N and K that computes the power N^K, where N and K are unsigned integers. Have your procedure return the result in AX. If the product cannot fit into 16 bits (or if N = K = 0, so that N^K is undefined), print an error message to the screen, including the values of N and K, and exit the program and return to DOS. Write an assembly-language main program to test your procedure.

4. Alter Program 4.1 so that the Fibonacci numbers are stored in 32-bit strings, i.e., two words for each number instead of one, thus greatly increasing the maximum value of N that we can set in the pseudo-op EQU.

5. In Program 6.1 and Figure 6.1, we saw how to implement the addition of **double-precision** integers—i.e., two words for each integer instead of one. Generalize this technique to integers of size N words, i.e., integers of size 16*N bits. In other words, write an assembly-language procedure NWADD having the following three parameters:

> N, the number of words in each integer
>
> X, the (offset of the) source addend
>
> Y, the (offset of the) destination addend

NWADD must be general—i.e., it must work for general values of N, X, and Y. It will implement Y = X + Y, where X and Y are N-word integers. The more significant words have lower offset values; e.g., if N is 3, then X is the most significant word and X + 4 is the least significant word.

Test NWADD with an assembly-language main program that calls NWADD twice. The first call will be for two-word integers A and B, in which are stored 2AB6FF04 and 110A31E2, respectively; your answer should be 3BC130E6. The second call will be for three-word integers C and D, containing 4004ABCD0011 and 644A1111AAAA, respectively. Initialize the arrays in your data segment declaration, e.g., with

```
C DW 4004H,0ABCDH,0011H
```

Finally, explain why there seems to be no good way to take advantage of the ADC instruction here.

6. Write an assembly-language procedure, callable from C or Pascal, to do an efficient copy of one two-dimensional array to another, using the MOVSW instruction with an REP prefix. (*Note*: You will first need to determine whether your compiler implements two-dimensional arrays in row-major or column-major order.) Then write a C or Pascal calling program to test your procedure. Finally, devise and conduct a timing experiment similar to the one in Program 6.26 and the programs that follow it, to see how much of an improvement your procedure yields.

7. Write an analogue of the procedure DISPBX in Program 4.1 that displays the contents of BX in 16 bits instead of in four hex digits.

8. Rewrite the macro PREPREGS in Program 6.24 as a procedure instead of as a macro. Be *very* careful with the stack! Test your code by linking it to Program 6.23, to make sure you have been careful enough.

9. The language C has built-in operations similar to the AND, OR, and NOT instructions in the iAPX (and most other) instruction sets, but Pascal does not. Write assembly-language procedures, callable from Pascal, that provide these operations. For example, write an assembly-language procedure that would be declared in the Pascal program as

```
procedure AndOp(var X:integer; Y:integer); extern;
```

and that would perform X ← X AND Y, where Y would typically be given in hex if the compiler allows hex constants. Microsoft Pascal allows such constants, specified via the prefix '16#'. Thus, the call

```
AndOr(A,16#FFFE);
```

would clear bit 0 of the variable A and leave the other bits of A unchanged. Write the assembly-language procedures, and write a Pascal program to test them.

10. At the beginning of Section 6.2.9 on segment overrides, there is an example in which we desire to copy the contents of absolute memory address 2AD46 to the BX register. A problem arises in that this location will probably not be within the "reach" of the current value in the DS register. Write an assembly-language procedure that will determine whether this is in fact so. The two parameters will consist of the lower 16 bits and upper 4 bits of the 20-bit address that we wish to access under the current value in DS. The procedure will return its "answer" in AX, with a value of 1 meaning that the given location is reachable and 0 meaning that it is not.

11. It was mentioned in Section 6.1.2 that some C compilers do not produce code to check for overflow, even as an option, and thus, we would have to write an assembly-language procedure to do such checks. Write such a procedure. Its declaration in the C calling program will be

```
extern int far SUM( int , int , int * );
```

The first two parameters are the values to be added, and the third is the place where the sum is to be stored. Also, the procedure will return an error code of 1 or 0, with 1 meaning that an overflow occurred. Write a C program to test your procedure.

12. Redo Programming Project 8 in Chapter 5 to concatenate two strings, using the MOVSB instruction with the REP prefix.

13. Rewrite Program 4.2 so as to allow a larger value of the variable MAX. (See Analytical Exercise 6.)

14. As mentioned in Section 6.3.1, some CPUs, including all the iAPX models except the 486, do not have instructions for performing floating-point arithmetic. In that case, floating-point operations must be done via software, i.e., using more primitive instructions. Write an assembly-language procedure to do floating-point addition. Assume the 32-bit format described in Section 1.2.2, and assume that the calling program will point SI and DI to two double-word items in the current data segment which will be our operands. The double word pointed to by SI is to be added to the one pointed to by DI.

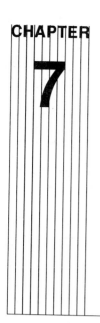

CHAPTER
7

Input/Output

During the early days of computers, input/output (I/O) was of very little importance: computers, as the name implies, were used primarily to *compute*. A typical application might involve huge mathematical calculations needed for some problem in physics. The I/O done in such an application would be quite minimal, with the machine grinding away for hours at a time with little or no I/O being done.

Today, we have just the opposite situation. I/O plays a crucial role in most modern computer applications. In fact, applications in which I/O plays an important role can arguably be viewed as the most powerful "driving force" behind the revolutionary rise to prominence of computers in the last decade or so. Today we make use of computers in numerous aspects of our business and personal lives—and in the vast majority of such uses, the programs center around I/O operations.

In some of these applications, the use of a computer is fairly obvious: credit-card billing, airline reservations, word processors, spreadsheets, automatic teller machines, real estate data bases, and drafting programs for architects come immediately to mind. Possibly less obvious is the existence of computers in automobiles and in such household items as washing machines and autofocus cameras. However, whether the computers in these applications are obvious or hidden, the common theme behind them is that they all are running programs in which I/O plays an important role, often the *dominant* role.

In short, if your career is in computer science, computer engineering, or another field in which you will design applications of computers, a thorough understanding of I/O concepts is of fundamental importance. Accordingly, I/O issues are the focus not only of this chapter, but also to a large extent of Chapter 8. And, as we might already have guessed, our "look under the hood" metaphor will be even more important than it was in prior chapters.

In the introduction to the text, it was mentioned that an understanding of what is "under the hood" is necessary no matter at which level our work is done:

- Even if we work solely in a high-level language, such as Pascal or C, we still need to know what is happening at the machine level so that we can write efficient code and detect subtle bugs.

- In many applications, we need to work at the machine level directly—say, in order to increase the speed of a crucial procedure.

These same considerations—and again, even more so—hold for I/O. A thorough knowledge of I/O is important regardless of the level at which we work:

(a) If we do I/O at a high level, meaning that we merely request I/O services through the facilities available in a high-level language, a lack of insight into what is happening at the machine level could result in an unacceptably slow-running program.

(b) In some applications, we need to do I/O directly at the machine level, either to gain extra speed or because we are working with a special I/O device that is not recognized by the ordinary facilities of our high-level language.

An example of Point (a) above was given in the Introduction, in which lack of sufficient understanding of the way the operating system handled I/O led to a drastic— and unacceptable—slowdown in the execution speed of the program.

Concerning Point (b), Chapter 2 mentioned an example, in which we might be developing a machine to dispense regional railway tickets. This machine would have a number of nonstandard I/O devices, such as an optical scanner, to sense and check the paper money which the customer feeds into the machine. Another example of Point (b) will be seen in the current chapter; it shows how one can write to the screen of an IBM PC-family machine much faster via direct access than by calling the services of the operating system.

In this chapter, we will look at I/O essentially "from the bottom up," i.e., starting with a discussion of basic I/O hardware operations and then continuing to viewpoints at increasingly higher levels. The basic I/O hardware operations will be presented in Section 7.1, which covers I/O **ports**, chips through which the CPU communicates with I/O devices. Then Section 7.2 covers **interrupt-driven I/O**. Section 7.3 looks at the next higher level, which is performing I/O via operating system services, and, finally, Section 7.4 introduces the topic of doing I/O via primitive operations in high-level languages.

7.1 INTRODUCTION TO I/O PORTS AND DEVICE STRUCTURE

An I/O device connects to the bus through **interface ports**, sometimes called **I/O registers**. I/O ports are usually eight-bit registers. (Do not, however, confuse them with the CPU registers: they are external to the CPU, and have a different structure than do CPU registers.) I/O ports have addresses, just like words in memory do, and these addresses are given meaning through the address bus, just as is the case for words in memory.

The latter remark gives rise to a potential ambiguity. Suppose we wish to communicate with port 50, which is connected to some I/O device. The CPU will place the value 50 on the address bus. Since all items that are connected to the address bus will "see" what is on the bus, how can they distinguish this 50 from a value of 50 meant to address word 50 of memory? In other words, how can the CPU indicate that it wants to address I/O port 50 rather than memory word 50? The two fundamental systems for handling this problem are described in the next two subsections.

7.1.1 I/O Address Space Approach

In many computers, the control bus has a special line or lines to indicate that the current value on the address bus is meant to indicate an I/O port, rather than a word in memory. On IBM PC/XT/AT models, for example, the control bus includes lines named IOR (I/O Read) and IOW (I/O Write), which are counterparts of the other control bus lines, MEMR (MEMory Read) and MEMW (MEMory Write), mentioned in Chapter 2. (On PS/2 models, the problem is handled by lines that are somewhat different, but essentially similar, to these.) Then, to access I/O port 50, the CPU will assert either IOR or IOW (depending on whether it wants to read from or write to that port), while to access word 50 in memory, the CPU will assert either MEMR or MEMW. In either case, the CPU will place the value 50 on the address bus, but the values it simultaneously places on these lines in the control bus will distinguish between I/O port 50 and word 50 of memory.

The programmer controls which of the foregoing lines will be asserted by choosing which instruction to use. Instructions such as MOV will result in MEMR or MEMW being asserted, as described in Chapter 2. To assert IOR and IOW instead, we use the instructions IN and OUT, respectively.

For example, suppose, for simplicity, that c(DS) is 0000, so that the instruction

```
MOV AL, [x]
```

has its source operand at $16*c(DS) + x = x$. Then the instructions

```
MOV AL, [50H]
```

and

```
IN AL,50H
```

will both make the value 50H go out onto the address bus. (Since the instruction IN treats its source operand as a pointer, it would have been more consistent to require brackets around it in the mnemonics, but the designers of the assembly language unfortunately did not choose to do so.) And in both cases the response will be sent back via the data bus. But the MOV will assert the MEMR line in the control bus, while the IN instruction will assert the IOR line in that bus. As a result, MOV will result in copying the memory byte at address 50 to AL, while IN will copy the byte from I/O port 50 to AL.

Since the lines IOR/IOW and MEMR/MEMW allow us to distinguish between I/O ports and memory words having identical addresses, we can say that the I/O ports have a separate **address space** from that of memory. Thus, we will call this approach the **I/O address space approach**.

Figure 7.1 is a picture of a typical IBM PC/XT bus and I/O system. The word "typical" is used here because details vary from one IBM microcomputer to another, although generally the newer models of the IBM microcomputer family are upwardly compatible with the earlier ones, as mentioned in Chapter 2. We will use this earlier model for our examples here, to keep things from getting too detail ridden, but due to upward compatibility, what is said will apply to the later models, too.

Do not try to understand all of the components in the figure at this time, since they will be introduced gradually in this section and the next one. For now, note, for example, that the printer has ports with addresses 3BCH, 3BDH, and 3BEH and the keyboard has ports with addresses 60H, 61H, and 62H. As an example of the use of the keyboard addresses, the instruction

```
IN AL,60H
```

would copy a character from the keyboard's data port, which has address 60H, to the AL register.

Figure 7.1 is a simple block diagram, showing only "what is connected to what." A complete discussion of the configuration is beyond the scope of this book, but a brief description is feasible. A typical PC will have a **motherboard** as its foundation. The motherboard will include the CPU, some RAM memory, some ROM memory for the BIOS procedures (see Section 7.3), some I/O ports, the 8259A and 8253 chips, the clock, and the bus itself. The motherboard will also typically include a few **expansion slots**, in which **expansion boards** (or **cards**) may be inserted. Typical expansion boards contain ports for an extra I/O device, such as a modem or a mouse, or contain extra memory. These additional items make their connection to all system components through the expansion slots by attaching to the bus.

7.1.2 Memory-Mapped I/O Approach

The other major approach to the problem of duplicate I/O and memory addresses is the memory-mapped I/O approach. This approach is used in many computers, including those in the VAX family and those using the Motorola 68000 family of CPUs. The way the memory-mapped I/O approach solves the problem is simply by avoiding duplicate addresses! Whoever builds the computer must make sure that there are no duplicate addresses between I/O ports and memory cells. Thus, there would be no I/O port and memory word which both have, say, the address 50.

Under the memory-mapped I/O approach, there are no special lines in the control bus to indicate I/O access versus memory access (although there still must be one or

iAPX CPU

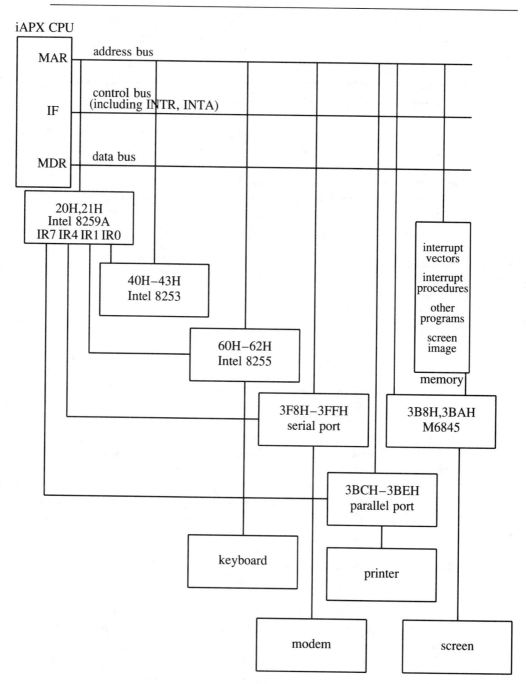

Figure 7.1

two lines to distinguish a read from a write, of course). Thus, there are no special I/O instructions, such as IN and OUT. One simply uses ordinary instructions, such as MOV, whether one is accessing I/O ports or memory.

For example, in the PDP-11 computer family, an older family from which the VAX family evolved, to read a character into a memory location CHARBUFFER from the keyboard, we would use

```
MOV 177562,CHARBUFFER
```

where 177562 is the address of the keyboard data port in octal—i.e., base-8—notation, as was customary for PDP-11 computers. (PDP-11 mnemonics are in opposite order from those of the iAPX family; this instruction represents a move *from* 177562 *to* CHARBUFFER.) Since this is an ordinary MOV instruction, the CPU is "fooled" into thinking that the keyboard data port is a memory location that the MOV is reading. But of course, it is not memory at all.

One advantage of the memory-mapped approach to I/O port addressing is that one can access the ports from the language C directly, by taking advantage of the fact that the * operator in C allows access to specific memory locations. For example, the preceding operation on a PDP-11 could be done in a C program by having the declaration

```
char CharBuffer,*KDataPtr;
```

and then the code

```
KDataPtr = 65394;
CharBuffer = *KDataPtr;
```

where $177562_8 = 65394_{10}$. The declaration says that CharBuffer will be a character variable, while KDataPtr will be a variable that *points to* character variables. The statement

```
KDataPtr = 65394;
```

then points KDataPtr to "memory address" 65394, i.e., to the keyboard data port. The statement

```
CharBuffer = *KDataPtr;
```

then says, "Get the contents of the character pointed to by the variable KDataPtr, and copy them to the variable CharBuffer." The effect is quite analogous to the iAPX instruction

```
IN AL,60H
```

mentioned just before Figure 7.1.

Note that we can even do memory-mapped I/O on a machine that is not designed for the task, mapped I/O, such as the IBM PC. All we have to do is wire the I/O port in question to MEMR and MEMW instead of IOR and IOW and use MOV instead of IN and OUT in our program. On the other hand, the reverse is impossible—for example, we can't do non-memory-mapped I/O on a PDP-11, since it doesn't have the IN and OUT instructions nor the IOR and IOW lines in its control bus.

7.1.3 I/O Ports and Device Structure in the IBM Microcomputer Family

For the rest of the chapter, we will concentrate mainly on the IBM microcomputer family, which, as we have seen, has a separate address space for I/O ports. As a first example of how I/O ports are used, we will look at the printer interface. As mentioned before, the printer has three ports:

The Printer Data Port, Address 3BCH.   If this port is filled with the ASCII code for a character, and the output control and printer status ports are set correctly (see shortly), that character in the data port will be printed on the printer.

The Printer Control Port, Address 3BEH.   This port provides the necessary control over the output of characters to the printer. Each bit in the port has a specific function. We will be interested here in bits 0, 2, 3, and 4.

Bit 0 is called the start bit. The setting of this bit to 1 tells the printer to print the character contained in the data port. The printer circuitry requires that this setting be done for 0.5 microsecond, before we clear it back to 0 again.

If we clear bit 2 to 0, the printer will initialize itself. This is done by the operating system when we first turn on the computer (see Chapter 8), so ordinarily we keep this bit set at 1. Bit 3 will not be explained here, but for our purposes must also always be set to 1. Bit 4 is the interrupt enable bit, which will be discussed in Section 7.2.

The Printer Status Port, Address 3BDH.   This port gives the status of the printer. We are most concerned here with bit 7, the ready bit. If this bit is 0, the printer cannot accept any more characters to print at the time. The printer has a **buffer area** in which it keeps characters that are queued for printing. If we send the printer too many characters in a short period of time, the buffer area will become full and the printer will clear the ready bit to 0 to indicate that we should not send it any more characters until some buffer space becomes available, a condition the printer will indicate by setting the ready bit to 1.

There are other bits in the printer status port, such as the out-of-paper indicator, bit 5, but we will not discuss these here.

Program 7.1 is code that will result in printing the character 'A' to the printer. Note the loop that begins at the line labeled TOP. We just loop around until the printer signals to us that it is ready, by setting the ready bit to 1. For obvious reasons, this is called **wait-loop I/O** or **busy-wait I/O**. (Sometimes it is called **polling**, referring to the fact that we constantly "poll" the printer as to its current buffer status, just as people are polled, for example, to ask about their opinions on some political issue.)

```
              MOV     DX,3BDH
       TOP:
              ; get a copy of the contents of status port
              IN      AL,DX

              ; if ready bit is still 0, loop again
              AND     AL,80H
              JZ      TOP

              ; put 'A' in data port
              MOV     AL,41H
              MOV     DX,3BCH
              OUT     DX,AL

              ; set and clear start bit in control port
              MOV     DX,3BEH
              IN      AL,DX
              OR      AL,01H
              OUT     DX,AL
              AND     AL,0FEH
              OUT     DX,AL
```

Program 7.1

After finally exiting the loop, we are ready to print out a character, say the letter 'A'. The next three instructions,

```
MOV     AL,41H
MOV     DX,3BCH
OUT     DX,AL
```

prepare for this by placing the ASCII code for 'A', 41H, in the printer data port.
The next six lines,

```
MOV     DX,3BEH
IN      AL,DX
OR      AL,01H
OUT     DX,AL
AND     AL,0FEH
OUT     DX,AL
```

have as their main purpose briefly setting the start bit of the printer control port to 1. Recall that this setting, provided it is held for a duration of at least 0.5 microsecond, will cause the character in the printer data port to be printed out. Note that we have used OR and AND here, so as to change bit 0 but leave the other bits, which control other functions, unchanged.

Program 7.1 does only the task of printing a single character 'A'. Thus, it is overly simple, but actually, even a *general* program to do printing would have most of

Program 7.1 as its core. Incidentally, such a program is called a **device driver**, the device in this case being the printer.

Now, what about the keyboard? Again, the keyboard interfaces to the computer through ports. In Figure 7.1, these ports have addresses 60H, 61H, and 62H, which serve as the keyboard data port, keyboard control port and keyboard status port, respectively, in analogy to the printer ports just described. These three keyboard ports, which in IBM literature are called PA, PB, and PC, are implemented in an Intel 8255 **parallel I/O chip**. The term "parallel" here means that there are eight lines connecting the keyboard to the computer, so that all eight bits of a character can be sent in parallel. This arrangement is in contrast to a **serial** connection, in which there is only one line and the bits in a character (or other item) must be sent serially, i.e., one at a time along the single line.

Incidentally, an I/O chip such as the 8255 is sometimes itself called a "port," which is a little confusing since it actually contains many ports. This confusion is often avoided by using the term "registers" for the latter and the term "port" for the chip as a whole. We will continue to use the term "port" in both ways, but the meaning will always be clear from context.

Just as we *send* a character to the printer by writing the ASCII code for that character to the printer data port, we *receive* a character from the keyboard by reading from the keyboard data port. However, unlike many computers, in which the keyboard places the ASCII code of the key into the keyboard data port, on IBM microcomputers a different code is used, called the **scan code**. The scan code is the identification number of a key under a special key numbering system that IBM developed for its keyboards. For example, the scan code for the 'q' key is 16, while the ASCII code for 'q' is 71H.

IBM microcomputer systems as a whole *do* use the ASCII system for character coding, e.g., in the printer examples discussed earlier in this chapter and also in displaying characters on the monitor screen in earlier chapters. The keyboard, with its use of scan codes instead of ASCII, is the only exception. Thus, the program controlling the keyboard—i.e., the **keyboard driver** (recall the term "device driver")—must do a conversion from the scan code to ASCII, in order to achieve consistency with other parts of the system. Accordingly, the keyboard driver program would include a table in its data segment and perform the conversion by doing a table lookup. In some of the more advanced IBM microcomputers, there is also special hardware that does the conversion automatically, and the ASCII code is available to the programmer in an extra keyboard port beyond the ones described here.

There is considerable variation among keyboard configurations in IBM microcomputers, but again, later models are upward compatible with earlier models. Thus, the material that follows, which applies to the original IBM PC, is compatible with the later models. Software based on this material—e.g., software that uses the scan codes and port numbers listed in what follows—will run on later, as well as earlier, models.

The keys on the IBM PC/XT keyboard are numbered from 1 to 83. A list of the 83 scan codes is given in Appendix I. Actually, each key has *two* scan codes, one for when the key is pressed and the other for when the key is released. Every time a key is *pressed*, the keyboard circuitry causes the *base* scan code, as listed in Appendix I, to be placed in port PA. Whenever a key is *released*, the base scan code *plus 128* is placed in PA. The addition of 128 is done so that the keyboard driver can distinguish between a key stroke and a key release if needed.

Remember that more than one key might be pressed at a time. For example, suppose we wish to type the capital letter 'T'. Then the keyboard will send four scan codes in all, corresponding to the following four actions: shift key pressed, 't' key pressed, 't' key released, shift key released. The keyboard driver will thus be executed four times.

Having separate executions of the keyboard driver for key pressings and releasings facilitates checking for simultaneous pressings, such as that of the shift and 't' keys being pressed simultaneously. In this way, the *software* is taking over a function "normally" (i.e., in many other computers) handled by the *hardware*: simultaneous key pressing is detected by the keyboard driver program instead of the keyboard circuitry.

The keyboard hardware "expects" the keyboard driver program to acknowledge each key action (stroke or release). This acknowledgment lets the keyboard know that the previous key action was noticed by the driver, so that the keyboard can now report a new key action without worrying that the keyboard driver will confuse this action with the previous one.

After the driver has read the scan code placed by the keyboard into PA, the driver must make some sense out of this code. In most cases, this means converting the scan code to standard ASCII code, but in some cases special actions must be taken. For example, if we are running the DOS operating system and the keyboard driver discovers that the Ctrl, Alt, and Del keys have been pressed, the driver must jump to a routine that resets the system, since Ctrl–Alt–Del is a DOS command to reset the system.

Program 7.2 shows what the core of a keyboard driver program looks like. Some further details will be discussed in Section 7.2. To simplify matters, the program handles only letters, and no other characters. As another simplification, we will examine only pressings of keys, and not releasings.

```
DSEG SEGMENT       ;       data segment
G     DB 0,0,0,0,0,0,0,0,0,0,0,0,0,0,0,0
      DB 'qwertyuiop',0,0,0
      DB 0,'asdfghjkl',0,0,0
      DB 0,0,'zxcvbnm',0,0,0,0,0
      DB 0,0,0,0,0,0,0,0,0,0,0,0,0,0
      DB 0,0,0,0,0,0,0,0,0,0,0,0,0,0
DSEG ENDS

CSEG SEGMENT
KDRIVE PROC FAR       ;       code segment

      ; lots of code here, not shown

      ; here is the core of the code

      ; get scan code from PA, and store temporarily on stack
        IN AL,60H
```

```
            PUSH AX

    ; send acknowledge signal to keyboard hardware
            IN AL,61H          ; read PB
            OR AL,80H          ; set ACK signal
            OUT 61H,AL         ; send ACK signal
            AND AL,7FH         ; reset ACK signal
            OUT 61H,AL         ; restore original PB

            POP AX             ; get back key number
            TEST AL,80H        ; see if this was a key release
            JNZ XIT

            MOV BX,OFFSET G    ; set up for XLAT instruction
            XLAT               ; convert contents of AL to ASCII

    XIT:
```

Program 7.2

Again, this is just the core of the driver. For example, it does not show the processing of the character after the ASCII code is found.

Let us consider the data segment DSEG first. The array G will serve as a conversion table, to convert from the scan code to ASCII code. At assembly time, MASM responds to the declaration of G by setting up an array with the first 16 bytes (count them!) filled with zeros, the 17th byte filled with the ASCII code for 'q', the 18th byte filled with the ASCII code for 'w', and so on. Why 16 bytes? Because the scan codes for 'q', 'w', etc., are 16, 17, and so on. So we have arranged things such that the ASCII code for the key having scan code x is stored at the byte $G+x$, and table lookups can be done in the manner of the instructions in the code segment CSEG.

A difference, both between IBM keyboard and printer I/O, and between IBM keyboard I/O and the keyboard I/O of some other machines, is that on the IBM keyboard one cannot do wait-loop I/O. On at least the basic IBM microcomputers, such as the PC and XT, there is no analogue of the printer's ready bit. If such an analogous bit existed, as it did for example on PDP-11s, it would signal us that a new character has arrived from the keyboard. Thus, wait-loop I/O for the keyboard would consist of looping until this bit indicated the arrival of a new character. However, in modern systems, wait-loop I/O is seldom used in the case of keyboards, and thus, the designers of the original IBM PC did not include a "ready bit" analogue for the keyboard, even though they had done so for the printer. Instead, they relied on **interrupts** to signal the arrival of a new character. We will discuss interrupt-driven I/O in Section 7.2.

Disks are also accessed through I/O ports. Figure 7.2 depicts a typical disk and its drive. All the files you create on the computer are stored on disks such as the one shown in the figure. Each bit of a file is stored by magnetizing some position on the disk. The disk rotates, and a bit is read by the **read/write head** positioned over the disk. As the bit passes under the head, the motion of the magnetic bit induces a current in the head, which becomes the bit to be read.

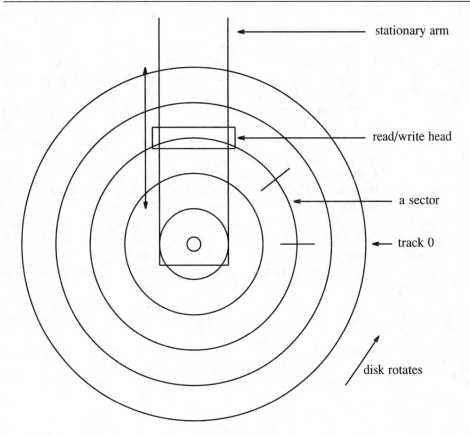

stationary arm

read/write head

a sector

track 0

disk rotates

Figure 7.2

The storage areas for bits on the disk consist of concentric rings called **tracks**. The tracks are numbered, with the outermost one called track 0, the next one track 1, and so on. (In a multidisk system, a collection of all tracks having a given number is called a **cylinder**.) Each track is then subdivided into regions called **sectors** (or, on many machines, **blocks**). So, in the file system directory that the operating system maintains, the entry for any given file name must list all the track numbers and sectors at which the bits of that file are stored. (Note that the disk hardware "knows" nothing about these files. It just treats each sector as a stream of bytes and does not "know" where one file ends and another begins. The interpretation of the various sectors as storage regions for files comes from the operating system—i.e., the software—and not the disk hardware. This will be discussed in Section 8.3.)

The read/write head can be positioned above only one track at any given time. If we want to access a different track, the read/write head must be moved laterally along the stationary arm shown in Figure 7.2 and positioned above the desired track. This movement is called a **seek**. So a disk access starts with a seek; then comes the

rotational delay, i.e., the time spent waiting for the desired sector to rotate around to the read/write head, and finally, the **data transfer time**, during which the data are actually read or written. An entire sector must be read or written, even if we need only part of a sector. Note that this implies that if we want to write to only part of a sector, we must first do a *read*: we read the entire sector to an array in memory, make the desired change in the array, and then write the entire array back to the sector.

Disks are **direct access** devices. On such a device, if the data we want to access are in a track different from the one at which the read/write head is currently positioned, we can go directly to the other track, without having to read all the data in the intervening tracks. By contrast, a **tape** access is strictly **sequential**.

IBM disks either of the **fixed** (**hard**) or of the **floppy** variety and have 512 bytes as their sector size. All other parameters, though, exhibit a wide variation from one model to another. A typical seek time is on the order of tens of milliseconds, with the rotational delay being of a similar order of magnitude. Typical storage capacities are now near or above 1 **megabyte**, i.e., 1 million bytes, for a floppy disk and tens of megabytes for hard disks.

The I/O ports for a disk drive are both more numerous and more complex than those for a printer or keyboard. A detailed description of them is beyond the scope of this book, but the reader can easily imagine what the ports would be like. For example, one port might be used to specify what track is desired, and another port could specify the sector on that track.

The seek time and rotational delay for a typical disk are on the order of tens of milliseconds, i.e., tens of thousandths of seconds. This is quite short from the point of view of us humans, but painfully long compared to the access time of main memory, which is on the order of hundreds of *nano*seconds—i.e., hundreds of *billionths* of seconds. Thus, in rough terms, main memory operations are thousands of times faster than disk operatiions. This extreme slowness in disk access time means that system developers, such as developers of data-base management systems (DBMSs), must find clever ways to minimize the time the data-base programs spend on disk access.

For example, a bank checking account data-base program might make hundreds of millions of disk accesses every day. If the program were inefficient, it might not be able to keep up with such a pace. Aside from using faster disk technology—e.g., using a multihead disk, which can do several accesses at once—several things can be done to speed things up:

- As mentioned in Section 2.3.5.1, the software—either the operating system or the DBMS programs themselves,—can include a **software cache**, which attempts to keep copies of the most frequently accessed sectors in main memory. (This should not be confused with a **hardware cache**, which keeps copies of frequently accessed areas of main memory inside the CPU, thus reducing the number of times a program must access main memory.)

- The DBMS can try to order its many disk accesses by track number, instead of using a first-come, first-serve order. For example, suppose the next three accesses are reads in tracks 29, 4, and 362 and the read/write head is currently positioned over track 6. Then we would execute the read in track 4 first, then the one in track 29, and finally the one in track 362, instead of performing the read requests in the order in which they arrived. This would minimize the total seek time.

*   The DBMS can store the most frequently accessed data in the central tracks of the disk and the less frequently accessed data in the inner and outer tracks. This again reduces seek time.

The third approach would probably require bypassing the operating system (OS) services: If we used those services, we would have no control as to where on the disk the OS stored the data. So here again, as in the rest of this book, we see that in some applications we must not only be able to "*look* under the hood," but also be able to "*work* under the hood."

The earlier IBM microcomputer models handled disk read/write via a method called **direct memory access** (DMA), which involved the Intel 8237 DMA chip. The reason for using this chip is that the earlier iAPX CPUs were too slow to access the disk. The DMA chip handled disk access much faster, by *directly* transferring characters to and from memory and from and to the disk, instead of making a stop at the CPU in between accessing memory and the disk. Later models, though, use CPUs that are both faster in general and faster due to the inclusion of the INS ("input string") and OUTS ("output string") instructions. These instructions are extensions of the IN and OUT instructions to the family of string instructions discussed in Section 6.3.3. Used in conjunction with the REP prefix described there, INS and OUTS provide a very fast method for inputting and outputting a string of many characters, such as that residing in a sector in a disk. Thus, some later IBM microcomputers are able to use these instructions instead of DMA for disk access.

Another class of I/O devices is the **display screen** or **monitor**. There is a wide variety of monitors available—e.g., color versus monochrome, graphics versus character only, and so on. In the material that follows, we will discuss how characters are written to the screen. The discussion will apply without modification to most monitors used with IBM microcomputers.

A typical monitor displays 25 rows consisting of 80 characters each. For convenience, we will number the rows from 0 to 24, starting from the top of the screen, and number the columns within a row from 0 to 79, starting from the leftmost column. (Unless stated otherwise, we will specify row and column numbers using base-10 values, rather than in hex.)

Since an image on the screen fades quickly, it must be **refreshed** frequently and regularly. Screen refresh is accomplished in the following way. At any given time, there are 25*80 = 2,000 characters displayed on the screen. (Keep in mind that even a blank space is a character, with ASCII code 20H.) These characters are stored in main memory, starting at a given location, which for the screen described here is B8000H. (For some screens this address is B0000H, in which case what follows will still apply if all occurrences of the segment address B800 are replaced by B000.) The characters are stored in the even-numbered bytes B8000H, B8002H, B8004H, B8006H, and so on. Support circuitry, including a Motorola 6845 chip (ports 3B8H and 3BAH; see

Figure 7.1), constantly scans these locations and copies the characters in them to the proper locations on the screen. Again, this happens repeatedly, many times per second, even if the contents of the screen are not changed, because otherwise the image would quickly fade away.

Interspersed with the storage of these characters in memory are **attribute bytes** for the characters, at the odd-numbered locations B8001H, B8003H, B8005H, B8007H, and so on. These bytes specify the manner in which we want the characters displayed, e.g., "ordinary" display versus blinking or highlighting (reverse video—say, black on a white background instead of white on a black background). The attribute code byte contains the bit fields shown in Table 7.1.

TABLE 7.1

Bit Positions	Contents
0–2	Foreground intensity
3	Highlight specifier
4–6	Background intensity
7	Blink specifier

The ASCII code for the character in row 0, column 0, of the screen is stored in location B8000H, and its attribute is stored in B8001H; the character in row 0, column 1, is stored in location B8002H, and its attribute is in B8003H; and so on. In general, the character in row i, column j has its ASCII code stored at location

```
B8000H + 2 * (i*50H + j)
```

and the attribute code for the character is stored at location

```
B8000H + 2 * (i*50H + j) + 1
```

Note that the quantity 50H comes from the fact that 50H = 80D.

(The reader should confirm the foregoing using DEBUG or some other debugger that can access specific memory locations.) The reader can use DEBUG to put the ASCII code for, say, the letter 'G' into location B8000H, using the DEBUG command

```
E B800:0000 47
```

and watch how the character in the upper left corner of the screen will immediately change to 'G'.)

This arrangement of characters and their attributes in memory can be exploited by the programmer to produce extremely fast access to the screen, which, of course, is very important for programs that involve screen-oriented applications, such as text editors and on-screen airline reservation systems (not to mention video games). Again, the operating system provides services that may be called from a program that needs to perform screen access—e.g., service 21/09 in MS-DOS. But we can write to the screen *much* faster if we bypass the operating system and write directly, by making use of the information in the preceding paragraphs. Since the characters at B8000H, B8002H, etc., are constantly copied to the screen, if we want to change the screen, we simply write to the proper one of these memory locations, and that change will immediately be reflected on the screen.

To see the difference in speed between the two techniques the reader should read and run Programs 7.3 and 7.4. Both programs fill the screen with asterisks. But Program 7.3 takes several seconds to do so while Program 7.4 acts virtually instantaneously. Program 7.3 uses a DOS call (set up by the compiler in translating our Pascal call to the **write** procedure) to access the screen, whereas Program 7.4 writes to the screen directly. It is also quite interesting to look at the relative sizes of the .EXE files for the two programs: 16,000 bytes for Program 7.3, but only 742 bytes for Program 7.4!

```pascal
program Stars(input,output);

    var i,j : integer;

begin
  for i:=0 to 24 do
      for j:=0 to 79 do write('*')
  end.
```

Program 7.3

```asm
SSG SEGMENT STACK
   STK DW 100D DUP (?)
SSG ENDS


CSG SEGMENT
   ASSUME CS:CSG,SS:SSG

MAIN PROC FAR

   ; point ES to screen storage area
   MOV AX,0B800H
   MOV ES,AX

   CLD  ; want incrementing in the increasing direction
   MOV DI,0  ; start at the beginning of the storage area
   MOV AL,'*'  ; want to print stars
   MOV AH,07H  ; normal attribute code (no blinking, etc.)
   MOV CX,2000D  ; want to loop around once for each of the 2,000 characters
```

```
    ; OK, write to the 2,000 locations
    REP STOSW

    ; normal exit
    MOV AH,4CH
    INT 21H
MAIN ENDP
CSG ENDS

END MAIN
```

Program 7.4

So Program 7.4 is another example in which working at a lower level in a computer system can produce much better results than working at a higher level. Clearly, one would not want to use the approach of Program 7.3 if one were writing a text editor or other application in which fast action was needed in writing to the screen. Nor would we use Program 7.3 if memory space were tight.

Another example of how I/O devices interface to a computer is the speaker on IBM microcomputers. The speaker is controlled by the same 8255 chip that is used to control the keyboard and, in fact, by the keyboard control port at address 61H within that chip. Some bits within that port are wired to the keyboard, but some other bits are wired to the speaker. So, by setting the latter bits properly, we can make the speaker emit sound, just as setting the bits in, say, the printer control port properly activates the printer. Furthermore, whatever settings are necessary can be done in conjunction with the 8253 **timer chip** (port addresses 40H–43H in Figure 7.1), so as to turn the speaker on and off very frequently at specified intervals–and thus produce a sound of any desired pitch.

As mentioned earlier, an I/O device can be interfaced to a computer with a **parallel** or a **serial** connection. The former transmits several bits in parallel, while the latter transmits only one bit at a time. In Figure 7.1, the printer is connected to a parallel port on the machine. This means that the cable leading to the printer has eight lines, enabling us to transmit all eight bits of a character to the printer simultaneously. Some printers connect to the serial port instead and thus are sent characters one bit at a time.

Cords with parallel lines become difficult to use over distances of more than a few feet. They become bulky, and slight timing discrepancies among the lines can become problematic. Thus, serial connections are common for many types of devices, and a given computer might have several serial ports (each at a different address, of course), even though in Figure 7.1 only one such port is shown.

The figure also shows a **modem** connected to the serial port. A modem allows remote communication via telephone lines. For example, suppose you have a terminal in your home and wish to connect it up with a computer in some other location. When you hit a key on your terminal, the code for that character is sent, bit by bit, to the modem that is connected to your terminal. The modem then emits tones into the phone line—a high pitch for a 1 bit and a low pitch for a 0 bit. The computer on the other end of the phone line also has a modem connected to it. The computer's modem will "hear" the high- and low-pitched sounds "spoken" by your terminal's modem, convert them back to 1's and 0's, and send those bits to the computer. The process is reversed when the computer sends a character to your terminal.

Instead of a terminal, you might have an IBM (or other) microcomputer at your home. If so, you could buy a **communications program** to run on your microcomputer that would allow it to act as a terminal in communicating with the remote computer. Such a program would use IN and OUT instructions to access port addresses 3F8H–3FFH, in a manner similar to that shown in Programs 7.1 and 7.2. Of course, a similar program must be running on the computer at the other end, controlling the modem attached there.

Thousands of computers are connected via phone lines and modems, many of them on a continuous, 24-hour basis, thus forming a **wide-area network** (WAN). Among other things, WANs enable a banking system to transfer data quickly between many banks in widely geographically dispersed areas, an airline reservation system to coordinate reservations on a nationwide and even worldwide basis, and university researchers to share information easily.

By contrast, a **local-area network** (LAN) serves a much smaller geographical area—say, an office building or a university campus. A LAN is typically used for sharing resources. As an example, suppose we have an office with several PCs, an expensive printer, and a large disk drive containing a centralized data base. We would connect all these components using a LAN. The printer and the disk drive would be connected to one of the PCs, and that PC would in turn be connected to the LAN, so that *all* the PCs could access the printer and the disk drive.

Each PC in a LAN would have a set of **network interface chips** that connect the PC to the network. Again, these chips have port addresses and thus are controlled by the programs running on the PCs, using IN and OUT instructions in the manner seen in Programs 7.1 and 7.2. And again, both the "consumer" and "producer" PCs must be running programs to make the operation work. To share the printer, for example, the PC that has the printer connected to it needs to run a program that will accept printing tasks sent via the LAN from the other PCs, and those other PCs need to run a program that will send those printing tasks to the PC with the printer.

7.2 INTERRUPT-DRIVEN I/O

Wait-loop I/O, such as that in Program 7.1, is very wasteful. Usually, the speed of an I/O device is very slow compared to the speed of the CPU. This is particularly true for I/O devices that are mainly of a mechanical rather than a purely electronic nature, such as printers and disk drives; these devices are usually orders of magnitude slower than the CPU. Accordingly, if we use wait-loop I/O, the CPU must execute the wait loop many times between successive I/O actions.

For example, in Program 7.1, suppose we must execute the three-instruction loop starting at the line labeled TOP 100 times before the ready bit changes to 1. There are nine other instructions in that program, so altogether we will execute 100*3 + 9 = 309 instructions, of which 100*3 = 300 consist of unproductive waiting! In other words, approximately 97% of this program's execution time is spent doing unproductive looping. The CPU *could* be doing other useful work during this time—running some other program instead of just looping and waiting for the printer to finish.

A commonly used analogy is the following. Suppose you are expecting an important phone call at the office. Imagine how wasteful it would be if phones didn't have bells—you would have to repeatedly say "Hello, hello, hello,..." into the phone until the call actually came in! This would be a big waste of time. The bell in the phone frees you from this; you can do other things around the office without paying attention to the phone, because the bell will notify you when a call arrives.

Thus, it would be nice to have an analogue of a telephone bell in the computer. One such analogue is an **interrupt.** It takes the form of a signal sent to the CPU by an I/O device. The signal forces the CPU to suspend—i.e., "interrupt"—the program that is running, say, "X," and switch execution to another procedure, which we term the **interrupt service routine** (ISR) for that particular I/O device.*

Note that the ISR may or may not have any relation to X, the interrupted program; we will see examples of both cases. But the key point is that at some time the ISR will need to be run, and from the point of view of program X, that time is unpredictable. That time will occur when some instruction of program X is executing, but the person who wrote X does not know which instruction that will be. Indeed, if X is run several times, the interrupt might occur at a different instruction of X each time. (In fact, typically, there will be several interrupts occurring within *each* run of X.)

Thus, program X is *incapable* of invoking the ISR on its own, through one of its instructions (e.g., CALL or JMP), since it has no idea when that should be done. This is where our "telephone bell" becomes crucial—the "bell" serves as an *external* mechanism to force the CPU to run the ISR at the time the ISR needs to be run. Again, Program X does not *initiate* the execution of the ISR; on the contrary, Program X is rudely *interrupted* by this "bell," and suspended until the ISR finishes execution.

Let us next look at a couple of examples in which the "bell" is useful:

(a) This example was suggested in the preceding discussion of the printer. Here, the ISR would consist mainly of the nonloop portion of Program 7.1 (i.e., the code that accesses the data and control ports, and not the status port). Program X would be some other program that probably would have no relation to the ISR. For example, X might be a game program, which we would like to play while we are waiting for our printing to get done. Most of the time X would run, but whenever the printer was ready to accept another character, the printer would send an interrupt signal to the CPU, upon which X would be suspended and the ISR would run. The ISR would initiate the printing of the next character and then would return control of the CPU to X, whereupon X would resume execution at the point at which it was interrupted.

---

*This type of interrupt is called a **hardware interrupt** or **external interrupt**. It should not be confused with the INT *instruction*, which is a **software interrupt** or **internal interrupt**. We will discuss INT in Section 8.1.

Again, whoever writes program X in this example would have no idea when the printer would be ready to accept another character. True, the programmer could sprinkle checks of the printer's status port at lots of different places in X, but clearly that would be a nuisance, to say the least, especially if X has no connection to the ISR. Indeed, if there is no connection, we want to be able to write X for *general* use. For example, if X is a game program, we certainly do not want to limit playing this game to times when the printer is being used! So again, the *external* nature of interrupts, in which the printer's signal is what forces the switch of execution to the ISR, is absolutely crucial.

(b) In some other applications, the ISR may have a relation to X. Let us again use a game as our example. Imagine a game in which some kind of object is moving around the monitor's screen. Suppose the user can make the object change directions by typing the proper keys whenever desired. Note carefully the word "whenever" here: in writing X, we have no idea when in fact this will be. We certainly cannot use an ordinary Pascal **read** or a C **scanf** here; if we did, the program would simply stop until the user typed a key, which is not what we want at all. What we want is for the object to keep moving on the screen, until the user types a key to make the object change direction. To accomplish this aim, we could use interrupts from the keyboard. (Another approach is also possible, via BIOS service number 16H, which relies on DOS's own keyboard ISR.)

Later on, we present a program that uses interrupts in the intended manner. Program X will consist mainly of a loop that keeps moving the object on the screen. When the user hits a key to order a change of direction, the striking of the key will result in the keyboard sending an interrupt signal to the CPU, so that X will be suspended and the ISR will be run. The ISR will read the keyboard and change a variable in X that stores the current direction of movement of the object on the screen. Then the ISR will return control to X. The whole thing will happen "instantaneously" from the game player's point of view: he or she will not notice the suspension of X at all, since it will be extremely brief.

7.2.1 Basics of the Interrupt Sequence

This section is the most detailed in the book, but if you keep the following summary in mind, it will be much easier to learn (we will continue to speak of "program X" and the ISR, as we have just done):

> There is an **interrupt request line**, called INTR, in the control bus. By asserting this line, an I/O device can force the CPU to interrupt execution of program X and make the ISR program run instead. The ISR is actually the driver for that I/O device and thus will service it. Whoever wrote the ISR will have inserted a **return from interrupt** instruction, IRET, at the end of the ISR. Execution of this instruction causes resumption of execution of program X.

So, in Example (a), instead of running a wait-loop program, which wastes its time watching the printer's ready bit, we could arrange things to work as follows. The ready bit would be permanently wired to the INTR line. We would initiate execution of some other program X while the printer is busy. When the printer finally became free, the change in the status of the ready bit would result in assertion of the INTR line. The CPU will have been designed to respond to the assertion of the INTR line by interrupting the execution of the program that is currently executing and switching execution to the printer's ISR. The latter, which consists mainly of the nonloop portion of Program 7.1, would initiate printing of the next character and then execute its last instruction, which would be an IRET instruction, as mentioned earlier. The latter action would make the CPU switch execution back to program X, which would resume execution at the point at which it had left off, with "no harm done" to it by the interruption.

With this kind of arrangement, whose details will be presented subsequently, the CPU would be freed up to do useful work while the printer was busy. The INTR line would serve as the "bell" which would signal the CPU that the printer has become ready.

A couple of points need to be clarified here, before presenting actual code to do this kind of operation. First, how does the CPU "know" to which ISR to switch execution when it notices that INTR has been asserted? After all, a typical computer system has many I/O devices, most of which utilize interrupts for their service, and each such device has its own ISR. So, to which ISR should the CPU switch execution? As an example, suppose the game program in Example (a) is also the one in Example (b). Then there would be two ISRs, for the printer and the keyboard, and both of these I/O devices could request an interrupt. How, then, is the CPU to "know" which ISR to run when INTR is asserted? Also, what if two or more I/O devices request interrupts simultaneously? How can we arrange things so that some devices have a higher priority for service than do others?

The answer to both of these questions lies in the Intel 8259A **interrupt controller chip**. All I/O devices are connected only *indirectly* to the INTR line: they are connected to the 8259A, which in turn is connected to the INTR line (see Figure 7.1). (The connections to inputs IR0 and IR1 lie in the motherboard, while the connections to IR2–IR7 are made via the control bus, which has lines named IR2–IR7.) When a device wants to request an interrupt, instead of asserting INTR by itself, it will assert its IR*i* input to the 8259A, which will in turn assert INTR *on behalf of* the I/O device. The reason for setting things up this way is that doing so allows the 8259A to enforce priorities if several devices request interrupts at the same time. After "seeing" that INTR is asserted, the CPU will "ask" the 8259A which ISR it should switch execution to. Not only does this arrangement resolve the issue of which ISR to jump to, but it also answers the concern raised on how priorities can be enforced. The details of the operation will be given shortly, but the main point for now is that the 8259A acts as a "manager" of such things.

Second, think about program X, the program that gets interrupted. Again, the CPU must eventually resume execution of X "with no harm done"—i.e., so that the program will still work correctly in spite of the fact that it had been suspended for a while. Thus, when the CPU first suspends execution of X, the CPU must record the exact status of X at that moment, keeping information such as what would have been the next instruction to be executed at that time. This information is recorded in the following way. The CPU, upon seeing the INTR assertion, will copy the current IP, CS, and FR values to the stack. Later, the IRET instruction will pop those values off the stack and restore them to the IP, CS, and FR registers, so that the program that was interrupted resumes execution at the proper place, with even the flags set in exactly the way they were when the interrupt occurred. Note that the ISR will have to save and later restore X's values in any other registers the ISR uses, again so that when X resumes execution, it will do so in precisely the same environment that it was in at the time it was interrupted.

As shown in Figure 7.1, the 8259A has eight interrupt lines leading into it, labeled IR0 to IR7. Each line is attached to a particular I/O device. For example, the printer is attached to the interrupt line IR7. We call this number the **interrupt level** of the I/O device—7 for the printer. After the 8259A asserts the INTR line and the CPU "notices" this assertion, the CPU asserts the **interrupt acknowledge line** (INTA), also in the control bus. This signal informs the 8259A that the CPU is willing to accept the interrupt (i.e., its IF flag is set; see shortly). After receiving the signal, the 8259A will send to the CPU the interrupt level of whichever device has requested the interrupt (or, if there were several such devices, whichever device the 8259A decides should be given priority). The interrupt level number will tell the CPU where the proper ISR is, in a manner to be described momentarily.

Now, recall the normal instruction cycle, which the CPU paces through continually (see Chapter 2): step A, fetch instruction; step B, decode instruction; and step C, execute instruction. What we did not mention earlier is that there is also a step D which the CPU does after every step C; in other words, the fetch/execute cycle consists of step A, step B, step C, step D, step A, step B, . . . , not step A, step B, step C, step A, step B, ... And the actions the CPU takes during step D depend on whether the IF bit in its FR has been set—say, by putting an STI instruction in the program. Now, there are some circumstances under which we want the CPU to ignore external interrupts. We can arrange for this by clearing the IF bit, say, by a CLI instruction. In other words, c(IF) = 0 means "do not disturb," but if c(IF) = 1, the CPU will react to assertions of the INTR line—i.e., it will grant interrupt requests.

With this information about IF in mind, we can set forth what step D consists of. Figure 7.3 shows the sequence of instructions that execute during step D. After step D comes the usual step A. If there has been an interrupt, the last part of step D listed changes the CS and IP registers to point to the ISR, so the instruction fetch in step A will fetch the first instruction in the ISR—in other words, the ISR will now be running! This is how the transfer of control between programs—from program X to the ISR—takes place.

```
Check the INTR line and the IF bit in the FR
If INTR is asserted and IF is set, then
   Push c(FR) onto the stack
   Push c(CS) onto the stack
   Push c(IP) onto the stack
```

```
Clear IF
Assert INTA
Read the value v = i + 8 sent by the 8259A on the data bus (IRi is asserted)
Copy c(4*v) to IP and c(4*v + 2) to CS
```

Figure 7.3

The last point raises the question of how the ISR returns control to program X when the ISR is finished. As indicated earlier, this is done by making the last instruction of the ISR an IRET instruction. An IRET instruction is almost the same as a long RET instruction for procedures: a long RET pops the top two elements of the stack and puts them in IP and CS, while an IRET pops the top *three* elements of the stack and puts them in IP, CS, and FR. These actions of IRET are *exactly what we want*, as the substeps of step D plainly show: the FR, CS, and IP values of the interrupted program were saved onto the stack, and now the IRET instruction will pop those three values from the stack and restore them to the respective registers. The result will be that the program which was interrupted will resume execution in exactly the same environment that it was in when the interrupt occurred.

At this point, we will go through a concrete illustration of the concepts outlined so far. Many real-life ISRs are difficult to fit into a textbook, since they either are highly complex (e.g., DOS's keyboard ISR) or are for specialized I/O devices that require extensive supplementary explanation. However, the game program mentioned earlier in Example (b) provides a very simple and convenient illustration of the concepts we have been discussing. Even more than most concepts dealing with computers, learning the concept of an interrupt relies vitally on the principles of "learning by doing" and "seeing is believing," so having a simple but concrete example is vital. With all this in mind, we present Programs 7.5 and 7.6.

```
/*  This program will serve as the foundation of a video game. In this
    "bare-bones" form, it is not yet a game. Readers are
    invited to make a full game out of it.

    The cursor will move around the screen, changing direction
    only when the user requests it, by typing either u, d, l, or
    r—for up, down, left, and right, respectively. It will continue
    until the user types s, for "stop."

    The speed at which the cursor moves is set by the user, via
    the variable Delay.  */


/*  The source file here contains the code to keep the
    cursor moving and also the code for setting the keyboard interrupt
    vector properly. The keyboard interrupt service routine is in an
    assembly-language file.  */
```

```
extern int far INIT(char far*);


#define StartLoc 0xb8000000  /* location of start of screen memory */


long Delay;
long FullDelay;  /* number of iterations in pause loop */


int Row,Col;  /* current or new position of cursor */
int OldRow,OldCol;  /* old position of cursor */


char Dir ;  /* current direction */


void BlankScreen()

{   int I;
    char far *ScreenPtr;

    ScreenPtr = (char far *) StartLoc;
    for (I = 0; I < 2000; I++)   {
       *ScreenPtr = ' ';
       ScreenPtr += 2;
    }
}


void PutBlank(R,C)
    int R,C;

{   char far *ScreenPtr;

    ScreenPtr = (char far *) StartLoc + 2*(R*80+C);
    *ScreenPtr = ' ';
}


void PutCursor(R,C)
    int R,C;

{   char far *ScreenPtr;

    ScreenPtr = (char far *) StartLoc + 2*(R*80+C);
    *ScreenPtr = '*';
}


void Pause()

{   long I;
```

```
    /* do nothing, many times */
    for (I = 0; I < FullDelay; I++) ;  /* note that loop is empty */
}


main()

{ char far *p;

    printf("enter delay (try 10)\n");  scanf("%ld",&Delay);
    FullDelay = 10000*Delay;
    p = &Dir;
    INIT(p);
    BlankScreen();
    /* initially at top left corner, going down */
    Row = 0;  Col = 0;  Dir = 'd';

    while (1)  {
        OldRow = Row;  OldCol = Col;
         switch (Dir)  {
            case 'u' :  Row--;  if (Row < 0) Row = 24; break;
            case 'd' :  Row++;  if (Row > 24) Row = 0; break;
            case 'l' :  Col--;  if (Col < 0) Col = 79; break;
            case 'r' :  Col++;  if (Col > 79) Col = 0; break;
        }
        PutBlank(OldRow,OldCol);
        PutCursor(Row,Col);
        Pause();
    }
}
```

Program 7.5

```
SETDS MACRO
    ; goal is to point DS to our local data segment, GDSG,
    ;    saving C program's DS on the stack
    PUSH DS
    MOV AX,GDSG
    MOV DS,AX
ENDM


SENDEOI MACRO
    MOV AL,20H
    OUT 20H,AL
ENDM


KEYBDACK MACRO   ; send acknowledge signal to keyboard
    IN AL,61H
```

```
        OR AL,80H
        OUT 61H,AL
        AND AL,7FH
        OUT 61H,AL
ENDM


NEWDIR MACRO C
        PUSH BX
        PUSH ES
        MOV BX,OFFDIR
        MOV ES,SEGDIR
        MOV BYTE PTR ES:[BX],C
        POP ES
        POP BX
ENDM


GDSG SEGMENT
        DOSKVO DW (?)  ; saved DOS keyboard ISR offset
        DOSKVS DW (?)  ; saved DOS keyboard ISR segment
        OFFDIR DW (?)  ; offset of Dir
        SEGDIR DW (?)  ; segment of Dir
GDSG ENDS


GCSG SEGMENT

        ASSUME CS:GCSG,DS:GDSG
        PUBLIC _INIT

_INIT PROC FAR

        ; pick up offset and segment of Dir
        PUSH BP
        MOV BP,SP
        MOV BX,[BP+6]
        MOV CX,[BP+8]

        SETDS

        ; save offset and segment of Dir
        MOV OFFDIR,BX
        MOV SEGDIR,CX

        ; set up ES to point to low memory
        MOV AX,0
        MOV ES,AX

        ; save DOS keyboard interrupt vector
        MOV AX,ES:[4*9]
        MOV DOSKVO,AX
        MOV AX,ES:[4*9+2]
```

```
        MOV DOSKVS,AX

        ; point keyboard interrupt vector to KISR
        MOV WORD PTR ES:[4*9],OFFSET KISR
        MOV WORD PTR ES:[4*9+2],SEG KISR

        ; leave
        POP DS
        POP BP
        RET
_INIT ENDP

KISR PROC FAR

        PUSH AX

        SENDEOI

        SETDS

        ; get scan code, and save temporarily on stack
        IN AL,60H
        PUSH AX

        KEYBDACK

        ; retrieve scan code
        POP AX

        ; test if it's a key release, in which case leave
        TEST AL,80H
        JNZ XIT

        CMP AL,1FH  ; request to stop?
        JZ STOP
        CMP AL,16H  ; request for up direction?
        JZ UP
        CMP AL,20H  ; request for down direction?
        JZ DOWN
        CMP AL,26H  ; request for left direction?
        JZ LEFT
        CMP AL,13H  ; request for right direction?
        JZ RIGHT
        ; must be an erroneous command, so just leave
        JMP XIT

STOP:   ; arrange to stop

        ; restore DOS keyboard interrupt vector
        MOV AX,0
        MOV ES,AX
        MOV AX,DOSKVO
        MOV ES:[4*9],AX
```

```
        MOV AX,DOSKVS
        MOV ES:[4*9+2],AX

        ; we're done, so leave program and go back to DOS
        MOV AH,4CH
        INT 21H

UP:  ; change to up direction
        NEWDIR 'u'
        JMP XIT

DOWN:  ; change to down direction
        NEWDIR 'd'
        JMP XIT

LEFT:  ; change to left direction
        NEWDIR 'l'
        JMP XIT

RIGHT:  ; change to right direction
        NEWDIR 'r'

XIT:  ; prepare to leave

        ; restore registers and leave
        POP DS
        POP AX
        IRET
KISR ENDP

GCSG ENDS

END
```

Program 7.6

Programs 7.5 and 7.6 form the basis for a video game. An asterisk moves along the screen in a certain direction, continuing in that direction until the user makes it change directions, by typing either 'u', 'd', 'l', or 'r', for "up," "down," "left," and "right," respectively. Typing 's' makes the game stop. As indicated in the first comment in Program 7.5, the program in the form given here is not a very interesting game, and the reader is strongly encouraged to add various features to it to make it a "real" game. But for our purposes, it will do fine.

Programs 7.5 and 7.6 will be compiled and assembled, respectively, and then linked together to produce a single .EXE file. The reader should complete these steps and then run the program before going into the details in the paragraphs that follow. Again, "seeing is believing (and understanding)," and you will understand the program—and the general concept of an interrupt—much better if you actually run the program before reading about it. Also, review Program 2.1, which shows how we can access the screen memory from the language C.

Let us consider Program 7.5 first. Its first statement indicates that another module—which, of course, is Program 7.6—contains the procedure INIT, which Program 7.5 will use. The call to INIT is near the beginning of main( ), but there is no call to KISR. The reason for the absence of this call is that KISR will be the keyboard's ISR, so it will not be executed by a CALL instruction *or, in fact, by any other instruction in Program 7.5.* Instead, KISR will start execution as a result of the keyboard's sending an interrupt signal to the CPU, as we will see in a little while.

The functions BlankScreen, PutBlank, PutCursor, and Pause deal with the game itself and should be easy to follow. In the declaration that follows, the **char** variable Dir controls the direction of motion of the object on the screen (an asterisk, which we will refer to here as the "cursor"). The role of Dir can be seen in the **switch** statement in main( ). To change the direction of the cursor, the contents of Dir must be changed. But except for the assignment statement

```
Dir = 'd';
```

which initializes the cursor to a downward motion, nowhere in Program 7.5 is Dir changed! You will see shortly that KISR is the entity via which this change is made.

Note next the call to INIT. The parameter p notifies INIT of the location—i.e., the offset and segment values—of the variable Dir. INIT will store these values in the variables OFFDIR and SEGDIR in Program 7.6's data segment, GDSG. KISR uses those two variables to change Dir. (Another method, which would generally be better, would be, in effect, to declare Dir 'public' in Program 7.5 and EXTRN in Program 7.6, but we did not use this method here, to avoid getting sidetracked by the complex details of how the C compiler creates data segments.)

Now we examine INIT in Program 7.6. As noted in the first comment, the first four instructions,

```
PUSH BP
MOV BP,SP
MOV BX,[BP+6]
MOV CX,[BP+8]
```

pick up the offset and segment values of Dir from the stack, where they were placed as parameters, and store them temporarily in BX and CX. We wish to put those values into OFFDIR and SEGDIR, but first we need to point DS to the segment GDSG that contains these variables, so we call the macro SETDS.

Most of the remainder of INIT is devoted to dealing with the keyboard **interrupt vector**. This is a pair of words in low memory that is used to point to the keyboard's ISR. Note that MS-DOS (or, more properly, the BIOS) has a keyboard ISR of its own, which you have been using (without realizing it) all along! We will replace the DOS keyboard ISR with our own—namely, KISR.

The keyboard interrupt vector is at locations 00024H and 00026H in memory. The reason that these particular locations are associated with the keyboard is as follows. Recall from Figure 7.3 that after an interrupt from a device connected to input IR*i* of the 8259A interrupt controller, the 8259A will wait for the INTA acknowledge signal from the CPU and then send the value $v = i + 8$ on the data bus, after which the CPU will copy the contents of memory words $4v$ and $4v + 2$ to the IP and CS registers, respectively. From Figure 7.1, for the keyboard, $i = 1$, since it is connected to input IR1 of the 8259A. Thus, the CPU will look at memory words

```
4*(1 + 8) = 00024H
```

and

```
4*(1 + 8) + 2 = 00026H
```

and copy those values to IP and CS, thus causing a jump to the location 16*c(26H) + c(24H). Of course, we want that jump to be to KISR! So the procedure INIT must store OFFSET KISR and SEG KISR into locations 00024H and 00026H. To do this, it puts 0000 into the ES register and executes the code

```
MOV WORD PTR ES:[4*9],OFFSET _KISR
MOV WORD PTR ES:[4*9+2],SEG _KISR
```

(DOS service 21/25 is available to perform this operation for you.) The code immediately preceding this, namely,

```
MOV AX,ES:[4*9]
MOV DOSKVO,AX
MOV AX,ES:[4*9+2]
MOV DOSKVS,AX
```

had saved the address of the DOS keyboard ISR. We need to save this address, since we will want to use the DOS version of the keyboard interrupt vector after executing our game program. At that time, the code in KISR,

```
MOV AX,0
MOV ES,AX
MOV AX,DOSKVO
MOV ES:[4*9],AX
MOV AX,DOSKVS
MOV ES:[4*9+2],AX
```

will restore the address of the DOS ISR back to the keyboard interrupt vector. (Make sure you understand thoroughly the need for such a restoration; without it, the keyboard would be useless after the game program finished executing.)

Now consider the other portions of KISR. First, there is the macro SENDEOI. As indicated earlier, a typical computer system has several I/O devices that are capable of generating interrupt requests, and thus, questions of priority arise. One such question is whether we should allow an ISR itself to be interrupted. For example, we entered KISR as the result of an interrupt request from the keyboard while Program 7.5 was running, and now that KISR is running, it is certainly possible that there will be another interrupt request from some other device. Should that interrupt request be granted immediately, or should we wait for KISR to finish executing first? The macro SENDEOI deals with this question, which we will return to in Section 7.2.2. (Some instructors or readers may choose to skip that subsection due to lack of time. If so, keep in mind that SENDEOI *is* required in ISRs for IBM microcomputers.)

The macro KEYBDACK performs the keyboard-acknowledge function we have already seen in Program 7.2. Such a function is crucial; if we had omitted it, KISR would work only once, for the first keystroke, since the keyboard would not send interrupts for the succeeding keystrokes.

The pair of instructions

```
TEST AL,80H
JNZ XIT
```

make the program respond to key strokes but ignore key releases, again as in Program 7.2.

The next few lines, consisting of several CMP and JMP instructions, check the scan code of the key the user has hit—was it one of the s, u, d, l, or r keys? If u, d, l, or r was the key that was hit, then we execute the macro NEWDIR, which puts 'u', 'd', 'l', or 'r', respectively, into the variable Dir in Program 7.5. This solves the mystery of how Dir controls the direction of the cursor without ever being changed in Program 7.5. We see now that KISR makes this change.

After NEWDIR, we JMP to XIT, where we restore the registers and do an IRET. The latter instruction is the same as a far RET, except that IRET pops three items from the stack, instead of two. The popped items go into IP, CS, and FR and result in a return to Program 7.5, since the values of that program that were in these registers were pushed onto the stack when the interrupt occurred.

Putting all these separate actions together, here is what transpires. Program 7.5 will be executing, looping around in its **while** loop in main( ), and the cursor will move on the screen in whatever direction the variable Dir currently indicates, say, downward. Suppose the user hits the u key, to change the direction of movement to upward. Then the following sequence of events will occur:

- The keyboard will assert the IR1 input to the 8259A.
- The 8259A will then assert the INTR line in the control bus.
- Meanwhile, the CPU has been busy executing one of the instructions in Program 7.5 (Again, we cannot predict which one.) In step D of the fetch/execute cycle, the CPU will check the INTR line and find that it is asserted. The CPU will then assert the INTA line and will also push the current values of FR, CS, and IP onto the stack.
- The 8259A will see that the INTA line is asserted and thus will send its "$i + 8$" value, 9, along the data bus.
- The CPU will receive the value 9 in the MDR and will copy the contents of words $4*9 = 00024H$ and $4*9 + 2 = 00026H$ to the IP and CS registers, respectively.

- Since the INIT procedure had previously put the offset and segment values of KISR into words 00024H and 00026H, at the next step A of the fetch/execute cycle we will be executing KISR!

- KISR will change the value of the variable Dir in Program 7.5 to 'u'.

- KISR will then perform IRET, which pops the previously saved values of FR, IP, and CS of Program 7.5, so we return to that program exactly where we left off, i.e., at the instruction following the one at which the interrupt occurred. So now Program 7.5 is executing again, and the cursor resumes its movement, but in an upward direction!

Note again that this entire sequence occurs in a very small fraction of a second. The user will *not* see the cursor "slow down" at all.

But why does the CPU, in step D of the fetch/execute cycle, save the value in the flags register FR, and why does the IRET instruction restore that value? To see why— indeed, to see that such actions are *absolutely necessary*—suppose that just before the interrupt occurred, Program 7.5 had been executing an instruction

```
CMP DX,BX
```

(which would be some instruction in the machine-language version of Program 7.5). Recall that the result of this comparison is reflected in the flags. Whatever values the flags have must be preserved and restored when Program 7.5 resumes execution, so that the instruction following the comparison, say, something like

```
JZ TOP
```

will work correctly. Keep in mind that when the interrupt causes Program 7.5 to be suspended temporarily, and KISR runs instead, the instructions in KISR will themselves affect the flags register, destroying whatever was put there by Program 7.5's CMP instruction and thus causing the JZ instruction that follows to execute with invalid information about the flags. So the design of the CPU includes saving the value of FR along with those of CS and IP, and the IRET instruction includes restoring the value of FR.

Note that KISR (including its macros) uses the AX, BX, DS, and ES registers. Thus, the old values put in them by Program 7.5 before the interrupt occurred must be carefully saved and later restored.

In considering the foregoing scenario, think about the roles of the Intel chip designers, the IBM system designers (who selected and put together the Intel chips to make the whole IBM microcomputer system), and the programmer:

- The Intel chip designers designed the iAPX CPU and the 8259A, giving these chips certain capabilities that Program 7.5 exploits. They designed the circuitry in the CPU so that the CPU checks the INTR line at the beginning of every step D in the fetch/execute cycle. They designed the circuitry in the 8259A so that if IRi is asserted, the 8259A asserts INTR and later sends $i + 8$ along the data bus when it "sees" INTA asserted. And they designed the circuitry in the CPU to make such an assertion and to jump to the ISR pointed to by the words at addresses $4*(i + 8)$ and $4*(i + 8)+ 2$, first saving the current values of FR, CS, and IP on the stack.

- The IBM systems design people knew about the capabilities of the iAPX CPU and the 8259A chip and designed IBM microcomputers to include these chips. They also chose to assign the keyboard to ports 60H–62H and to attach the keyboard to the IR1 input of the 8259A.

- The programmer, knowing that the Intel people designed the CPU and the 8259A to do as just described, and knowing that IBM had connected the keyboard to the IR1 pin in the 8259A, realized that the CPU would look for the ISR pointer at the words at addresses $4*(1 + 8) = 24H$ and $24H + 2 = 26H$. Thus, the programmer made sure to put code in INIT to set up $c(24H)$ and $c(26H)$ to point to KISR.

As a further variation on this theme, consider an alternative setup. We could design the CPU circuitry to save *all* CPU register values upon receiving an interrupt request, rather than just the FR, CS, and IP values. In other words, the entire **CPU state**—FR, CS, IP, DS, SS, ES, SP, BP, AX, BX, CX, DX, SI, and DI—would be saved on the stack during step D of the fetch/execute cycle. As a matter of fact, some CPUs *are* designed in this way. Now, what would be the pros and cons of such an approach? Well, on the plus side, it would save work on the programmer's part, since we would not need all those PUSH and POP instructions in KISR. On the other hand, it would be wasteful, since KISR does not need to save all these register values; it only needs to save the values of AX, BX, DS, and ES (and FR, CS, and IP, which the iAPX CPUs do save).

As an intermediate approach between the two presented, the designers of the iAPX family added PUSHA ("push all registers") and POPA ("pop all registers") instructions to the instruction set on all members of the family, except for the original 8086 and 8088 models. These instructions do push and pop the entire CPU state (except for DS, SS, and ES). The Motorola 68000 family has a similar instruction, called MOVEM, that is even more flexible, allowing the programmer to specify which registers should be saved and which should not.

Incidentally, interrupt vectors should be changed with great care. The reader can imagine what disasters might occur if a given I/O device requests an interrupt during the time we are changing the interrupt vector for that device. It is safe practice to precede code that changes an interrupt vector by a CLI instruction and follow it with an STI. The code from INIT in Program 7.6, for example, would then look like the following:

```
CLI     ;     "do not disturb"
MOV AX,0                  ; change ES to segment 0
MOV ES,AX
MOV WORD PTR ES:[4*9],OFFSET _KISR
MOV WORD PTR ES:[4*9+2],SEG _KISR
STI     ;    interrupts OK now
```

There is a DOS service, number 21/25, that will change interrupt vectors. To use it, put 25H into AH, the interrupt number (9 in the example here) into AL, and the segment and offset of the new ISR (_KISR here) into DS and DX. Then issue an INT 21H instruction.

7.2.2 Arranging Priorities among Devices

Consider the following two questions:

- Q1: Suppose I/O devices A and B ask for interrupts at the same time, i.e., during the execution of the same instruction. How do we give priority to one of these two (or more) requests?
- Q2: Suppose, during the execution of the interrupt routine for I/O device A, I/O device B requests an interrupt. How can we arrange things so that B's request is granted—or not granted?

These questions of priority are crucial. For example, suppose we are using interrupt-driven I/O for a disk drive. A disk drive is *many* times faster than a keyboard: characters will arrive from the disk at a rate at least on the order of thousands per second, whereas they will arrive from the keyboard at the rate of at most ten per second. If we were to give the keyboard priority over the disk for interrupt service, we would lose characters from the disk: a character in the disk data port might be overwritten by a newly arriving character before we would have a chance to process the old character. It thus would be much safer always to give the disk priority when the disk and the keyboard contend for interrupts. This contention will last only for as long as the disk transfer takes place (one sector's worth, i.e., 512 bytes), which will be done long before the next character arrives from the keyboard. Thus, there is little danger of losing characters from the keyboard (unless more disk accesses immediately follow).

IBM microcomputer disk drives—even the floppies—do not use interrupts for their I/O operations. Thus, the discussion in the preceding paragraph is moot, but it does illustrate the point: I/O devices exhibit a vast range of speeds, and among those which use interrupts, we must service the faster ones first.

IBM microcomputers provide a variety of ways to implement priorities. We will just give an overview of them here. Often, several ways are used in combination, depending on a particular application's needs. The situation is just like when one writes any other kind of program: many different algorithms can be used to accomplish the same goal, and which one is chosen is a matter of taste or other considerations.

With this in mind, let us look at the mechanisms that are available.

(i) Interrupt Enable Bit in the Control Port of the I/O Device.   For example, bit 4 of the control port of the printer controls whether the printer will request an interrupt. If the bit is set, interrupts will be enabled from the printer; if the bit is cleared, interrupts are disabled.

Hence, if, in Program 7.6, we did not want to allow any interrupts to be requested by the printer during the execution of KISR, we could include the following code there:

```
MOV DX,3BEH
IN AL,DX
```

```
AND AL,0EFH
OUT DX,AL
```

(ii) Interrupt Levels. As we have seen, the 8259A has eight lines coming into it, named IR0–IR7. These lines are connected to the interrupt request pins of various I/O devices. Following is a partial list, corresponding to what is shown in Figure 7.1:

> The 8253 timer chip is connected to IR0.
>
> The keyboard is connected to IR1.
>
> The serial interface is connected to IR4.
>
> The printer is connected to IR7, the lowest (i.e., least urgent) of all priority levels.

Thus, each device has a certain "hardware priority," e.g., priority 4 for IR4. Note that smaller numbers mean higher—i.e., more urgent—priorities. For example, the foregoing numbering scheme identifies the printer as the least urgent of the I/O devices on the PC, which does make sense. After all, no characters will be lost if we delay in using the printer.

Incidentally, the fact that there are only eight interrupt levels would at first appear to be quite limiting, since modern usages of even microcomputers tend to include a large number of I/O devices. But actually, this is not the case at all. On the IBM AT, and on all models of the PS/2 series, the device that is connected to IR2 is another 8259A! And that second 8259A can have eight devices connected to *it*. Thus, the **cascading** of the two 8259A devices allows us to have as many as 15 I/O devices in our system.

Now, suppose a device of interrupt level i and one of interrupt level j, where $i < j$, both request an interrupt within the execution of the same instruction. (Say, one makes its request during step B and the other during step C of the fetch/execute cycle.) Then the 8259A will give preference to the device of interrupt level i. What this means is that when the CPU notices the interrupt request on the INTR line and acknowledges it on the INTA line, the 8259A will respond by sending $i + 8$ (rather than $j + 8$) to the CPU, resulting in the CPU's switching execution to the ISR of the device of interrupt level i (rather than the one of level j).

(iii) The 8259A Interrupt Mask Register. This register is located at port address 21H. By placing a 1 at bit i, we can tell the 8259A to ignore assertions of IRi. For instance, suppose we wanted no interrupts from the printer during the execution of KISR. The following code would suffice to give us just that:

```
IN AL,21H
OR AL,80H
OUT 21H,AL
```

(iv) EOI Code. The value 20H is a code understood by the 8259A as meaning "end of interrupt" (EOI). This code must be sent to the port at address 20H. (An unfortunate and confusing coincidence is that the EOI code and the port address to which it is supposed to be sent are both 20H.) The 8259A is designed so that once it sends an

interrupt request to the CPU, by asserting the INTR line in the control bus, it will not send an interrupt of lower or equal priority (i.e., of less or equal urgency) interrupt until it receives an EOI code. Knowledge of this feature can be used as another method for implementing priorities.

To see how this method would work, suppose I/O device A, having interrupt level i, asserted IRi, the 8259A then asserted INTR, the CPU then responded with INTA, and the ISR for device A is now executing. Suppose also that another I/O device B, having interrupt level j, asserts IRj. Will the 8259A now assert INTR on behalf of B, interrupting A's ISR? The answer is as follows:

If A's ISR has *not* yet sent the EOI code, then the 8259A will assert INTR if and only if $j < i$.

If A's ISR *has* already sent the EOI code, then the 8259A will assert INTR, no matter which of i and j is smaller.

Thus, if we do not want the ISR for device A to be interrupted by a less urgent device, we can write A's ISR so that it doesn't send out an EOI until the end of the routine. That is, in writing the ISR, we would put the instructions to send the EOI code just before the IRET instruction. On the other hand, if we don't mind that A's ISR may be interrupted by some less urgent device B, we can put the EOI-emitting instructions right at the beginning of A's ISR (as we did in KISR in Program 7.6).

Note that if device B does interrupt device A, everything works the same as before in this case. When A's ISR is interrupted, the CPU will save the values of FR, CS, and IP as usual, so that when B's ISR finishes and executes its IRET, we will return to A's ISR and resume execution exactly at the point where the interruption occurred. The LIFO property of the stack is again crucial here, just as it was for nested procedure calls.

In the mode initialized by DOS, the 8259A insists on getting an EOI code at some point. It will not process further interrupts of equal or less urgency than the current interrupt until it receives that code. For instance, if KISR in Program 7.6 had omitted sending the EOI, KISR would execute only once: the second and succeeding interrupts from the keyboard would not be forwarded by the 8259A to the CPU.

(v) Interrupt Enable Flag.   There is an interrupt enable flag IF in the iAPX CPU's flags register FR. If this flag is 0, the CPU will ignore the 8259A's assertions of INTR. The flag can be set and cleared by the STI and CLI instructions.

Whenever an interrupt request occurs and the CPU accepts it (by asserting INTA), the CPU hardware will automatically clear the IF to 0. This action protects the ISR from itself being interrupted by some other I/O device. If we do not want such protection—i.e., if we want the ISR to be able to be interrupted, we must put an STI instruction at the beginning of the ISR.

Recall that the IRET instruction in the ISR will restore the original (preinterrupt) flag values, including that of the IF. Since that IF value must have been 1—after all, the interrupt is what brought us to the ISR in the first place—the IF will be restored to 1 automatically during execution of IRET.

Be careful not to confuse approaches (i), (iii), and (v). A device's interrupt enable bit determines whether the device will *request* an interrupt. The corresponding bit in the 8259A's interrupt mask register controls whether the 8259A will *accept* an interrupt request from the said device. The CPU's interrupt enable flag in turn controls whether the CPU will *process* an interrupt request relayed by the 8259A.

A number of other modes are available in the 8259A to implement complex priority schemes. For example, a rotating priority scheme, in which the 8259A makes the devices connected to it take turns, in order, can be chosen. The 8259A also has an automatic-EOI mode. These approaches are beyond the scope of this book.

For each pair of devices, say, A and B, there are different priority systems related to questions Q1 and Q2 posed earlier. If A and B ask for an interrupt at the same time, which one should have its request granted? If the CPU is currently executing the ISR of one of them, say, B, should the other, A, be allowed to interrupt it? Then, what happens if we have *n* I/O devices, where there will be a very large number of possible orderings? We can combine the various tools in numerous clever ways to answer these questions.

As an exercise, you should try a few examples. However, keep in mind that the interrupt level of a device is at least semipermanent: we certainly do not want to keep reconnecting the I/O devices to different IR*i* pins. Thus, changing the interrupt level is not a good way to achieve a certain pattern of priorities. But given a fixed set of interrupt levels, we can use approaches (i), (iii), (iv), and (v) in various combinations in order to achieve various priority systems.

7.3 I/O THROUGH SYSTEM CALLS

Performing I/O operations through direct access to the I/O hardware, as in the preceding two sections, is sometimes necessary—say, for special-purpose I/O devices such as the railway-ticket vending machine example given at the beginning of the chapter. It also is sometimes necessary for the sake of speed, as shown in Programs 7.3 and 7.4. And in any case, one at least needs to understand how I/O is done at the hardware level.

However, for "ordinary" applications, i.e., those without special I/O devices or special speed requirements, *convenience* becomes more important. We simply do not want to "reinvent the wheel" by writing device drivers for ordinary applications. Instead, we work at a higher level of abstraction, turning to OS procedures that make use of the device drivers already present in the OS. These procedures, calls to which are termed **system calls**, are the topic of this section. For example, instead of writing our own device driver for the keyboard, we can simply make system calls to OS procedures that make use of the OS's own keyboard driver.

In many OSs, the idea of multilevel machines, in which one works at the lower levels for special applications but uses the high levels for convenience in ordinary applications, is applied even to system calls. IBM microcomputers have such a feature. The low-level procedures are called **BIOS functions** and the high-level ones are called **DOS functions** ('BIOS' stands for Basic Input/Output System). The BIOS procedures are written by the manufacturer of the computer, whether IBM or a company specializing in IBM-compatible equipment, and are stored permanently in ROM inside the computer.

We have already been using DOS calls in programs in earlier chapters, such as Program 4.1, where we used DOS calls to print individual characters (service number 21/2) and character strings (service number 21/09). We also used some DOS calls for non-I/O operations, such as returning to OS control at the end of a program (service number 21/4C). For example, suppose we want to use the printer to print a character. DOS service number 21/05 will do this for us; it waits until the printer is ready and then sends the character to be printed. This DOS function requires us to pass the character to be printed to the DL register, as shown in Program 7.7. But if we want to be a little bit more careful, the BIOS functions are more versatile. For example, BIOS service number 17/02 will report the value in the printer status port, thus allowing us to check for anomalies such as an out-of-paper condition before sending the character to be printed. The requisite code is shown in Program 7.8. Of course, we could do this ourselves directly through the code shown in Program 7.9, without a BIOS call, as we did in Sections 7.1 and 7.2. But this would require us to know the address of the printer status port, 3BDH, and it is more convenient not to have to know that information.

```
MOV AH,5
MOV DL,character to be printed
INT 21H
```

Program 7.7

```
MOV AH,2
;    this BIOS service requires the printer number to be in DX
MOV DX,printer number
INT 17H
;    check bit 5 for out-of-paper condition
TEST AH,30H
JNZ NOPPR   ;  suppose we have code at that label which prints an error message
;    now print the character, using BIOS service number 17/00
MOV AH,0
MOV AL,character to be printed
MOV DX,printer number
INT 17H
```

Program 7.8

```
MOV DX,3BDH
IN AL,DX
```

```
TEST AH,30H
JNZ NOPPR
;    et cetera
```

Program 7.9

There is another advantage to not having to know the address of the printer status port: it makes the given BIOS call independent of that address. To see how important this is, consider the implications of the fact that some "PC clones"—i.e., microcomputers that are advertised as being compatible with IBM PCs or other IBM microcomputers—are not totally compatible with their exemplars. For example, a clone would still have an iAPX family CPU (or at least a copy of it), but it might have its printer ports at different addresses than those shown here, or the ports themselves might have a different structure from that of the originals. Program 7.9 would then not work on such a clone, because the machine instructions (MOV, IN, TEST, JNZ, etc.) would work fine, but they would access the wrong addresses. On the other hand, Program 7.8 would have no problem, because the company that produced the clone would write the code for its BIOS service number 17/02 to access whatever addresses its printer ports have. Since the form of the *call* is the same across all manufacturers of IBM and IBM-compatible microcomputers, Program 7.8 will work on all of them. Note that Program 7.7 will work on all of these machines, too, since the DOS functions invoked there typically call their BIOS counterparts.

Another example in which DOS provides a more convenient but less flexible service than does the BIOS is reading from the keyboard. DOS service 21/01 reads a character from the keyboard and automatically echoes it to the monitor screen. DOS services 21/06 and 21/08 do the same thing but with no echo (a capability that is useful if our program reads in a secret password, for example). BIOS service 16/00 also can read without echo. (Of course, the programmer can always include code for an echo.) But its sister service 16/01 can also do something more delicate, namely, check whether a character has even been typed at all. (Recall that this ability was needed in Program 7.5).

Both DOS and BIOS services provide other capabilities that are not available at the C or Pascal level. For example, C's **scanf** and Pascal's **read** cannot read the non-standard characters from the IBM keyboard, such as F1–F12, PageUp, PageDown, and so on. But the DOS and BIOS functions *can* read these characters; in BIOS service 16/00, for instance, the scan code of the character read is put in the AH register.

Programs 7.10 and 7.11 show an example of the finer control afforded by these services, control that is sometimes not possible with C or Pascal. The two programs comprise a **forms program**, meaning a program that displays something like a company employment application form to the monitor screen, allowing the user to fill in the form. At least one commercial product does this for federal income tax forms: the various forms appear on the screen; the user fills in the blanks, sometimes revising what was filled in earlier if a mistake is found; and finally, the user prints the contents of the screen and mails in the tax return to the Internal Revenue Service.

```
extern void far PUTCURSOR( int , int );
extern char far READC();


#define TRUE 1
#define FALSE 0


char Cmd;   /* user command */


void PrintForm()

{   char far *P;
    int I;

    /* erase the screen first */
    P = 0xb8000000;
    for (I = 0; I < 2000; I++)  {
       *P = ' ';
       P += 2;
    }

    /* now print the labels for the blanks */
    PUTCURSOR(2,0);   printf("Surname: ");
    PUTCURSOR(2,40);  printf("Given Name: ");
    PUTCURSOR(3,0);   printf("Address: ");
    PUTCURSOR(4,0);   printf("Phone: ");
    PUTCURSOR(4,20);  printf("Birth Date: ");

    /* print menu */
    PUTCURSOR(8,0);
    printf("menu:  s(urname), g(iven name), a(ddress), p(hone), b(irthdate) or q(uit)");
}


void PromptUser()

{   PUTCURSOR(9,0);
    printf("enter command: ");
}


main()

{   int I,Done;
    char C;

    PrintForm();
    Done = FALSE;
    while (!Done)  {
       PromptUser();
```

```
    Cmd = READC();
    switch(Cmd)   {
        case 's':   PUTCURSOR(2,9); break;
        case 'g':   PUTCURSOR(2,52); break;
        case 'a':   PUTCURSOR(3,9); break;
        case 'p':   PUTCURSOR(4,7); break;
        case 'b':   PUTCURSOR(4,31); break;
        case 'q':   Done = TRUE;
    }
    if (!Done)
        /* now the user will fill in the blank */
    do
        scanf("%c",&C);
    while (C != 0x0a);
    }
}
```

Program 7.10

```
PUBLIC _PUTCURSOR, _READC

CSG SEGMENT

    ASSUME CS:CSG

_PUTCURSOR PROC FAR   ; puts cursor at the row and column given in the parameters
    ; usual preamble
    PUSH BP
    MOV BP,SP
    ; get row number and put it in DH
    MOV DX,[BP+6]
    MOV CL,8
    SHL DX,CL
    ; get column number and put it in DL
    MOV CX,[BP+8]
    MOV DL,CL
    ; call the BIOS service
    MOV AH,2
    MOV BH,0
    INT 10H
    ; restore BP and leave
    POP BP
    RET
_PUTCURSOR ENDP

_READC PROC FAR

    ; this procedure reads a character with echo but gives no
    ;     opportunity for the user to backspace or take other actions
    ; the advantage of the procedure is that the character
```

```
;      will be read immediately, unlike the case for C's
;      scanf function or Pascal's read procedure

   MOV AH,1
   INT 21H
   RET  ; character will be in AL
_READC ENDP

CSG ENDS

END
```

Program 7.11

As usual, we have kept the example very simple. It consists of an application form with blanks labeled "Surname," "Given Name," "Address," "Phone," and "Birth Date." More elaborate forms would be handled using the same principles. A nice enhancement for this program would be to save a partially filled-in form to a disk file, enabling the user to return in another session to complete the remaining blanks in the form.

The program consists of a main program in the language C, and two assembly-language procedures. The user is urged to run the program before reading on, in order to get a feeling for what actions it takes. It first erases the screen and then displays the application form—item labels followed by blanks. At the bottom of the screen, the program displays a menu asking which blank the user wishes to fill in next; the user types 's' for Surname, 'g' for Given Name, and so on. Upon reading the user command, the program will move the screen cursor to the specified blank, such as the blank in which surnname is to be filled in if the user types 's'.

Note that the positioning of the screen cursor is also done via a BIOS service, service 10/02. This service requires that the calling program put the desired screen row and column numbers in the DH and DL registers, respectively, and the **video page number** in BH. The latter is normally zero, but can be checked by calling BIOS service 10/0F, which will return the page number in BH. (An alternative method for positioning the cursor, even from C or Pascal programs, is to use the ANSI.SYS file if your system has it, although the file may be inefficient.)

The forms program has been set up so that when the user fills in a blank, he or she terminates the entry by hitting the carriage return key. The code that handles this aspect is

```
do
  scanf("%c",&C);
while (C != 0x0a);
```

However, when the user submits the command to choose which blank to fill in, we want the response—i.e., the movement of the cursor to the specified blank—to be immediate; we do not want to burden the user by insisting that he or she follow the command with a carriage return. Thus, we have used DOS service 21/02 to read Cmd, rather than using C's **scanf** function:

```
Cmd = READC();
```

Here, READC is an assembly-language procedure that is in Program 7.11.

By contrast, the C statement

```
scanf("%c",&Cmd);
```

would not have worked as well. The **scanf** function (and Pascal's **read** procedure) works in **cooked mode**, in which special characters are given special processing. For example, the backspace character, which has ASCII code 8, is given special treatment, and a "backspace action" is performed. In **raw mode**, this character is just ASCII 8, with no special meaning. The point is that in cooked mode no input is considered final until the user hits the return key, since prior to that time the user can always revoke previously typed characters by using the backspace key. Thus, with **scanf**, the user would have to hit the return key after typing the command, instead of getting instant response. Moreover, we would need **scanf** to read the return character, too. (On the other hand, some C compilers offer functions to perform I/O in raw mode.)

A number of the system calls involve disk access. These calls tend to be placed at both low and high levels. The low-level calls are explicit accesses of a disk, such as BIOS service number 13/02, which does a read of a floppy disk, at the track and sector specified by the programmer in the CH and CL registers, into a memory buffer specified by the programmer in the ES and BX registers. (There are some other parameters, too.) The high-level calls deal mainly with the abstraction of files. They cite file names, alleviating the programmer of having to know track and sector numbers for the desired file; the code in these DOS functions will look up this information itself and, in turn, call the proper BIOS routines.

This is yet another example of the notion that a programmer might have to work at different levels for different applications. For a large, complex data base, for example, the programmer may need to use the BIOS functions directly, in order to minimize overall seek time, while in an "ordinary" application it would be much more convenient to use the DOS functions.

Program 7.12 illustrates a few of the DOS functions for high-level disk file access. The program reads in a file and produces a copy of that file which is identical to the original, except that all uppercase letters have been converted to lowercase. (Programmers accustomed to the Unix environment might prefer the latter, and thus, they might find such a program useful.) The program uses the following DOS functions:

Service 21/3C: create new file
Service 21/3D: open file
Service 21/3E: close file
Service 21/3F: read from file/device

Service 21/40: write to file/device
Service 21/09: write character string to monitor
Service 21/4C: exit to DOS

```
DSG SEGMENT

    IPROMPT DB 'enter name of input file',0DH,0AH,'$'
    OPROMPT DB 'enter name of output file',0DH,0AH,'$'

    INFNAME DB 15D DUP (?)  ; name of input file
    OUTFNAME DB 15D DUP (?)  ; name of output file

    C DB (?)  ; character which was read from input file

    INFH DW (?)  ; input file handle
    OUTFH DW (?)  ; output file handle

DSG ENDS

SSG SEGMENT STACK
    STK DW 100D DUP (?)
SSG ENDS

CSG SEGMENT 'CODE'

    ASSUME CS:CSG,DS:DSG,SS:SSG

MAIN PROC FAR

    ; standard preamble to set DS

    MOV AX,DSG
    MOV DS,AX

    ; get file names
    MOV AX,OFFSET IPROMPT
    PUSH AX
    MOV AX,OFFSET INFNAME
    PUSH AX
    CALL GETFNAME
    MOV AX,OFFSET OPROMPT
    PUSH AX
    MOV AX,OFFSET OUTFNAME
    PUSH AX
    CALL GETFNAME

    ; open input file
    MOV AH,3DH  ; DOS service number 21/3DH
    MOV AL,00H  ; open for read access
    MOV DX,OFFSET INFNAME  ; point to file name
    INT 21H  ; make the call, which will return the file handle in AX
```

```
    MOV INFH,AX  ; save the file handle

    ; create output file
    MOV AH,3CH  ; DOS service number 21/3CH
    MOV CX,00H  ; normal file attribute, i.e., not a hidden or system file
    MOV DX,OFFSET OUTFNAME  ; point to file name
    INT 21H  ; make the call, which will return the file handle in AX
    MOV OUTFH,AX  ; save the file handle

    ; main read/write loop, processing one character at a time for
    ;    simplicity (though less efficient, since it greatly increases
    ;    the number of DOS calls to be made)
LP: CALL READINF  ; read a character from the input file
    CMP AX,0  ; check for end of file
    JE EOF  ; leave loop if end of file encountered
    CALL LC  ; check for capital letter and change to lowercase if capital
    CALL WRITEOUTF  ; write the character to the output file
    JMP LP  ; back to top of loop

EOF:  ; all done, so close the files
    MOV AH,3EH  ; DOS service number 21/3EH
    MOV BX,INFH  ; input file handle
    INT 21H  ; make the call
    MOV AH,3EH  ; DOS service number 21/3EH
    MOV BX,OUTFH  ; output file handle
    INT 21H  ; make the call

    ; standard code to return to DOS
    MOV AH,4CH
    INT 21H
    MAIN ENDP

GETFNAME PROC

    MOV BP,SP

    ; display prompt
    MOV AH,09H  ; DOS service number 21/09H
    MOV DX,[BP+4]  ; put pointer to string in DX
    INT 21H  ; call display-string service

    ; read name
    ; first, input string from keyboard
    MOV AH,3FH  ; DOS service number 21/3FH (read from file/device)
    MOV BX,0  ; the keyboard has handle number 0
    MOV CX,15D  ; allow for the string to be as long as 15 characters
    MOV DX,[BP+2]  ; put pointer to string buffer in DX
    INT 21H  ; call read-device service, returning in AX the number of bytes read
    ; then put a null byte to demark the end of the name, making sure to
    ;    account for the CR and LF at the end of the input string
    MOV BX,DX
    ADD BX,AX
    SUB BX,2
```

```
   MOV BYTE PTR [BX],0

   RET
GETFNAME ENDP

READINF PROC
   MOV AH,3FH  ; DOS service number 21/3FH (read from file/device)
   MOV BX,INFH  ; input file handle
   MOV CX,1  ; read one character
   MOV DX,OFFSET C  ; buffer for the character
   INT 21H  ; call service
   ; the call will set AX to the number of bytes read, which will
   ;   be 0 in case the end of file has been encountered
   RET
READINF ENDP

WRITEOUTF PROC
   MOV AH,40H  ; DOS service number 21/40H (write to file/device)
   MOV BX,OUTFH  ; output file handle
   MOV CX,1  ; write one character
   MOV DX,OFFSET C  ; buffer for the character
   INT 21H  ; call service
   RET
WRITEOUTF ENDP

LC PROC
   ; check to see if C contains a capital letter
   ; if so, change it to lowercase
   CMP C,41H  ; 41H is ASCII code for 'A'
   JL XIT  ; not a capital
   CMP C,5AH  ; 5AH is ASCII code for 'Z'
   JG XIT  ; not a capital
   ; if reach this point, C does contain a capital, so change it to lowercase
   ADD C,20H
XIT: RET
LC ENDP

CSG ENDS

END MAIN
```

Program 7.12

Note that the file-manipulation services use **file handles**, which serve as temporary names that the program will use to specify each file. For example, consider the input file, i.e., the one containing the capital letters, which will be changed to lowercase in the output file. When the input file is first opened, by making a call to DOS service 21/3D, that call returns a number called the file handle, which we are storing in the variable INFH. Later, when the program reads the input file by making a call to DOS service 21/3F, one of the parameters of the call is the file handle; this is the mechanism used to let the DOS service "know" which file we desire the service to treat. Then, when the file is closed, using DOS service 21/3E, one of the parameters again is the file handle.

Earlier versions of DOS used another method of specifying parameters for DOS disk-access services, called a **file control block** (FCB). Later versions retained this method, but also added the file-handle method used here; the method is borrowed from Unix.

Note that system calls usually include quite a bit of overhead. On a 286 machine, for example, the INT instruction alone takes at least 23 clock cycles. Thus, our use of DOS service 21H/3F above is *highly* inefficient, because it reads the characters one at a time, incurring overhead on each character. A much-improved version of the program would read many characters at a time. The reader is invited to ponder the details of how this could be done.

As mentioned before, the BIOS and DOS services are *programs*, consisting of the same instructions you use in your own programs, such as MOV, ADD, JMP, and so on. (Figure 8.1 shows the first few instructions for the service family 21H.) As such, these services are liable to use the registers, which raises the question as to whether we should save our register values before calling a service. For example, if our calling program had something important in BX, we might want to have an instruction PUSH BX preceding our INT instruction and a POP BX following the INT. Fortunately, none of this is necessary: almost all the BIOS and DOS services do their own register saving and restoring.

Incidentally, the BIOS system has been extended with a supplement, NetBIOS, which consists of basic services for accessing a LAN, such as opening a connection with another PC on the network, sending data, and so on. The details are beyond the scope of this book.

7.4 I/O IN HLLS

Here we look at a still higher level of abstraction in I/O than performing it through direct access to hardware or through system calls. Recall the example of DOS services for disk file manipulation illustrated in the last section. A disk itself deals only with tracks and sectors; thus, the BIOS disk services are specified only on that level, whereas the higher level DOS services allow the programmer to specify files. The whole point of those higher level services is to remove the burden the programmer would otherwise have of breaking down a file access to a sequence of detailed accesses to the specific tracks and sectors in which the given file is stored.

Similarly, in an HLL, we can read or write objects that are more complex than characters. For example, consider the Pascal **read** procedure, which is a built-in procedure included with the Pascal compiler. Suppose our program includes a declaration

```
var n : integer;
```

and a statement

```
read(n);
```

(Of course, all of what we say here will also apply to the C-language **scanf** function and variables of type **int**.) At first glance, this **read** statement looks quite innocent. But in reality, it is quite complex.

The code for **read** makes calls to OS services that read in characters from the keyboard. The **read** procedure itself must then process these characters to form the value to be stored in the **integer** variable n. Now, we know that the keyboard is physically capable of transmitting only characters, not integers. If the user wants n to be 25, for example, he or she will type the '2' key and then the '5' key. This means that our program must somehow take the ASCII codes for these two characters, namely, 00110010 and 00110101, and compute from them the binary form of the number 25, namely 00011001.

Programs 7.13 and 7.14 show how the read(n) statement *could* be translated by the compiler. We say "could" because the code is not general enough (e.g., it doesn't allow n to be negative), but it is sufficient to get an idea of what kind of code is necessary. Program 7.13 is a Pascal-like pseudocode outline. It is just for *descriptive* purposes, to make it easier to read the assembly language that follows in Program 7.14.

```
set sum to 0
do
 read a character
if the character is a nondigit (space or carriage return)
 then leave the loop
else
 begin
 convert the character from ASCII to the actual number for that digit
 multiply sum by 10
 add the latest digit to sum
 end
until done
```

Program 7.13

In Program 7.13, consider again what happens when the user wants to input the value 25 for n. The value of 'sum' is initialized to 0. Then the machine will read the character '2', which is ASCII code 50D. We subtract 48 to get the numeric equivalent, i.e., 2. (The byte was originally 00110010 and, after subtraction, will be 00000010.) We add the 2 to 'sum', so sum = 2. Then we read in the next character, which is '5'. The value of the character will be 53, which will change to 5 after subtracting 48. We then multiply 'sum' by 10, yielding 20, and add the 5, yielding 25. Then we read the next character, which happens to be a carriage return (ASCII value of 13, recognizable as a nondigit), and we are done.

In Program 7.14, the assembly-language implementation of the pseudocode, we store the sum in BX (though occasionally copying it to AX, e.g., since the MUL instruction needs it). Note that we use a system call, DOS service number 21/01, to read the individual characters from the keyboard. This service waits for a key to be struck, reads a character from the keyboard, puts the ASCII code of the character read into AL, and echos the character to the screen. The test for whether the character read is a digit or a nondigit is done by CMP AL,30H, since the ASCII codes for the digits '0' through '9' are 30H through 39H (48 through 57 decimal).

```
        MOV CH,0
        MOV BX,0  ;  initialize sum to 0
        MOV DI,10D  ;  for our multiplication by 10

T:      ;  get character
        MOV AH,1
        INT 21H
        ;  non-digit, indicating end of input?
        CMP AL,30H
        JL XIT
        ;  convert digit from character to numeric
        SUB AL,30H
        ;  copy digit to CX, since MUL needs multiplicand in AX
        MOV CL,AL
        ;  sum ← 10*sum
        MOV AX,BX
        MUL DI
        ;  copy the sum back to BX
        MOV BX,AX
        ;  add digit to sum
        ADD BX,CX
        ;  process the next digit
        JMP T

        XIT:
```

Program 7.14

For Pascal variables of type **real** (or C variables of type **float**), the code in the procedures built in to the Pascal compiler, i.e., **read** and **write** (or their C cousins, **scanf** and **printf**), would be even more complicated than the code for integers. For example, both the forms 25.4 and 0.254e02 would have to be allowed.

Of course, HLLs such as Pascal and C offer built-in procedures for accessing disk files, too. These procedures call the corresponding DOS services, which do the actual work. But once again, the HLL procedures allow the programmer to work at a higher level of abstraction, using file names instead of file handle numbers to indicate which file is being accessed.

File access in standard Pascal is rather limited, but most Pascal compilers offer extensions to the standard, so that various types of file access can be done. However, access varies from one compiler to another, so once again, the portability of the language C is an important advantage.

Program 7.15 is an introductory example of file manipulation in C. It is a C-language version of Program 7.12, which inputs a file, changes all capital letters to

```
#include <stdio.h>


FILE *InPtr,*OutPtr;
char C,InName[10],OutName[10];


main()

{  printf("enter name of input and output files, separated by one blank0);
   scanf("%s %s",InName,OutName);
   InPtr = fopen(InName,"r");
   OutPtr = fopen(OutName,"w");
   while (!feof(InPtr))  {
      fscanf(InPtr,"%c",&C);
      if (C >= 'A' && C <= 'Z') C += 32;
      fprintf(OutPtr,"%c",C);
   }
   fclose(InPtr);
   fclose(OutPtr);
}
```

Program 7.15

lowercase, and outputs the result to a new file. The #include statement directs the compiler to include in its compilation the compiler file stdio.h, which contains definitions related to various I/O services and, among other things, a definition of the new data type FILE. We have declared the variables InPtr and OutPtr as pointers to that data type, since most of the file functions require such a pointer.

We first read in the names of the files the user wishes to be accessed. The names are stored in arrays of characters and read in using the **%s** ("string") format. Then the corresponding files are opened, one for read access and the other for writes.

The **while** loop reads and processes characters from the input file until an end-of-file condition is reached. Each character is written to the output file, after changing the character if it is found to be uppercase. Reading and writing are done with the built-in C functions **fscanf** and **fprintf**, which operate on files the way that **scanf** and **printf** do for the keyboard and screen.

The language C offers a very wide variety of file access services. A book on C reveals details. And again, many Pascal compilers also offer some of those services. Check the compiler manual.

ANALYTICAL EXERCISES

1. Determine where the DOS keyboard ISR starts, and report the first few instructions in it.
2. Look at Figure 7.3, and give the history of the contents of the address bus, data bus, and control bus (in the latter case, for the lines described in this book) during step D of the CPU

cycle, assuming INTR is asserted and IF is set. Since this is a general analysis, you will need to use the c( ) notation for your answer, instead of specific numbers. Be careful! Make sure you cover *all* activity on the bus.

3. Suppose we have an I/O device that is connected to the IR5 pin of the 8259A interrupt controller. The ISR for this device will be named W. The last instruction of W is IRET, but there is also another instruction in W, labeled L in the source file, which is IRET, too. In other words, there are two possible places at which we can exit W. Suppose we want to set things up so that, if we exit at L, then all subsequent interrupts will result in our entering W right after L, instead of at the beginning of W. Write code, to be placed just before L, that will accomplish this goal. Assume that the source code line following L is labeled L1 and that W saves the values of AX and BX on the stack upon entry.

4. Use DEBUG to view the boot loader program (review Section 4.3), and give an example of specific code there which initializes the 8259A interrupt chip.

5. Give a DEBUG command that will place an exclamation point at the upper-right corner of the monitor screen.

6. Rewrite Program 7.12 so that it works more efficiently, with each read/write action being for an entire disk sector instead of a single character. Then run timing experiments (see Program 6.7) to compare your version of the program with the original one, and analyze the sources of the difference in timing. Also, discuss why the existence of the disk cache means that Program 7.12 is not inefficient in its access of the disk.

7. Suppose an interrupt were to occur during execution of the instruction CALL 0060, with the register contents just before step A of the instruction being as shown in Figure 4.6. Show the contents of the top three elements of the stack after step D and also the five-hex-digit addresses of those stack elements.

8. Write code that will make the 8259A ignore interrupts from the printer. Your code must not affect the status of the other I/O devices.

9. Consider the third OUT instruction in Program 7.1. State what values will appear on the various bus lines during step C of that instruction.

10. Consider an I/O device that is tied to the IR6 pin of the 8259A chip. Suppose we have placed an ISR for the device in ROM at absolute address C024B. Give assembly code to initialize the interrupt vector.

PROGRAMMING PROJECTS

1. Adapt Program 7.12 so that it will report how many lines are in a file specified by the user. It will do this by counting the number of instances of carriage-return characters, ASCII 0AH, in the file.

2. Adapt Program 7.12 so that it will search the file specified by the user for a given character string, printing out all lines containing that string.

3. Modify Program 7.14 so that it allows input of both positive and negative numbers and so that it detects the input of a number outside the range of numbers representable in 16 bits. In case of an error, display an error message and exit the program back to DOS.

4. Convert Program 7.5 so that instead of directly using interrupts from the keyboard to signal the existence of a keystroke, it uses BIOS service number 16/01. This service reports the

keyboard status via the ZF bit in the flags register. If ZF is set, then the user has typed a character, which is in AL in ASCII form. If ZF is cleared, then no character has been typed.

5. Write an assembly-language procedure SILENT, callable from C or Pascal, which inputs a string of characters without echoing them to the screen. For example, such a procedure could be used for input of a secret password. Use BIOS service 16/00. (Put 00 in AH, and issue an INT 16H instruction. Upon return, AH contains the scan code of the character read and AL contains the ASCII code.) Assume that the input string will be terminated by the user hitting the carriage return key. SILENT should have a single parameter: the offset at which the string should be returned to the calling program. Write a C or Pascal main program to test your procedure.

6. Write an enhanced version of the picture-drawing program in Programming Project 1 of Chapter 2. The enhanced version will have these new features:
   * The user will enter draw-line commands one at a time, instead of all at once, as in the old version of the program. Each time the user submits a draw-line command, the program *immediately* draws that line, instead of waiting for the user to tell the program the whole set of lines to be drawn.
   * The user will specify the starting point of a line to be drawn by moving the cursor to that point, instead of giving numerical coordinates, as in the old version of the program.
   * The user will be allowed to erase previously drawn lines.
   * The user will be allowed to save the current picture in a disk file, in order to be able to return to the program at another time and continue to draw the picture.

At the beginning of the execution of the program, it will ask the user whether to load the picture from a previously saved file to the screen; if the user has no such file, the program will erase the screen. Then the program will place the cursor at the middle of the screen, say, row 12 and column 40. From then on, the user will submit single-character commands, selected from the following list:

   u—change current direction to up

   d—change current direction to down

   l—change current direction to left

   r—change current direction to right

   m—move the cursor one space in the current direction

   M—move the cursor ten spaces in the current direction

   s—draw a star at the current cursor postion, and then do m

   S—do s ten times

   b—draw a blank at the current cursor position, and then do m

   B—do b ten times

   v—save the current picture in a file

   q—quit the program

In the case of the v command, the program will move the cursor to the bottom of the screen; print a message there asking for the name of the file; read the user's response; save the picture to the file named; and finally, move the cursor back to row 12 and column 40, ready to accept more commands.

Write as much as possible of your program in C or Pascal. Pattern the program after Programs 7.10 and 7.11, to avoid scrolling the picture upward after the user hits a carriage return. Also, note that you will not want the user commands to be echoed (except for the entry of the file name).

7. Add features to Program 7.5 to make it a "real" game. Use your own creativity here. If you need to generate random numbers—say, to make the cursor change direction at random times—use the algorithm that follows in Programming Project 8.

8. This project illustrates how *interrupts* can be used to make the computer appear to do two jobs at once, in a way similar to that of example (a) near the beginning of Section 7.2. (A much more general method for doing this will be presented in Section 8.4.2, but it will use the same basic technique as that described here.) Keep in mind, however, that the computer is not *really* doing two jobs simultaneously; it just "fills in" the time in which an I/O device is not ready to send or receive characters.

Recall that, from the point of view of "human efficiency" and convenience, one generally tries to write in an HLL instead of in assembly language. But sometimes we need assembly language either for extra speed or for special access to I/O devices. So, in such cases, we write as much of the program as possible in an HLL and write the special parts of the program in assembly language. This will be the case here. Your "INIT" and ISR programs will be in assembly language, and your "Program X" will be in C or Pascal.

Your "Program X" will generate a random array and sort it. The code to generate the array is as follows:

```
seed = 9999;  /* seed is an integer variable */
for (i = 0; i < n; i++)  {
  seed = (25173*seed+13849) % 16384;
  x[i] = seed;
}
```

"Program X" will use a bubble sort to do the sorting, with the following pseudocode as a basis:

```
for (i = 0; i < n-1; i++)
   for (j = i+1; j < n; j++)
      if (x[i] > x[j]) then trade x[i] and x[j]
```

(A bubble sort is inefficient, but it is fine for our purpose here, which is to demonstrate the idea of interlacing the execution of two unrelated programs.)

How many numbers should you sort? Do some experimentation, and choose a value of n that results in a sort time of one or two minutes. When the sorting is finished, a message, "sort is done," should be output to the screen.

Your ISR program will read in some sentences (consisting of lowercase letters, spaces, and carriage returns), from the keyboard, store them in an array in memory, and finally write them to a file. Use the F1 key as an end-of-input signal to the program. (Your program must watch for this.) Then ISR will close the file and write a message, "file closed," to the screen.

Your INIT program will do initialization, and you should put INIT and ISR in the same
.ASM file.

Since one of the goals of this project is to demonstrate that we can get Program X and the
ISR to run "concurrently" (though not simultaneously), run your program several times, with
the same sorting going on but with sentences of different lengths being input. Show one run
of the program in which "sort is done" appears before "file closed" and another run in which
the opposite occurs, so that you are clearly demonstrating the concurrent running of X and
ISR.

Development Hints.   Most of the program is already written for you. The INIT and
ISR programs will be very similar to those in Program 7.6, while the file-manipulation
aspects are very similar to those in Program 7.12. Here are outlines of the programs:

```
prog_x:    call init
        generate the array
        sort it
        print out "sort is done"

init:    record OS keyboard interrupt vector value (why?)
        point keyboard interrupt vector to kisr
        RET

kisr:    push register values
        get character from keyboard port
        send acknowledge to keyboard
        if char is not F1 and not a key release then
                convert to ASCII
                append to the character array
                send EOI to 8259A
        else
                STI (due to interrupt from disk when it's done)
                send EOI to 8259A   (due to interrupt from disk when it's done)
                create the file
                write to the file
                close the file
                restore OS keyboard interrupt vector (why?)
                print out "file closed"
        IRET
```

Make sure you understand Programs 7.6 and 7.12 thoroughly before attempting this project.
Omission of any detail will probably result in the failure of your program to work, with mys-
terious "symptoms."

Debugging Hints.   Debugging will be very difficult in this project. The use of
DEBUG will be impossible at all but the earliest executing parts of your program—if your
keyboard routine has problems, there is no way to type commands to DEBUG! We suggest
the following as aids instead.

Use a "confirmatory" approach to debugging: a general truism is that quite often the bug
turns out to be in the one place that you are most sure is correct! So be sure to check all

such "definitely correct" quantities, to confirm that they do indeed have the correct value—often they don't! Perform this confirmation by calling the procedure DISPBX in Program 4.1 and by using DOS service number 21/09 to print out messages like "I did reach line 29" to confirm that you really got to a certain point in the code. In particular, make sure that you got into KISR; if you find that you never entered KISR, your interrupt-preparation code in INIT is probably wrong.

Note. The DOS keyboard ISR does many things that you take for granted, e.g., "echoing" the characters you type to the screen and obeying backspace commands. Keep in mind that you will lose these services by switching to your own keyboard routine (unless you write your routine to include them, which is not necessary). For the same reason, CTRL–ALT–DEL will not work. If your program has a problem—for example, if it gets into an infinite loop—you will be unable to use CTRL–ALT–DEL to kill the program. If this happens, use your computer's RESET button if it has one; otherwise you will have to turn the machine off and then on again.

9. Suppose in the game program, Programs 7.5 and 7.6, we want to put a five-minute time limit on the game. Implement this by borrowing code from Program 8.3.

8

Introduction
to Operating Systems

In this chapter, we will examine computer operating systems (OSs), both in function and in implementation. Concerning the latter, a recurring theme will be that certain features of the hardware, especially interrupts, will play a crucial role in supporting the OS.

As mentioned in Section 2.2, OSs are programs, and thus, several different OSs can be developed to run on the same hardware. For example, among the OSs developed for IBM microcomputers are MS-DOS, the OS we have used most in this book, OS/2, and several versions of Unix. On the other hand, viewing an OS as a collection of services available to programs, we can see that essentially the same OS can be developed for (**ported** to) several quite disparate types of hardware.

Does a computer *need* to have an OS? Some computers, used in special settings, do not. For example, in **embedded applications**, such as a computer controlling a bank's automatic teller machine or a car's fuel system, there is only one program, in ROM and running continuously. So the services of an OS are not needed. But in general-purpose computer systems, it is much more convenient to draw upon the services of an OS. For example, in the "good old days" in the history of computers (not really so long ago!), people loaded a program into memory literally bit by bit, using toggle switches on the front panel of the machine. It certainly is much more convenient to have an OS load the program for us!

But of course an OS provides much, much more than just program-loading services. The reader can get a good idea of what OSs do by looking at some of the section titles in this chapter: " 'Cooking' Services"; "File Systems"; "Process Management"; and "Memory Management." Once again, all of these sections will follow the "look under the hood" theme of the book, giving the reader a look at the methods of implementing various computer operations that the reader has probably taken for granted in the past. For example, in Section 8.1, we will take a closer look at the methods by which the OS provides service procedures, especially for I/O; in Section 8.3, we will get a glimpse of how the OS relieves casual users of the burden of providing parameters such as track and sector numbers when accessing files; in Section 8.4, we will see how **time-sharing** OSs such as OS/2 and Unix give the user the illusion that many users are simultaneously running programs, even though a machine usually has only one CPU; and in Section 8.5, we will see how a combination of the OS and special hardware can protect against certain programming errors and can produce another useful illusion, that we have more physical memory than actually exists.

Again, various features of the hardware play a crucial role. For example, interrupts come into play in all but one of the examples mentioned in the preceding paragraph. Furthermore, the material in Section 8.5, depends heavily on special hardware that is present in more advanced computers; in the iAPX family, this special hardware exists only in the 286/386/486 subfamilies, not in the iAPX 86 subfamily.

In the latter regard, it will be very important in this chapter to recall from Chapter 1 that CPUs in the 286/386/486 subfamilies run in one of two modes. In **real mode**, these CPUs run essentially like those of the iAPX 86 type, albeit it much faster and with some additional instruction types available. In **protected mode**, on the other hand, a 286/386/486 processor uses an extended and more useful interface to memory, which we will discuss in Section 8.5. (Incidentally, these CPUs operate in real mode on powering up. To change to protected mode, a special flag in an adjunct to the FR must be set. There is a BIOS call to help set up the flag, which we will not describe here.)

Once again, keep in mind that the OS is a *program*. It consists of the same instructions, such as CMP, JMP, MOV, CALL, ADD, and so on, that you use in your own programs. True, it usually is so large and complex that it is written by a team of programmers instead of by an individual, but it nevertheless is a program, and that is all.

8.1 MECHANISMS TO CALL OS SERVICES

A typical example of a mechanism to call an OS service is DOS service number 21/09, which writes a character string to the terminal screen. One calls this service by placing the offset of the string in the current data segment into DX, placing 9 into AH, and executing the INT instruction with operand 21H. Program 8.1 gives the assembly-language code.

```
MOV DX,offset of string
MOV AH,9
INT 21H
```

Program 8.1

The actions of the INT instruction are similar to those which occur during step D of any instruction during whose execution the INTR line has been asserted. Specifically, for the instruction

```
INT n
```

(where n is the operand), the following occur in step C (not step D) of the CPU cycle:

- The values in FR, CS, and IP are pushed onto the stack.
- The IF in FR is cleared.
- The contents—say, v and w—of memory locations $4n$ and $4n + 2$ are fetched.
- v and w are placed into IP and CS, thus forcing a jump to $w{:}v$.

So, for the INT 21H instruction, for which $n = 21$H, a jump is made to the location

```
16*c(86H) + c(84H)
```

That location is where the OS put the instructions for this DOS service group when the OS was first loaded into the machine (recall Section 4.3), and of course, at that time it initialized memory locations 84 and 86 to point to these instructions.

Keep in mind that an INT instruction *is* an instruction; it has an op code and an operand. For example, from line 76 of Figure 4.4, INT 21H has the machine code CD21, where CD is the op code and 21 is the operand. So in spite of having actions similar to the response to an external interrupt sent along the INTR line, the INT is *software*. For this reason it is sometimes referred to as a **software interrupt**. And for the same reason, the actions in the aforementioned list occur in step C instead of step D—they comprise the actions of an *instruction*. (There will be a step D here, too, just as with any instruction, but since the IF will be cleared in step C, checking IF in step D will produce nothing (see Figure 7.3).)

As you can see, though, INT is simply a fancy variant of the CALL instruction. And, since a DOS or BIOS service is typically "called" using an INT instruction instead of a CALL instruction, the service's last instruction will be an IRET instead of an RET. But why take this indirect approach? Why not just use CALL and RET?

One of the major answers to this question lies in the notion of portability across machines, or even across different versions of an OS. A particular service might be stored at different locations on different machines or on different OS versions running on the same machine. Let us use service number 21 as an example. Where does the code for this service begin? Since the code is reached via an INT instruction, we can determine its location by inspecting the interrupt vector, which is in words 00084H and 00086H in memory. So we type

```
D 0:84
```

in DEBUG (since 4*21H = 84H). The author tried this on an IBM AT-compatible machine, with the following result (we show only the first line here):

```
0000:0080              1C 02 16 12-F5 02 AF 16 2E 03 AF 16
```

We want the contents of *words* 84H and 86H, so, recalling that the D command displays words with the bytes reversed, we see that the code for DOS service number 21 begins at offset 021C in the segment beginning at 1216. However, typing in D 0:84 for an NEC 386SX machine yields the information that on that system DOS service number 21 begins at segment 02F2, offset 1460.

The same problem might occur even on the same machine, say, for MS-DOS, version 3.3 versus version 4.0; both versions would offer the service but might store it at different addresses. Using INT instead of CALL solves this problem. The OS for a given machine can place the code for service number 21H at any memory address and then simply fill memory locations 4*21H and 4*21H + 2 to point to that address. (The OS initializes the interrupt vectors when the OS is first booted into memory, as described in Section 4.3.) *The advantage of this approach is that the a program that makes a call to service number 21H will work on any IBM (or IBM-compatible) microcomputer running MS-DOS, even if the code for that service number is at different places on different machines.* Some other IBM microcomputer OSs work this way, too. For example, Xenix, a Unix OS developed for these machines, uses INT 5 for its system calls in the same way that MS-DOS uses INT 21H for many of its calls.

The same is generally true for other hardware as well. For example, the Motorola and VAX CPU families have a TRAP instruction that works similarly, and OSs running on those machines typically implement system calls using that instruction or one of several other similar instructions. (TRAP is also used to change privilege levels on those machines.) On the other hand, the OS/2 OS, which is a more sophisticated alternative to MS-DOS for iAPX 286/386/486 CPUs, uses something termed a **call gate**, which will not be described here.

Let us make these ideas a bit more concrete by using DEBUG to take a peek at the actual code of INT 21H on, say, the NEC machine mentioned earlier. We will use the DEBUG U command, but first let us see whether we can predict what that code will look like, using the reasoning in the following paragraph.

As we have seen for the last few chapters, some of the BIOS and DOS services are arranged in families, with service family 21H being a prime example. Service number 21/09 prints a character string to the monitor, 21/4C terminates a program and effects a return to the DOS command reader, and so on. Now recall that the service subnumber, say, 09H or 4CH, is put into the AH register by the programmer. Thus, you can imagine the beginning of the code for service family 21 to be like a big Pascal **case** statement or C **switch** statement, using c(AH) as the basis for making a decision among the alternatives.

A look at the code for INT 21 on the NEC machine, shown in Figure 8.1, confirms our conjecture. For example, if c(AH) = 51H, corresponding to DOS service 21/51 ("get PSP segment"), then we will jump to offset 140D of the current code segment, which apparently has the code that implements that particular service. (For the more commonly used DOS services, say 21/02, it turns out that the check for the value of c(AH) is buried deep in the procedure, because a lot of saving of registers, changing of segments, and so on must be done first. But if you are patient in stepping through the procedure using DEBUG, you will see that eventually all values of AH are checked.)

```
-U 02F2:1460
02F2:1460 2E            CS:
02F2:1461 3A26FF0D      CMP     AH,[0DFF]
02F2:1465 77DC          JA      1443
02F2:1467 80FC51        CMP     AH,51
02F2:146A 74A1          JZ      140D
02F2:146C 80FC62        CMP     AH,62
02F2:146F 749C          JZ      140D
02F2:1471 80FC50        CMP     AH,50
02F2:1474 7491          JZ      1407
02F2:1476 80FC33        CMP     AH,33
02F2:1479 7498          JZ      1413
02F2:147B 80FC64        CMP     AH,64
02F2:147E 74BA          JZ      143A
```

Figure 8.1

Incidentally, almost all the DOS and BIOS service procedures do their own saving and restoring of registers. Thus, if your program has a "live" value in CX before a call to a DOS or BIOS service, you do not need to save that value before the call. The procedure itself will save and restore the value, and the value will therefore still be intact upon return from the call. (There are a small number of exceptions to this "rule," such as the procedures for DOS services 25 and 26. Check a DOS manual if you are unsure in a particular case.)

8.2 "COOKING" SERVICES

Typically, an OS offers other services which the user may not be aware stem from the OS, rather than the hardware. For example, you are accustomed to see an **echo** on the screen of any character you type at the keyboard. On most systems these days, that echo is done, not by the keyboard/monitor hardware, but rather by the software, i.e., the OS. And the same is true for the backspace key: the backspace action comes from the OS (more specifically, the keyboard interrupt routine, which is part of the OS), and not from the hardware in the keyboard or the screen. Here is an outline of how an interrupt routine could be written for the keyboard for IBM microcomputers:

```
get the scan code of the key pressed and put it in AX
send the ACK signal to the keyboard
see if c(AX) = scan code for ← key
if so, JMP to label A
see if c(AX) = scan code for carriage return key
if so, JMP to the OS command reader to indicate that a complete command is ready
increment count of number of characters in the current line
```

```
convert scan code to ASCII code
write character to the screen
            .
            .
            .

IRET
```

```
A:    decrement count of number of characters in the current line
      change the character in the current position on the screen to a blank
      move the cursor one position to the left on the screen
      IRET
```

Another example is the use of control-S and control-Q, which under many OSs (including MS-DOS and Unix), stops and restarts the scrolling of what is on the monitor.

After the OS preprocesses the characters input from the keyboard, the resulting characters are said to be in **cooked mode**. Typically, an OS will also provide system calls under which the user can request **raw mode**, i.e., no preprocessing. For example, DOS function 21/01 reads from the keyboard in cooked mode, while function 21/06 does so in raw mode.

8.3 FILE SYSTEMS

Recall from discussions in Sections 1.2 and 7.1.3 that the concept of a **file** is not inherent in disk hardware; instead, it is an abstraction provided to the user by the OS. Hence, if two consecutive sectors on a disk happen to belong to the same file, the OS is aware of this fact—since it put them there in the first place—but the disk hardware is quite ignorant of it; to it, they are merely two sectors, each containing 512 bytes.

So again, we see the OS's role as a provider of a service. If there were no OS, we would have to manage our own data storage on disk, keeping track for ourselves which sectors we are using for which data sets. Instead, the OS allows us to give a name to a data set—a **file name**—and leave the OS to worry about which sectors that data set is stored in.

In most cases, users are quite grateful for this convenience the OS provides. But in some applications, such convenience is an obstacle to the efficient use of the machine. As noted in Section 7.1.3, the fact that the operation of a disk drive is primarily mechanical rather than electronic implies that the disk drive is the slowest component in a computer system. For example, a file might be stored in sectors on many different tracks of the disk, and moving from one track to another—a **seek**—takes time. If we access the file in a very naive way that completely ignores the track positions of the various parts of the file, the total seek time may be significant. But if we get more actively involved and use information about track positions, we may be able to reduce the total seek time significantly. And in any case, it is helpful to know how things work at the level of the OS, even for those who rarely write code at that level. Thus, in this section we will once again "look under the hood," to see how DOS maintains files and keeps records of the locations on the disk where the files are stored.*

---

*Some of this material must be altered slightly if DOS version 4.0 is used.

First, let us review the numbering systems for IBM disk sectors. The system we described in connection with BIOS service number 13H specifies a sector by using two numbers: the track number and the sector number within the track. (Actually, the situation is even more complex than that, since a side number and other information must be given.) It is easier, however, to deal with **logical** sector numbers than these physical sector numbers. Accordingly, all sectors of a disk are aggregated into a single numbering system: sector 0, sector 1, sector 2, and so on.

DOS services 25H and 26H use the latter system and thus are easier to use than BIOS service number 13H. To read a given sector using DOS service number 25H, one uses code patterned on the following outline:

```
MOV AL,drive number
MOV CX,number of sectors to be read
MOV DX,logical sector number of first sector to be read
MOV BX,offset of array to which the sector bytes will be copied
INT 25H
POP AX
```

This code assumes that the array to which the sector bytes will be copied is in the current data segment. The POP is required because this particular DOS service, unlike the others, returns via a far RET instruction, rather than with IRET. Also unlike other DOS services, this one changes all the registers except the segment registers, so if, for example, the surrounding code uses SI, the value of SI should be pushed and popped before and after the preceding code. On the other hand, this DOS service, as well as its companion for writes, DOS service number 26H, is more convenient to use than the BIOS services for disk read/write–number 13H–since the latter do not use the logical sector numbering system used by the DOS service. (In working those programming projects at the end of this chapter which require low-level reading of disk sectors, it is therefore recommended that you use service 25H instead of 13H.)

Program 8.2 uses service 25H for quick, informal examination of disk sectors. It will display to the screen any bytes from any sector of the disk, as specified by the user. We will use this program to illustrate the concepts pretaining to file systems presented in the remainder of this section. Actually, the DEBUG program also provides a means for such examination, and we will use it in a couple of cases, but for the most part we will use Program 8.2. Besides serving as an example of how to use service 25H, Program 8.2 is more convenient and provides a cleaner form of output than the DEBUG program.

```
SECSIZE EQU 512D


READSP MACRO   ; reads one blank
    MOV AH,1
    INT 21H
    ENDM
```

```
PRCRLF MACRO  ; prints carriage return and line feed
   MOV AH,2
   MOV DL,0DH
   INT 21H
   MOV DL,0AH
   INT 21H
   ENDM


DSG SEGMENT
   PROMPT DB '? $'
   SECTOR DB SECSIZE DUP (?)  ; the sector contents will be copied to this array
   SECTNO DW (?)   ; sector number
   OLDSN DW 0FFFFH  ; old value of sector number
   BYTENO DW (?)  ; at what byte to start printing
   NBYTES DW (?)   ; number of bytes to print
DSG ENDS


SSG SEGMENT STACK
   STK DW 100D DUP (?)
SSG ENDS


CSG SEGMENT

MAIN PROC FAR
   ASSUME CS:CSG,DS:DSG,SS:SSG

   ;   standard preamble to set DS
   MOV AX,DSG
   MOV DS,AX

   ; main loop

   ; print prompt
TOP:  MOV DX,OFFSET PROMPT
   MOV AH,9
   INT 21H
   CALL READBX  ; read SECTNO
   MOV SECTNO,BX
   CMP BX,0FFFFH  ; "sector" FFFF means quit
   JE EXIT
   READSP  ; one space between input parameters
   CALL READBX  ; read BYTENO
   MOV BYTENO,BX
   READSP  ; one space between input parameters
   CALL READBX  ; read NBYTES
   MOV NBYTES,BX
   PRCRLF  ; go to next line on screen
   ; ready to read sector, but bypass the read if we already have that sector
   MOV AX,OLDSN
   CMP SECTNO,AX
```

```
        JE DBTS
        MOV AL,0   ; read from drive A
        MOV CX,1   ; read one sector
        MOV DX,SECTNO   ; read sector number SECTNO
        MOV BX,OFFSET SECTOR   ; copy what is read to the array SECTOR
        INT 25H   ; do the read
        POP AX   ; service 25 returns with RET instead of IRET, so clean up the stack
DBTS:   CALL DISPBYTS   ; display the bytes requested
        MOV AX,SECTNO   ; update OLDSN
        MOV OLDSN,AX
        JMP TOP   ; ready for next user command

EXIT:
        ; standard code to return to DOS
        MOV AH,4CH
        INT 21H
MAIN ENDP

READBX PROC   ; reads a hex value from keyboard to BX

        ; note: must be a 4-digit number, so put in leading zeros if needed,
        ;       and must use lowercase for digits a-f

        ; method:
        ; set BX to 0, then loop around 4 times, once for each hex digit
        ; for each digit, multiply BX by 16, convert the ASCII to the numeric
        ;     version, and add to BX

        MOV DI,4   ; loop around 4 times, with DI being the loop counter
        SUB BX,BX   ; set BX to 0

RLP:

        ; prepare to multiply c(BX) by 16D
        MOV AX,BX
        MOV CX,16D
        MUL CX   ; multiply c(AX) by c(CX), putting the result in AX

        MOV BX,AX   ; store back to BX, where we are accumulating the sum

        CALL READCHAR   ; read digit from keyboard

        ; have to convert the ASCII to numeric
        CMP AL,39H   ; 0-9 or a-f? ASCII for the character '9' is 39H
        JG LETTER   ; if a-f, go to a-f code
        SUB AL,30H
        JMP UPDATE
LETTER:  SUB AL,57H   ; ASCII for 'a' is 61H, and 61H - 57H = 10D = 0AH

UPDATE:   ; now add this to BX
        MOV AH,0   ; make sure nothing is in the high part of AX
        ADD BX,AX
```

```
                ; done with loop?
                SUB DI,1
                JNZ RLP  ; if not, go back to read another digit

                ; all done, so return to caller
                RET
        READBX ENDP

        READCHAR PROC
                ; we will use DOS service 21/01, which reads a single
                ;   character from the keyboard, placing it into AL
                ;   and echoing it to the screen
                MOV AH,1
                INT 21H
                RET
        READCHAR ENDP

        DISPBYTS PROC

                ; point DI to first byte to be displayed
                MOV DI,OFFSET SECTOR
                ADD DI,BYTENO

                ; loop once for each byte
                MOV SI,NBYTES

        DING: ; get byte
                MOV DL,[DI]

                ; put upper nibble in BH, lower in BL
                MOV BH,DL
                MOV CL,4
                ROR BH,CL
                AND BH,0FH
                MOV BL,DL
                AND BL,0FH

                ; print the two nibbles
                MOV CL,BH
                CALL PRNIB
                MOV CL,BL
                CALL PRNIB
                MOV AH,2
                MOV DL,' '
                INT 21H
                INC DI
                DEC SI
                JG DING

                ; all done, so print out carriage return and line feed, and leave
                PRCRLF
                RET
        DISPBYTS ENDP
```

```
PRNIB PROC
   CMP CL,9  ;  is it 0-9 or A-F?
   JG A_F
   ADD CL,30H  ;   ASCII codes for the characters '0'-9' are 30H-39H
   JMP WR_CHAR
A_F: ADD CL,37H  ;   ASCII codes for the characters 'A'-F' are 41H-46H
   WR_CHAR: MOV DL,CL
   MOV AH,2
   INT 21H
   RET
PRNIB ENDP

CSG ENDS


END MAIN
```

Program 8.2

The reader should run the program before continuing reading. Assuming a file name of PROG82.ASM, assemble and link from that source file, and then put a floppy disk into drive A. Then type

```
> PROG82
```

at the DOS prompt. Each time the program displays its ? prompt, enter the following three four-hex-digit numbers, separated by one space each (make sure to type leading zeros—e.g., type 0025 instead of just 25):

- The sector number to be read.
- The byte number at which to start reading.
- The number of bytes to be read.

For example,

```
? 0002 00fa 0004
```

would mean that you wish to read four bytes in sector 2, starting at byte FA within that sector. To leave the program, type ffff.

Now let us begin our exploration of the DOS file system. The author loaded a floppy disk into drive A and typed DIR, yielding the display given in Figure 8.2. Three files are shown: the familiar MASM executable file; a subdirectory, GY; and an .ASM source file, PRIME.ASM, which happens to be the source file for Program 4.2 in Chapter 4.

MS-DOS has a **hierarchical**, tree-structured file system similar to that of Unix. The structure allows the user to organize files into meaningful groups. For example, if

```
Volume in drive A has no label
 Directory of  A:
MASM     EXE    110703   2-01-88   1:00p
GY            <DIR>      5-05-90   4:20p
PRIME    ASM     6060    4-28-90   2:45p
         3 File(s)      643072 bytes free
```

Figure 8.2

the user has two projects, named, say, 1 and 2, then he or she might create two sub-directories, say, PROJ1 and PROJ2, and keep all files related to project 1 in PROJ1 and all related to project 2 in PROJ2. The CD ("change directory" command can be used to enter any given subdirectory.

The files at the top level of the MS-DOS tree form the **root directory** of the system. Some of those files represent subdirectories, as is GY in Figure 8.2, but they are still files in their own right; their "data" simply consist of lists of the various files in them.

Now let us look "under the hood" of Figure 8.2. First, it is essential to know that the sectors of a floppy disk are arranged as shown in Figure 8.3. We will see what these items are later on. The first one, though, should be familiar from Section 4.3: the boot record, sector 0 on the disk, is loaded into memory automatically when the computer is powered up; it contains a short program whose job it is to read in the OS and do some initialization. Let us take a look at the first 16 bytes of that sector, using Program 8.2:

```
? 0000 0000 0010
EB 34 90 4E 45 43 49 53 33 2E 33 00 02 01 01 00
```

Boot record
File allocation tables
Directory index sectors
File data clusters (called cluster 2, cluster 3,...)

Figure 8.3

Recall from Section 4.3 that this particular sector contains a program, the boot loader program. Thus most of the sector contains program instructions. This is certainly so for the first two bytes, EB34, which is a JMP forward of distance 34H bytes, i.e., to the instruction beginning at byte

```
0000 + 2 + 34 = 0036
```

Byte 0036 happens to be FA:

```
? 0000 0036 0001
FA
```

which is a CLI instruction.

The bytes between the JMP and the CLI, i.e., bytes 02H–35H in the boot record, happen to be data, not code, set up according to a format that is uniform across all PC and PC-compatible floppy disks. These data consist of miscellaneous pieces of information needed for initialization of the OS, especially concerning disk configuration.

In particular, bytes 02–32H form the BIOS parameter block (BPB). Let us examine a few of the parameters stored there:

- First, word 0BH (i.e., bytes 0BH–0CH) of the boot sector contains the number of bytes per sector:

  ```
  ? 0000 000b 0002
  00 02
  ```

Recall that iAPX machines are **little-endian** in their addressing scheme: *word n* consists of *bytes n* and $n + 1$, with byte $n + 1$ the more significant one. Thus, in our setting here, word 0BH consists of bytes 0BH and 0CH, with the latter the more significant one. In other words, we have just found that the number of bytes per sector for the disk in question is 200H = 512D.

- Next, byte 0DH contains the number of sectors per **cluster**:

  ```
  ? 0000 000d 0001
  01
  ```

A cluster is a set of consecutive sectors (more on this shortly). We see, then, that there is one sector per cluster.

- Byte 10H stores the number of copies of the **file allocation table** (FAT):

  ```
  ? 0000 0010 0001
  02
  ```

The FAT lists which clusters our files are stored in and which clusters are currently unused and thus available when new files are created. We see that two copies of the FAT are stored on this disk; if one of them gets corrupted, we may be able to use the other to recover our files.

- Byte 11H stores the number of **directory index** entries:

  ```
  ? 0000 0011 0001
  E0
  ```

So the disk we are examining has 0E0H = 224D directory index entries. This means that we can have as many as 224 files, including subdirectories, in our root directory. The entries in the directory index give information on file names, sizes, and so on (see shortly).

* Word 16H gives the size of the FAT, in sectors:

```
? 0000 0016 0002
07 00
```

Again, since this is *word* 16H, the individual bytes will be displayed in reverse order. So each FAT is seven sectors long.

Now let us look at the directory index for the disk. Where on the disk is it? From Figure 8.3, we see that it follows the FATs, which in turn follow the boot record. We found that there are two FAT copies, each taking up seven sectors. The boot record is in sector 0, so the FATs then occupy sectors 1–14D. That means the directory index starts in sector 15D.

Where does the directory index end? We can reason as follows. As you will see shortly, each directory index entry is 20H = 32D bytes long. We found that there are 0E0H = 224D entries. Thus, the entire directory index occupies 224 * 32 = 7,168 bytes, and since each sector is 512 bytes long, the directory index occupies 7,168/512 = 14 sectors.

In other words, the directory index begins at sector 15D and extends through sector 28D. Let us take a look at that first sector. This time we will use DEBUG, since it prints out both hex and ASCII values, which will be more convenient here than using Program 8.2, which prints out hex values only.

To see the contents of sector 15D, we use DEBUG's L ("load from disk") command and then use its D command to display what was loaded. We tell DEBUG to load one sector, beginning with sector 0FH (15D) from drive 0 (i.e., drive A), starting at offset 0000 of the current data segment. Then we ask DEBUG to display what was loaded there. The result is:

```
-L 0000 0 F 1
-D 0000
13E6:0000  4D 41 53 4D 20 20 20 20-45 58 45 20 00 00 00 00   MASM    EXE ....
13E6:0010  00 00 00 00 00 00 00 68-41 10 02 00 6F B0 01 00   .......hA...o...
13E6:0020  47 59 20 20 20 20 20 20-20 20 20 10 00 00 00 00   GY         .....
13E6:0030  00 00 00 00 00 00 9B 82-A5 14 04 00 00 00 00 00   ..............
13E6:0040  E5 49 4E 4B 20 20 20 20-45 58 45 20 00 00 00 00   .INK    EXE ....
13E6:0050  00 00 00 00 00 00 40 29-67 10 DC 00 03 00 01 00   ......@)g.......
13E6:0060  50 52 49 4D 45 20 20 20-41 53 4D 20 00 00 00 00   PRIME   ASM ....
13E6:0070  00 00 00 00 00 00 B7 75-9C 14 5D 01 AC 17 00 00   .......u..].....
```

We see the names of the files we have stored on this disk—both the ones we saw in Figure 8.2, i.e., MASM.EXE, GY, and PRIME.ASM, *and* another one, with the strange name .INK.EXE, strange because it begins with a period.

If we were to look further in this directory, we would find a few more files listed, but after those, the entries in the file name fields would be zeros. The zeros indicate that there is room in the directory for additional files to be created. The directory has room for 224 files in all, and of course, there may be additional files in the GY subdirectory, subsubdirectories, and so on.

Each directory index entry is 20H = 32D bytes long, as is plain from the fact that the beginning offsets of successive entries are spaced 20H bytes apart—MASM.EXE at 0000, GY at 0020, and so on. As with the BPB, the 20H bytes store specific information in specific fields, including those shown in Figure 8.4. Here, d is the byte number of the directory entry. For the disk in question, d = 0000 for MASM.EXE, d = 0020 for GY, and so on.

File name: bytes d + 0H through d + 07H
File name extension (EXE, ASM, etc.): bytes d + 08H through d + 0AH
Attribute byte: byte d + 0BH
First cluster: word d + 1AH

Figure 8.4

Let us look at these fields in more detail. The file name and file name extension need no explanation, except in the case of .INK.EXE. If a file name listed in the directory index has a period as its first character, as in this case, then the file has been removed, using the ERASE command. Here, the file was LINK.EXE, and the command was

```
ERASE LINK.EXE
```

Because it was erased, the file did not appear in Figure 8.2.

In carrying out the ERASE command, the OS replaced the 'L' in the name by E5H, a non-ASCII character that appears as a period when displayed on the monitor screen. But contrary to what you might guess from the command name ERASE, the file LINK.EXE was *not* erased. It is still there on the disk. Upon issuance of the ERASE command, the OS set the file's entries in the FAT to zeros, which means that the space occupied by the file on the disk is now available for use when we create new files. But until the space *is* reused, the file will still be there.

We might even be able to reconstruct the "erased" file if we regret having removed it. We could we do this changing the entry in the directory, using service 26H to write to the appropriate disk sector. First, we would change the period in the name back to 'L'. The rest would be a matter of changing the FAT entries from zeros back to the cluster numbers where the file is stored. Determining these would be a matter of searching through the disk sectors, using, say, Program 8.2 or DEBUG, until we found the sectors for the file. Doing this would be a rather delicate job, which we will not describe any further here, but the point is that the file *is* still there and, thus, is recoverable. Commercial "unerase" programs, such as those of the Norton Utilities, use methods similar to that just described.

Let us look at the other two directory index fields mentioned in Figure 8.4. The attribute byte, 0BH, contains the following information:

Bit 0: read-only file
Bit 1: hidden file (will not appear in DIR, though not removed)
Bit 2: system file
Bit 3: volume label
Bit 4: subdirectory
Bit 5: archive

Each bit will be 1 or 0 according to whether the file has the given characteristic.

As an example, let us examine the attribute byte for the file MASM.EXE. Recalling that the directory begins at sector F and that the attribute byte for a file is at offset B within the directory entry for that file, we type

```
? 000f 000b 0001
```

and the computer returns

```
20
```

The value is 20H, i.e., 00100000. The only bit that is set is bit 5, the archive bit, which means that the file MASM.EXE should be copied if a file-backup process is performed.

Things are different for the file GY, as we will see by examining its attribute byte. Since GY's directory entry begins at byte 0020 of sector F, Figure 8.4 shows that the attribute byte for GY will be at byte 002B. To see what is there, we type

```
? 000f 002b 0001
```

and the computer returns

```
10
```

The attribute byte is, then, 10H, i.e., 00010000. Here bit 4 is set, indicating that GY is a subdirectory (as we saw in Figure 8.2), rather than an "ordinary" file. Again, GY is still a file in its own right, just like the other files we see in Figure 8.2. The only difference is that the "data" in GY file are actually another directory index similar to the one we are viewing here, with that index listing the 20-bytes-per-file information for whatever files exist in the GY subdirectory.

Again consulting Figure 8.4, we see that word d + 1AH in the directory listing entry for a file contains the cluster number at which the data for that file begin. For example, for the file PRIME.ASM, we use the fact that the file has d = 60 (see the DEBUG output on page 328) and type

```
? 000f 007a 0002
```

The computer returns

```
5D 01
```

Again keeping in mind the "little-endian" factor, we find that the file is stored begining at cluster 15DH, i.e., cluster 349D. To examine this cluster, we must know the logical sector number of the first data cluster on the disk. Figure 8.3 shows that the file data areas follow the end of the directory index; the first file data cluster is called cluster 2, the second cluster 3, and so on.

Earlier, we found that the directory index ends at sector 28D. Thus, cluster 2 starts at sector 29D. And since the BPB told us that there is one sector per cluster, cluster 2 ends there, too. Cluster 3 is then sector 30D, cluster 4 is sector 31D, and so on; in general, for the disk, cluster n is sector $(n + 27D)$.

So we can now finally look at the data in PRIME.ASM! The data start in cluster 349D, which, from the last paragraph, we now know means sector 376D, i.e., Sector 178H. Because PRIME.ASM is an ASCII file, let us again use DEBUG instead of Program 8.2, since DEBUG prints in both hex and ASCII. The result is shown in Figure 8.5. The figure does indeed reveal our file, PRIME.ASM. Recall that we mentioned after Figure 8.2 that PRIME.ASM happened to be the source file for Program 4.2. A check back to that program will show that PRIME.ASM is one and the same file. For example, Program 4.2 started with the line

```
MAXPRM EQU 1000D
```

and this is the output shown in Figure 8.5.

```
-L 4000 0 178 1
-D 4000
3816:4000   0D 0A 0D 0A 4D 41 58 50-52 4D 20 45 51 55 20 31   ....MAXPRM EQU 1
3816:4010   30 30 30 44 0D 0A 0D 0A-44 53 47 20 53 45 47 4D   000D....DSG SEGM
3816:4020   45 4E 54 0D 0A 0D 0A 20-20 20 4E 20 44 57 20 28   ENT....   N DW (
3816:4030   3F 29 20 20 3B 20 74 68-65 20 63 75 72 72 65 6E   ?)   ; the curren
3816:4040   74 20 6E 75 6D 62 65 72-20 62 65 69 6E 67 20 74   t number being t
3816:4050   65 73 74 65 64 20 66 6F-72 20 70 72 69 6D 65 6E   ested for primen
3816:4060   65 73 73 0D 0A 20 20 20-4D 41 58 20 44 57 20 28   ess..   MAX DW (
3816:4070   3F 29 20 20 3B 20 74 68-65 20 6C 61 72 67 65 73   ?)   ; the larges
```

Figure 8.5

Again, the disk hardware does not "know" that the file PRIME.ASM begins at sector 178H of the disk; for that matter, the hardware does not even "know" of the existence of that file or any other. All the hardware "knows" is that certain bytes, in this case,

```
0D, 0A, 0D, 0A, 4D, 41, 58, ...
```

are stored in Sector 178H. So it is the *OS*, not the disk hardware, which "knows" and manages the file system. The OS—on request from the VI editor, which executed a DOS service call when the author was using VI to create PRIME.ASM—created a directory index entry for this file, put the first 512 bytes of the file in sector 178H, and made a record of this in the directory index.

What about the rest of the file, say, the *next* 512 bytes of it? Where are they stored? Recording this information is the purpose of the FAT. The number for the *first* cluster of a file is given in word $d + 1AH$ of the directory index entry for that file, as we have just seen. But the numbers for all other clusters are given by the FAT. Specifically, the FAT is a linked-list data structure, with the entry for the *k*th cluster of a file containing a link pointing to the $(k + 1)$st cluster of that file.

So, in order to determine where the *second* cluster of the file PRIME.ASM is, we need to look at the FAT entry for the first cluster of that file. Let us take a look at the first few bytes of the FAT. Recall that it starts in sector 1. We have:

```
? 0001 0000 0010
F9 FF FF 03 50 00 FF 6F 00 07 80 00 09 A0 00 0B
```

The very first byte, F9, is a code that indicates certain characteristics of the disk, e.g., whether its a floppy vs. a hard disk, whether it is single vs. double density, and so on. The main importance of this is that it determines the size of each FAT entry, which is either 12 or 16 bits. The code F9 indicates that the FAT has 12-bit entries (which is true for most floppy disks). Unfortunately, 12 is not a multiple of 8; so each FAT entry will take up 1.5 bytes, and the non-integer nature of this value becomes a bit of a nuisance, but nothing too terrible, so let us proceed to find the first FAT for the file PRIME.ASM.

Since each FAT entry is 1.5 bytes long, a noninteger value, it is easier to think in terms of *pairs* of FAT entries, because a pair will be 3 bytes long, which *is* an integer value. With this in mind, here are the rules to use:

- The FAT entries for clusters $2n$ and $2n + 1$ are stored in bytes $3n$, $3n + 1$ and $3n + 2$ of the FAT.
- If we denote the hex forms of those three bytes as *uv*, *wx*, and *yz*, respectively, then the FAT entry for cluster $2n$ is 0x*uv* and that for cluster $2n + 1$ is 0*yzw*.

(If you are puzzled by the strange-looking grouping here, you should again review the discussion of the "little-endian" nature of iAPX addresses, which, for example, results in DEBUG's D command displaying word-sized quantities "backwards." The principle is the same here, with bytes and nibbles playing the roles of words and bytes, respectively, in the discussion in Section 4.1.)

Let us apply the rules to our file PRIME.ASM. We found that the first cluster for the file was cluster 349D. Thus, by the first rule, the even-odd pair it belongs to is the pair of clusters 348D and 349D, with $n = 174D$. So the second rule tells us that the FAT entries for this pair are at bytes 522D, 523D, and 524D, i.e., bytes 20AH, 20BH, and 20CH of the FAT. Accordingly, we type

```
? 0001 020a 0003
```

and the computer responds with

```
00 E0 15
```

In the notation of the rules, we have $u = 0$, $v = 0$, $w = E$, $x = 0$, $y = 1$, and $z = 5$. The FAT entry for cluster 349D is thus $0yzw = 015E$. In other words, the *second* cluster of the file PRIME.ASM is cluster 015EH, i.e., cluster 350D. This happens to be right next to the *first cluster* of the file, cluster 349D.

Now that we know where the second cluster of the file is, let us examine it. Remember that we found that cluster m is sector $m+27D$, so cluster 350D is sector 377D, i.e., sector 179H. Loading the sector into DEBUG, we find the following display:

```
-L 5000 0 179 1
-D 5000
8076:5000   77 6F 72 6B 2C 20 73 69-6E 63 65 20 74 68 65 20   work, since the
8076:5010   70 72 69 6D 65 20 74 65-73 74 69 6E 67 20 77 69   prime testing wi
8076:5020   6C 6C 20 62 65 20 64 6F-6E 65 20 77 69 74 68 0D   ll be done with.
8076:5030   0A 20 20 20 3B 20 20 20-66 65 77 65 72 20 70 6F   .   ;    fewer po
8076:5040   74 65 6E 74 69 61 6C 20-64 69 76 69 73 6F 72 73   tential divisors
8076:5050   0D 0A 20 20 20 3B 20 42-79 74 65 20 50 52 49 4D   ..   ; Byte PRIM
8076:5060   45 2B 49 20 77 69 6C 6C-20 62 65 20 73 65 74 20   E+I will be set
8076:5070   74 6F 20 31 20 6F 72 20-30 2C 20 61 63 63 6F 72   to 1 or 0, accor
```

This, of course, is more of the file PRIME.ASM.

In the foregoing manner, one can follow through the chain of clusters set up by the FAT to get the entire list of clusters for a file. (The last cluster in the chain is indicated by a FAT entry containing a value in the range 0FF8–0FFF.) Again, in ordinary applications we do not have to burden ourselves with this work, because the OS will do the work for us. If our program will read *sequentially* through a file, as, for example, was the case with the program in Section 7.3 to convert capital letters to lowercase, the DOS services we call will follow through the chain of clusters without our having to do so ourselves. On the other hand, if we are doing random access of a disk file and are trying to minimize total seek time, such as in a large data-base application, we must access specific sectors of the file directly and will need the information from the FAT to do so.

If the FAT entry for a cluster contains 0000, the cluster is free for assignment to a new file. When your program submits a call to DOS service 21/3C, which creates a new file, the OS will search the FAT for entries that contain 0000, i.e., for space at which the OS can allocate the new file (and, of course, will change the FAT entries accordingly).

Finally, why differentiate between clusters and sectors? The answer is that, although in the example we have considered there is only one sector per cluster, there could be two or more. The advantage to having more than one sector per cluster is that we can make storage for a file more contiguous. In the example we presented, the first two sectors of the file PRIME.ASM happened to be adjacent on the disk. Thus, if we access them sequentially, no seek will be needed to read the second sector after the first. But in general, storage of consecutive portions of the file will *not* be in contiguous sectors of the disk.

This problem can be solved by having, say, two sectors per cluster. Since the several sectors in a cluster are contiguous by definition, having two sections per cluster will force the desired contiguity. The drawback, though, is that if one has a large number of small files—say, less than one sector in size—each file would take up *two* sectors, since they could not occupy only part of a cluster. Thus, space on the disk would be wasted.

Unix file systems are largely similar to the MS-DOS system we have been discussing. Both DOS and Unix treat a file merely as a long stream of consecutive bytes. If the file is a **text** file, meaning that its bytes are supposed to be interpreted as characters, the *user* will think of the file as being broken down into lines of text, and utility programs such as the VI text editor will display the file in this way on a monitor screen. But from the OS's point of view, the carriage return and line feed characters—which define those lines that the user sees—are just characters, with the ASCII codes 0DH and 0AH, respectively, and are no different from the alphabetical or other characters. All that the OS must do is find space on the disk for these characters—in noncontiguous sectors if necessary—and maintain a list of pointers showing where these sectors are. There is no concept in DOS or Unix of lines in a file, even an ASCII file.

In some other OSs the structure of a file may be quite different: the OS itself may keep track of "lines" within the file (called **records**), and keep pointers to each line. But in the DOS system we have presented here, DOS does not record where, say, the 124th line of a text file begins; all we can do is read the file from the beginning, counting carriage return and line feed characters until we accumulate 123 such pairs. Of course, we *can* write our program so that it creates a table of correspondences between line numbers and sectors for our file, if we will access the file by line number often enough to make it worthwhile to create such a table. But the point is that DOS and Unix do not do this for us, whereas some OSs do. On the other hand, those OSs may waste space, either by storing such a table or by making sure that all lines are the same length, say, 80 characters per line (padded with blanks if necessary). Some OSs do the latter so that we can find the position of a certain line just by multiplying by 80.

8.4 PROCESS MANAGEMENT

It is often very useful to have several user programs alternate execution. In Example (a) of Section 7.2, for instance, we briefly discussed a situation in which one might run a game program to entertain oneself while waiting for a print program to complete its work of printing out a large file. An extension of this concept that will be familiar to many readers is **time-sharing**, an environment in which many users (or one user running several programs) appear to be running programs simultaneously, but are actually alternating the programs in execution.

In this section, we will discuss how to set up the alternation of several such programs. MS-DOS offers the capability of writing **terminate-and-stay-resident** (TSR) programs, which would enable us to run the previously mentioned game program and print program "simultaneously." We will present an example of TSR programming in Section 8.4.1. MS-DOS does *not* offer time-sharing services, but the IBM microcomputer hardware is capable of them, and several OSs available for IBM microcomputers, such as OS/2 and Xenix, MINIX, and other Unix OSs for PCs, do implement time-sharing. We will show how time-sharing is done in Section 8.4.2.

First, we introduce the notion of a **process**. This might be defined as an instance of execution of a program. The word "instance" is important, because if several users, (say six) are currently using the same program, they account for six processes, rather than one. Thus, in the discussion that follows, we will speak in terms of various processes being active, instead of various programs.

Incidentally, a given user might have several different processes active at the same time. For example, readers who have used Unix may have had some experience with the '&' command, such as in the command line

```
% cc g.c &
```

The '%' is the prompt symbol on many Unix systems. The command

```
cc g.c
```

specifies that we want to run the C compiler on a source file named g.c. The symbol '&' means that we wish to be able to submit new commands while the compilation is in progress. If we now type

```
% vi x
```

to use the vi editor on the file x, we will initiate a new process, with the vi editor, in addition to the process cc.

Again, process management strongly depends on the availability of interrupts, both hardware and software, but especially hardware.

8.4.1 TSR Programming

In TSR programming, we terminate a program but tell the OS to keep it in memory. Consider DOS service number 21/4C, which we have been using all along to terminate our programs, i.e., with the familiar sequence

```
MOV AH,4CH
INT 21H
```

Our program has finished execution, and we use this DOS service to return to DOS, which will then print out the usual '>' prompt, inviting us to submit our next command.

But this service also does something else: it notifies DOS that we no longer need the program in memory, and thus, DOS is free to overwrite it by loading some other program in the same area of memory.

By contrast, DOS offers terminate-and-stay-resident services, such as DOS service number 21/31 and DOS service number 27. (We will use the latter, but the two are very similar.) These services enable us to return to DOS but tell DOS *not* to overwrite the area of memory occupied by our program.

For instance, in the game-and-printer example mentioned earlier, the printer program would initiate the printing of the first character and then terminate and stay resident. The terminate action would allow us to submit another command at the '>' prompt, in this case, the command to run the game program. But the stay-resident action would mean that the printer program would stay resident in memory: once the printer was ready for more characters to print, the printer program would be right there in memory, ready to supply the printer. We are, in effect, telling the OS not to overwrite the printer program with anything else.

As outlined earlier, the key to switching back and forth between the new program and the TSR program is interrupts. In the game-and-printer example, we would start the printer program first. It would then start the printing of the first character and perform a TSR exit. We would then start the game program. When the printer became ready for more characters, it would send an interrupt, which would suspend execution of the game program. The printer program would then initiate some more printing and, subsequently, let the game resume. And the person playing the game would probably not notice any slowdown in computer response during this switching between programs.

Program 8.3 is a program that constantly displays the time of day at the top-right corner of the monitor screen—no matter what program we are running. The display is done by a TSR program that runs whenever there is an interrupt from the Intel 8253 timer chip, which occurs 18.2 times per second. DOS's ISR for this chip includes a call to BIOS service number 1CH, which is actually a dummy procedure consisting only of an IRET instruction. (The reader is urged to verify this by using DEBUG.) We will instead point the interrupt vector for INT 1CH toward our TSR, which will refresh and update the time-of-day display at the top-right corner of our screen.

Let us suppose Program 8.3 is in the file TOD.ASM. We would assemble and link the program. Then we would produce a .COM file from the .EXE file, using the EXE2BIN utility:

```
> EXE2BIN TOD TOD.COM
```

(For technical reasons we will not present here,TSR programs should be run as .COM files instead of as .EXE files.)

We would then run TOD, typing

```
> TOD.COM
```

upon which the program will almost instantly "finish" (it is not really finished, since it will be repeatedly reactivated, 18.2 times per second), and we will see the DOS '>' again. Suppose we then use the VI editor, typing

```
    > VI Z.C
```

to edit some file Z.C (having no relation to TOD.ASM). Then, while viewing the file Z.C on our screen, the time of day would appear there, too, even as the time changes, because our TSR will update the displayed time every five seconds.

The reader should assemble, link, and <u>run</u> the TOD program to get a feel for what it does. The latter is extremely important; make sure to run this program before reading about it. Especially vital are the interrupts, so make sure you understand their role thoroughly.

```
CSG SEGMENT
    ASSUME CS:CSG,DS:CSG
    ORG 100H

NTRYPT:  JMP INIT

NTICKS DW (?)   ; number of timer ticks

INT1C PROC

    ; since this procedure is called by an INT, we need to reallow interrupts
    STI

    ; save registers
    PUSH AX
    PUSH BX
    PUSH CX
    PUSH SI

    ; increment count of clock ticks, and check if ready to redisplay time
    INC NTICKS
    CMP NTICKS,100D
    JL XIT

    ; read real-time clock
    MOV AH,2
    INT 1AH

    ; display time
    MOV BX,CX
    MOV SI,152D
    CALL ADISPBX

    ; start over
    MOV NTICKS,0

XIT:
    POP SI
    POP CX
    POP BX
```

```
      POP AX
      IRET
INT1C ENDP

ADISPBX PROC    ;  adaptation of DISPBX in Program 4.1

      PUSH AX
      PUSH BX
      PUSH CX
      PUSH DX
      PUSH ES

      ;  point ES to screen memory
      MOV AX,0B800H
      MOV ES,AX

      ;  each nibble to be printed will be taken from bits 15-12 of BX
      ;  so we will keep rotating BX by 4 bits at a time, each time
      ;     moving a new nibble into bits 11-8

      ;  this will have to be done 4 times, for the 4 nibbles of BX,
      ;     and we will use DH as the loop counter, starting at 4,
      ;     then 3, 2, and 1
      MOV DH,4

      ;  the rotation of 4 bits will be indicated by CL, so put 4 there
      MOV CL,4

  LP: MOV DL,BH  ;  put a copy in DL, to work on it there

      ;  prepare the nibble for printing
      AND DL,0F0H  ;  put 0's in the lower 4 bits of DL, leaving our nibble unchanged
      ROR DL,CL  ;  rotate so that the nibble is in bits 3-0 of DL

      CALL APRNIB  ;  print that nibble

      ROL BX,CL  ;  rotate BX to get to next nibble

      ;  decrement loop count and check if we are done with all nibbles yet
      DEC DH
      JNZ LP

      POP ES
      POP DX
      POP CX
      POP BX
      POP AX
      RET  ;  return to calling program
ADISPBX ENDP

APRNIB PROC   ;  adaptation of PRNIB in Program 4.1

      ;  must convert numeric value in DL, which is in the range 0-F, to ASCII
```

```
      CMP DL,9   ;   is it 0-9 or A-F?
      JG A_F   ; if so, go to the code to handle the A-F case
      ;   if not, we are in the 0-9 case
      ADD DL,30H   ;   ASCII codes for the characters '0'-'9' are 30H-39H
      JMP WR_CHAR   ;   OK, ready to write to screen
A_F:  ADD DL,37H   ;   ASCII codes for the characters 'A'-'F' are 41H-46H

      ; here is where the actual writing to the screen takes place
      WR_CHAR:
      MOV BYTE PTR ES:[SI],DL
      ADD SI,2

      ;  OK, nibble printed, so return to caller
      RET
APRNIB ENDP


INIT PROC NEAR

      ; set DS
      PUSH CS
      POP DS

      ; point ES to low memory
      MOV AX,0
      MOV ES,AX

      ; set vector for INT 1C
      CLI   ; don't allow interrupts while changing vector
      MOV WORD PTR ES:[4*1CH],OFFSET INT1C
      MOV WORD PTR ES:[4*1CH+2],CS
      STI   ; reallow interrupts

      MOV NTICKS,0   ; start count

      ;  OK, terminate program but stay resident
      ;  first set program size
      MOV DX,OFFSET INIT
      INT 27H
INIT ENDP

CSG ENDS

END NTRYPT
```

Program 8.3

A requirement for .COM files is that they fit into a single segment. Thus, no separate data segment is declared in Program 8.3; instead, the data (here consisting of only one item, NTICKS) is simply declared in the code segment. Another requirement is that the code begin at offset 100 of the segment, which the pseudo-op ORG 100H accomplishes.

DOS service 27, at the end of the program, performs the TSR operation. Its parameter in DX is the number of bytes to be reserved in memory. Since the INIT procedure, as indicated by its name, does only initialization, we do not need it to stay in memory; we only need what precedes it, and there are OFFSET INIT bytes in that portion of the program.

Now let us look at INT1C, our ISR for INT 1CH. The 8253 timer issues an interrupt 18.2 times per second. Whatever program we are running at the time—say, VI—will thus be interrupted 18.2 times per second, and the procedure INT1C will run each time. INT1C keeps track of how many timer ticks have occurred, and after every 100th tick—approximately every five seconds—it prints the time of day on the screen. It acquires the time of day from the **real-time clock**, via BIOS service number 1A/02. (The real-time clock is available on most machines; however, even those machines which do not have a real-time clock can still keep track of the time by using the 8253 timer itself, again by counting ticks within the 8253's ISR.)

Many popular commercial products are TSR programs. For example, the so-called "hot key" applications, in which a certain key can be used to suspend the current program suddenly and temporarily take some other action, rely on the TSR approach. One could make a TSR program that provides access to a dictionary stored on disk. Then the person writing the "Great American Novel" using a word-processor program, or the person playing a word-game program, could quickly access the dictionary by typing a given key—say, F1—without having to "pack up and leave" the program he or she was using.

The typical pattern is to replace a DOS or BIOS ISR. For example, consider the disk cache application discussed in Section 2.3.5.1. BIOS service number 13 reads and writes disk sectors. We could record the original value of this interrupt vector, so that we remember where the BIOS ISR for INT 13H is, but change the vector to point to our TSR. The TSR would check to see whether the given sector is in the cache (which itself would be an array declared within the TSR); if not, the TSR would relay the request to the original BIOS ISR for INT 13H, which would do the work of accessing the sector on disk. (The TSR would "call" the original BIOS 13 routine by simulating an INT, via a PUSHF and a far CALL.)

A caveat is necessary here: do not make calls to any DOS services from within your ISR in a TSR program. If a DOS service is in progress when an interrupt occurs, and then the ISR calls a DOS service too, there is a high risk that the stack will be ruined. It is possible to write the program to sense whether another DOS procedure is in progress before entering DOS, but the code is extremely delicate; it is better to limit calls for OS services in your TSR program's ISR to BIOS routines.

8.4.2 The Infrastructure of Time-Sharing

In time-sharing, the most important hardware interrupt is that of a timer, such as the Intel 8253 timer. This chip will generate periodic interrupts, and since in a time-sharing OS the timer's interrupt service routine (ISR) is part of the OS, the OS has periodic opportunities in which to "take a look around" and decide whether to switch control of the CPU to another process.

Let us make the latter notion more concrete. Suppose that users X and Y are using the same computer, from different terminals attached to that computer. Suppose also that user X requests a program to be run that will have an execution time of five hours, and a split second after X hits the return key, user Y requests a program to be run that will finish after only one second. It would be terribly unfair to have Y wait five hours for X's program to finish.

To avoid such an inequity, time-sharing systems make processes take turns running. A turn is called a **time slice**, or a **quantum**. The **quantum size** is a fixed time interval, say 50 milliseconds (ms). In the example in the last paragraph, suppose, for simplicity, that neither X's nor Y's program has any system calls and that those two programs are the only two processes in the system right now. Then X's process would run for 50 ms, then Y's process would run for 50 ms, then X would have another 50-ms turn, then Y again, and so on. This scheduling policy, which is called **round robin**, will result in Y's program being done after 20 turns and with Y being delayed only by one second (due to waiting during X's first 20 turns), instead of having to undergo a five-hour delay.

The other big advantage to time-sharing is that the computer is not wasting time in wait-loop I/O operations. If, say, user X's program has reached a **readln** operation in its Pascal source code, we certainly do not want our expensive computer to waste its time looping until the user types a key. Instead, we give some other program a turn and rely on the keyboard interrupt to notify the OS when user X finally gets around to hitting a key. In other words, time-sharing generalizes the ideas suggested in example (a) in Section 7.2.

Note again that even in single-user systems, the typical case in PC applications, the one user could have several programs active at once. This is in fact one of the major reasons for the interest in extensions of MS-DOS such as OS/2 and Windows 3.0—a desire for easily setting up several program executions at once. Thus, even though we have been speaking in terms of several users, what really counts is that several programs are active at once, whether they are invoked by different users or all by the same user. So we will just refer to *programs* X and Y in what follows rather than to *users* X and Y. (Referring to *processes* X and Y would be even better.)

To see why the timer interrupt is so important, suppose that the OS, during its initialization period, programs a timer to interrupt 60 times per second. Then three such interrupts will occur during a 50-ms turn. Thus, we can write our timer ISR to count these interrupts and to end the turn when the count reaches 3.

The reader should convince him- or herself that we simply could not implement this taking-turns policy without timer interrupts. For example, without the timer interrupts, once program X got control of the CPU, it would simply run for five hours to completion. The OS could not intervene and stop that program, since *that* program would be running, not the OS. The CPU would be, as always, simply stepping repeatedly through its step A, step B, step C, etc., cycle, so without interrupts, X would continue to run, and the OS would be completely dormant—completely powerless to stop X. The timer interrupt is thus crucial in forcing the process to relinquish the CPU to the OS.

Program 8.4 is an outline of how the timer's ISR might be written for a time-sharing OS for an IBM microcomputer. As indicated earlier, it keeps a count of timer interrupts that have occurred so far in the current program's turn and ends the turn when this count reaches 3. This is evident in the code

```
INC TICKS ; TICKS contains # of timer interrupts so far this turn
CMP TICKS,3 ; see if this is the third timer interrupt
JE ENDTRN  ; if so, then end current program's turn
```

When a turn is over, say, for program X, OS will record X's current values of IP, CS, FR, AX, BX, etc.—that is, all the registers in the CPU. Clearly, recording these values is necessary, so that when X's next turn comes, X will be able to resume execution in precisely the same setting as existed when its last turn ended. The OS keeps a record of all processes in a table; we will call this table the process table. For each process, the process table will include a pointer to a "save area" in memory for that process; all the register values will be saved there.

After saving X's register values, the OS will look at its process table to determine which process should be given a turn next. If program Y is due to run, the OS will need to restore all of Y's saved register values first, as indicated in the comments in the latter portion of Program 8.4. After restoring these values, the OS will give control of the CPU to Y, and Y's turn will begin.

It is worth noting how the OS passes control to Y. As can be seen at the end of Program 8.4, control is passed via an IRET instruction. But the operation is not quite as simple as it may seem. To see why, look at the KISR procedure in Program 7.6. It, too, ends with an IRET instruction. But the difference is that KISR is entered when Program 7.5 is interrupted, and the IRET in KISR will make us return to Program 7.5. In other words, our entry to and return from KISR involve the same program, Program 7.5.

By contrast, when CLKINT in Program 8.4 executes for the third time during X's turn, we will *return* from CLKINT to Y's program, even though we *entered* CLKINT from X's program! This may seem strange at first, but it becomes clear if one notes by that before the IRET there is code in which the OS restores Y's SS and SP values. Thus, it will be Y's stack that will be popped during the execution of IRET, not X's stack, and we will return to Y, not X, since Y's stack will contain Y's IP and CS values that were saved at the end of Y's previous turn.

This whole sequence of ending X's turn and starting a turn for Y is called a *context switch*: we have changed the "context" of the machine—i.e., the set of values in all the registers—from that of X to that of Y. Note that this switch-over period is time that is unproductive—necessary overhead in order to achieve the illusion of simultaneity between X and Y. Some CPUs, such as those of VAX machines, have the capability to do all the saving and restoring within the same single special instruction, thus reducing the overhead.

The code in Program 8.4 has been simplified, to make the presentation easier to follow. The use of the word "restore" in the comments (e.g., just above MOV TICKS,0) assumes that all the processes that are currently running programs (actually, taking turns running programs) have already had at least one turn. So there should be code to check

```
CLKINT:   PUSH DS
          ; move OS's data segment location into DS (code not shown),
          ;  so that OS can access its own variables, e.g., Process Table,
          ;  TICKS, etc.
          INC TICKS ; TICKS contains # of timer interrupts so far this turn
          CMP TICKS,3  ; see if this is the third timer interrupt
          JE ENDTRN  ; if so, then end current process' turn
          POP DS     ; if not, then restore current process' DS value
          IRET       ;    and return to current process

ENDTRN:   PUSH BX
          ; look at process table and determine where current process' save area
          ;  is, and point BX to it (code not shown)
          PUSH BX
          MOV [BX],AX        ;save current process' AX value
          ADD BX,2
          POP AX;            ;recover current process' BX value
          MOV [BX],AX        ;save current process' BX value
          ADD BX,2
          ; save current process' CX, DX, DI, SI in the same way (code not shown)
          ; save current process' DS, SS, and SP values (code not shown)
          ; note that at this point, SS and SP are still pointing to
          ;  current process' stack, and current process' values of IP, CS
          ;  and the flags register are still on current process' stack
          ;  so we do not have to save those as we did the other registers
          ; look on the process table for a new job, the "next" process
          ;  to start a turn for (code not shown)
          ; restore next process' AX,BX,CX,DX,DI,SI,SS, and SP (code not shown)
          MOV TICKS,0  ;   initialize the number of interrupts this process' turn
          ; restore next process' DS value (code not shown)
          ; next process' values of IP, CSs, and the flags register are still
          ;  on next process' stack, left over from this user's last turn
          ;  (so no code needed for restoring values of these from the
          ;  process' entry in the OS process table)
          ; so the IRET below will take us back, exactly to the point
          ;  which was executing when this user's last turn ended
          ;but first, send EOI to 8259A (code not shown)
          IRET
```

Program 8.4

whether the next process has already had a turn, and if it has not, then other code would be executed, with all the references to "restore" changed to "initialize" instead.

In illustrating round robin scheduling with programs X and Y, we made the simplifying assumption that neither of the programs makes any system calls and that no other processes are currently in the system. Let us now discuss what happens in general.

Clearly, there may be more than just two processes in the system, perhaps many more. In its simplest form, round robin scheduling will service each process in turn, in circular fashion. In more sophisticated OSs, more complicated priority systems might be imposed.

Furthermore, a process' turn often ends early, before 50 ms have elapsed. Suppose X occasionally makes system calls. Since such calls execute procedures within the OS, X is voluntarily relinquishing control of the CPU to the OS. This ends X's turn early, before 50 ms are up. Since most system calls deal with I/O, and since I/O is a relatively slow operation, it makes sense to start a new turn for another process—say Y—rather than to wait patiently for X's I/O request to be completed. In fact, after the new turn for Y is completed, X's I/O request may *still* not be complete, so we could then give Y another turn or a give a turn to some third process. Of course, another possibility is that X's system call is, say, in MS-DOS, to DOS service number 21/4C. In that case, X will have finished execution and will not need the rest of its turn.

More detailedly, in addition to its process table, the OS will keep a ready list. This list shows which processes are ready to get another turn. Those which are not ready are waiting for something, e.g., completion of an I/O operation. Assuming an equal-priority system, the OS would simply continue to gives turns cyclically to all processes on the ready list. When a process' turn ends—due to 50 ms elapsing, not due to making a system call—it simply joins the end of a queue, and the OS gives a turn to whichever process is currently at the head of the queue.

As an example, suppose that the system currently has three processes, A, B, and C, and that A is executing and B and C are on the ready list. Suppose A reaches a system call, say, to read a character from the keyboard. The system call, in the form of a software interrupt as in Section 8.1, transfers control to the OS. The OS ends A's turn and puts A on a blocked list, where **blocked** refers to the fact that A could not run right now even if the OS were to give it another turn—A is blocked by its pending I/O action. The OS then looks on the ready list for a program that is ready to start a new turn. The OS then starts a turn for B, since B is at the head of the list. After that, the ready list consists of C only.

Suppose that B's turn ends after the normal 50 ms—that is, B had no system calls during this time. Then again, the OS takes over, due to the interrupt from the timer, and again, the OS looks at the ready list, seeing C. The OS starts a turn for C and puts B on the ready list; now the ready list consists of B only.

Suppose now that during the middle of C's turn, the user running process A finally types a character. The keyboard will generate an interrupt, and again, the interrupt routine will be some section of the OS. The OS notes from the blocked list that A was waiting for this I/O, and thus, the OS puts A back on the ready list. Then C's turn will be resumed, and after C has run 50 ms, the turn will be over, and B's next turn will start. Then the next turn will be A's, since it has now rejoined the ready list.

Once again, it is very important to keep in mind the role of interrupts in passing control from a user program to the OS. Control can be passed via a hardware interrupt, either from the timer or from an I/O device, or via a software interrupt, when the currently executing process makes a system call. Keep in mind that *the OS has no power whatsoever when a user program is running.* The OS cannot simply "step in" and stop a user program; either an I/O device forces the user program to relinquish control of the CPU, or the program voluntarily does so, via an INT instruction.

8.5 MEMORY MANAGEMENT

Memory management is one of the most vital features of a time-sharing OS, even an OS designed to be used by only one user at a time. (Recall that a single user might have several processes in the system at one time.) Among the questions to be addressed in memory management are the following:

 (i) How can many processes run the same copy of the same program at the same time? For example, the VI editor takes up several hundred thousand bytes of memory, so in a multiuser system, it would be desirable for all users who are using the VI editor at a given time to share the same copy of a program, so as to conserve memory.

 (ii) Can we prevent one process from accidentally (say, due to a programming error) writing to the memory area belonging to another process?

(iii) What if the collective size of all the processes to be run at a given time exceeds the available memory space?

We will see that with the iAPX 86 subfamily of CPUs, only question (i) can be answered satisfactorily. However, with more advanced hardware, such as CPUs in the iAPX 286/386/486 class, or the Motorola 68030 and 68040 processors (or external chips that can be paired with earlier members of the 68000 family), all three questions may be dealt with quite well. Thus, the *hardware* is what makes this possible. Note, however, that the *software*—specifically the OS—must take advantage of the hardware in order to get the benefits. Even running on a machine having an iAPX 286/386/486 CPU, MS-DOS does not provide solutions to the three problems listed; OS/2 does.

With this in mind, let us look at each of these problems in turn. Before beginning, it will be helpful to recall from Section 4.3 that the OS maintains a memory-usage table, listing which parts of memory are currently occupied and which are currently free. When it is first booted into memory, the OS is the only program occupying memory (except for ROM, which, being permanent storage, is always "occupied"). The OS "knows" which parts of memory it itself occupies, and each time it loads a new program into memory or marks space formerly used by some program as now being free, it will update the memory-usage table accordingly.

8.5.1 Memory Sharing

Suppose we have an IBM microcomputer running a time-sharing OS with several terminals, and user A types

```
> VI G
```

to use VI on a file G. Suppose that VI.EXE is not currently in memory. The OS will then go to disk, read VI.EXE into some area of memory not currently in use, and update its memory-usage table. Let us say that the OS loads VI's code segment at 20000, data segment at 25000, and stack segment at 60000.

Now suppose that user B types VI Q. In order to save memory, the OS could assign the identical code segment region to user B as to user A—i.e., that starting at 20000—but assign regions for user B's data and stack segments that are separate from those of user A. In that manner, A and B would share their code and save memory. Note again that the OS would assign data and stack segment areas to B which are separate from those of A. The OS might assign the area starting at, say, 85000 for B's data segment. You should convince yourself that this separation is necessary. For example, the declaration of VI's data segment might look something like that shown in Program 8.5. In this program, the array FILE_CHARS would hold the actual characters in the file that VI is working on, e.g., the file G for user A and the file Q for user B. The variable N_CHARS would record the current number of characters in that file. If, say, user B submits the 'x' command to VI, which is a command to delete whatever character is currently pointed to by the screen cursor, VI will decrement the value of N_CHARS by one. Clearly, the processes for users A and B need to have separate data segments, since they have completely different values stored in FILE_CHARS and N_CHARS. But again, they can share the same code segment, since they are running the same program. (Of course, they will not be running the same *instructions* at the same time; that is, they will have different values of IP, which will be saved between turns as described in Section 8.3.2.)

```
DSG             SEGMENT
FILE_CHARS      DB  10000 DUP (?)
N_CHARS         DW  ?
                 .
                 .
                 .
DSG             ENDS
```

Program 8.5

Thus, memory sharing is easy to set up on machines whose CPUs come from the iAPX family. In fact, the segmented nature of memory address formation on these CPUs, which sometimes is a cumbersome feature, is in this case the very source of the solution to the memory-sharing problem! On the other hand, essentially the same solution could be applied, though perhaps less elegantly, with any CPU that allows something similar to the iAPX family's based addressing mode. Even though most non-iAPX CPUs do not have the notion of a program as consisting of separate code, data, and stack segments (they simply view a program as one indivisible monolith), we can still implement these notions on our own, by writing our program as described in the next couple of paragraphs.

Recall from Section 6.2.6 that in based addressing mode we specify a register and a constant. To implement separate data areas on a non-iAPX machine, we would simply make sure that we write our program (or for HLL programs, the compiler makes sure to produce the machine language programs) so that all accesses to data use based addressing mode, with the register pointing to the start of the data area and the constant part being the distance of the desired data item from the start of the data area. If, for instance, the aforementioned users A and B were to use VI done on a non-iAPX machine, the register would point to 25000 during A's turns and to 85000 during B's turns. The constant part of the based addressing mode accesses would be 0 for FILE_CHARS, 10000 for N_CHARS, and so on.

As an example, suppose we have a machine that has a Motorola 68000 series CPU. Then we might use register A6 as a pointer to the current user's data area, and the part of the program that implements VI's 'x' command might have the following code to do the decrementing of N_CHARS:

```
DEC A6@(10000)
```

(The syntax of 68000 assembly language is different from that of iAPX machines. For based addressing mode, the constant is inside the parentheses and the register is on the outside. But it is the same idea as that which we saw in Section 6.2.6 for iAPX machines.) Under this setup, the value of A6 would change when the context is switched from user A to B, say, but N_CHARS will always be 10,000 bytes past the place pointed to by A6.

Once again, these same considerations apply to a single-user system. A single user might, for example, be running *two* VI processes at the same time, on each of two files.

8.5.2 Virtual Addressing

In earlier chapters, especially Chapter 2, we mentioned that although the iAPX 286 is set up for 24-bit addresses, allowing a memory size of 16 million bytes, and the 386/486 models are set up for 32-bit addresses, allowing 4 billion bytes (though most current systems would not use nearly this much), in real mode they only use 20-bit addresses, allowing for only 1 million bytes of memory. In order to take advantage of the full address space of these CPUs, a program must run in protected mode.

When an iAPX 286/386/486 CPU is run in protected mode, the mechanism for forming memory addresses changes from that applicable to real mode. For example, consider the address of an instruction. In real mode, this takes the familiar form

```
instruction address = 16*c(CS) + c(IP)
```

But in protected mode, the address will be

```
instruction address = DT[c(CS)] + c(IP)
```

where DT is the **descriptor table**, a table that the OS maintains in memory. (Actually, there are two such tables, but for now, assume there is only one.) The notation DT[*n*] means the contents of the *n*th entry in the DT.

Suppose, for example, that c(CS) = 5022 and c(IP) = C406. On a machine of the iAPX 86 series, or in real mode on a 286/386/486 machine, this would mean that the code segment begins at address 50220, so that the instruction is at 50220 + C406 = 5C626. But in protected mode on a 286/386/486 machine, it means that the code segment begins at DT[5022]. So if, say, entry 5022 in DT is 3A1564 then the code segment begins at 3A1564 and the instruction will be at 3A1564 + C406 = 3AD96A.

Physical segment addresses in the DT entries have lengths equal to the full address size of the machine, i.e., 24 bits for a 286 and 32 bits for 386/486 machines. In this manner, the entire address spaces of these machines can be used, instead of only the 1 million bytes that are accessible in real mode.

The same is true for the other segment registers: DS, SS, and ES. They no longer contain the segment addresses. Instead, they serve as pointers to entries in the DT, and the latter contain the segment addresses. Once the segment addresses are determined, though, the offsets within segments are specified as before. For instance, the value of C406 for c(IP) in the foregoing example had the same meaning in both real and protected mode: the instruction was a distance C406 from the beginning of the code segment, wherever that is. Similarly, BX and BP, in the instructions

```
ADD AX, [BX]
```

and

```
MOV CX, [BP]
```

still have the same interpretations as they did before, i.e., as offsets into the data segment and stack segment, respectively; all that has changed in protected mode is the method for determining where those segments are.

In addition to enabling us to use the full memory space on an advanced Intel machine, the addressing scheme used in protected mode allows more flexibility. Recall from Section 4.3 that when we wish to run a program, the loader must find a chunk of memory at which to load the program. Suppose sufficient memory is available to load a certain program, but the memory exists as several smaller chunks, instead of one large unused region. In real mode, we would not be able to load the program at all, since loading in real mode is done only in contiguous segments in memory. In protected mode, we can split the segments up, putting different ones in different, noncontiguous memory locations. (Actually, this could be done in real mode, too, but DOS is not set up to do so.)

Even in protected mode, offsets are 16 bits wide in the 286. Thus, a segment is still limited to 64K bytes in size, and a large program might need more than one code segment or more than one data segment. If so, the program would continually have to change the value of CS or DS back and forth when switching from one segment to another—a real inconvenience.

On the 386 and 486 models, however, offsets are 32 bits wide. And in protected mode, registers such as IP, BX, BP, and so on are 32 bits wide, too, so that they can be used to specify offsets. Thus, one can have a segment fill the entire address space, so there is no need to have multiple code segments or multiple data segments. In fact, we could even have the entire program, including code, data, and the stack, in one single segment; no matter how large those components are, if they collectively fit into the available memory, we can enclose them in one large segment.

The skeptical reader will by now have noticed an inherent drawback of the addressing scheme in protected mode as we have described it so far: we need to make an extra read of memory—to the DT—in order to access the desired item. To fetch an instruction, for example, we must read the DT first, to determine where the code segment is, and then read memory a second time to get the instruction itself. This dual reading would represent a large—and quite unacceptable—slowdown in the operation of the machine. As the use of the word "would" here implies, this is not what is actually done. Instead, whenever we load a segment register, say DS, as in the second MOV in the code

```
MOV AX,DSG
MOV DS,AX
```

at the beginning of Program 4.1, the circuitry that implements the MOV instruction is designed *also* to load into the segment register a copy of the corresponding DT entry. (The segment register contains extra bits in which this copy is stored.) So, in every subsequent reference to an item in the data segment, the CPU can avoid checking the DT, since it has a local copy of that DT entry right in the DS register. And the same is true for CS, SS, and ES. Thus, we do not have to make an extra trip to memory after all.

The term **virtual addressing** refers to the fact that in protected mode, addresses only *appear* to have a certain value. (The word "virtual" in this context means "apparent.") In the foregoing example, for instance, it *appeared* that our code segment began at 50220, since c(CS) = 5022, but actually, it began at 3A1564. Incidentally, 3A1564 is called the **physical address**, of the code segment, in contrast to the virtual address 50220.

So far, we have been presenting virtual addressing as a means by which the more advanced iAPX CPUs break out of the 20-bit address restriction of the original iAPX 86 family. However, there is much more to the scheme than this: it turns out also to be the key to answering questions (ii) and (iii) posed at the beginning of Section 8.4.

Let us first consider question (ii), which concerned the ability to protect a process' memory region from being accidentally written to by another process (or even from being read by another process, by another user trying to break security). The virtual addressing scheme in protected mode allows us to enforce read/write privileges (thus the name "protected" mode) in two ways.

First of all, in addition to a DT entry's containing a base field, which contains the physical address corresponding to a given virtual address, the entry also contains a limit field, which contains the size of the segment. For the segment DSG in Program 4.1, for example, this size would be 28H, becaue DSG consists of only 28H bytes (as can be seen in line 14 of Figure 4.4). Think what would happen if, due to a programming error, our program were to generate an offset in the data segment that is greater than 28H. For example, if, in line 42 of Figure 4.4, our source code had been the incorrect

```
MOV BX,FHDR
```

instead of

```
MOV BX,OFFSET FIBNUM
```

then BX would get a copy of what is in the word FHDR, i.e., 4669H (see line 10 of Figure 4.4.). Then line 45 of the figure,

```
MOV WORD PTR [BX],1
```

would result in writing to offset 4669H of DSG, which of course is *far* outside the declared 28-byte limit of DSG. This would be a major error, but in real mode the hardware would not notice that error. Instead, the hardware would obediently add 4669H to c(DS) to get a memory address and then write 1 to that address, even though the address is not in DSG or even in any other part of the program.

In protected mode, the hardware would catch this error. The limit field for the DSG segment's entry in the DT would contain the value 28H. The circuitry in the CPU is designed to check the limit field any time it accesses a segment. If it detects an error, i.e., a memory request having an offset larger than 28H, the CPU will generate an internal interrupt similar to that of a divide-by-zero condition. The ISR will be part of the OS, of course, and the OS will print out an error message and terminate the program.

Another way in which memory protection is implemented is through the use of two kinds of DTs. There is a global DT (GDT), which is accessible by all processes, and each process also has its own local DT (LDT). The GDT lists segments that are meant to be shared by several processes, as with the code segment in the VI example in Section 8.5.1. A process' LDT lists segments that are accessible only by that process. Thus, if it accidentally attempts to access a segment it shouldn't—i.e., it tries to load the wrong segment value into a segment register—the hardware will fail to find that segment in either DT, and the potentially destructive segment access will be avoided.

As we have done many times before, let us again review "who does what." The OS is the entity that fills in the DT entries, while the CPU hardware is the entity that checks the DT at every memory reference made by a user program. Keep in mind that the OS cannot do the latter, since the OS is not running when the user program is running. (Only one program can be executing at any given instant, assuming there is only one CPU.) When a program is first loaded into memory by the OS, the OS will set up the tables properly so that the program will only be able to access the proper segments, which the hardware will then monitor.

Still another method of implementing memory protection in protected mode is that of **privilege levels**. These, however, are quite complex and beyond the scope of this book.

Finally, what about question (iii) at the beginning of Section 8.5, which asked what, if anything, can be done if the collective size of all programs that are currently active exceeds our physical memory size. Again, the answer lies in DT entries. The DT entry for a given segment includes a present bit. When a program generates a memory access to the segment, the CPU hardware checks the present bit. If the bit contains a 1, then the segment is physically present in memory and the requested memory access will be made. On the other hand, if the bit contains a 0, the segment is not currently

resident in memory due to lack of space, but rather, exists on a disk. In this case, which is called a **segment fault**, the hardware will again generate an internal interrupt, and the ISR will again be in the OS. The OS will then bring in the segment from disk into main memory and update the DT entry for the segment accordingly; that is, it will enter the new physical address of the segment into the base field and set the present bit to 1.

Note, however, that in order to make room for the segment that is being brought in from disk, some other segment which is currently resident will have to be removed and its present bit cleared to 0. As in the case of block replacement in caches (see Section 2.3.4.1), this presents a problem: which segment must be removed from memory? Again as in the case of caches, most segment replacement policies are at least partially based on the LRU concept discussed in Section 2.3.4.1.

One difference here from the cache case is that the block replacement decision is made and carried out by software, not hardware. The hardware *is* the component which discovers that a segment replacement must be done, since the *hardware*—not the OS—is the component that checks the DT entry. But the *software*—i.e., the OS—decides which segment to replace and performs the replacement.

All this is still transparent to the ordinary (i.e., non-OS) programmer, since the OS does all the work. In fact, this setup is called **virtual memory**, meaning that it *appears* to the programmer that his or her entire program is resident in memory, even though it is not. Nevertheless, the cost of a segment fault is quite large, since disk access is so slow compared to CPU speeds, and thus, it may be helpful for the programmer to design the program so as to minimize the number of segment faults that occur. For example, the same problem noted with versions I and II of the matrix-summing program in Section 2.3.4.1 can occur here: one version may have many more segment faults than the other.

Many other machines, such as Suns, VAXes and most other types of CPUs of medium to advanced sophistication, also feature virtual memory. (The 'V' in 'VAX' stands for "virtual.") The principles of virtual addressing on these machines are very similar to what we have seen here for iAPX machines, with the main difference being due to the fact that on non-iAPX machines addressing does not use the segment-plus-offset form used in the iAPX family. Thus, a program is not broken into segments on these machines, but instead, memory is partitioned into fixed-size **pages**. Then, the analogue of iAPX's DT is called the **page table**, a segment fault is called a **page fault**, and so on.

Keep in mind, though, that even if the hardware has the capability for virtual addressing, memory protection, and virtual memory, the software must be written to take advantage of it. MS-DOS does not do so, but the new OS/2 extension of MS-DOS does. Some versions of Unix for the iAPX family take advantage of these hardware capabilities, and some do not.

ANALYTICAL EXERCISES

1. Use DEBUG to determine where BIOS service 13 resides on your machine, and display the first few instructions of it, using DEBUG's U command.

2. Consider the procedure CLKINT in Program 8.4. Write MASM code to set the interrupt vector to point to this procedure.

3. Use DEBUG to verify that the DOS routine set up for INT 1CH consists only of an IRET instruction.

4. It was noted in the text that since offsets in protected mode are 32 bits wide in 386/486 machines, a segment actually can cover the entire memory system, and thus, one could actually put an entire program in one segment. However, in some applications it may be useful to set up several segments—at least, separate code and data segments. Why is this?

5. Some of the BIOS and DOS functions return some of their results in the flags register, FR. For example, BIOS service 16/01, which gathers information on the status of the keyboard, puts a 1 or a 0 in the ZF flag, according to whether the user has hit a key or not. Using flags for returning information in this manner presents a problem for the programmer who must program these functions. For example, suppose you were the one who wrote the code for BIOS service 16/01. (Suppose you wrote the *procedure itself*, not the call to it.) Since this code is called via an INT instruction, the last line of the code must be IRET. But the problem is that IRET will pop the previously saved value of FR from the stack and put it into FR—thus ruining the value you have put into ZF indicating the presence or absence of a keystroke! How can this problem be solved?

PROGRAMMING PROJECTS

1. Write a program that will display on the screen the names of all subdirectories in the current directory. In the setting of Figure 8.2, for example, this program would display GY to the screen. You will probably want to use Program 8.2 as a basis for your program.

2. Modify Programming Project 1 so that it lists the names of all hidden files to the screen.

3. Modify Programming Project 1 above so that it lists to the screen the names of all files whose size is greater than the amount specified by the user. For example, in the setting of Figure 8.2, suppose the user types 50000. Then only the name MASM.EXE would be printed out. But if the user typed 2000, then both MASM.EXE and PRIME.ASM would be printed out.

4. Write a program that will display, to the screen, the numbers of all sectors in which a given file is stored.

5. Program 7.5 uses a crude method for implementing the delay between jumps of the cursor (see the function Pause). Alter Programs 7.5 and 7.6 so that the user can specify the precise amount of time between jumps, be it 0.5 second, 2 seconds, or whatever. To accomplish this, the program will take advantage of the Intel 8253 timer chip and its INT 1CH, as does Program 8.3 (although in this case you will not make the program a TSR). Your new version of Program 7.5 will read in a value from the user for a variable named JumpDelay, of type **float**. You will also have to alter Program 7.6, adding an ISR for INT 1CH and, of course adding code to the initialization part of that program accordingly. The function Pause in Program 7.5 will now just consist of a **while** loop that loops until a variable named JumpNow changes from 0 to 1. The ISR for INT 1CH will make the change to JumpNow when the number of ticks reaches the proper number. (You should review the manner in which KISR changed Dir in Program 7.6, or consult your C compiler manual on how to access C's global variables.)

6. The initials 'SR' in 'TSR' stand for "stay resident," meaning that the program will stay resident in memory even after we leave it to execute some other program. That *is* just what we want in some applications, but the disadvantage is that the program will stay resident in memory forever! For example, recall that Program 8.3 repeatedly displays the current time at the upper-right corner of the screen, no matter what other program we run. What if we no longer want this display? Short of rebooting the system, what can we do to disable Program 8.3 once we start it running? The key point is that the program is reactivated each time the 8253 timer emits an interrupt, because the timer's ISR includes an INT 1CH instruction, which calls our TSR. So, all that we need to do to "turn off" our TSR is to put an IRET instruction at the very beginning of it!

Write a program named KILTSR1C, meaning "kill a TSR that relies on INT 1CH." The program can be in C, Pascal, or assembly language; it does not matter, as long as you have access to absolute memory addresses. The program will put an IRET instruction at the location pointed to by the interrupt vector 1CH.

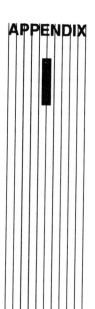
ASCII
and Scan Codes

For each entry, the character description, ASCII code, and IBM keyword scan code is given. Note that some of the items are left blank when not applicable: some keys do not correspond to ASCII characters (e.g., the F1 key), while some ASCII characters are generated via a combination of several keystrokes (such as 'A' being generated by holding down the Shift and 'a' keys).

ASCII	SCAN CODE	DESCRIPTION
00		
01		ctrl-a
02		ctrl-b
03		ctrl-c
04		ctrl-d
05		ctrl-e
06		ctrl-f
07		ctrl-g (often bell)
08		ctrl-h (often backspace)
09		ctrl-i (often tab)
0A		ctrl-j (often line feed)
0B		ctrl-k
0C		ctrl-l

ASCII	SCAN CODE	DESCRIPTION
0D		ctrl-m (often carriage return)
0E		ctrl-n
0F		ctrl-o
10		ctrl-p
11		ctrl-q (often start-scroll)
12		ctrl-r
13		ctrl-s (often stop-scroll)
14		ctrl-t
15		ctrl-u
16		ctrl-v
17		ctrl-w
18		ctrl-x
19		ctrl-y
1A		ctrl-z
1B	01	ESC
1C		
1D		
1E		
1F		
20	39	space
21	02	!
22	28	"
23	04	#
24	05	$
25	06	%
26	07	&
27	28	'
28	0A	(
29	0B	)
2A	09	*
2B	0D	+
2C	33	,
2D	0C	-
2E	34	.
2F	35	/
30	0B	0
31	02	1

ASCII	SCAN CODE	DESCRIPTION
32	03	2
33	04	3
34	05	4
35	06	5
36	07	6
37	08	7
38	09	8
39	0A	9
3A	27	:
3B	27	;
3C	33	<
3D	0D	=
3E	34	>
3F	35	?
40	03	@
41	1E	A
42	30	B
43	2E	C
44	20	D
45	12	E
46	21	F
47	22	G
48	23	H
49	17	I
4A	24	J
4B	25	K
4C	26	L
4D	32	M
4E	31	N
4F	18	O
50	19	P
51	10	Q
52	13	R
53	1F	S
54	14	T
55	16	U
56	2F	V

ASCII	SCAN CODE	DESCRIPTION
57	11	W
58	2D	X
59	15	Y
5A	2C	Z
5B	1A	[
5C	2B	\
5D	1B	]
5E	07	^
5F	0C	_
60	29	`
61	1E	a
62	30	b
63	2E	c
64	20	d
65	12	e
66	21	f
67	22	g
68	23	h
69	17	i
6A	24	j
6B	25	k
6C	26	l
6D	32	m
6E	31	n
6F	18	o
70	19	p
71	10	q
72	13	r
73	1F	s
74	14	t
75	16	u
76	2F	v
77	11	w
78	2D	x
79	15	y
7A	2C	z
7B	1A	{

ASCII	SCAN CODE	DESCRIPTION
7C	2B	|
7D	1B	}
7E	29	~
7F		(often DEL)
	0E	Back Space
	1C	Enter
	1D	Ctrl
	2A	Left Shift
	36	Right Shift
	37	Print Screen
	38	Alt
	3A	Caps Lock
	3B	F1
	3C	F2
	3D	F3
	3E	F4
	3F	F5
	40	F6
	41	F7
	42	F8
	43	F9
	44	F10
	45	Num Lock
	47	Home
	48	↑
	49	Page Up
	4B	←
	4D	→
	4F	End
	50	↓
	51	Page Down
	52	Insert
	53	Delete
	85	F11
	86	F12

The iAPX
Instruction Set

Following is a list of iAPX instructions. The list is complete, except for instructions that are special to 386/486 machines and for instructions that deal with privileged mode.

For each instruction, the field enclosed in parentheses ( ) shows which flags, if any, are affected by that instruction, while the field in brackets [ ] shows how many clock cycles the instruction takes; the latter is for 286 machines running in real mode and does not include instruction fetches if prefetch fails.

The following legend shows the abbreviations used in the machine code and timing information:

- 286+: available only on models 286 and above
- bt: byte
- ccc: lower 3 bits of coprocessor instruction op code
- CCC: upper 3 bits of coprocessor instruction op code
- d: direction bit (0 means source and destination fields exchange roles)
- disp: displacement
- dist: distance
- i: number of iterations
- jt: jump taken
- jnt: jump not taken
- m: memory
- m,i: immediate to memory
- mod: mode field:
    - 00: 0 bytes in disp field

01: 2 bytes in disp field, high byte is sign extension of low byte

10: general 2-byte disp field

11: r/m field codes an operand in register addressing mode, coded same as 'reg'

- m,r: register to memory
- nb: number of bit positions to rotate/shift
- ni: number of bytes in the next instruction
- r: register
- reg: register code, from Table 3.2, Chapter 3 (and remarks which follow it)
- r,i: immediate to register
- r/m: address mode field:

    000: c(BX)+c(SI)+disp if any

    001: c(BX)+c(DI)+disp if any

    010: c(BP)+c(SI)+disp if any

    011: c(BP)+c(DI)+disp if any

    100: c(SI)+disp if any

    101: c(DI)+disp if any

    110: c(BP)+disp if any (see exception)

    111: c(BX)+disp if any

    exception: if mod = 00 and r/m 110 then the operand offset is given in disp

- r,m: memory to register
- r,r: register to register
- s: sign-extend bit
- segreg: segment register (ES 00; CS 01; SS 10; DS 11)
- w: operand width (1 for word, 0 for byte)
- wd: word

AAA   ASCII Adjust for Addition (AF,PF,CF,SF,OF,ZF)

[3]:

00110111

AAD   ASCII Adjust for Division (AF,PF,CF,SF,OF,ZF)

[14]:

11010101	00001010

AAM   ASCII Adjust for Multiplication (AF,PF,CF,SF,OF,ZF)

[16]:

11010100	00001010

AAS   ASCII Adjust for Subtraction (AF,PF,CF,SF,OF,ZF)

[3]:

00111111

ADC   Add with Carry (AF,PF,CF,SF,OF,ZF)

Register/memory to/from register [r,r 2; m,r 7; r,m 7]:

000100dw	mod reg r/m	disp (0 or 2 bytes)

Immediate to register/memory [r,i 3; m,i 7]:

100000sw	mod 010 r/m	disp (0 or 2 bytes)	data (1 or 2 bytes)

Immediate to AX or AL [3]:

0001010w	data (1 or 2 bytes)

ADD   Add (AF,PF,CF,SF,OF,ZF)

Register/memory to/from register [r,r 2; m,r 7; r,m 7]:

000000dw	mod reg r/m	disp (0 or 2 bytes)

Immediate to register/memory [r,i 3; m,i 7]:

100000sw	mod 000 r/m	disp (0 or 2 bytes)	data (1 or 2 bytes)

Immediate to AX or AL [3]:

0000010w	data (1 or 2 bytes)

AND   Logical And (AF,PF,CF,SF,OF,ZF)

Register/memory to/from register [r,r 2; m,r 7; r,m 7]:

001000dw	mod reg r/m	disp (0 or 2 bytes)

Immediate to register/memory [r,i 3; m,i 7]:

100000sw	mod 100 r/m	disp (0 or 2 bytes)	data (1 or 2 bytes)

Immediate to AX or AL [3]:

0010010w	data (1 or 2 bytes)

BOUND   Check Array Bounds 286+ ( )

[jnt 13; otherwise use INT timing]

01100010	mod reg r/m	disp (2 bytes)

CALL   Procedure Call ( )

To near target [7+ni]:

11101000	dist (2 bytes)

To far target [13+ni]:

10011010	disp (4 bytes)

To a near target, indirectly specified [r 7+ni; m 11+ni]:

11111111	mod 010 r/m	disp (2 bytes)

To a far target, indirectly specified [16+ni]:

11111111	mod 010 r/m	disp (4 bytes)

CBW   Convert Byte to Word ( )

[2]:

```
10011000
```

CLC   Clear Carry Flag (CF)

[2]:

```
11111000
```

CLD   Clear Direction Flag (DF)

[2]:

```
11111100
```

CLI   Clear Interrupt Flag (IF)

[3]:

```
11111010
```

CMC   Complement Carry Flag (CF)

[2]:

```
11110101
```

CMP   Compare (AF,PF,CF,SF,OF,ZF)

Register/memory to/from register [r,r 2; m,r 7; r,m 6]:

001110dw	mod reg r/m	disp (0 or 2 bytes)

Immediate to register/memory [r,i 3; m,i 6]:

100000sw	mod 111 r/m	disp (0 or 2 bytes)	data (1 or 2 bytes)

Immediate to AX or AL [3]:

0011110w	data (1 or 2 bytes)

CMPS   Compare String (AF,PF,CF,SF,OF,ZF)

[8]:

1010011w

CWD   Convert Word to Doubleword (AF,PF,CF,SF,OF,ZF)

[2]:

10011001

DAA   Decimal Adjust for Addition (AF,PF,CF,SF,OF,ZF)

[3]:

00100111

DAS   Decimal Adjust for Subtraction (AF,PF,CF,SF,OF,ZF)

[3]:

00101111

DEC   Decrement by 1 (AF,PF,CF,SF,OF,ZF)

Register/memory [r 2; m 7]:

111111dw	mod 001 r/m

Register [2]:

01001 reg

DIV   Unsigned Divide (AF,PF,CF,SF,OF,ZF)

Register/memory [r bt 14; r wd 22; m bt 17; m wd 25]:

1110111w	mod 110 r/m	disp (0 or 2 bytes)

ENTER   Create Stack Frame 286+ ( )

[11+]:

11001000	size of frame (2 bytes)	procedure nesting level (1 byte)

ESC   Escape to Coprocessor ( )

[9-20]:

11011CCC	mod ccc r/m

HLT   Wait for External Interrupt ( )

[2]:

11110100

IDIV   Signed Division (AF,PF,CF,SF,OF,ZF)

Register/memory [r bt 17; r wd 25; m bt 20; m wd 28]:

1110111w	mod 111 r/m	disp (0 or 2 bytes)

IMUL   Signed Multiplication (AF,PF,CF,SF,OF,ZF)

Register/memory [r bt 13; r wd 21; m bt 16; m wd 24]:

1110111w	mod 101 r/m	disp (0 or 2 bytes)

IN   Input from I/O Port ( )

From fixed port [5]:

1110010w	port

From [DX] [5]:

1110110w

INC   Increment by 1 (AF,PF,SF,OF,ZF)

Register/memory [r 2; m 7]:

111111dw	mod 000 r/m

Register [2]:

01000 reg

INS/INSB/INSW   Input String from Port 286+ ( )

[5]:

0110110w

INT   Software Interrupt (IF,TF)

General interrupt number [23+ni]:

11001101	interrupt number

INT 3 [23+ni]:

11001100

INTO   Interrupt on Overflow (IF,TF)

[jt 24+ni; jnt 3]:

11001110

IRET   Return from Interrupt (AF,PF,CF,SF,OF,ZF,DF,IF,TF)

[17+ni]:

11001111

JA/JNBE   Jump if Above/Jump if Not Below or Equal ( )

[jt 7+ni; jnt 3]:

01110111	dist (1 byte)

JAE/JNB   Jump if Above or Equal/Jump if Not Below ( )

[jt 7+ni; jnt 3]:

01110011	dist (1 byte)

JB/JNAE   Jump if Below/Jump if Not Above or Equal ( )

[jt 7+ni; jnt 3]:

01110010	dist (1 byte)

JC   Jump if Carry ( )

[jt 7+ni; jnt 3]:

01110010	dist (1 byte)

JCXZ   Jump if CX is Zero ( )

[jt 8+ni; jnt 4]:

11100011	dist (1 byte)

JE/JZ   Jump if Equal/Jump if Zero ( )

[jt 7+ni; jnt 3]:

01110100	dist (1 byte)

JG/JNLE   Jump if Greater/Jump if Not Less Than ( )

[jt 7+ni; jnt 3]:

01111111	dist (1 byte)

JGE/JNL   Jump if Greater Than or Equal/Jump if Not Less Than ( )

[jt 7+ni; jnt 3]:

01111101	dist (1 byte)

JL/JNGE   Jump if Less/Jump if Not Greater Than or Equal ( )

[jt 7+ni; jnt 3]:

01111100	dist (1 byte)

JLE/JNG   Jump if Less Than or Equal/Jump if Not Greater ( )

[jt 7+ni; jnt 3]:

01111110	dist (1 byte)

JMP   ( )

To short target [7+ni]:

11101011	dist (1 byte)

To near target [7+ni]:

11101001	dist (2 bytes)

To far target [11+ni]:

11101010	disp (4 bytes)

To a near target, indirectly specified [r 7+ni; m 11+ni]:

11111111	mod 100 r/m	disp (2 bytes)

To a far target, indirectly specified [15+ni]:

11111111	mod 101 r/m	disp (4 bytes)

JNC   Jump if No Carry ( )

[jt 7+ni; jnt 3]:

01110011	dist (1 byte)

JNE/JNZ   Jump if Not Equal/Jump if Not Zero ( )

[jt 7+ni; jnt 3]:

01110101	dist (1 byte)

JNO   Jump if No Overflow ( )

[jt 7+ni; jnt 3]:

01110001	dist (1 byte)

JNP/JPO   Jump if No Parity/Jump if Parity Odd ( )

[jt 7+ni; jnt 3]:

01111011	dist (1 byte)

JNS   Jump if No Sign ( )

[jt 7+ni; jnt 3]:

01111001	dist (1 byte)

JO   Jump if Overflow ( )

[jt 7+ni; jnt 3]:

01110000	dist (1 byte)

JP/JPE   Jump if Parity/Jump if Parity Even ( )

[jt 7+ni; jnt 3]:

01111010	dist (1 byte)

JS   Jump if Sign ( )

[jt 7+ni; jnt 3]:

01111000	dist (1 byte)

LAHF   Load AH from FR ( )

10011111

LDS   Load DS Register ( )

11000101	mod reg r/m

LEA   Load Effective Address ( )

10001101	mod reg r/m

LEAVE   Dismantle Stack Frame 286+ ( )

[5]:

```
11001001
```

LES   Load ES Register ( )

```
11000100    mod reg r/m
```

LOCK   Lock Bus ( )

[0]:

```
11110000
```

LODS   Load String ( )

[5]:

```
1010110w
```

LOOP   Loop ( )

[jt 8+ni; jnt 4]:

```
11100010    dist (1 byte)
```

LOOPE/LOOPZ   Loop if Equal/Loop if Zero ( )

[jt 8+ni; jnt 4]:

```
11100001    dist (1 byte)
```

LOOPNE/LOOPNZ   Loop if Not Equal/Loop if Not Zero ( )

[jt 8+ni; jnt 4]:

11100000	dist (1 byte)

MOV   Move ( )

Register/memory to/from register [r,r 2; m,r 3; r,m 5]:

100010dw	mod reg r/m	disp (0 or 2 bytes)

Immediate to register/memory [3]:

1100011w	mod 000 r/m	disp (0 or 2 bytes)	data (1 or 2 bytes)

Immediate to register [2]:

1011w reg	data (1 or 2 bytes)

Memory to AX or AL [5]:

1010000w	disp (0 or 2 bytes)

AX or AL to memory [3]:

1010001w	disp (0 or 2 bytes)

Register/memory to segment register [r 2; m 5]:

10001110	mod 0 segreg r/m	disp (0 or 2 bytes)

Segment register to register/memory [r 2; m 3]:

10001100	mod 0 segreg r/m	disp (0 or 2 bytes)

MOVS/MOVSB/MOVSW   Move String Byte/Word ( )

[5]:

1010010w

MUL   Unsigned Multiply (AF,PF,CF,OF,ZF)

Register/memory [r bt 13; r wd 21; m bt 16; m wd 24]:

1110111w	mod 100 r/m	disp (0 or 2 bytes)

NEG   Negate (AF,PF,CF,SF,OF,ZF)

Register/memory [r 2; m 7]:

111011dw	mod 011 r/m	disp (0 or 2 bytes)

NOP   No-Operation ( )

[3]:

10010000

NOT   Logical Not ( )

Register/memory [r 2; m 7]:

111011dw	mod 010 r/m	disp (0 or 2 bytes)

OR   Logical Or (AF,PF,CF,SF,OF,ZF)

Register/memory to/from register [r,r 2; m,r 7; r,m 7]:

000010dw	mod reg r/m	disp (0 or 2 bytes)

Immediate to register/memory [r,i 3; m,i 7]:

100000sw	mod 001 r/m	disp (0 or 2 bytes)	data (1 or 2 bytes)

Immediate to AX or AL [3]:

0000110w	data (1 or 2 bytes)

OUT   Output to I/O Port ( )

To fixed port [3]:

1110011w	port

To [DX] [3]:

1110111w

OUTS/OUTSB/OUTSW   Output String to Port 286+ ( )

[5]:

0110111w

POP   Pop Stack ( )

Register/memory [5]:

10001111	mod 0 0 0 reg r/m

Register [5]:

01011 reg

Segment register [5]:

000 segreg 111

POPA   Pop All Registers 286+ ( )

[19]:

01100001

POPF   Pop Stack into FR ( )

[5]:

10011101

PUSH   Push onto Stack ( )

Register/memory [5]:

11111111	mod 1 1 0 reg r/m

Register [3]:

01010 reg

Segment register [3]:

000 segreg 110

PUSHA   Push All Registers 286+ ( )

[17]:

01100000

PUSHF   Push FR onto Stack ( )

[3]:

10011100

RCL   Rotate Left through Carry (CF,OF)

Register/memory, 1 bit [r 2; m 7]:

111011dw	mod 010 r/m	disp (0 or 2 bytes)

Register/memory, multiple bits specified in CL [r 5+nb; m 8+nb]:

1101001w	mod 010 r/m	disp (0 or 2 bytes)

Register/memory, number of bits specified in immediate form [r 5+nb; m 8+nb]:

1100000w	mod 010 r/m	disp (0 or 2 bytes)	immed data

RCR   Rotate Right through Carry (CF,OF)

Register/memory, 1 bit [r 2; m 7]:

111011dw	mod 011 r/m	disp (0 or 2 bytes)

Register/memory, multiple bits specified in CL [r 5+nb; m 8+nb]:

1101001w	mod 011 r/m	disp (0 or 2 bytes)

Register/memory, number of bits specified in immediate form [r 5+nb; m 8+nb]:

1100000w	mod 011 r/m	disp (0 or 2 bytes)	immed data

REP   Repeat Instruction ( )

[MOVS 5+4i; STOS 4+3i; INS 5+4i; OUTS 5+4i]:

11110010

REPE/REPZ   Repeat Instruction While Zero ( )

[CMPS 5+9i; SCAS 5+8i]:

11110011

REPNE/REPNZ   Repeat Instruction While Not Zero ( )

[CMPS 5+9i; SCAS 5+8i]:

11110010

RET   Return from Procedure ( )

From near target [11+ni]:

11000011

From far target [15+ni]:

11001011

Near return and parameter removal [11+ni]:

11000010	data (2 bytes)

From far target [15+ni]:

11001010	data (2 bytes)

ROL   Rotate Left (CF,OF)

Register/memory, 1 bit [r 2; m 7]:

111011dw	mod 000 r/m	disp (0 or 2 bytes)

Register/memory, multiple bits specified in CL [r 5+nb; m 8+nb]:

1101001w	mod 000 r/m	disp (0 or 2 bytes)

Register/memory, number of bits specified in immediate form [r 5+nb; m 8+nb]:

1100000w	mod 000 r/m	disp (0 or 2 bytes)	immed data

ROR   Rotate Right (CF,OF)

Register/memory, 1 bit [r 2; m 7]:

111011dw	mod 001 r/m	disp (0 or 2 bytes)

Register/memory, multiple bits specified in CL [r 5+nb; m 8+nb]:

1101001w	mod 001 r/m	disp (0 or 2 bytes)

Register/memory, number of bits specified in immediate form [r 5+nb; m 8+nb]:

1100000w	mod 001 r/m	disp (0 or 2 bytes)	immed data

SAHF   Store AH to FR (AF,SF,CF,ZF,PF)

```
10011110
```

SAL/SHL   Shift Arithmetic Left/Shift Logical Left (CF,OF)

Register/memory, 1 bit [r 2; m 7]:

1101000w	mod 100 r/m	disp (0 or 2 bytes)

Register/memory, multiple bits specified in CL [r 5+nb; m 8+nb]:

1101001w	mod 100 r/m	disp (0 or 2 bytes)

Register/memory, number of bits specified in immediate form [r 5+nb; m 8+nb]:

1100000w	mod 100 r/m	disp (0 or 2 bytes)	immed data

SAR   Shift Arithmetic Right (AF,PF,CF,SF,OF,ZF)

Register/memory, 1 bit [r 2; m 7]:

1101000w	mod 111 r/m	disp (0 or 2 bytes)

Register/memory, multiple bits specified in CL [r 5+nb; m 8+nb]:

1101001w	mod 111 r/m	disp (0 or 2 bytes)

Register/memory, number of bits specified in immediate form [r 5+nb; m 8+nb]:

1100000w	mod 111 r/m	disp (0 or 2 bytes)	immed data

SBB   Subtract with Borrow (AF,PF,CF,SF,OF,ZF)

Register/memory to/from register [r,r 2; m,r 7; r,m 7]:

000110dw	mod reg r/m	disp (0 or 2 bytes)

Immediate to register/memory [r,i 3; m,i 7]:

100000sw	mod 011 r/m	disp (0 or 2 bytes)	data (1 or 2 bytes)

Immediate to AX or AL [3]:

0001110w	data (1 or 2 bytes)

SCAS   Scan String (AF,PF,CF,SF,OF,ZF)

[7]:

1010111w

SHR   Shift Logical Right (CF,OF)

Register/memory, 1 bit [r 2; m 7]:

1101000w	mod 101 r/m	disp (0 or 2 bytes)

Register/memory, multiple bits specified in CL [r 5+nb; m 8+nb]:

1101001w	mod 101 r/m	disp (0 or 2 bytes)

Register/memory, number of bits specified in immediate form [r 5+nb; m 8+nb]:

1100000w	mod 101 r/m	disp (0 or 2 bytes)	immed data

STC   Set Carry Flag (CF)

[2]:

11111001

STD   Set Direction Flag (DF)

[2]:

11111101

STI   Set Interrupt Flag (DF)

[2]:

```
11111101
```

STOS   Store String ( )

[3]:

```
1010101w
```

SUB   Subtract (AF,PF,CF,SF,OF,ZF)

Register/memory to/from register [r,r 2; m,r 7; r,m 7]:

001010dw	mod reg r/m	disp (0 or 2 bytes)

Immediate to register/memory [r,i 3; m,i 7]:

100000sw	mod 101 r/m	disp (0 or 2 bytes)	data (1 or 2 bytes)

Immediate to AX or AL [3]:

0010110w	data (1 or 2 bytes)

TEST   Nondestructive Logical And Operation (AF,PF,CF,SF,OF,ZF)

Register/memory to/from register [r,r 2; m,r 6; r,m 6]:

100011dw	mod reg r/m	disp (0 or 2 bytes)

Immediate to register/memory [r,i 3; m,i 7]:

111011sw	mod 000 r/m	disp (0 or 2 bytes)	data (1 or 2 bytes)

Immediate to AX or AL [3]:

1010100w	data (1 or 2 bytes)

WAIT   Wait for Coprocessor Signal or Interrupt ( )

[3]:

10011011

XCHG   Exchange ( )

Register/memory and register [r,r 3; r,m 5; m,r 5]:

1000011w	mod reg r/m

Register and AX or AL [3]:

10010 reg

XLAT   Table Translation ( )

[5]:

11010111

XOR   Logical Exclusive-Or Operation (AF,PF,CF,SF,OF,ZF)

Register/memory to/from register [r,r 2; m,r 7; r,m 7]:

001100dw	mod reg r/m	disp (0 or 2 bytes)

Immediate to register/memory [r,i 3; m,i 7]:

100000sw	mod 110 r/m	disp (0 or 2 bytes)	data (1 or 2 bytes)

Immediate to AX or AL [3]:

0011010w	data (1 or 2 bytes)

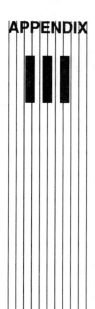

Commands for Assembling, Compiling, Linking and Debugging

This appendix lists selected commands for using the Microsoft DEBUG and CodeView debuggers, the assembler, the Pascal and C compilers, and the linker. Fields in brackets [ ] are optional. Only a few of the many available options are listed; for full details, consult the Microsoft manuals.

DEBUG:

Invoke DEBUG: DEBUG [file-name]

Display memory: D [[segment:]offset]

Enter values into memory: E [[segment:]offset] values-list

Display register: R register

Enter value into a register: R register carriage-return value

Display all registers: R

Run program: G [[segment:]offset]

Execute current instruction: T

Execute full procedure without pauses after instructions: P

Assemble source code: A [[segment:]offset] source-code extra-carriage-return

Unassemble: U [[segment:]offset]

Load bytes from disk: L [[segment:]offset] drive start-sector number-of-sectors

Quit: Q

CodeView:

Invoke CodeView: CV executable-file-name

F1: display help screen

F2: display/remove window which lists register contents

F3: change contents in display window from source to 'U' form or vice versa

F4: display the "user screen," i.e., the screen the user would see if the program were run directly, without a debugging tool

F5: execute until a breakpoint or end of program is reached

F6: move cursor from dialog window to display window or vice versa

F7: set a one-time-only breakpoint at line pointed to by cursor and execute to there

F8: same as DEBUG T command

F9: set/clear permanent breakpoint at the line pointed to by the cursor

F10: same as DEBUG P command

Most DEBUG commands work, such as D, E, R, A, U, and Q.

MASM:

To assemble a source file x.ASM, and link to produce the executable file x.EXE:

```
MASM /ZI x,x,x;
LINK /LI /MAP /CO x,x,x;
```

The /ZI and /CO options are for CodeView. Older versions of the assembler may not support this.

To run the program, type x.EXE or simply x.

Pascal:

To compile a source file y.PAS, and link to produce the executable file y.EXE:

```
PAS1 y,y,y,y
PAS2
PAS3
LINK /LI /MAP /CO y,y,y,library-directory;
```

The entry "library-directory" should be the complete path name for the location of your Pascal library, i.e., the location of the files such as PASCAL.LIB and MATH.LIB. If, say, they are in the directory \PASCAL of drive C:, then the link command would be

```
LINK /LI /MAP /CO y,y,y,C:\PASCAL\;
```

(make sure to type the trailing backslash and semicolon).

The /CO option is for CodeView; on older versions of the compiler, not all Code-View features are accessible. Note too that on later versions of the compiler, a compile-and-link command PL, similar to the CL command for C listed below, is available.

To run the program, type y.EXE or simply y.

C:

To compile a source file w.C, and link to produce the executable file w.EXE:

```
CL /I include-directory /Zi /Fc w.C /link library-directory
```

The include-directory and library directory contain files such as STDIO.H and SLIBCE.LIB. If for example, they are in the directories \MSC51\INCLUDE and \MSC51\LIB in drive C, your command would be

```
CL /I C:\MCS51\INCLUDE /Zi /Fc w.C /link C:\MSC51\LIB\
```

To run the program, type w.EXE or simply w.

APPENDIX IV

Selected DOS and BIOS Service Routines

BIOS Service 10/02: position screen cursor

AH: 02; BH: page number (usually 0); DH: row (0–24D); DL: column (0–79D)
call with INT 10H

BIOS Service 16/00: read keyboard character

AH: 00
call with INT 16H
on return, AH contains the scan code and AL contains the ASCII code (if any)

BIOS Service 16/01: get keyboard status

AH: 01
call with INT 16H
on return, the Zero Flag will be either cleared or set, according to whether a key
has been struck; if ZF is cleared, then AH contains the scan code and AL contains
the ASCII code (if any)

BIOS Service IA/02: read real-time clock

AH: 02
call with INT 1AH
on return, CH, CL and DH contain the time in hours, minutes and seconds

DOS Service 21/01: read single character from keyboard with echo

AH: 01
call with INT 21H
character is returned in AL

DOS Service 21/02: display single character to monitor

AH: 02; DL: ASCII code of the character to be displayed
call with INT 21H

DOS Service 21/05: print character

AH: 05; DL: character to be printed
call with INT 21H

DOS Service 21/09: display character string to monitor

AH: 09; DX: offset of string in current data segment; string must be terminated
with a '$' character
call with INT 21H

DOS Service 21/25: set interrupt vector

AH: 25; AL: interrupt number; DS:DX: pointer to new ISR
call with INT 21H

DOS Service 21/3C: create new file

AH: 3C; CX: file attribute (usually 0); DS:DX: pointer to file name
call with INT 21H
file handle returned in AX

DOS Service 21/3D: open file

AH: 3D; DS:DX: pointer to file name
call with INT 21H
file handle returned in AX; Carry Flag is cleared or set, according to whether the
file-open was successful

DOS Service 21/3E: close file

AH: 3E; BX: file handle

call with INT 21H

DOS Service 21/3F: read from file/device

AH: 3F; BX: file handle; CX: number of bytes to read; DS:DX: pointer to buffer area

call with INT 21H

on return, the Carry Flag will be cleared or set, according to whether the read was successful; if successful, AX will contain the number of bytes read

DOS Service 21/40: write to file/device

AH: 40; BX: file handle; CX: number of bytes to write; DS:DX: pointer to buffer area

call with INT 21H

on return, the Carry Flag will be cleared or set, according to whether the write was successful; if successful, AX will contain the number of bytes written

DOS Service 21/4C: end program execution and return to DOS

AH: 4C

call with INT 21H

space occupied by the program will now be eligible for being overwritten by a new program

DOS Service 25: read disk sector

AL: drive number (0 for A, 1 for B, etc.); CX: number of sectors to be read; DX: logical number of starting sector

call with INT 25H

file handle returned in AX

DOS Service 27: terminate program but keep program resident in memory (TSR)

DX: number of bytes to be kept in residence

call with INT 27H

space occupied by the program will *not* subsequently be overwritten

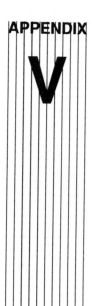

APPENDIX

V

Pascal/C Tutorial

As mentioned in the introduction, this book is designed for the reader who knows *either* Pascal *or* C. Knowledge of one of these languages is sufficient for reading and understanding the examples written in the other language, because Pascal and C are so similar (this similarity stems from the fact that they are both descendants of the langauage Algol).

For the purpose of *reading* the example programs, the relevant correspondences between Pascal and C constructs are developed within the text itself, after each program. Those explanations should suffice. However, some readers may wish to actively learn the "other" language, not just to acquire a reading knowledge in it. In particular, the readers who know Pascal may wish to acquire a *writing* knowledge of C, since C has come to play a central role in the modern computer software industry.

This appendix is intended to facilitate such learning. First, a table of Pascal/C correspondences is presented (reproduced by permission from *Operating System Concepts: Volume I, The XINU Approach*, by D. Comer and T. Fossum, 1988, Prentice Hall). Afterward, two sample programs are given. They both perform the same function, one in Pascal and the other in C, so that the reader may see the correspondences "in action."

Further details may be found in the many available Pascal and C texts.

388

C construct	Explanation	Pascal equivalent
`int a;`	declarations: integer	`var a: integer;`
`char b;`	character	`var b: char;`
`char *c;`	pointer to character	`var c: ↑ char;`
`int(*x)();`	pointer to procedure that returns integer	-none-
`char d[10];`	array of characters	`var d: array[0..9] of char;`
`char e[10][12];`	2-dimensional array	`var e: array[0..9,0..11] of char;`
`char*f[5]`	array of pointers	`var f: array[0..4] of ↑char;`
`char**g;`	pointer to pointer	`var g: ↑↑char;`
`'a'`	character constant	`'a'`
`'\014'`	character constant with value 014 (octal)	-none-
`"abc"`	string constant Array of contiguous characters terminated by a null byte (i.e., 'a', 'b', 'c', '\0'). Newline and tab denoted by \n and \t. Value is the address of the first character	-none- (some Pascal compilers use '...')
`123`	decimal constant	`123`
`0123`	octal constant (has leading zero)	-none- (decimal value is 83)
`0x123`	hexadecimal address	-none- (decimal value is 291)

`struct x {`
`  int f1;`
`  char f2;`
`}`
	structure (record) declaration with fields f1 and f2	`x = record`
		`  f1: integer;`
		`  f2: char`
		`end`

`struct x y[2];`	y is array of struct x	`var y: array[0..1] of x;`
`#define A v`	symbolic constant	`const A = v;`
`#define A(x) v(x)`	parameterized macro	-none-

`#ifdef A`
`  X`
`#endif`
	conditional compilation code X is compiled only if symbol A defined	-none-

C construct	Explanation	Pascal equivalent

`#ifndef A`
  `X`
`#endif`
	negative conditional compilation; X compiled only if A not defined	-none-

`#include src`	source file inclusion (if *src* is "*path*" then path is relative to curent directory; if <*path*> then relative to system directory)	-none-
`=`	assignment operator	`:=`

`+-*`
`/`
`%`
	arithmetic operators
	division (C does integer division on integers)
	modulus or remainder
		`+-*`
		`/div`
		`mod`

`var op= exp` `v += 9`	operation and assignment example: add 9 to variable v	`var := var op exp` `v := v + 9`

`==`
`!=`
`>`
`<`
`<=`
`>=`
	test equality
	test inequality
	test greater than
	test less than
	test less than or equal
	test greater than or equal
		`=`
		`<>`
		`>`
		`<`
		`<=`
		`>=`

`*x`	pointer dereference (whatever x points to)	`x`↑
`sizeof(x)`	size of data object x in bytes	-none
`&x`	address of object x (when used as a unary operator)	-none-

`&`
`|`
`~`
	bitwise and (when used as binary operator)
	bitwise or
	bitwise (1's) complement
		-none-
		-none-
		-none-

`&&` `||`	Boolean and Boolean or	`and` `or`

C construct	Explanation	Pascal equivalent
!	Boolean not (&& and || are evaluated left-to-right with early termination)	not (Pascal does not use early termination)
x[i]	array reference	x[i]
s.f	reference to field f in structure s	s.f
p->f	reference to field f in structure pointed to by p	p↑.f
e ? a : b	conditional expression (if e is nonzero, value is a else value is b)	-none-
++x	preincrement	x := x+1
x++	postincrement	x := x+1
--x	predecrement	x := x-1
x--	post decrement (when used in an expression ++x refers to the value of x after incrementing; x++ refers to the value before incrementing)	x := x-1
p(e1,e2,...,en)	procedure invocation	p(e1,e2,...,en)
while (exp) S;	indefinite iteration	while exp <> 0 do S
if (exp) S;	conditional	if exp <> 0 then S
if (exp) S1; else S2;	2-way conditional	if exp <> 0 then S1 else S2
{S1 ; S2 ;...; Sn ; }	compound statement (note semicolons)	begin S1 ; S2 ;...; Sn end
for(S1; exp; S2) S3;	indenfinite iteration with initialization and reinitialization (S1, exp and S2 are optional – if exp is omitted, infinite loop results)	S1; while exp <> 0 do begin S3; S2 end
return	procedure return	finish executing procedure

C construct	Explanation	Pascal equivalent
`return(exp)`	return exp to caller as function value	*function name* `:=exp;` finish executing function
`name(formals)` declaration of formals `{` declaration of local variables; statements `}`	procedure declaration	procedure name(formals); declaration of locals; `begin` statements `end;`
type name(formals) declaration of formals `{` declaration of local variables; statements `}`	function declaration	function name(formals) : *type*; declaration of locals; `begin` statements `end;`
`for(i=0; i<N ; i++)` `...x[i]...`	typical loop to search array x, assuming x has size N	`for i := 1 to N do` `...x[i]...`
`*x++`	idiomatic expression for pointer x: its value is whatever x points to; x is incremented after the reference according to pointer arithmetic	-none-
`(type)exp`	type casting the type of expression exp is changed.	-none-
`1 + (int) &x`	Example: make the address of x an integer before adding 1 to it (i.e., use integer, not pointer, arithmetic)	
`/*...*/`	Comment	`(*...*)` or `{...}`

The sample programs are presented below. Each of then reads in a sequence of numbers into an array, and reports the minimum and maximum values found. Here's the Pascal version:

```
program Calc(input,output);

        type Ary = array[1..10] of real;

    var X : Ary;
        Max,Min : real;
        I : integer

    procedure MinMax(var A:Ary; var Mn,Mx:real);
            var J : integer
    begin
        Mn:=A[1]; Mx:=A[1];
        for J:=2 to 10 do
            if A[J]< Mn then Mn:=A[J]
            else if A[J]> Mx then Mx:=A[J]
    end;

begin
    for I:=1 to 10 do read(X[I]);
    MinMax(X,Min,Max);
    write(Min,' ',Max)
end
```

Here's the C version:

```
float X[10],Max,Min;

int I;

void MinMax(A,MnP,MxP)
    /* need to declare the paramters as pointers;
            see Section 5.3.1.*/
    float A[],*MnP,*MxP;
{   int J;

    *MnP = A[0]; *MxP = A[0];
    for (J = 1; J < 10; J++)
        if (A[J] < *MnP) *MnP = A[J];
        else if (A[J] > *MnP) *MxP = A[J];
}

main()

{   for(I = 0; I < 10; I++) scanf("%f",&X[I]);
    MinMax(X,&Min,&Max);
    printf("%f %f",Min,Max);
}
```

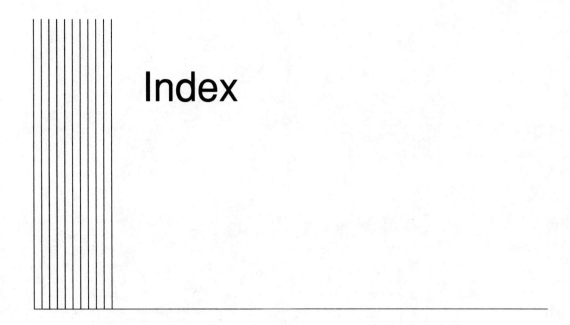

Index

2's complement, 9–12
68000 (*see* Motorola 680x0 CPU family)
8253 timer chip, 294, 336–40
8259A interrupt controller, 279–96

A

Actual parameter, 160
Addressing mode (*see* individual modes,
     e.g., Based addressing)
ALU, 38–39, 204, 205, 207
Architecture, 1, 56, 59, 138, 204, 231, 232
Argument, 160
ASCII, 14
.ASM files, 98
Assembler, 89, 91–3
Assembly language, 3, 15, 89, 91–139
Assembly-time, 110–11, 114, 128, 140, 159,
     160, 167
Attribute byte, 274

B

Based addressing, 114, 135, 154, 221–23,
     225, 346
.BAT files, 120–21
BIOS, 263, 296–306
BIOS services (*see* DOS and BIOS services)
Bootloading, 139–40, 326–27
Branch, 75
Breakpoint, 127–28, 192
Buses, general information, 35–38, 49–52,
     262–64, 279–92
Bus lines, iAPX:
   address lines, 37, 40, 49–52
   control lines, 37, 49–52, 279–92
   data lines, 37, 49–52, 281
   INTA line, 279–92
   INTR line, 279–92
   IOR line, 262
   IOW line, 262
   MEMR, 37, 40, 49–52, 262, 263–64
   MEMW, 37, 40, 49–52, 262, 263–64

Busy-wait I/O, 266

C

C 'define', 242
C functions:
  fprint, 309
  fscanf, 309
  malloc, 24
  print, 17, 27, 206–7
  scanf, 54, 206, 308
C I/O formats:
  %c (character), 17
  %d (decimal, i.e., signed integer), 17, 27
  %s (string), 309
  %u (unsigned integer), 17, 27
  %x (hexadecimal), 18
C language, general, 4, 16, 26–29, 46–47,
    177–78, 185–86, 189–90, 241–44,
    308–9
C operators:
  * (pointer), 27–29, 45–48, 177–78,
    186–87, 246–48
  & (address), 27–29, 45–48, 177–78,
    186–87, 247
  & (bitwise 'and'), 243–44
  ! ('not'), 235, 243
  / (division), 243
  % (mod), 243
  << (left shift), 243
  >> (right shift), 243–44
  +=, −=, &=, etc., 207, 243–44
  ++, 186, 247–48
  sizeof, 24
C 'Ox' symbol, 27
C statement types:
  'for' loops, 186
  goto, 15
C variable and function types:
  boolean, lack of, 27
  char, 23
  far pointers (iAPX machines), 45–48
  FILE, 309
  float, 6
  int, 21
  long, 22
  pointers, 27–29, 45–48, 177–78, 186–87,

    246–48
  register, 213–14
  struct, 26, 223
  unsigned char, 23
  void, 242–43
Cache, disk, 62–63
Cache, memory, 59–62
Call-by-reference, 171
Call-by-value, 171
CF (flag), 205–7
Chip, 44
Cleared, 8
Clock cycle, 58
Clone, 298
Code View, 125–28, 192–93
.COD files, 172–74
Compiler, 1, 2, 3, 16–18, 21–29, 45–48, 68,
    69, 97, 143–44
CPU, 4–5, 12, 18–20, 23–24, 35–52, 55,
    56–62, 68–78, 82–83, 94–95, 139,
    142, 144, 153–56, 162, 204, 211, 212,
    214, 231–32, 245, 254, 261–65,
    277–96, 316, 318, 341, 345–51
Cray, 4, 58, 232
Cylinder, 271

D

DEBUG, 90–95, 97–98, 121–28, 142–43,
    190–92, 207, 211, 328
Destination, 73
Device driver, 268
DF (flag), 245
Direct addressing, 116, 214–15
Directive, assembler, 117
Disks, 4, 62–63, 270–73, 320–34
DISPBX procedure, 101–2, 109, 136–38
Displacement, 75–76
DMA, 37, 273
DOS, 5, 53–56, 62–63, 114–15, 118–21,
    139–44, 156, 162, 176, 197, 269,
    296–306, 306–9, 315–51
DOS and BIOS services, general information,
    114, 162, 296–306, 316–19
DOS and BIOS services, specific:
  10/02, 301
  10/0F, 301

13/01, 321, 340
13/02, 321, 340
16/00, 298
16/01, 298
17/02, 298
1A/02, 340
21/01, 138, 307–8
21/02, 115
21/05, 297
21/06, 298
21/08, 298
21/09, 115
21/31, 336
21/3C, 302–6, 333
21/3D, 302–306
21/3E, 302–306
21/3F, 302–306
21/40, 302–306
21/4C, 117, 335–36
25, 321
26, 321
27, 336–40

E

EBCDIC, 14
Embedded applications, 3, 315
EOI, 294–95
.EXE files, 118–21

F

Formal parameter, 160
FR (flags register) (*see* Registers, iAPX,
    specific)
Functions, 108

H

Hexadecimal, 7–8
HLL variables, storage of, 9–14, 21–29

I

IF (flag), 295

Immediate addressing, 74, 214
Indexed addressing, 135, 215–21
Indirect addressing, 73, 215
Instructions, iAPX:
    ADC, 206–7
    ADD, 73
    AND, 137, 233–35, 236–44
    BOUND, 220–21
    CALL, 109, 156–60
    CLC, 212
    CLD, 212, 245
    CLI, 212, 295
    CMP, 74
    CMPSB, 251
    CWD, 227–28
    DEC, 136
    DIV, 135, 226–28
    ENTER, 178–79
    ESC, 232
    FADD, 231–32
    FSIN, 231–32
    HLT, 256
    IDIV, 227–28
    IMUL, 227–28
    IN, 262–63
    INC, 135
    INS, 273
    INT, 114–15, 316–17
    IRET, 115, 282, 317
    JAE, 211
    JC, 208
    JGE, 211
    JMP, 82
    JNC, 206
    JNO, 208
    JNS, 75
    JNZ, 78
    JO, 208
    JS, 97
    JZ, 97
    LAHF, 212
    LEA, 253
    LEAVE, 178–79
    LOCK, 254–56
    LOOP, 251–53
    LOOPNE, 252
    LOOPNZ, 252
    LOOPZ, 252

Instructions, iAPX (*cont.*):
  LRET, 176
  MOV, 80
  MOVSB, MOVSW, 245–51
  MUL, 135, 226–28
  NOT, 235
  OR, 233–35, 236–44
  OUT, 262–63
  OUTS, 273
  POP, 155–56
  POPA, 292
  POPF, 212
  PUSH, 154–56
  PUSHA, 292
  PUSHF, 212
  REP prefix, 245
  RET, 109, 160
  ROL, 137, 236–44
  ROR, 236–44
  SAHF, 212
  SAL, 228–30
  SAR, 228–30
  SBB, 206
  SCASB, 251
  SHL, 228–30
  SHR, 228–30
  STC, 212
  STD, 212, 245
  STI, 212, 295
  STOSB, STOSW, 251
  SUB, 72
  TEST, 235
  WAIT, 232
  XCHG, 253
  XLAT, 253
  XOR, 235–36
INTA line (*see* Bus lines, iAPX)
Interrupt, 277–96
INTR line (*see* Bus Lines, iAPX)
IOR, IOW (*see* Bus lines, iAPX)
ISR (interrupt service routine), 278

L

Label, 97
LIFO property of stacks, 157, 295
LINK, 118–21

Little-endian, 70
Loader, 139–44
Load-time, 110

M

Macintosh, 35, 55
Macro, 193–97
Malloc (*see* C functions)
MAR, 40–41
MASM, 98–121
MASM programming and data constructs:
    arrays, 106–7
    'for' loops, 136
    if-then-else, 136
    'while' loops, 136
MDR, 40–41
Megahertz, 58
Memory-mapped I/O, 263–66
MEMR line (*see* Bus lines, iAPX)
MEMW line (*see* Bus lines, iAPX)
Microsteps, 50, 58
Minix, 55, 140
Modem, 36, 276–77
Monitor screen, 46–48, 273–76
Motorola 680x0 CPU family, 5, 18, 19, 36,
        48–49, 55, 58, 68, 83, 84, 170, 263,
        292, 318, 347
MS-DOS (*see* DOS)

N

Nanosecond, 58
Near CALL, RET, 159–60
Nibble, 8

O

Object code, 96
.OBJ files, 118
OF (flag), 207–11
Op code, 79–80
Operating systems, 53–56, 62–63, 139–44,
        315–51

OS/2 55, 116, 351

P

Packed 23, 236
Parallel I/O, 276
Parallel operations, 56–58, 232, 254–56
Parameter, 160–90
Pascal extern (Microsoft-specific), 179–80
Pascal functions:
  indexck (Microsoft-specific), 219
  mathck (Microsoft-specific), 209
  read, readln, 28, 55, 306–9
  write, writeln, 16–17, 28, 177
Pascal operators:
  and, 234
  nor, 235
  or, 233
Pascal subprogram parameters, 171
Pascal variable types:
  ads (Microsoft-specific), 47–48
  array, 21
  boolean, 21
  char, 21
  integer, 21–22
  integer4 (Microsoft-specific), 22
  pointers, 27–28
  real, 21
  record, 26, 222
Polling, 266, 277–78
Portable, 48, 55
Prefetch, instruction, 57, 214
Procedures, 108, 151
Protected and real modes, 20, 41, 44, 316, 347–51
PS/2, 4–5
Pseudo-ops (MASM):
  @@, 175
  ASSUME, 108
  BYTE PTR, 113
  DB, 107
  DUP, 106
  DW, 106–7
  END, 106, 110–11
  ENDS, 105
  EQU, 105
  EXTRN, 165
  FAR, 159–60
  NEAR, 159–60
  OFFSET, 112
  PROC, 108
  PUBLIC, 124, 166–67
  SEG, 112
  SEGMENT, 105
  WORD PTR, 113

R

RAM, 36
READBX procedure, 137–38
Real mode (*see* Protected and real modes)
Register addressing, 97, 212–14
Registers, iAPX, general information, 41–5, 68–78
Registers, iAPX, specific:
  BP, 153–54, 221
  BX, 73, 113–14, 215, 221
  CS (*see* Segments, general information)
  DI, 215–17, 245
  DS (*see* Segments, general information)
  ES (*see* Segment override)
  FR, 40, 42, 71–78, 204–12, 295
  SI, 215–17, 245
  SP, 152–56
  SS (*see* Segments, general information)
ROM, 36, 139, 263, 315
Run-time, 110

S

Scan code, 268–69
Sector, disk, 270–73, 320–34
Segment override, 224–26
Segments, general information, 42–48, 105–6, 110, 347–51
Serial I/O, 276
SF (flag), 71–73
Signed-magnitude representation, 9
Sizeof (*see* C operators)
Source code, 96
Source operand, 73
Stack, 152–63, 280–82
Stack frame, 176, 179

Steps A, B, C, and D, 49–52, 281–82
Subprogram (*see* Procedures)
Subroutine (*see* Procedures)
Sun Microsystems, 36, 55, 232, 351
Symbol table, 29, 105, 108, 114, 119, 124,
    166, 190
SYMDEB, 124–25, 190–92
System call, 296

T

TF (flag), 211

U

Under the hood, 1–5, 54–55, 112, 152, 171,
    244, 261, 273, 315–16, 320, 326

Unix, 5, 55–56, 62, 90, 118, 180, 190, 197,
    210, 220, 315–16, 318, 320, 325, 334,
    335, 351

V

VAX, 4, 5, 18, 19, 55, 56, 58, 62, 68, 84,
    143, 170, 251, 252, 263, 318, 342

W

Wait-loop I/O (*see* Polling)

Z

ZF (flag), 73, 78